Covenant
for a
New
Creation

STUDIES IN ETHICS

Center for Ethics and Social Policy
GRADUATE THEOLOGICAL UNION

Editorial Committee

Charles S. McCoy, Series Editor

GRADUATE THEOLOGICAL UNION:

- American Baptist Seminary of the West
- Church Divinity School of the Pacific
- Dominican School of Philosophy and Theology
- Franciscan School of Theology
- Jesuit School of Theology at Berkeley
- Pacific Lutheran Theological Seminary
- Pacific School of Religion
- San Francisco Theological Seminary
- Starr King School for the Ministry

Covenant
for a
New
Creation

ETHICS, RELIGION, AND PUBLIC POLICY

Edited by
Carol S. Robb and Carl J. Casebolt

ORBIS BOOKS

Maryknoll, New York 10545

GTU

Graduate Theological Union

The Catholic Foreign Mission Society of America (Maryknoll) recruits and trains people for overseas missionary service. Through Orbis Books, Maryknoll aims to foster the international dialogue that is essential to mission. The books published, however, reflect the opinions of their authors and are not meant to represent the official position of the society.

Copyright © 1991 by Orbis Books
Published by Orbis Books, Maryknoll, NY 10545 in cooperation with the Graduate Theological Union, 2465 LeConte Avenue, Berkeley, CA 94709

Library of Congress Cataloging-in-Publication Data

Covenant for a new creation: ethics, religion, and public policy /
   edited by Carol S. Robb and Carl J. Casebolt.
      p.   cm.
   Includes bibliographical references.
   ISBN 0-88344-740-1
   1. Creation.   2. Human ecology—Religious aspects—Christianity.
I. Robb, Carol S.   II. Casebolt, Carl, 1931-
BT695.C58   1991
241'.691—dc20   90-27013
                                                              CIP

Contents

v

Acknowledgments

We have been brought into partnership through the efforts of several people related to the Center for Ethics and Social Policy of the Graduate Theological Union in Berkeley, California. Phil Joranson, Harlan Stelmach, Ed Voris, and Charles McCoy have worked with the Center in many capacities through the years, and through their conversations with the Dean of the GTU, Judith Berling, and Orbis Books, particularly Robert Gormley, Eve Drogin, and Robert Ellsberg, the idea of this anthology emerged to carry on the Environmental Ethics Project of the Center.

Initially, we were asked to collaborate on a volume updating Phil Joranson and Ken Butigan's *Cry of the Environment* (Santa Fe, N.M.: Bear, 1984). Carl's political experience is with grassroots peace and environmental groups and with church bodies attempting to voice concern on environmental policy at the federal level. Carol's experience is teaching environmental ethics in the context of theological education and the preparation of persons for ministry. It is the mission of the Center for Ethics and Social Policy to keep church people, political actors, and academics talking to each other about social policies that shape our lives together. And in asking the two of us to collaborate, the Center asked us to find a way to mesh our very different perspectives and the contacts we had to articulate these perspectives for a reading public. In that mesh we found we were creating a very different kind of book than *Cry of the Environment*, one that depends on it, while exploring different territory. Here we want to acknowledge that we were cradled in the arms of the Center for the Ethics and Social Policy and the prior work of people related to the Center, particularly Charles McCoy, and Phil Joranson.

Additionally, Carol wants to acknowledge the stimulation of students who have worked together in the environmental-ethics courses at San Francisco Theological Seminary—students who are sometimes from Oregon and have a long tradition of ecological consciousness; from Southern California, where outdoors is the mall; from Richmond and Oakland, where environmentalists are perceived as wealthy, white, and skiers—all these students have been looking over her shoulder in this work. Fran Elton, Don Steele, and Karin Case have given support very directly by word processing, proofreading, and critical reading of works in progress, and all the while keeping their own careers as students afloat. Carol also thanks the San Francisco Theological Seminary and the Graduate Theological Union for supporting this work through grants for research assistance and word processing, and through the work of several people: Pat Lista-Mei, Faculty Communicator, Mary Poletti, Assistant to the Dean, and Linda Buquia, Mail Room and Copying Coordinator. Carol acknowledges the work that has taken place over the dinner table with Bill Mayer, with whom she also has increased motivation for a sustainable future for this world because of their child, Duncan, who is to inherit it.

Carol and Carl both would like to give a special word of thanks to Philip Joranson for all of his assistance on this book, as well as for other gifts of insight, friendship, and inspiration. His perseverance in his work and his concern for the creation, in spite of numerous obstacles, gave his participation a special relevance.

Particularly helpful to Carl were all the folks associated with the Peace and Environment Convention Coalition and the Peace and Environment Project. While all cannot be named, indispensable help came from Lucile Green Isitt and the World Citizens, Tam Beeler, Michael Closson, Allen Cohen, Edythe Colello, Ruthann Corwin, Henry S. Dakin, Bruce Dearborn, Bill Hough, Cliff Humphrey, Amy Kelly, Eleanor LeCain, Susan LeFever, Danny Moses, Steve Rauh, Leon Regelson, Nancy Strohl, and Ben Young. Advice on consensus building and political negotiation was generously and effectively given by Bob Russell. Throughout the years of work on peace and environmental agendas, Carl's wife Cathy has given advice and support. He is especially grateful for her support and sacrifice, which made it possible to move from California to Washington, D.C., to take advantage of opportunities in the capital city. We are also appreciative of Susan Perry and Catherine Costello of Orbis Books, whose intelligent shepherding turned our many manuscripts into this book.

In citing passages from Scripture, we have used a variety of translations, including our own paraphrasing of some passages.

CAROL S. ROBB

CARL J. CASEBOLT

Introduction

CAROL S. ROBB
with CARL J. CASEBOLT

No one of us lives apart from the natural world. As children of the earth and sea and sky, we are nourished and sheltered by the world's lively goodness, its dynamic presence, and its continual creation and recreation. ... [Yet] nature is less often conceived as "creative matrix" and more often grasped, in the spirit of realism and "utility," as our property to be used and used up.
   — Philip Joranson and Ken Butigan, *Cry of the Environment*[1]

THE NEED TO REVALUE CREATION

One of the purposes of developing creation theology has been to revalue the segments of the created universe besides the human species. This revaluation must continue to make possible genuine inclusiveness in the universe of moral discourse about what human beings responsibly are to do and be with our powers and talents. Since nontalking creation cannot present arguments in its own behalf, we talkers must expand our moral imagination to consider "the good of" the rest of creation in public attitudes and in all social policy that will have effects on it.

Part of the moral, spiritual, and theological effort at revaluing, however, must be the analytical discipline of assessing the causes of the devaluation of the created nonhuman world. While the dynamics at work in modern societies toward the nonhuman world are complex, it is our perspective that sexism, racism, and class oppression are political dynamics used to justify privileged access by elites to the goods of this earth created by God/ess[2] for the well-being and harmony of the whole created order.

For instance, Vandana Shiva[3] wondered why it was that when the U.N. Decade for Women ended, women in the developing world were in worse circumstances than before it began. Women's relative access to economic resources, incomes, and employment worsened, their burden of work increased, and their relative and even absolute health, nutritional, and educational status declined.

1

She concluded that development itself was the cause of women's worsening position. Development projects appropriated or destroyed the natural-resource base needed for sustenance and survival. They destroyed women's productivity by removing land, water, and forests from their management and control and by destroying soil, water, and vegetation systems, so that nature's ability to renew itself was impaired. In Shiva's analysis, development was based on measurements in which destruction meant "production" and the regeneration of life meant "passivity." Fragmentation and uniformity were the hallmarks of development that destroyed the living forces that arise from relationships within the "web of life," and the diversity in the elements and patterns of these relationships.

> In actual fact, there is less water, less fertile soil, less genetic wealth as a result of the development process. Since these natural resources are the basis of nature's economy and women's survival economy, their scarcity is impoverishing women and marginalized peoples in an unprecedented manner.[4]

The cultural assumption of a secondary status for women, an economic theory based on cash flow rather than quality of life, and a view of nature as passive—all these forces embedded in development theory result in the destruction of nature, while creating inequality among women in relation to men.

In another instance of privilege for elites resulting in the degradation of the earth, the Commission for Racial Justice of the United Church of Christ published in 1987 a national report on the racial and socio-economic characteristics of communities in the United States with hazardous-waste sites. This report indicated there were

> clear patterns which show that communities with greater minority percentages of the population are more likely to be the sites of such facilities. . . . [There is] an inordinate concentration of such sites in Black and Hispanic communities, particularly in urban areas.[5]

Three out of every five black and Hispanic Americans live in communities with uncontrolled toxic-waste sites. Racial-ethnic communities and the poor pay the price of the polluting by-products of manufactured goods. They have to live close to these by-products in their groundwater, soil, and air. It is not a fair price to pay, as these communities do not benefit proportionately from the production, either in profits or by the use of the produced goods. If wealthy and white communities were saddled with the true costs of production, including having to live with toxic wastes, one wonders how long it would take to change production methods in accord with more benign models.

The ideology of a passive and devalued nature is extended to enfold women, working and poor people, and racial-ethnic people. This ideology is a symptom of the elites' privileged access to the goods of the earth. We will not be able to heal the damage already accomplished on this earth, and justified by this ideology, without confronting and healing the effects of the social misuses of power over majority segments of the population and the nonhuman world.

In 1863, the Emancipation Proclamation decreed an end to slavery in all states still at war with the Union. In 1871, wife beating was declared illegal for the first time in the United States (in Alabama and Massachusetts). Both slavery and wife beating were social practices dependent upon the assumption that some people were other people's property and could be used as resources for economic development and/or personal well-being. The degradation of the biosphere today is the result of an "ownership" mentality as our economy still functions for the well-being of those with property rights, who see nature in terms of utility, as property to be used.

> Theologically and practically, ecological threats and injustice are inseparable. Neither can be pursued in isolation from the other. The biblical vision of shalom (peace) assumes such a holistic integration.[6]

In biblical times, natural catastrophes were seen as God's response to sin. In later times, these occurrences were seen as unrelated to divine action — part of natural processes. Now, we are coming again to understand natural disasters as results of human activity. Floods happen when forest catchments are denuded. Drought follows deforestation and creates desertification. Violent storms are connected to climate change and carbon dioxide buildup in the atmosphere. The possibility of severe changes in climate, accompanied by the loss of coastal communities to rising ocean levels, will surely affect people's perceptions of humanity's relationship to nature and nature's creator.

REVALUING THROUGH COVENANT RELATIONSHIPS

Covenant relationships may offer a context within which to meet the challenges of the current crisis with discipline and hope. The Eco-Justice Working Group of the National Council of Churches suggested *A Covenant Group for Lifestyle Assessment*[7] as a way to bring light on how one should arrange one's personal household and life. A business leader reflecting on covenantal relationships noted:

> Covenantal relationships induce freedom, not paralysis. A covenantal relationship rests on shared commitment to ideas, to issues, to values, to goals and to management processes. Words such as love, warmth, personal chemistry are pertinent. ... They fill deep needs and they enable work to have meaning and to be fulfilling. Covenantal rela-

tionships reflect unity and grace and poise. They are an expression of the sacred nature of relationships.[8]

The most often used meaning of covenanting is within the context of interpersonal relations; however, we are proposing a reappropriation of the covenant with God/ess as the theological dimension of *social* relations and social policy. Of what use is covenantal faithfulness as a basis for ecological living and an environmental ethic? This is an interesting question and one we push, although not in a historical vacuum. The whole question of the relevance or usefulness of the Hebrew Scriptures and the New Testament for ecological consciousness is still much debated.

This question was raised by Lynn White, Jr. in 1967 with his article, "The Historical Roots of Our Ecologic Crisis."[9] In his analysis, the Bible, particularly the Genesis creation story, has served as a worldview for all cultures affected by it, justifying the exploitation of nature for human consumption and interests. In the creation account, "man" is created in the image of God and given dominion over and charged to subdue a profane nature.

One response to White is that of the "stewardians." They read the Genesis account to say *not* that human beings were to dominate nature, but rather that our unique status in creation gives us particular responsibilities, powers, and privileges — to dress the garden and keep it, to be stewards of the earth. This interesting debate has been going on for more than twenty years and is a serious challenge to reflect on our assumptions about humankind's status in relationship to the rest of creation.

However, the power of White's thesis rests most heavily on the first rather than the second Genesis creation story. The first creation story is *younger* than the second and was written by the same "source," person or persons, who are known today as "P," standing for the priestly writers.[10] The priestly history appears in certain passages in Genesis and Exodus, virtually the whole of Leviticus, and about three-fourths of Numbers. The priestly writers were from a line of priestly elites whose social status probably originated in political proximity to Solomon, his court, and the temple. Much later, maybe after the Exile, in the sixth century B.C.E., P amended the J source, written earlier by David's court theologian. The P creation story was placed before J for emphasis, and it supports a view of the way society should be organized — the way in which distinctions and separations are crucial to social order. The P version, Genesis 1:1–2:4a, contains these passages:

> In the beginning God created the heavens and the earth. Now the earth was a formless void, there was darkness over the deep, and God's spirit hovered over the water.
> God said, "Let there be light," and there was light. God saw that light was good, and God divided light from darkness. God called light

"day," and darkness he called "night." Evening came and morning came: the first day. . . .

God said, "Let the earth produce every kind of living creature: cattle, reptiles, and every kind of wild beast." And so it was. God made every kind of wild beast, every kind of cattle, and every kind of land reptile. God saw that it was good.

God said, "Let us make humankind in our own image, in the likeness of ourselves, and let them be masters of the fish of the sea, the birds of heaven, the cattle, all the wild beasts and all the reptiles that crawl upon the earth."

God created humankind in the image of himself, in the image of God he created them, male and female he created them. . . . Evening came and morning came: the sixth day.

Thus heaven and earth were completed with all their array. On the seventh day God completed the work he had been doing. He rested on the seventh day after all the work he had been doing. God blessed the seventh day and made it holy, because on that day he had rested after all his work of creating.

According to P, the world prior to creation was disordered. In this account, God created things in a particular order, an order to be maintained by priests. In writing this creation story, the priests were writing a job description for themselves to separate, to make distinctions, and to establish categories for a social order in which, by the way, they stood to reap privileges. Their distinctions *justified* their privileges.

The J creation account, beginning at Genesis 2:4b, immediately follows the P account and contains passages such as these:

At the time when Yahweh God made earth and heaven there was as yet no wild bush on the earth nor had any wild plant yet sprung up, for Yahweh God had not sent rain on the earth, nor was there any man to till the soil. However, a flood was rising from the earth and watering all the surface of the soil. Yahweh God fashioned man of dust from the soil. Then he breathed into his nostrils a breath of life, and the man became a living being. Yahweh God planted a garden in Eden which is in the east, and there he put the man he had fashioned. Yahweh God caused to spring up from the soil every kind of tree, enticing to look at and good to eat, with the tree of life and the tree of the knowledge of good and evil in the middle of the garden. . . .

Yahweh God said, "It is not good that man should be alone. I will make him a helpmate." So from the soil Yahweh God fashioned all the wild beasts and all the birds of heaven. These he brought to the man to see what he would call them; each one was to bear the name the man would give it. The man gave names to all the cattle, all the birds of heaven, and all the wild beasts; but for the man there was not found a helper as his partner.

J is concerned to locate the beginning of the people in the geographical circumstances of the bedouins and to make a connection between them and the rain-agriculture geography and people characteristic of the new nation under David's reign. David depended upon the support of the bedouins to gain the throne.

The Genesis creation stories are key for many people who search the Scriptures for clues to the "biblical" treatment of the relationship between humanity and the rest of creation, as is reflected in Baird Callicott's and (to a degree) Martha Ellen Stortz's essays in this collection. It might be more to the point, however, to say that the authors of the creation stories were just as interested in the configuration of political and economic power in Palestine, for it was they who also wrote versions of most of the covenants. We must give attention to the covenants, but not ignore the fact that the two creation stories were written by two different authors to support two different political configurations that are described only later in the Bible.

We believe remembrance of the covenants in the Hebrew Scriptures and the New Testament — and recommitment to them — is necessary for passionate Christian involvement in healing creation. However, the covenants, as we have access to them in Scripture, are also part of the problem. They need to be thoroughly reviewed and criticized and need to be, in effect, renegotiated. Such review, renegotiation, and recommitment is itself a continuation of the biblical treatment of covenants, which is why there is more than one. We need a commitment to a new covenant in order to heal and sustain a new creation.

This is an audacious claim, because one of the most consistent threads of covenantal history is that the biblical *God* initiates all the covenants and sets the terms for them. Yet for those who have eyes to see and ears to hear, creation is groaning all around us, and God/ess is inviting us to a new relationship to heal the earth. In trying to articulate the basis for a new covenant, we are straining to hear properly and to see fully what the new covenant entails.

In this collection, Charles McCoy develops the theme of the Bible's openness to revision of the covenant in an additional way. He comments that the covenant provides a basis and boundaries for humankind's creativity and that God's covenant is not static. We inherit certain purposes and possibilities from the history of the covenantal tradition, but our creativity is divinely expected and invited.

We have a biblical tradition to examine critically and with which to become acquainted, if not reacquainted. But reader beware: the attempt to harvest a basis for environmental ethics from the Scriptures is fraught with difficulties. We make the attempt for two reasons. Ours is a culture marked deeply by Christianity, and we feel we must find resources within that tradition to foster mythoreligious change that must accompany the political and economic changes necessary for a new world garden. Secondly, there are many people today, particularly women, whom we respect, like Marti Kheel, whose essay appears in this collection, who have given up finding a positive role for Judaism and Christianity in healing the earth because these traditions are so thoroughly patriarchal. Upon hearing of the covenantal perspective that undergirds this particular collection, Marti said, "The center of the covenant is circumcision, and circumcision has nothing to do with me." On the face of it, Marti is correct, and Carl and I feel accountable to her and those for whom she speaks to expose the difficulties involved in harvesting a basis for environmental ethics from the Scriptures. But at the same time we are following an impulse that has been nourished by our own experience with progressive people who hold themselves accountable to the Bible and its traditions.

What are the difficulties in using Scripture and its treatment of the covenants as a theological grounding for environmental ethics? First, the *forms* the covenants take in Scripture are quite varied. Covenants are essentially the basis for social order and interaction, and, thus, every time a new political or social organization is depicted, it is described in terms of a new covenant with the biblical god. So "covenant" is a way of talking about a social group's view of what is justice, or a just social, economic, and political order. Hence the relevance of the covenants as a biblical foundation for social ethics, where justice is perennially the most salient principle.

THE COVENANT WITH NOAH

The first covenant depicted in the Bible is the covenant of Noah (Gen. 9), for which the sign is a bow—a rainbow, and a bow for shooting arrows.[11] After the waters of the flood receded and Noah and all those on the ark disembarked, God said,

> "Never again will I curse the earth because of the [albeit continuing] evil heart of these humans. Nor will I ever again strike down every living thing as the flood did."

> Then God blessed Noah and his sons, saying to them, "Be fruitful and multiply and fill the earth. Be the terror and the dread of all the wild beasts and all the birds of heaven, of everything that crawls on the ground and all the fish of the sea; they are handed over to you. Every living and crawling thing shall provide food for you, no less than the foliage of plants. I give you everything, with this one exception: you must not eat flesh with life, or that is to say blood, in it."

Among the limitations stipulated for those entering the covenant is a prohibition against the shedding of human blood, which is a prohibition on revenge. This covenant is a *universal* covenant, that is, with Noah and his descendants and with every living creature that came out of the ark. There are no stipulations in this covenant as to what obligations people who enter into it incur. It is given graciously, but in response to the injustice that characterized the preflood political order.

This covenant is the one that sanctions meat eating. In the context of the relatively wealthy industrialized nations, meat eating is an environmental issue in itself. The food and fiber required for beef raising, for instance, could be distributed widely as protein sources for people who do not have the minimum daily requirements. This same issue affected the people of Palestine, who—with the exception of the wealthy—ate meat only on rare occasions.

THE COVENANT WITH ABRAHAM

The Abrahamic covenant is similar in form to the covenant with Noah in that it binds only God, El Shaddai. This covenant is described in Genesis 12, 15, and 17. In Genesis 17, the sign of the covenant is circumcision.

"Here now is my covenant with you: You shall be the ancestor of a multitude of nations. You shall no longer be called Abram; your name shall be Abraham, for I have made you the ancestor of a multitude of nations. I will make you most fruitful. I will make you into nations, and your issue shall be kings. I will establish my covenant between myself and you, and your descendants after you, generation after generation, a covenant in perpetuity. . . . I will give to you and to your descendants after you the land where you are now an alien, the whole land of Canaan, to own in perpetuity, and I will be your God."

God said to Abraham, "You on your part shall maintain my covenant. Now this is my covenant which you are to maintain between myself and you, and your descendants after you: all your males must be circumcised. . . . When they are eight days old all your male children must be circumcised. . . . The uncircumcised male, whose foreskin has not been circumcised, such a man shall be cut off from his people: he has violated my covenant."

God said to Abraham, "As for Sarai, your wife, you shall not call her Sarai, but Sarah. I will bless her and moreover give you a son by her. I will bless her and nations shall come out of her; kings of peoples shall descend from her."

This covenant is not universal, but particular. From all the descendants of Noah, El Shaddai chooses one man and one woman and their descendants with whom to covenant. To emphasize the particularity, the covenant promises the land with no conditions of any substance. Circumcision is required of the males, but it is a mark, a sign. In this sense, the Abrahamic covenant contains a potentially dangerous ideal that Abraham's "people" were a chosen people without concomitant obligations or responsibilities.[12] Fred Kirschenmann's essay in this collection explores further the problem with Abrahamic consciousness.

THE COVENANT WITH MOSES

The covenant of Moses, on the other hand, follows a very different form. In Exodus 6, Yahweh announces the covenant, and in Exodus 20, Yahweh lays down its stipulations.

In Exodus 6, Moses had been trying to convince Pharaoh to release the Hebrew people who had been pressed into slave labor for Egypt's court. But Pharaoh made even greater demands on the workers to increase their productivity without providing more raw materials. God spoke to Moses and said to him,

> Say this, then, to the Israelites, "I am Yahweh. I will free you of the burdens which the Egyptians lay on you. I will release you from slavery to them. . . . and I will be your God. Then you shall know it is I, Yahweh your God, who have freed you from the Egyptians' burdens. Then I will bring you to the land I swore that I would give to Abraham, and Isaac, and Jacob, and will give it to you for your own; I, Yahweh, will do this!"

After their exodus from Egypt and when they had come to Sinai, the people agreed to the covenant; and God gave them the Decalogue, which includes the remembrance of the sabbath.

> Remember the sabbath day and keep it holy. For six days you shall labor and do all your work, but the seventh day is a sabbath for Yahweh your God. You shall do no work that day, neither you nor your son nor your daughter nor your servants, men or women, nor your armies nor the stranger who lives with you. For in six days Yahweh made the heavens and the earth and the sea and all that these hold, but on the seventh day he rested; that is why Yahweh has blessed the sabbath day and made it sacred. (Exodus 20:8–11)

The sabbath is the sign of the Mosaic covenant, as it was one of the ten stipulations known as the Decalogue. The *form* of this covenant is very similar, if not identical, to that of ancient suzerainty treaties.[13] Such treaties contain a *preamble*, the historical prologue in which it is claimed that one country has a bigger army than the other and could be victorious on the field of battle, although it will not come to that; *stipulations*, which essentially apply to the vassal rather than the overlord, and, in effect, say the vassal will be loyal and have no independent foreign policy; *provisions for deposit of the text and for public reading*; *divine witnesses to the treaty*; and *blessings* and *curses*, blessings for those who maintain the covenant and curses for those who do not. This is not a treaty between equals. The overlord intends to behave in an upright way, but there is nothing in writing stipulating his obligations, and thus no chance of taking him to court before the gods if he offends the vassal king.

The Mosaic covenant's parts are very faithful to the model of the suzerainty treaties. The Decalogue contains the stipulations, indicating that each Israelite has certain obligations toward other Israelites that stem from their common allegiance to Yahweh. Faithfulness to Yahweh *requires* right relationships among the people.[14]

Is this model appropriate for a new covenant? Are we willing to view ourselves as subordinates to our Lord? It would seem quite appropriate that we hold our own actions accountable to the biblical principles we have investigated and found consistent with moral living and the betterment of the common good. To do so is to act autonomously, in the sense of acting without coercion, but according to moral values we have affirmed as consistent with our best selves and the best community we can imagine. We submit to moral guidelines because we have tested them, or our community has, and found them to be necessary for who we want to become, personally and in relationships.

A vassal-overlord relationship is not at all implied by such moral autonomy, and, in fact, is antithetical to it, when autonomy is understood as the freedom to be responsible. For when we submit our actions, and characters, for that matter, to moral scrutiny in the terms of the principles we uphold, we do it because we find these principles to be right, not because there is an unequal power relationship between ourselves and God/ess or ourselves and the Bible. The principles are right by virtue of their moral properties and the effects that will be produced by following them.

Having become sensitive to how compromised is the suzerainty model, we can denounce the *underpinnings* of such covenants and begin to renegotiate a covenant to include newly recognized citizens of the world garden, those who have been treated as property heretofore, including nonhuman creation, conquered peoples, women, and children. The renegotiated covenant would be among parties for whom the relationship is mutual respect and accountability, and the recognition that different citizens have different contributions to make in the world garden and to the source of our being.

Two other covenants, at least, are mentioned in the Hebrew scriptures. At Shechem an assembly of elders and other leaders participated in a *renewal* of the covenants of both Abraham and Moses. Joshua 24 portrays not a new covenant, but all the people facing a choice whether to serve Yahweh with the obligations entailed at Sinai. In this sense, the Shechem assembly affirms the form of covenant associated with the suzerainty treaty. In the covenant with David (2 Sam. 7), Yahweh promised to David that he and his descendants would always have the throne. Again, this covenant was unconditional and eternal, and similar in form to the covenants with Noah and Abraham.

We propose using the tradition of the covenants, in the face of this plurality of forms, with this comment: the covenants that are unconditional gifts of grace do not clearly require us to change our current course of history or model of economic development. Yet we know our current course is leading straight to devastation. The Mosaic covenant explicitly contains stipulations that are obligations for those entering the covenant and seems most directly tied to the social ethics of ecology, whereby we can make claims on each other for the way we lead our lives and govern ourselves. Yet the covenant at Sinai was modeled after the suzerainty treaty, involving an overlord and a vassal, in dominant-subordinate relationship. How can we challenge with any moral consistency the social-economic relations of domination and subordination we witness now in gender, race, and class dynamics without a new understanding of the "sovereignty of God," wherein sovereignty is defined not as "power over" but as "the power we share"? Just as the biblical writers borrowed language from their secular experience, our mythoreligious language is borrowed in large part, if not totally, from *our* secular experience. Mythoreligious language either confronts secular experience or baptizes it. *Our* secular experience of liberation movements has sensitized us to the oppressive effect of belief in a sovereign god who relates to persons as overlord to vassal.

On the other hand, while the covenant with Noah was one of promise, it is the only one that was universal. The others were made between the biblical god and Abraham and Sarah and their descendants. Because the degradation of the biosphere is a matter of direct significance to all species in the world, regardless of national boundaries, our new covenant must be universal.

In this regard, the period of Israel's history that constituted the tribal federation is instructive. Before there was a king who bound the tribes together under central authority and a centralized cult, the twelve tribes were in federation, each free to work out the specific policies of cult and community as it found best. Not all members of those tribes were blood kin. They were diverse groups, some, if not most, having no history in the exodus from Egypt. Yet those diverse groups were nevertheless brought together for a significant period, their only link being their mutual bond with Yahweh through the covenants.[15] It boggles the mind to imagine a personality of God/ess that could covenant with every people and nation, with their own gods, non-gods, and goddesses. Yet the cosmos of Yahweh was constituted by the known world of the Israelites. That cosmos has expanded in this era, when a nuclear accident affects people, plants, and animals all over the world. There is a *material* basis for a mythic structure tying together the peoples of different "tribes." The question is whether or not we have the moral imagination and depth of piety to respond to the creation that cries in agony, for there is no possibility of "election" of one people out of many in this historical period. We will thrive together in appropriate models of sustainable technology and agriculture, or we will all be poisoned, although at varied rates and sequences.

THE SOCIAL CONTEXT OF THE EARLY COVENANTS

A second matter to be addressed in harvesting the scriptures for environmental ethics is the social location of their different authors. These writers had dissimilar stakes or political interests, and one cannot help wondering whether their motivations were self-aggrandizing. Still (with reference to Hebrew Scriptures), at this point biblical scholars identify four authors, or circles of authors, whose texts were later combined. J, the Yahwist, is the oldest source. E, who uses "Elohim" as the name for the biblical God, is next oldest. P, the priestly writer, is third oldest according to some. And D, the Deuteronomist, is either the youngest source or trades position with the priestly writer.[16] All of the writers incorporated earlier traditions, some oral and some written, in formulating their distinctive approaches. And their specific identities made a difference in the way each portrayed the covenants.

J was a court theologian to David. His role was to legitimate David's rule. This was accomplished by scripting a creation story, the second in Genesis, and by writing a history of the people of Palestine in such a way as to portray Abraham, a bedouin, as the father of the nation. J was trying to consolidate the bedouins' loyalty to David in order to compensate for the lack of support of the traditional power brokers of that time. The most important story in J is the rebellion and escape of the workers from Egypt. The nation under David was a nation of laborers, whose freedom from exploitation, as J portrayed it, depended upon the rule of David, in a time when that nation was constantly threatened.[17] In J's depiction of the history of the nation, the law had its source in Yahweh and the Mosaic covenant, not in David's threat to use coercive power.[18]

J wrote about the covenants with Noah, Abraham, and Moses. So did P. The priestly writer added sections to the portrayal of all three covenants, representing his (their) particular interests as "a class of Jerusalem priests exiled to Babylon after the destruction of Solomon's temple and then reenfranchised under Persian rule."[19] The priestly writers were members of the ruling class. Their duties included being butchers of sacrifices, cult petitioners, taboo specialists, artists, scribes, lawyers, judges, counselors, prophets, and warriors.[20] An important function of the priests was to make sharp distinctions between the holy and the common and between the clean and the unclean. In making these distinctions, the priests defined social relations. Of course, people who were "unclean" were socially inferior to those who were "clean" and by virtue of their "cleanness" had access to public ritual and displays of power.

The priests used their right to distinguish what was holy or common to sanction their privileged access to meat. Only the best of the herd could be sacrificed at the altar, and, through the sacrifices of animals at the temple, priests gave themselves access to large quantities of good meat. This was an extraordinary privilege in the ancient eastern Mediterranean, as it would be today for rice- and bean-eating people. The social basis for the priests' class privileges was sanctioned mythically by the distinctions between holy and common, clean and unclean, and the entire ritual system.

In the covenant with Abraham, P wrote the stipulation regarding circumcision and in so doing wrote in a role for the priests in directing the proper control of the discharge of blood. Priest-controlled blood discharge was deemed clean. Blood not controlled by the priests was unclean, as in murder, or even menstrual flow. Women had a very ambiguous stake in the proper fulfillment of the Abrahamic covenant, as women's normal menstrual flow and flow after childbearing marked them as unclean and therefore untouchable. Women participated in the covenant primarily by being mothers, producing sons and kings, yet their reward was their untouchability. Ann Marmesh remarks that the essence of covenant making appears to have been the multiplication of males.[21]

In the Mosaic covenant, P scripted a heavy portion of the stipulations regarding community law and ritualistic observance. The seven-day week in Western culture comes from these priestly writers. The day of rest called "sabbath" that existed in Israel prior to the P rendition fell on the full moon—once every twenty-nine days. By increasing the number of sabbaths, the priests increased the number of sabbathlike feast days, maybe fourfold, and strengthened their position as elites who were privileged to consume meat on a regular basis.

In addition, the seventh year was renamed the sabbath and applied to fallow, although not to the remission of debt, which was extended from every seventh to every forty-ninth year. Not being farmers, the priests must have overestimated the carrying capacity of the Palestinian land, for it actually needed fallowing every two or three years. Yet one day of rest in seven seems better than one in twenty-nine from a worker's point of view, providing cultic responsibilities did not deplete one's resources four times faster. And further, the Mosaic covenant acknowledged that there were rhythms of nature that must be respected in order to assure sustainable food production. Time to renew ourselves as producers, as well as nature's own capacity to produce, and respect for rhythms of productivity alternating with rest are two elements to affirm in a new covenant.

The overriding interest of the priests was in the cult of sacrifice.[22] This cult and their privileged role in it were legitimated by the creation account. In the priestly view, the promulgation of the cult was a way of reinforcing God's acts of creation.

As a ruling elite, the priests were also interested in rules for social justice. In their conception, the world God created was an ordered world in which justice prevailed.[23] However, if injustice becomes the dominant aspect of a social order, the creator God can and does uncreate the world. The creation falls apart in the face of injustice. This direct connection between creation doctrines and social-justice commitments is developed further by Charles McCoy in his essay.

P had a particular perspective on social justice and tended to emphasize fair judicial process and the alleviation of the consequences of debt. Both of these concerns are crucial to contemporary formulations of environmental ethics, as Herman Daly, Jim Lockman, Drew Christiansen, and Carol Robb illustrate in their essays.

It is difficult, however, to avoid the conclusion that P's understanding of social justice was significantly skewed by P's social location as the temple elite. P drew on older practices of periodic remission of debt, release of debt slaves, and return of land held in security for debt. The earlier law provided for the remission of debt and restoration of security, whether labor or real estate, every seven years. P drew on this ancient law, but reassigned such remission to the forty-ninth year.

The purpose of the jubilee year was to protect the land and homes of the villagers, the bulk of the population, but it seems likely that the priestly formulation of the seventh year fallow, in the absence of a seventh year of debt remission, may have exacerbated the vulnerability of the villagers.[24]

To boot, the rules of social justice are promulgated in the holiness law of Leviticus 17–25. The holiness law prohibits incest, adultery, and idol worship, but it also contains prohibitions against making love to a menstruating woman, trimming one's beard, and a man lying with a man as though with a woman, which many people read to be a prohibition against homosexual relations.

On the one hand, we find in Leviticus 25 some of the most explicit imagery of the connection between covenantal obligations to social justice and environmental integrity. Describing the jubilee, Yahweh says to Moses on Mount Sinai:

> You will declare this fiftieth year sacred and proclaim the liberation of all the inhabitants of the land. This is to be a jubilee for you; each of you will return to your ancestral home. . . .
>
> Land must not be sold in perpetuity, for the land belongs to me, and to me you are only strangers and guests. . . . If your relative falls on evil days and has to sell their land, the nearest relative shall come and exercise the right of redemption on what had to be sold. . . . If there is no one to exercise the right of redemption, the property will remain in the possession of the purchaser until the jubilee year. In the jubilee year, the latter must relinquish it. . . .
>
> If you live according to my laws, if you keep my commandments and put them into practice, I will give you the rain you need at the right time; the earth shall give its produce and the trees of the countryside their fruits; you shall thresh until vintage time and gather

grapes until sowing time. You shall eat your fill of bread and live secure in your land.

Along with the principles of social justice come negativity regarding women's bodies and homosexual men. The writers of the law of holiness are in good company with the segments of the church today who see no contradiction between the impulse to control women's and sexual minorities' activities and the impulse to protect the economically vulnerable.

Similar treatment could be given to E's and D's identities and how their political interests affected their contributions to the covenants, but quite enough has been said about basing one's moral stance on polemical sources—written to justify particular configurations of sociopolitical power. Insofar as we are able to know whose interests, agendas, or projects were at stake in these sources, we may be able to discern the most fruitful correlations with efforts to achieve ecological justice in our historical situation.

We would be the first to admit that the value of written traditions that have survived a span of centuries is not limited altogether by the motivations behind them. Motivations are generally complex, mixing self-aggrandizement and genuine concern for the health of the community, but the limitations of the writers' motivations tend to survive in their effects on communities as well.

On the other hand, it is not our intent to criticize the biblical authors for *having* political interests. Everyone does. We do. It is not possible to take a moral stand that is unfettered by social location, although through moral imagination people are able to extend their viewpoints to consider others' welfare. Rather, we encourage participants in all social and moral debate to contribute and to be aware of their particular identities at the same time as they listen to contributions from different social locations. This is probably the only way we can achieve a measure of "objectivity" — by constructing it together.[25]

THE NEW TESTAMENT COVENANT

The final covenant to be considered here is the new covenant given through Jesus the Christ and depicted in the New Testament. The new covenant, which Christians believe Jesus mediated and embodied, was messianic, that is to say, it looked forward to an apocalyptic period wherein God would overthrow the Roman Empire and institute God's rule with Christ as the governor. While Jesus, as a Jew, and all his friends and relations, as Jews, identified themselves as heirs of the covenants, the laws had become massive, complicated, and burdensome. The priests were the lawyers, interpreting the covenants, and they continued to emphasize the purity codes instituted by their predecessors.

Words attributed to Jesus speaking to his disciples at the Last Supper are extremely enigmatic. They are recorded variously in Matthew 26:26–29, Mark 14:22–25, Luke 22:15–20, and Paul's 1 Corinthians 11:23–25. We face the same issues in the New Testament as we did in the Hebrew Scriptures, in that the New Testament authors have different stakes or interests, and knowing these interests helps to understand their portrayal of covenantal relationships. Matthew's agenda, for instance, was to emphasize the continuity of the Christian cult with the Hebrew Scriptures. His version of Jesus' words at the Last Supper reads:

> Now as they were eating, Jesus took some bread, and when he had said the blessing he broke it and gave it to the disciples. "Take it and eat," he said. "This is my body." Then he took a cup, and when he had returned thanks he gave it to them. "Drink all of you from this," he said, "for this is my blood, the blood of the covenant, which is to be poured out for many for the forgiveness of sins. From now on, I tell you, I shall not drink wine until the day I drink the new wine with you in the kingdom of my Father."

While the reference to blood is covenant language of an ancient lineage, it is used here in a new way. During the giving of the Sinai covenant, Moses used the blood of sacrifices to bring the curse into effect should the people break the covenant. Jesus seems not to be talking about bringing the disciples under a curse, but rather of a sacrifice made on their behalf. In Matthew, as in Luke and 1 Corinthians, the tie to the older covenants is most direct through Jeremiah's prophecy (31:31–34) of a new covenant

> not like the covenant which I made with their ancestors on the day I took them by the hand to bring them out of the land of Egypt. They broke that covenant of mine, so I had to show them who was master. ... Deep within them I will plant my Law, writing it on their hearts. Then I will be their God and they shall be my people. ... They will all know me, the least no less than the greatest — It is Yahweh who speaks — since I will forgive their iniquity and never call their sin to mind.[26]

The "new covenant" language in the New Testament focuses on the central role of Jesus the Christ in mediating God's forgiveness, rather than a pact that links God and the people, with responsibilities and obligations necessary for the people to uphold their end of the covenant.

However, Luke's Jesus depicts his own ministry as the promulgation of the jubilee year, the fiftieth year, stipulated in the Mosaic covenant. The jubilee year, a major aspect of covenantal economic policy, functioned to put lower limits on poverty as well as upper limits on the accumulation of wealth. It was so significant that the priests worked overtime to find ways to skirt it, for to implement the jubilee year on its regular basis would have thrown the world of finance into chaos. For Jesus to announce a jubilee year made God's forgiveness of guilt of a significance second only to God's forgiveness of debt. In this respect, Jesus' threat to the political power of Rome and Rome's Judean overseers was rooted, in part, in his *insistence* on the authority of the Mosaic covenant, or so Luke would have us believe. He, too, was concerned to emphasize the continuity of the Christian cult with the Hebrew Scriptures.

We cannot understand the significance of Jesus solely in terms of his announcement of God's forgiveness and his promulgation of the jubilee year. We also need to see him as the one who challenged the hierarchical and elitist elements of all prior covenants. The new covenant was in this sense Jesus' claim that he was the "new humanity," seated at the right hand of God, that is, coenthroned with God and participating in God's transcendence and creativity. Furthermore, Jesus claimed that we are also the new humanity, also coenthroned with God and participating in God's transcendence and creativity. The Samaritan woman at the well (John 4) was the person who first elicited this perspective from Jesus. Because she brought her neighbors to meet him and share in her "paradigm shift to horizontality," she is, in effect, the new Moses.[27]

A significant component of Jesus' teachings and ministry involved setting aside major sections of the purity code, particularly with reference to associations with the unclean, including table fellowship with them. The social hierarchy of the patriarchs was turned on its head in Jesus' teachings, which changed the role of women to active involvement in the "Jesus movement," which no longer treated women primarily as property, and which altered the status of children.

> By making the child—not the father—the model for entry into the reign of God, Jesus again negated the family structure of the society and reversed the hierarchical assumptions that governed all of life.[28]

Given that the burdensome quality of the Mosaic code centered in large measure on the purity code—which drew boundaries between Israel and the uncircumcised and served to draw boundaries between at least four different Jewish sects at the time—Jesus' way was indeed a source of liberation for many people. The suspension of the purity laws made possible the spread of the Christian sect to non-Jews.

Parts of the New Testament seem to emphasize the discontinuity between the old and new covenants, particularly the letters of Paul. The book of Hebrews, on the other hand, portrays the new covenant as better than the Sinai covenant, but not contradicting it; rather, it fulfills it and reveals its deepest meaning.[29] John Calvin took this latter approach in the sixteenth century. Regarding the similarity of the Old and New Testaments, Calvin said,

Both can be explained in one work. The covenant made with all the patriarchs is so much like ours [Christians'] in substance and reality that the two are actually one and the same. Yet they differ in mode of dispensation."[30]

In any case, early Jewish Christians owed to the Hebrew Scriptures their basic law from the Mosaic covenant, which provided a framework for community social structures and norms they shared with their peers not involved in the Jesus movement. Expecting the last days, as they did, they had not bothered to address the matter of normative community structures.

A NEW COVENANT FOR ENVIRONMENTAL ETHICS

For our purposes, it seems appropriate to comment that the contributions of Jesus and his followers can be important for environmental ethics: within the overall assumption of covenantal ties with God, Jesus challenged the implementations of the covenants that reinforced hierarchical relations of dominance and subordination in the religious, social, political, and economic realms. By challenging those implementations, he challenged the authority of the lawyerly priests' purity code. We can affirm these developments, despite the way they were tamed by the early bishops, and at the same time be humbled by the record—the knowledge that one who preaches the invalidity of such power relations will not be welcomed by the constituted authorities.

In the face of formidable tasks, we continue to assert the positive value of bringing forward from the past a moral image to help us move into the future. The image or model of the covenant may serve as a corrective to the alienation and atomism of contemporary culture. However, it cannot serve this purpose unless the unjust property relations are named as the roots of our alienation and confronted in both the political and mythoreligious spheres.

An aspect of covenantal history worth appropriating in negotiating a *new covenant* is public oath taking to a sustainable technology and agriculture: the acknowledgment of the value of the rhythms of nature, which must be respected in order to assure sustainability of ourselves as persons, of our institutions, and of our ecology; and, as a corollary, the recognition of the value of *fallowing*, of rest for renewal.

Building on the implications of our being the "new humanity," participating with God/ess as cocreators of the universe, the new covenant points to not less but more responsibility for the direction of nature's history than may be gathered from the Mosaic covenant. Having been gifted by God/ess with this partnership in the new creation, we have no higher power to hold responsible for the biospheric crisis, nor its possible healing.

Another aspect to affirm is the accountability of all property use to the common good. The Mosaic covenant placed a limit on the extent to which extremes of wealth and poverty could develop, and held the expectation (unfulfilled in practice) that all privately held property would be redistributed periodically to once again achieve equality in property holdings. Here there are two assumptions: land is owned ultimately by the biblical God and the community is accountable to God for its use; and extremes of wealth and poverty are incompatible with community cohesion. Alan Miller and Ann Marie Bahr's essays reflect on the limitations of a notion of ownership that has no accountability to the common good. Accountability for the common good, when the good of all nature is included, is a necessary component of a covenant for a new creation. When acting for one's own benefit to the neglect of other people's or species' benefit is generally acknowledged to be unrighteous, we will be able to say that a restored relationship with God/ess rests on new lines of accountability among people.

Also worth affirming is the collective aspect of covenant making, involving individual commitment to public accountability. The freedoms enjoyed by the propertied elites, and abstractly guaranteed to many who have not had the material wherewithal to use them, affect not only the social order but the other citizens of the world garden. One reason covenantal history has not been a major component of U.S. public mythology and valuing is that it has been supplanted by an ideology of contractual freedom. Such freedom well undergirds atomic individualism, but is insufficient by itself for a sustainable world community, as Alexandra Allen's essay documents.

Yet another component of the biblical covenants to affirm is the personality of God/ess as, among other things, our judge. Our actions should be righteous, not because they follow laws legalistically, in the sense of being without spirit, but because they fulfill the demands of social, including ecological, relationships. God/ess functions as judge to help those who have had their rights taken from them to regain such rights. The purpose of such judgment is the preservation of the community of the people and the rest of creation. The purpose of the judgment is also to create new possibilities for right relationships to arise and be given social standing.

Women, particularly, have no stake in a covenant in which the principals are men, while women are viewed as property. Nor do women have a stake in covenantal ties that engender obligations defined by patriarchs. Women need a new covenant protecting their freedom to be responsible, which is to say, a covenant supporting public policy that will undergird their moral autonomy. Such public policy should guarantee women's rights to bodily integrity. Ina Praetorius Fehle and her colleagues suggest ways in which women have a different history than men in undermining covenantal responsibility.

And, finally, from the covenantal tradition and the Jesus movement, we can derive the practice of mutual respect and egalitarian power relations. We wish to *extend* membership in the covenantal community, not only to gentiles, but also to other species, all world-garden citizens. This inclusion does not disregard the possibility of conflict of interest among species. That is the reason for ethics, and some people are already beginning the task of clarifying what respect for the good of other species means in the practical area.[31] It will require us, however, to cease viewing the land and other species as the backdrop against which the really important stuff — "our" history — takes place. Nature also has history, partially due to human interaction with it; today nature, the biosphere, is saying more clearly than ever before that nature has demands on humans, with dire consequences should we not honor them.[32]

As editors of this collection, Carl Casebolt and I have been charged with the theological and theoretical tasks of exploring what covenantal responsibility to Creator God/ess means in the contemporary U.S. context. Fully aware that no solutions to the threat to the biosphere can emerge from one nation alone, we are nevertheless profoundly sobered by the slowness of our nation and its citizens to face up to the major impact we have on the world's ecosystems. We are convinced that no creation consciousness can emerge with any practical consequence for our national life until we grapple with the structures creating racism, sexism, and poverty. These structures develop economic wealth at the expense of justice for the vulnerable among us and future generations, and leave ecological damage in their wake. Covenantal faithfulness to the biblical God/ess is undermined and made impossible by these structures of injustice.

There is evidence of an emerging appreciation among faith communities for the need of a new covenant that will take account of the crisis of the biosphere and will express the human commitment required to realize a renewed creation. Two examples are the Justice, Peace, and Integrity of Creation movement of the World Council of Churches, as well as the development of the interfaith "Rainbow Covenant" (October 1987), that came out of the meeting in 1986 at Assisi.[33] These efforts speak of a yearning to express comprehensive commitments of the human community within the context of current knowledge, hopes, and goals. Yet the initial products of covenant writing fail to satisfy the need. In the first case, significant environmental and social issues that must be addressed were ignored.[34] In the second case, there was an assumption that environmental integrity can be reestablished without addressing racism, sexism, and poverty.

The writers in this collection of essays explore a wide field in the conviction that far-ranging, comprehensive change is called for. If this breadth of change is to be supported effectively, a broad consensus willing to support it will need to emerge. We conceive of this consensus as convenantal in nature. In preparation, it is critical to stimulate an informed discussion about historical covenants and what should be in a renegotiated covenant.

Topics around which the negotiation will focus will likely include new forms of ownership, new relationships with the rest of creation, and new theories of justice to hold together a society that is sustainable. The three major sections of this book look at each of these tasks from the varied perspectives of the authors.

Part I, New Models of Ownership, explores ways in which property relationships in a primarily market economy can be held accountable to the common good, including the good of the rest of nature: limits to income and poverty, accountability guidelines for bio-technology, and sustainable agriculture. Biblical commitments to hold private property accountable to the common good are major aspects of the "covenants."

Part II, Re-Visioning Relationship with the Rest of Nature, tangles with the ideology that justifies treating the earth and other species primarily as "resources" for human use. Altogether these authors point to ways an ethic that assumes human citizenship with other species, rather than superiority over them, will challenge some of the rationale for species, gender, race, and class domination.

Part III, Reconstructing Justice for Environmental Ethics, examines a major principle for evaluating politics and economics — justice — and asesses its relevance for a social ethic that is ecologically sound. Perhaps because ecological integrity is currently barred by economic and political structures, and also because justice can be understood as right relationship, the need for justice claims in ecological praxis has not abated.

Each section contains perspectives relevant to convenantal responsibility to transform politics, economics, culture, and religious beliefs. No less a project is required to heal the earth.

NOTES

1. Philip Joranson and Ken Butigan, *Cry of the Environment: Rebuilding the Christian Creation Tradition* (Santa Fe, N.M.: Bear, 1984), p. 1.

2. We are building on the biblical practice of referring to deity in such a way as to signal the community out of which testimony is made. El Shaddai, Yahweh, Yahweh is Sabaoth, God, and Abba are all names of deity used in Scriptures. They all in some way reflect the historical context of the worshipping community. Rosemary Ruether's suggestion that the worshipping community appropriate "God/ess" as the name for deity, for reading if not speaking, is a wise one in this historical context. We have become aware of the sexual politics of worship, including the way we refer to the source of all value and power. While we agree that "God" is unlimited by gender, we think the freight of that name is male. "God/ess" helps us communicate about divinity without easily imaging deity as father only. See Rosemary Radford Ruether, *Sexism and God-Talk*: *Toward a Feminist Theology*, (Boston: Beacon, 1983).

3. Vandana Shiva, *Staying Alive: Women, Ecology and Development* (London: Zed Books, 1988). This passage summarizes material on pages 3–4.

4. Ibid., p. 13.

5. Commission for Racial Justice, United Church of Christ, *Toxic Wastes and Race in the United States* (New York: UCC, 1987), p. 11.

6. Wesley Granberg-Michaelson, "Preserving the Earth," *One World* (November 1989), p. 12. This article is a summation of Christian interest and work on

Justice, Peace, and the Integrity of Creation and general environmental issues.

7. William E. Gibson, *A Covenant Group for Lifestyle Assessment*, United Presbyterian Program Agency, 1981. Dieter T. Hessel revised and updated the manual as *Shalom Connections in Personal and Congregational Life* (Ellenwood, Ga.: Program Agency, Presbyterian Church U.S.A., 1986).

8. Max DePree, *Leadership Is an Art* (New York: Doubleday, 1989), p. 51.

9. For more treatment of this debate see J. Baird Callicott's essay in this collection.

10. Much of the treatment of P and J in this introduction depends heavily upon Robert B. Coote and David Robert Ord's *Creation in Seven Days: The Priestly History* (Minneapolis: Fortress, forthcoming) and Robert B. Coote and David Robert Ord's *The Bible's First History* (Philadelphia: Fortress, 1989).

11. Robert Coote and David Ord's *Creation in Seven Days* describes each of the covenants in terms of its sign and name for God.

12. See Delbert R. Hillers, *Covenant: The History of a Biblical Idea* (Baltimore, Md.: Johns Hopkins University Press, 1969), p. 65.

13. This is the comparison made by Delbert Hillers and it is his framework that we are following here. See pp. 29–64.

14. Ibid., pp. 50–51.

15. Hillers makes this point on pp. 68–69.

16. Richard Elliott Friedman, in *Who Wrote the Bible?* (New York: Summit, 1987) dates these sources as follows: J, writing between 848 and 722 B.C.E.; E, writing between 922 and 722 B.C.E.; P, writing between 722 and 609 B.C.E.; and D, writing between 622 and 580 B.C.E.. However, Robert B. Coote and Mary P. Coote date these sources differently. J is dated 1000–960 B.C.E.; E is dated 930–920 B.C.E.; D is dated 622–560 B.C.E.; and P is dated 540–520 B.C.E.. See *Power, Politics, and the Making of the Bible* (Minneapolis: Fortress, 1990).

17. See Coote and Ord, *The Bible's First History*, pp. 304–7.

18. See Coote and Coote, *Power, Politics, and the Making of the Bible* pp. 25–31.

19. Ibid., p. 7.

20. We are indebted for this description of P to Coote and Ord, *Creation in Seven Days*.

21. Ann Marmesh, "Anti-Covenant," in Mieke Bal, ed., *Anti-Covenant: Counter-Reading Women's Lives in the Hebrew Bible* (Sheffield, England: Almond Press, 1989).

22. Coote and Ord, *Creation in Seven Days*, chapter 10.

23. Ibid.

24. Ibid.

25. See Beverly Wildung Harrison, *Making the Connections* (Boston: Beacon, 1985), p. 250.

26. See Hillers, *Covenant*, pp. 179–88.

27. This perspective we owe to Herman Waetjen in conversation, August 22, 1990.

28. William Countryman, *Dirt, Greed, and Sex: Sexual Ethics in the New Testament and Their Implications for Today*. (Philadelphia: Fortress, 1988), p. 188.

29. Hillers, *Covenant*, p. 182.

30. John Calvin, *Institutes of the Christian Religion*, ed. John T. McNeill (Philadelphia: Westminster Press, 1960), II, 10.2, p. 429.

31. See particularly Paul Taylor, *Respect for Nature: A Theory of Environmental Ethics* (Princeton: Princeton University Press, 1986).

32. We do not mean to imply that humankind is not part of nature.

33. The Rainbow Covenant reads as follows: "Brothers and sisters in creation, we covenant this day with you and with all creation yet to be: with every living creature and all that contains and sustains you. With all that is on earth and with the earth itself; with all that lives in the waters and with the waters themselves. With all that flies in the skies and with the sky itself. We establish this covenant that all our powers will be used to prevent your destruction. We confess that it is our own kind who put you at risk of death. We ask for your trust and as a symbol of our intention we mark our covenant with you by the rainbow. This is the sign of the covenant between ourselves and every living thing that is found on earth." The Rainbow Covenant, an interfaith statement of commitment to protect the creation, emerged out of the 1986 Assisi, Italy, meeting of the World Wildlife Fund and senior representatives of Christianity, Buddhism, Judaism, Hinduism and Islam. It was formally adopted at a meeting in 1987 at the Winchester Cathedral in England and was affirmed at the Festival of Creation at the Washington National Cathedral following the Intercontinental Conference on Caring for Creation, May 16-19, 1990 in Washington, D.C.

34. The Justice, Peace, and Integrity of Creation covenants enunciated in Seoul, Korea, focused on global warming as the environmental challenge, ignoring other environmental and social issues.

Agenda for a Healthy, Just, and Sustainable Society

CARL J. CASEBOLT

A new phase in human evolution, long hoped for, yet for most of the twentieth century seeming very remote, has now begun. Some of the characteristics of this new phase can already be discerned: greater sensitivity to the earth, to life, and to ecosystem maintenance; greater reliance on consensus building in local, national, and global forums; growing awareness that peace is the fruit of justice; and the emergence of positive feminine influence and power joining positive masculine attitudes in the nurture and promotion of life.

While the strength of this new way of being and living is still in formation and therefore fragile, it is encouraging that for more than two decades individuals and organizations in the United States and in many other countries have been debating and evaluating the shape and content of this new era. We do not yet have a new or even a renewed creation, but clearly this is what is being discussed as a goal—a realizable goal. The discussion has centered on what a healthy, just, and sustainable society might look like. In conferences, legislatures, articles, and books, questions have been raised about how health is related to industrial activity and pollution, how justice is connected to peace and environmental quality, how the biosphere is affected by human impact, and what future there will be for life on the planet. These discussions and activism for the environment have not operated in a vacuum. Rising concern in the general public is clearly observable. Earth Day 1990, commemorating the twentieth anniversary of the first Earth Day, was an occasion for two hundred million people from nearly every nation to celebrate the earth and to think about how to preserve and protect it. Poll takers tell us that increasing numbers of people support strong action to protect the environment. In 1981, 45 percent of the U.S. citizens agreed with the statement that "protecting the environment is so important that standards and requirements cannot be too high and continuing environmental improvements must be made regardless of cost." In July of 1988 the same question was agreed to by 65 percent of respondents.

Religious communities are being energized. Pope John Paul II's encyclical letter *Sollicitudo Rei Socialis* (*On Social Concern*), issued in 1988, addressed ecological matters and was warmly received by environmentalists. The World Council of Churches Seventh Assembly in Canberra, Australia, in February 1991, chose as its theme "Come Holy Spirit, Renew the Whole Creation." Offices focusing on environmental issues are now established in the Vatican and in Geneva at the World Council of Churches. Interfaith cooperation on environmental issues was a focus of the twenty-fifth anniversary celebration of the World Wildlife Fund in Assisi, Italy, in 1986. That meeting gave birth to a network on conservation and religion that has since issued quarterly bulletins on news, events, and progress in interfaith work to preserve and protect the environment.

Of course, it is the desperate plight of the environment that has awakened people to the need for action. The litany of problems is now fairly familiar — air, ground, and water pollution, soil loss and desertification, ozone depletion, carbon dioxide buildup and global warming, tropical and temperate forest destruction, species losses, unsustainable development, and increased population demands on a shrinking resource base.

Concerned environmentalists and responsible agencies have approached these issues directly and have proposed and worked for solutions to these particular problems. The implied belief is that these problems can be solved and a sustainable society/environment developed without addressing such social evils as racism, sexism, and extremes of wealth and poverty. Other observers, claiming to see a more complex picture, have pointed to disharmonies and injustices in our culture that are blocking an effective resolution. Steady-state economists, the ecofeminist movement, and certain religious communities are documenting how environmental problems need to be seen in the context of other economic and social realities. They are suggesting that a successful strategy must incorporate improvements in gender, race, and economic relations, address biotechnology, consider economic and political structures, and rethink assumptions about "ownership" and "stewardship."

A comprehensive program is essential now because we may be at the most propitious moment in history to make significant progress toward the goal of a healthy, just, and sustainable society. The danger is that the momentum of events and the manifold crises pressing upon societies could precipitate partial, incomplete solutions.

What should be on a comprehensive agenda for this new society? Informed people are concerned about what will be put in and what will be left out of this new program. What direction is taken and whether their cause will be remembered matters profoundly to oppressed persons and people who are in poverty.

We cannot build an agenda in a vacuum as though nothing has been done. Work in the United States started in the late sixties, and we have already benefited from the incorporation of numerous proposals into law and public policy. If we are to have confidence in an adequate agenda, we need to know what has gone before and what additions and improvements are needed to make it comprehensive and ultimately successful.

This essay will look at the emergence of major environmental concerns in the last two decades, consider the National Council of Churches Eco-Justice evaluations of one of the major U.S. studies, *An Environmental Agenda for the Future*,[1] review the programs of international commissions on environment and development, examine the consensus platform of the Peace and Environment Project, and conclude with a look at the task ahead.

BEGINNINGS OF A NEW ENVIRONMENTAL MOVEMENT

Following on the interest generated by the 1972 United Nations Stockholm Conference on the Human Environment, the Club of Rome studies *The Limits to Growth* (1972)[2] and *Mankind at the Turning Point* (1974),[3] Gerald Barney and sixty-three leading environmentalists from the United States published *The Unfinished Agenda*,[4] a citizens' guide to environmental issues. This agenda recommended programs for family planning and population stabilization, energy conservation, renewable energy, recycling of automobiles, air- and water-pollution control, implementation of a toxic-substance control act for new chemicals and for those already in the environment, protection of endangered species, strict controls on bioengineering, and the advocacy of societal decision making in favor of the environment.

While this consensus document was not endorsed by major environmental organizations, it was widely read and critiqued by knowledgeable authorities. Its recommendations have helped guide the movement and generate support for environmental legislation. *The Unfinished Agenda* focuses on solving environmental problems in isolation, but it does recognize that educational issues are involved in the present crisis, particularly the role of the media in promoting the consuming over the conserving society.

Lester Brown of the Worldwatch Institute published *Building a Sustainable Society* in 1981.[5] This study gave enough facts on the deterioration of the environment to establish that a cross-over point had already been passed. Basic biological systems stayed ahead of population demands only until the 1960s. Indicators of decline since then are: population growth outstripped forest growth after 1964; world fish catch per person has fallen 13 percent since 1970; grasslands production of beef, mutton, and wool began to fall behind population growth in the 1970s when population exceeded four billion; and overfishing, overgrazing, and overcutting of forests have become widespread.[6]

By raising the question of sustainability, Brown gave a new and important name for the goal being sought by the environmental movement. While demonstrating the unsustainability of our present course, the study showed how it is possible to make the changes to put us on a sustainable path.

Since 1984, the Worldwatch Institute has published annual State of the World reports. While all categories have shown deterioration each year since, the institute maintains that all the elements necessary to establish a sustainable society are still present.

Recognizing that the environmental movement would benefit from direct participation in the policy dialogue preceding the presidential conventions of the major political parties in the United States, grassroots environmental groups joined with peace groups for the first time in 1983–84 to develop a consensus document, *Platform for Peace and Common Security and for a Healthy and Sustainable Environment*.[7] This document was the work of the Peace and Environmental Convention Coalition (PECC), formed in San Francisco in July 1983. PECC included more than eighty groups, sixty-five of which endorsed the platform. It was used as a basis for negotiations with the California Democratic party and with the national Republican and Democratic parties. It was also given to representatives of the Union of Soviet Socialist Republics. Copies were shared with other grassroots organizations in the United States and with international groups. The endorsers urged the next adminstration to adopt strong policies with respect to foresight capability, sustainable development, biological diversity, hazardous wastes, water resources, clean air, solid waste, pesticides and herbicides, energy, land and wilderness protection, oceans and the law of the sea, and population planning. Its major concern was for the United States and Union of Soviet Socialist Republics to immediately abandon the arms race and cooperate in the "environmental recovery race."[8] The recommendation that the superpowers start cooperating on environmental issues for mutual benefit was acted upon, and in the summer of 1984 the United States and Union of Soviet Socialist Republics revived the agreement to cooperate on environmental issues that had been sundered in the wake of the invasion of Afghanistan. This agreement and others added at the Geneva summit in the next year have played a role in creating the new climate of cooperation between the superpowers.

AGENDA OF MAJOR ENVIRONMENTAL GROUPS AND ECOJUSTICE RESPONSES

Although leading environmental organizations engaged in a lively debate on public policy before the 1984 election, no comprehensive consensus emerged from these discussions. This left it up to the grassroots organizations and to the Peace and Environmental Convention Coalition to put together a comprehensive consensus on environmental issues.

The problem of finding recommendations for an environmental agenda acceptable to members and governing boards was finessed in 1985 by developing *An Environmental Agenda for the Future*. This consensus was the work of the chief executive officers of ten main-line environmental groups.[9] Funded by five foundations, it does not speak for the entire movement but does represent the overall approach to public policy taken by the ten organizations.

Major recommendations of the *Agenda* include:

1. Moratorium on all nuclear-weapons production
2. Stabilization of population, with sustainable management of resources and reasonable quality of life for all people
3. Shift from nonrenewable to renewable energy
4. Protection of water resources from unsustainable use and contamination
5. Reduction of sulfur emissions by 50 percent and EPA action on other air pollutants
6. A five-year $12-billion extension of Superfund
7. Government measures to reduce production of hazardous wastes
8. Creation of a permanent soil conservation reserve

Recognizing the potential influence of this publication, members of the Eco-Justice Working Group of the National Council of Churches responded by lifting up concerns that they saw as either omitted or inadequately addressed.[10] The working group, a creation of the National Council of Churches and the Joint Strategy and Action Committee, seeks to embody and deepen the concern of the churches for ecology and justice and to foster communication and collaboration between religious and environmental bodies. The working group approved nearly all of the *Agenda* recommendations. Criticisms were mainly about perspective and what was left out. For instance, there was an assumption that poor countries generate population problems and bear the main responsibility for change. Dieter Hessel noted that for more than a decade denominations in the National Council of Churches have stressed five interrelated causes of poverty, malnutrition, and rapid population growth:

> 1) unjust economic structures that are a legacy of colonialism, 2) lack of appropriate agricultural and economic development in the two-thirds world, 3) consumptive use of resources by the rich countries, 4) religious or cultural opposition to effective family planning methods, and 5) paltry multilateral investment in a strategy to meet basic human needs through food distribution, programs of literacy, maternal and infant health care, and employment.[11]

Regarding the perspective toward water, Owen Owens was concerned about the idea in *Agenda* of water as a "resource" (a concern that is also applicable to the chapter on "Wild Living Resources").

> Conservationists who uncritically begin by thinking of streams and lakes as resources, have already taken a major step toward seeing them as mere entities to be used .... Streams and lakes are gifts of

the Creator, sources of life, and are to be approached with fundamental respect.[12]

Another flaw in the water section is the failure to mention the existence
of the United Nations Water Decade program and the neglect of its funding
by the United States and other industrialized countries. More than a billion
people are affected by water-related diseases, and more than twenty-five
million people die each year in developing countries because of water pollution.[13] The U.N. Water Decade effort aimed at providing adequate supplies of clean water to everyone.

The working group noted that the genetic engineering section overlooked the economic injustice that agrigenetic research and development
intensifies. A Congressional Office of Technology Assessment report
recently pointed out that a shift to biotechnology would accelerate small-
farm bankruptcies. The working group suggested that support should be
given to public-policy initiatives that would place limits on biotechnology
to avoid injustices and counterproductive developments.

Agenda's $12-billion recommendation for hazardous-waste cleanup is
considerably under official estimates of need. The EPA, in 1984, placed
the costs at $22.7 billion. The Office of Technology Assessment estimated
in 1985 that total costs would run to $100 billion. Concern was expressed
that the full magnitude of the problem be faced and that recommended
expenditures be closer to estimated need.

Regarding soil erosion and degradation, *Agenda* failed to mention the
disturbing global trends toward desertification, which, according to U.S.
and U.N. estimates, affect from one-half to one billion people. The U.N.
Food and Agriculture Organization estimates that sixty countries will be
unable to feed their people by the year 2000 if present trends continue.
The U.N. Plan To Combat Desertification, started in 1977, aimed to raise
$2.5 billion per year for reforestation and soil-conservation programs. By
1985 that would have come to $20 billion. Instead the plan was largely
ignored, and receipts totaled $48,524(!), with $26 million reported coming
in through auxiliary programs.[14]

Regarding sustainable development, the working group would have liked
to have seen an acknowledgment that the

> market-oriented model of development fostered by the U.S. Govern-
> ment in the 1980s ... has accelerated trends of economic injustice
> ... and ecological destruction ... [and] "developed" country behavior
> has contributed to this pattern by failing to provide poor countries
> and sectors adequate support for leadership development that can
> foster policies of self-sufficiency."[15]

In the way of general criticisms, William E. Gibson noted *Agenda's* failure to challenge existing structures. The authors missed a good opportunity

to build a case for reevaluating the prevailing ideology of economic growth. Acknowledging that polls show citizen opinion to be two-to-one in favor of environmental protection over economic growth if a choice must be made, *Agenda* declines to build a case on this finding and quickly offers the comforting reassurance that no choice is necessary. Continued economic growth is regarded as essential because "Past environmental gains will be maintained and new ones made more easily in a healthy (i.e., growing) economy than in a stagnant one with more continued high unemployment."[16] The working group asks: in the period of economic growth from 1983 to 1986, were environmental gains in fact maintained? The book is laden with evidence that they were not.

Taking note of the failure to acknowledge tension between profit seeking and earth keeping, the working group observed:

> A continuous monumental effort is required to transform the kind of narrow self-interest that drives development into a self-interest sufficiently enlightened to make it sustainable or to acknowledge its limits [because] the inherent tendencies of the economy (and the concept of the good life it promotes) work against commitment (to sustainability), just as they work against an equitable distribution of the fruits of the earth and products of human labor.[17]

In regard to financial requirements, *Agenda* does not examine the inadequate funding for environmental concerns in light of the money being spent for military purposes. Research indicates a need for $200–$300 billion globally per year — to provide for protection and conservation of soil, water, and forest resources, to maintain biological diversity, to control and reduce hazardous wastes, to reduce air pollution and carbon dioxide buildup, to establish foresight capability, to develop sustainable energy systems, and to move toward population stability. Actual funding in the United States and in the rest of the world is in the range of 10–15 percent of the need. *The Bulletin of Atomic Scientists* (April 1984) reported that overall federal spending had increased 41 percent since 1981 and that military spending had increased 70 percent. In the same period, there was a 44 percent decrease in federal spending for energy-conservation programs and a 19 percent decrease in federal spending for pollution control and abatement. Although such figures are missing from *Agenda*, there is acknowledgment that the "operating budget of EPA has declined since 1980 and now stands, in real dollars, where it was in 1975, when the agency had no responsibility for toxic substances or hazardous wastes."[18]

The sense of urgency that the facts seem to indicate and that the Eco-Justice Working Group is calling for is missing from *Agenda*. The working group sees lying ahead "a herculean task involving revolutionary changes in industrial methods, cessation of some kinds of manufacturing, and (probably) a lifestyle poorer for some in material things but (potentially) richer for everyone in quality."[19]

Various representatives of environmental organizations, some of whom are members of the Eco-Justice Working Group, were grateful for these contributions to dialogue and expressed an interest in a continued exchange of views.

Shortcomings aside, *An Environmental Agenda for the Future* was a giant step forward and it laid the groundwork for an even more ambitious and helpful project in 1987–88.

Following on the *Agenda* effort nine of the members (minus the Environmental Defense Fund) were joined by nine other groups (Defenders of Wildlife, Environmental Action, Global Tomorrow Coalition, Natural Resources Defense Council of America, Renew America, the Oceanic Society, Trout Unlimited, Union of Concerned Scientists, and Zero Population Growth) in producing a *Blueprint for the Environment*[20] in anticipation of the 1988 U.S. elections. The *Blueprint*, consisting of more than 700 specific recommendations, addressed these global environmental threats: global warming of the atmosphere; depletion of the stratospheric ozone layer; ocean pollution; environmental degradation in developing nations; loss of tropical forests and other wildlife habitats; population growth; wasteful and environmentally harmful use of energy; acid rain/air pollution; water pollution; and uncontrolled use of toxic substances.[21]

The group also proposed an environmental budget that called for additional spending of $5.455 billion. The breakdown included $2 billion for more energy efficient transportation, $1.1 billion for global-climate-change initiatives, $1.1 billion for saving tropical forests and conserving biological diversity, $400 million for energy conservation, $300 million for land- and water-conservation fund, $100 million for fish and wildlife service, $130 million for U.S. and international family planning, and $325 million to increase the Environmental Protection Agency's operating budget.

These recommendations were delivered to President-elect Bush after the November elections.

Blueprint represents a major breakthrough in consensus building. For the first time, these groups put aside disagreements (both large and small) to work together developing detailed guidelines for the nation to follow. Some of the flaws noted in critiques of *An Environmental Agenda for the Future* can also be seen in this effort, particularly in the modest proposals for increased funding for the environment. However, the groups reached out to the religious community and tried to make what recommendations survived consistent with that sector's values. Its detailed suggestions, specifically addressed to the appropriate government agency and giving all the information needed for implementation, make it a handy guide for policy makers and agency directors. It is a considerable service to the nation and to the world. The *Blueprint* makes several noteworthy recommendations.

Regarding debt loads in the two-thirds' world, it proposes a detailed study of outstanding loans owed to the United States by Third World countries, and a program under which they can be reduced or totally waived in a way that promotes environmentally sustainable economic development.[22]

Regarding health and environmental impacts of meat-centered diets, it requests the

Department of Health and Human Services, in cooperation with the Department of Agriculture, the Department of the Interior and the Environmental Protection Agency, should develop a comprehensive study on Diet Choices and the Environment, like the Surgeon General's report on Diet and Health, examining the impact of various diets on the environment.[23]

Such a study would look particularly at the impact of intensive animal husbandry on the environment and the health impacts of a meat-centered diet.

The administrator of the Agency for International Development should announce that the central theme of the Agency's entire foreign assistance program will be sustainable development, and that it will focus on three priority goals: sustainable economic growth, eliminating poverty and preventing environmental degradation.[24]

Blueprint will have a lasting value, as recommendations not implemented now can be revisited in future administrations. As will be seen, underlying needs will not go away just because they are ignored.

INTERNATIONAL COMMISSIONS

United Nations commissions on environment and development have helped build a consensus. Inquiries headed by Willi Brandt and Olof Palme preceded the 1987 World Commission on Environment and Development (WCED) report *Our Common Future*.[25] The Brandt Commission, reporting in 1980 and 1983, set out from an economic standpoint and found that world poverty was inextricably bound up with arms spending and the environment. The Palme report looked at what common security might be and offered the perspective that common security should replace "national security" in our interdependent world. The WCED closed the circle by showing that economic growth in both north and south depends on the health of the earth. It makes a plea for sustainable growth—development that meets the needs of the present, without compromising the ability of future generations to meet their own needs.[26] It explains the need for the developed world to abandon the armament culture and its rivalries and pay attention to and help the less-developed world in order to have a common future that is environmentally and economically more secure.

The WCED places its concern for those afflicted with poverty in the center of the dialogue. It notes that there are more people hungry in today's world than ever before — some 14 percent (340 million) more in 1980 than in 1970 with expectations of a continuing increase in years ahead.[27] It points out that while there were 18.5 million people affected by droughts annually in the 1960s, there were 24.4 million so affected yearly in the 1970s. Floods affected 5.2 million people each year in the 1960s but devastated 15.4 million annually in the 1970s. While statistics were not yet collected for the 1980s the WCED expects that they will continue the disturbing trend.[28] These millions are caught in the downward spiral of poverty leading to environmental degradation, which then leads to even greater poverty and greater environmental deterioration.

The commissioners note that "living standards that go beyond the basic minimum are sustainable only if consumption standards everywhere have regard to long-term sustainability. Yet many of us live beyond the world's ecological means, for instance in our patterns of energy use."[29] The WCED recommendation is for the developed world to reduce its consumption of fossil fuels by 50 percent over the next thirty to forty years while shifting to renewable sources. World consumption levels give a picture of the distribution problems.[30]

Table 1
Distribution of World Consumption, Averages for 1980–82

Commodity	Units of Per Capita Consumption	Developed Countries (26 percent of population)		Developing Countries (74 percent of population)	
		Share in World Consumption (percent)	Per Capita Consumption	Share in World Consumption (percent)	Per Capita Consumption
Food:					
Calories	Kcal/day	34	3,395	66	2,389
Protein	gms/day	38	99	62	58
Fat	gms/day	53	127	47	40
Paper	kg/year	85	123	15	8
Steel	kg/year	79	455	21	43
Other Metals	kg/year	86	26	14	2
Commercial Energy	mtce/year	80	5.8	20	0.5

Source: WCED estimates based on country-level data from FAO, UN Statistical Office, UNCTAD, and American Metal Association

The commissioners ask us to imagine providing for another human world the size of the present one within the next century and at a time when much of the world's quality resources have been degraded or used up. They speak of a "few decades" to make changes, and yet acknowledge that there are few institutions in place that are capable of making an adequate response.

The WCED recommended that regional hearings take place in the industrialized countries to focus on the crisis of sustainable development. Such a hearing was held in Los Angeles on November 3 and 4, 1989; one of its results was the paper "U.S. Citizens' Response to Sustainable Development," subsequently published by the Global Tomorrow Coalition.[31] This guide gives detailed recommendations on what individuals, institutions and governments can do. It also gives timetables as to when these actions should be accomplished.

The faith of the commissioners that present economic structures can modulate into sustainable policies and sustainable development is striking. Surely a major educational effort to transform our culture from a consuming to a conserving society is a necessary adjunct to such an undertaking. Society has yet to think through the environmental implications of affluent life-styles and the general acceptance of high consumption as "good." An important signal of economic and social responsibility in the developed, industrial world would be a recognition of the benefits of modest, conserving life-styles to the environment and to our descendants. The commissioners need to give this issue a high priority.

Also missing from *Our Common Future* are references to steady-state economics and how sustainable development differs from customary patterns of economic growth. A follow-up investigation by the World Commission of how to achieve value changes and economic restructuring would be very helpful.

CONSENSUS OF PEACE, ENVIRONMENTAL, AND RELIGIOUS GROUPS

The Peace and Environment Project (PEP), an outgrowth of the 1983–84 Peace and Environmental Convention Coalition, reached out to national organizations by establishing, in 1987, an office in the Washington, D.C., area. Following the same procedures adopted by the PECC in 1984, the project circulated drafts among interested parties and organizations and, through responses from a broad range of groups, developed their consensus positions, which were then transmitted to the political committees and party organizations of the Democratic and Republican parties. This time more than seventy national and regional groups endorsed the final draft. Among them were: SANE/FREEZE, National Jobs with Peace Campaign, Northern California Greens, East Bay Green Alliance, Friends of the Earth, Center for Ethics and Social Policy, Center for Economic Conversion, World Citizens, National Council of Churches Eco-Justice Working Group,

Church of the Brethren Washington office, and Unitarian-Universalist Association of Churches Washington office.

Context for the Development of the Consensus Platform

The groups working on the document developed a setting for their recommendations that was elaborated in "Toward Organic Security: Environmental Restoration or the Arms Race?"[32] This study noted that when the industrial revolution began (about 1760) humanity started taxing the earth's life-support system, then several billion years old, at a rate higher than it could replenish itself. Some two hundred years later, the demands of industrial culture—including those on the atmosphere's ability to absorb carbon dioxide emissions—have begun to strain severely the earth's capacity for renewal and life support. A graph developed by Cliff Humphrey and the Ecology Action Education Institute demonstrates the historical drawdown of the earth's resources and the potential of producing either a "survival gap" or, as we would now say, a sustainable society.

The optimistic future scenario is evident in the solid lines moving toward

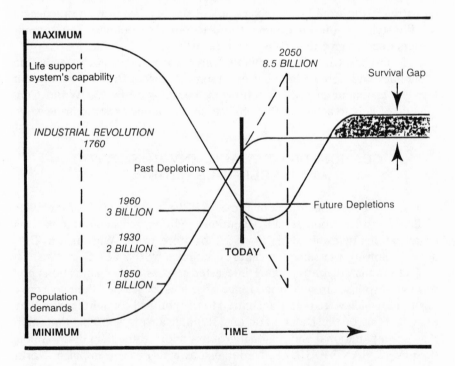

Ecology Action Education Institute, 1986.
Used by permission.

the survival gap; the pessimistic future view is indicated by the dotted lines for the continuation of current trends. The reality is that we are witnessing and participating in the continuation of the pessimistic trends.

The Peace and Environment Project study in 1986 and the United Nations 1987 Conference on the Relationship of Disarmament and Development came to the same conclusion: the continuation of present military outlays will preclude adequate expenditures for environmental and economic sustainability and development.

Development needs in the two-thirds world, now too often ignored, are urgent. Countries burdened with heavy debt and falling commodity prices often take a "way out" that involves exploiting resources to generate hard currency. This accelerates environmental decline and makes it less likely that they can become productive partners in trade relations in the future. The Peace and Environment Project recommends a comprehensive program to restore damaged ecosystems here and abroad and to provide assistance to countries seeking sustainable development.

Critique of Peace and Environment Project Platform

The platform follows the general outline of policies recommended by major environmental groups.[33] Unique to the Peace and Environment Project are the suggestions to provide assistance to low-income people to mitigate the rising costs of environmental protection; studies of and policies for ecological city development; a requirement that hazardous-waste producers implement waste reduction plans; the recommendation to spend $100 billion to clean up hazardous waste; the proposal for disposal taxes on goods that cannot be recycled, reused, repaired, or cleanly burned; a call for mandatory recycling; biotechnology restrictions; and a proposal for a development policy based on an ethic of fair and equal rights to the earth for all, with increases in land value being taxed for the benefit of the whole community.

The Peace and Environment Project, like its predecessor, the 1984 Peace and Environment Convention Coalition, recommended an immediate halt to the arms race, dramatically lowered defense budgets, and adequate funding to restore the environmental base for our society and economy. While defense-budget reductions seemed a remote possibility in 1984 and even in 1988, events in Eastern Europe and the Soviet Union have made this a possible goal for the immediate future, and the project deserves credit for making the case early and for building support for change.

PEP recommendations to address poverty at home and abroad are not forcefully or effectively made. The platform does call for support for the recommendations of the World Commission on Environment and Development. What it lacks are programs to move from present growth-economy models to a steady-state economy model, such as has been outlined by Herman Daly.

The platform is largely silent about problems of racism, although it recommends protection of tropical rain forests and their indigenous peoples. There is no mention of the relation of sexism and the environment. Various Green party documents in the United States and in Europe have addressed this issue, so it is disappointing not to have this in an environmental platform.

What is hopeful about this consensus is that initial steps have been taken to mobilize major segments of the citizenry to support an environmental reconstruction. Now that religious organizations and environmental activists are thinking these issues through and deciding which they can support, the way seems open for more cooperative work with mainline environmental organizations in coming struggles with economic and political power centers resistant to change.

As this is written, the religious community has yet to commit major resources and staff to the arduous task of influencing public policy in the direction of sustainability. While it has major commitments in justice, health, and peace, there has been a noticeable reluctance to move into environmental areas. Some religious leaders have contended that justice issues must be given priority over environmental issues, even though their interconnections have been carefully described by the Eco-Justice Working Group (of the NCC). There may also be a general assumption that mainline environmental groups are equipped for and capable of handling these issues by themselves. Environmental organizations do have considerable clout in the political arena, and this has grown as the environmental crisis has deepened. Yet experiences I have had in Washington, D.C., working on environmental policy have taught me that achievements in clean air, toxics, and agricultural policy are hard to come by, always contentious in Congress; they usually depend on extensive grassroots education and organization, as well as on dedicated advocacy among senators and representatives. Massive problems requiring international cooperation, such as global climate change, ozone depletion, and sustainable development in the two-thirds world, are now confronting a political establishment in the United States that has fallen short of meeting environmental standards in protecting its own population. Future successes will clearly require much greater involvement, not only by environmental groups but also by religious organizations and communities. By delaying its own education in environmental issues and its commitment of resources, the religious community is postponing, if not placing at risk, the achievement of a healthy, just, and sustainable society.

THE TASK AHEAD

Environmentalists and those segments of the religious community that follow environmental legislation are aware that, in spite of apparent public willingness to support strong laws and regulations to protect the environment, entrenched legislators in key committees and their allies in business are frequently able to thwart progress when economic interests seem threatened. Lawmakers are under the impression that one of their major obligations is to keep economic growth a first priority. Public understanding and acceptance of the need for a steady-state economy is probably going to have to precede its adoption by legislators.

Working out thorough consensus programs delineating what needs to be done to build a healthy, just, and sustainable society is a big step forward. But it is only that. It is a step in a process that may well be as difficult as the struggle for civil rights was in the 1960s and 70s. As with civil rights, the culture has waited too long to act.

While it is important to affirm components for environmental restoration and sustainability recommended in various agendas, the religious community has a larger vision that can be of real service to the world. Ina Praetorius Fehle, Susanne Kramer-Friedrich, Monika Wolgensinger, and Irene Gysel-Nef in their essay in this collection have stressed the role of sexism in aggravating environmental deterioration. It is becoming clearer to many that full participation of women in the society, in religious leadership, and in the economy would be of great benefit.

Racism is an environmental concern. The World Council of Churches document "Towards an Ecumenical Theological Affirmation on Justice, Peace and the Integrity of Creation" notes the terrible effects of racism on the people of South Africa and on indigenous peoples everywhere.

> All suffer increasing assaults upon their lives and sacred traditions. Although "development" and "national security" are reasons given for rejecting the land rights claims of indigenous peoples, the core cause of their oppression is racism. The unjust theft of their original lands, as well as their continued and increased oppression by dominant powers, causes them extreme spiritual, psychological and physical suffering.[34]

Ironically, it is indigenous peoples who have learned how to live most cooperatively on and with the land, and their destruction frequently leads to the destruction of the land itself.

What might happen if the need for broad-based changes does not elicit a response in contemporary society?

> If climate change, soil erosion, deforestation, and population growth continue along their current trajectories, the poverty rate will almost certainly skyrocket, perhaps doubling worldwide by the second half of the next century. In other words, without major changes in policy at every level, from multilateral institutions to the smallest villages, half of humanity could be living in absolute poverty some time between 2050 and 2075.[35]

Might it be possible to maintain islands of affluence in a rising sea of poverty and environmental degradation? Alan Durning, author of the Worldwatch study, is skeptical:

> Today, poverty is no longer only intolerable from a moral point of view. Failure to end its scourge will not only stain the history of our age, it will predestine the destruction of much of the shared biosphere. For, although environmental damage penalizes the poor more consistently and severely than it does the rich, the downward spiral eventually becomes a circle embracing all humanity, rich and poor alike.[36]

Moral admonitions from holy scriptures to care for the creation, the poor, the widow and orphan, and to do justice come to us now in different raiments. The clothes worn are those of *environmental necessity*. This is a twentieth-century revelation, and it may be realistic to hope that religious communities, sensing a new validation for their tradition and seeing the connection to environmental protection, will find renewed energy and inspiration for the tasks ahead.

For those who have been touched by the plight of the earth and of so many of its inhabitants, an active response will include life-style changes, organizing, resisting pollution and ecocide, and careful attention to public-policy remedies. Changes may come unevenly, haltingly, but every step along the way toward a healthy, just, and sustainable society can be beneficial and rewarding. If we were to chart the stages toward such a society, we could use a model pioneered by the Worldwatch Institute,[37] which could accept additional categories as our wisdom in these matters increases. From what is discussed and examined in this book, we could affirm the areas found in Table 2 on page 41 for action.

What about the timing of a major environmental, social effort? When the Environmental Policy Institute, the Oceanic Society, and Friends of the Earth joined forces in 1988, they gave as one of the reasons for working together that the next decade would bring the most significant years for environmental legislation. Such other authorities as the Worldwatch Institute and the World Commission on Environment and Development see the next thirty to forty years as a window of opportunity for the environment. Sentiment is building for casting the next ten years as the "turnaround decade." Obviously, the sooner we can make the necessary adjustments the less risk and suffering there will be. However, if this thirty- to forty-year window of maximum opportunity is broken down in segments it might be easier to envision how success could be achieved.

In the first decade, a strong emphasis on education for all segments of the society willing to listen should be coupled with public policy initiatives focused on environmental restoration, sustainability, reducing carbon dioxide buildup, and population planning. Progress is made in eliminating sexism and racism in the industrial, developed world.

Table 2

Category	Early Stage	Advanced Stage
Gender Roles	Equality for women, especially job opportunity and pay equity	Partnership
Race Relations	Equality, especially job opportunity, civil rights, and pay equity	Partnership
Poverty/Equity	Acceptance of poverty as environmental issue	More equitable sharing of earth's resources
Health Care	Health/environment connections established	Universal access
Economy	Disarmament/Conversion	Steady-state economy established
Life-style	Simplicity, frugality, and conservation emerge as social values	Esteem established for new life-styles
Energy	Conservation and sharing with less-developed countries	Reliance on renewable sources of energy
Foreign aid	Debt reduction and debt-for-nature swaps	Assistance in sustainable development
Population	Introduce family planning	Adopt family planning
Recyling	Voluntary	Mandatory
Transportation	Fuel efficient	Non-fossil-fuel energy and reliance on mass transit
Water	Nondegradation	Sustainable use
Forests	Halt deforestation	Sustainable use
Land	Introduction of sustainable agriculture	Adopt sustainable agriculture; land-use planning
Biotechnology	International dialogue on implications	Strict controls established
Attitude to Life	Respect for nature and life	Concern for the fulfillment of life universalized

In the second decade, the stress on education continues and steady-state economics is introduced in major industrial states. Continued emphasis is placed on public and international policy relating to restoration and sustainability. Sexism and racism are seen as barriers to progress as society commits itself to their eradication. Population-planning programs are now in place.

In the third decade, steady-state economics is adopted throughout the industrial world and assistance toward adopting steady-state economics is given to the developing world. Population stabilization trends become visible.

With a consensus developing around major aspects of environmental restoration and sustainability, the chances for substantial movement toward these goals are good. Promoting sustainable growth and development in the less-developed world while moving toward a steady-state economy in the developed world obviously requires new educational programs and new international arrangements. The small group of steady-state economists and the small group of religious observers aware of the need for economic changes must get a better hearing.

Coalition building will be an important part of the next phase of work. People working on racism, sexism, and poverty need to connect with environmentalists. Images of environmentalism as a "middle-class concern" or as "elitist" need to give way to seeing the interconnections between all the issues. Jesse Jackson emphasizes that "the environment is, in the final analysis, a political question. That means we must organize across and against lines of race, class, gender, nation and geography in order to save the earth and save ourselves."[38] It should be expected that this organizing will be difficult — if not impossible — without society's commitment to alleviating the injustices that have created misunderstandings, divisions, and wounds associated with race, class, gender, and nation.

That the global community has made progress in its efforts to become conscious of wounds and to start the healing process can be seen in the International Convention on the Elimination of All Forms of Racial Discrimination which has now been ratified by 129 countries. The U. N. Convention on the Elimination of All Forms of Discrimination Against Women has been ratified by 103 countries (13 members of the present U. N. Security Council's 15 members have ratified both Conventions).

Regrettably, the United States of America has not ratified either convention. Presidential administrations in office from 1981 through 1990 have declined to send either convention to the Senate for ratification.[39] It is difficult to see these lapses as anything other than intentional. Human rights activists were bitterly disappointed again when President Bush vetoed the 1990 Civil Rights Act. Quick action on both these treaties and on the Civil Rights Act would not only advance the cause of human rights, it would also prepare the culture for a major advance in its attitude to life and to its concern for the fulfillment of life.

To speak of the fulfillment of life, a new phase in human evolution, or a new creation in the circumstances that have developed in the wake of the Persian Gulf war may sound inappropriate. The war in the gulf and its repercussions will have negative environmental, economic, religious, and cultural effects for decades to come. Can war bring any peace to that troubled land? If so, it will be uncharacteristic of the region and its history.

The resort to war in the late twentieth century in Kuwait-Iraq with its overtones of conflict over oil is likely to influence attitudes toward the place of oil in the global economy as well as the efficacy of force to protect access to key natural resources. Cultures that have not learned to live within limits set by the natural environment are the ones that try to take by force what their unchecked appetites demand. In many cases, Middle Eastern instability is exacerbated by the slowness of industrialized nations to shift to reliance on renewable energy.

So far as we know, in the latter part of the twentieth century of our common era, Earth is the sole repository of life in the universe. The larger struggle we are now engaged in is to see whether life that has become conscious of itself and of what is needed to sustain life will develop the compassion, wisdom, and dedication required to enable life to continue and flourish. This is the challenge of our existence and our response to the will of God/ess that life—all life—shall be fulfilled.

The authors contributing to this collection of essays write out of an awareness of present realities that is also informed by a faith that humanity is capable of change and development. We see no survival value in pessimism and though our time be dark, we see strengths in our faith that have yet to be called on and that stand ready to help us in the present crisis/opportunity.

NOTES

1. John H. Adams, Louise C. Dunlap, Jay D. Hair, Frederick D. Krupp, Jack Lorenz, J. Michael McCloskey, Russell W. Peterson, Paul C. Pritchard, William A. Turnage, and Karl Wendelowski, *An Environmental Agenda for the Future* (Washington, D.C.: Island Press, 1985).

2. Donella H. Meadows, Dennis L. Meadows, Jorgen Randers, and William W. Behrens III, *The Limits to Growth* (New York: Universe Books, 1972).

3. Mihajlo Mesarovic and Eduard Pestel, *Mankind at the Turning Point.* (New York: E.P. Dutton/Reader's Digest Press, 1974).

4. Gerald O. Barney, ed., *The Unfinished Agenda* (New York: Thomas Y. Crowell, 1977).

5. Lester R. Brown. *Building a Sustainable Society* (New York: W.W. Norton, 1981).

6. Ibid., pp. 50, 51.

7. Peace and Environmental Convention Coalition, *Platform for Peace and Common Security and for a Healthy and Sustainable Environment* (San Francisco: Henry H. Dakin, 1984).

8. Ibid., p. 26.

9. Adams et al., *An Environmental Agenda for the Future.*

10. Material from individual position papers was incorporated by Carl Casebolt in a summary article, "An Eco-Justice Perspective on *An Environmental Agenda,*" which appeared in *The Egg* (Fall 1986).

11. Ibid.

12. Ibid.

13. Ibid.

14. Ibid, p. 9.

15. Ibid.

16. Ibid, pp. 4, 5.

17. Ibid, p. 5.

18. Ibid.

19. Ibid, p. 9.

20. T. Allen Comp, ed., *Blueprint for the Environment: A Plan for Federal Action* (Salt Lake City, Utah: Howe Brothers, 1988). A summary form is available through participating environmental organizations.

21. Ibid.

22. Ibid., p. 227.

23. Ibid., p. 123.

24. Ibid., p. 213.

25. World Commission on Environment and Development, *Our Common Future* (New York: Oxford University Press, 1987).

26. Ibid., p. 40.

27. Ibid., p. 29.

28. Ibid., p. 30.

29. Ibid., p. 44.

30. Ibid., see p. 33 for world consumption chart.

31. This report is available from the Global Tomorrow Coalition, 1325 G St., N.W., Washington, D.C. 20005-3014.

32. Carl Casebolt and Steve Rauh, "Toward Organic Security: Environmental Restoration or the Arms Race?" in Sierra Club *Yodeler*, June 1986.

33. Copies of the platform may be secured from Carl Casebolt, 13122 Parson Lane, Fairfax, Va 22033, for $3 each.

34. World Council of Churches, "Towards an Ecumenical Theological Affirmation on Justice, Peace and Integrity of Creation" (Geneva), paragraph 34.

35. Alan B. Durning, "Poverty and the Environment: Reversing the Downward Spiral," Worldwatch Paper 92 (Washington, D.C.: Worldwatch Institute, 1989), p. 53.

36. Ibid., p. 67.

37. See Brown, *Building a Sustainable Society*, p. 286, for the original model of this schema.

38. Quoted in January/February 1990 *Greenpeace* (Greenpeace USA: Washington, D.C.), p. 29.

39. President Jimmy Carter in 1980 forwarded the U. N. Convention on the Elimination of All Forms of Discrimination Against Women to Congress with his approval. Time ran out in that session of Congress (the 96th) before the Convention could be acted upon.

PART I

NEW MODELS
OF OWNERSHIP

1

A Biblical Economic Principle and the Steady-State Economy

HERMAN E. DALY

Building upon the thesis that the Bible's covenants are in some way binding on contemporary Christians, Dr. Daly posits the most salient economic principle as the prohibition of unlimited inequality in the distribution of private property. He believes it is necessary to implement this principle in order to establish the institutions and social practices needed for a steady-state economy. Steady-state economics is the only system compatible with ecological sustainability in Daly's view and in that of many other environmentalists.

INTRODUCTION

Everyone claims biblical support for his or her own pet economic ideas. Like the devil, the economist can quote Scripture to prove what is wanted. Some have argued that God is a socialist, a corporate syndicalist, a supply-sider, a Georgist single-taxer, a Reaganite, and so on. Now here I come trying to convince you that what God really likes best is a steady-state economy. Isn't this all rather tiresome and shouldn't we be doing something else?

On the contrary, I think we need far more of this discussion precisely because it is so muddled and contradictory. Christianity has coexisted with a wide range of economic systems, but do all economic systems merit its blessing (or condemnation) in equal measure? Do we not have some guidelines under both the Old and the New Covenant regarding what kind of economic order merits God's approval or, more frequently, disapproval? I believe that we Christians have a duty to try to influence the economic institutions and policies of our community, our nations, and our world, which is really God's world for which we are temporary stewards. Some policies reflect good stewardship, others do not. If we Christian stewards are to influence policy we must first know what we want. We must agree on basic principles. For these principles to command our agreement, our mutual assent, they must be authoritative. They must be rooted in Scripture, in the moral law written in our hearts, and they must not contradict the laws of nature that describe how God's creation works, insofar as we understand it. Furthermore, to the extent that such principles are revealed in Scripture they must be general and fundamental enough to be translatable from the agrarian economies of biblical Palestine and the Roman Empire to the modern industrial/information/capital-intensive economy of today.

Our task is twofold: first, to discover basic principles behind the economic institutions of the Covenant people, principles that we accept as part of God's revelation; second, to give those same principles a new institutional body through which to influence or leaven our modern economy. For example, it makes no sense for farmers today not to harvest the corners of their fields in order to leave something for wayfarers, sojourners, widows, and orphans. The food would rot or be eaten by insects. The practice is outdated, but the principle is timeless: make some provision for the poor. The old way is obsolete, so we look for a more fitting way. Even the categories of the needy change — in our time widows and orphans may be rather well-off heirs. Perhaps the colorless census term "unmarried head of household" comes closer to naming our disadvantaged brothers and sisters. I think everyone will agree on the twofold nature of the translation problem: What was the real meaning in the original setting? What in the modern setting means the same thing? If we moderns are to be a covenant people like the ancients who received the covenant, then we must face the translation problem. Although some differences of nuance or style are bound to arise between different "translators," there must be basic agreement on the meaning of the big ideas.

Perhaps there are a number of economic principles in the Scriptures that would command assent among Christians. I propose to deal with just one, which seems to me most basic, the most easily discerned, and most in need of a better institutionalization in today's world. It also partially overlaps with the institutions needed for a steady-state economy. In what follows I will first state the principle and the present evidence that it in fact was the guiding economic norm of the groups whose values are incorporated in Hebrew Scriptures and that its validity is reaffirmed in the New Testament. Second, I will suggest a new institution for better reincorporating that principle in the modern economy. Third, I will suggest some further implications of the principle and its relevance to a steady-state economy.

The principle, if it could be stated as an "eleventh commandment," would read: *Thou shalt not allow unlimited inequality in the distribution of private property*.

THE PRINCIPLE AND ITS BIBLICAL BASIS

The "commandment" presupposes the legitimacy of private property and of some inequality in its distribution. It simply insists that the degree of inequality be limited. Before considering the range of such limits, let us first say a word about private property itself, since its legitimacy is often contested. Christianity and Judaism both regard human persons as free and responsible agents, accountable for their own actions. Without private property the arena of individual freedom and responsibility would be exceedingly small. Also, the eighth commandment, "Thou shalt not steal," is often cited as an oblique support for private property. The Scriptures do, indeed, assume private property; but in the contemporary context, stealing does not only refer to taking someone else's private property—it could also refer to the private taking of public property.

Land was the primary factor of production, the basic source of wealth, in the economy of biblical Palestine; it was considered to belong to God, who created it. But the land was held, worked, and administered by families who had the right of usufruct as God's tenants in perpetuity. Some families prospered more than others. There were rich and poor. Riches were considered a blessing, poverty a misfortune. Absolute equality was neither a fact nor a goal, but the community could not tolerate unlimited inequality. There were definite limits to the degree of inequality. First, the distribution of land among families was equal, or at least just in some more inclusive sense. Second, if property is necessary for the exercise of freedom and responsibility, then it is clear that everyone should have some, or at least the right to glean the fields and harvest the corners, which is an attenuated form of property. The obverse of this position is the classical justification for private property as a bulwark protecting the individual against exploitation by others. A property owner has an independent livelihood and need not accept whatever conditions of employment are offered. If the legitimacy of property is based on either of these reasons, it is clear that its ownership should be widespread, indeed universal.

But the workings of an economy over time naturally generate inequality. Both success and failure tend to be cumulative. Ability is not evenly distributed, nor is soil fertility, nor good luck. Marriages are not economically random and usually result in further concentration of wealth. Dishonesty and exploitation are not required to explain inequality, although they certainly contribute to it. The Levitical answer to how much inequality is permissible was basically this: no more than could accumulate over fifty years, starting with a just initial distribution, and following basic laws of fair dealing, zero interest rate, sabbatical fallow, minimal rights of the poor, religious tithes, and the like. The jubilee, the sabbath of sabbaths, the fiftieth year, was a time for returning to the original distribution. The mere existence and expectation of the jubilee year tended to slow down the accumulation of the very inequalities that it would eventually correct. As the jubilee year approached, the incentive to accumulate was reduced, since current gains would soon have to be surrendered. Immediately after the jubilee, when the gains could be enjoyed for forty-nine years, the incentive to accumulate was greatest, just when the actual equality of distribution was also greatest. These considerations were reflected in the price of land, which was lowered as the jubilee approached, on the very modern principle that capital is the present value of a discounted future income stream ("For what he is selling you is a certain number of harvests"; Lev. 25:13–17). In conformity with the prohibition on interest, the future income stream was discounted at a zero rate, which is to say not discounted at all.

In addition to the overall long-run limits on social inequality implicit in the jubilee year, were there individual minimum and maximum limits in the short run? It seems that there were. Certainly at a minimum there were gleaning, and alms, and the rights of slaves and of widows, all of which can be interpreted as providing a floor below which no one was allowed to fall. Was there a corresponding ceiling on personal wealth? I submit that there was, because even the king, the person most likely to have unlimited rights of accumulation, was expressly denied such a right. Neither horses, wives, nor gold and silver was to be increased excessively by the king (Deut. 17:16ff.). The fact that from Solomon on this law was broken (as was the jubilee itself) simply gives rise to further support for the law in the repeated rebukes of the prophets. The basic philosophy of sufficiency, "enoughness," and limited inequality at the individual level is expressed in Proverbs:

> Give me neither poverty nor riches, but give me only my daily bread, Otherwise I may have too much and disown you and say, "Who is the Lord?" Or I may become poor and steal, and so dishonor the name of my God. (Prov. 30:8ff.)

The prohibition on interest, at least among members of the community, was a strong force for limiting inequality. Interest-bearing debt, with its explosive exponential compounding, is a powerful instrument of accumulation for the lender, and sometimes of impoverishment for the borrower.

Biblical scholars have a great deal more to say on these matters. My knowledge is limited and so is my purpose, namely, to offer some evidence that the general principle underlying the culturally specific laws of Israel's covenant community was that of limited inequality. In further support, I will cite one Old Testament scholar, C. J. H. Wright:

> There is, then, a strong link between Israel's theocratic monotheism (the central arch of her faith) and her tendency towards her own brand of socio-political and economic "egalitarianism." This did not obliterate differentials but attempted to confine them within the

proper limits of functional necessity for the harmony and peace of society.[1]

And one further supporting conclusion from Cambridge economist A. B. Cramp can be cited:

The fundamental principle enshrined in the many-sided, detailed provisions, then, seems to be one that would set limits to the accumulation of capital by individuals (not necessarily the same thing as limiting total accumulation by society as a whole), and would make serious provision for the difficult matter of redistribution of capital when, inevitably, some citizens fare better than others in the economic process.[2]

I have concentrated on the Old Testament because that is where economic organization is most explicitly discussed. The New Covenant is not only a general reaffirmation of the Old, but provides a much sharper and more personal warning on the danger of riches and an even stronger injunction to have a special concern for the poor. It seems to me therefore that the Old Testament principle of limited inequality is forcefully reaffirmed in the New Testament, albeit in a less legalistic and more personal way. Legal structures are necessary, but not sufficient, for community and shalom. A change of heart, a renewal of the mind at the individual level, is also required lest the law become dead. This renewal of the mind is urged at the individual or local level by Paul in 2 Corinthians 8:13–15:

This does not mean that to give relief to others you ought to make things difficult for yourselves: it is a question of balancing what happens to be your surplus now against their present need, and one day they may have something to spare that will supply your own need. That is how we strike a balance: as scripture says: "The man who gathered much had none too much, the man who gathered little did not go short."

Here is a New Testament affirmation of the principle of limited inequality based on an explicit reference to its Old Testament roots (Exod. 16:18): "The man who had gathered more had not too much, the man who had gathered less had not too little." The gathering refers to manna, which also had the property of spoiling if accumulated beyond need, thus reinforcing the idea of limits to accumulated inequality.

That no one has a right to luxury while others lack necessities is a basic requirement of community, whether the basis of community is God's gift of the land or the gift of God's Son. How might we incorporate the principle of limited inequality in today's economy in some reasonable and effective way? What are the further implications of doing it?

THE PRINCIPLE IN THE MODERN WORLD

Before searching for new institutional forms of the limits-to-inequality principle, we should ask whether or not the jubilee year itself could be revived in our time. I think not, even though international debtors and creditors may be forced to arrange something like a "jubilee" forgiveness of international debt in the near future! But the jubilee presupposes an initial just distribution of land among particular families that was established by God's authority within historical memory. That is not the case now. Furthermore, most wealth today is not in the form of land, but rather in the form of capital, including human capital (skills, education). Because of the enormous importance of capital and the associated complex debt structure, the imposition of a zero interest rate would be unrealistic, to put it mildly.

Also, the jubilee system seems to assume a steady-state economy, which we emphatically do not have now, no matter how strongly some of us advocate it as a goal. The initial distribution can be reestablished only if the size or number of families does not grow and if the resource (the land) is not depleted over time. These two conditions were more closely approximated in ancient Israel than in our day. Naturally high death rates kept the population from growing very fast, and a pastoral-agrarian economy did not deplete the resource base rapidly, especially when supplemented by laws requiring sabbatical fallow for the land.[3] Today the prior existence of a steady-state economy cannot be taken for granted, but must be taken as a goal of policy—as something to be reestablished in modern form. Establishing the principle of limited inequality is a necessary, but not sufficient, condition for achieving a modern steady state. But more of that in the next section. For now, we must look for a way to institutionalize limits to inequality without a God-given initial distribution. What range of inequality is necessary to reward real differences in irksomeness of work and in initiative and responsibility? What is the actual range of inequality? How might the actual be brought into conformity with the functionally necessary and just degree of inequality?

We must begin by admitting that we have no God-given definition of what the limits to inequality should be. Do we therefore face a hopeless task? I don't think so. A democracy has no clear-cut objective rule for determining the minimum voting age. We feel that it should be early adulthood, but whether or not that should be defined as eighteen or twenty-two could be argued endlessly. The point is that the exact limit is largely arbitrary. The important thing is that there be some defined and accepted minimum age—whether eighteen or twenty-two is not really significant. Likewise, the exact limits to inequality are much less important than the principle that limits be placed somewhere corresponding to a reasonable, functional, and just degree of inequality. But what is that reasonable, functional range? The minimum income would be some culturally defined amount sufficient for food, clothing, shelter, and basic health and education. The maximum might be ten times the minimum. Plato thought the factor should be four. Why do I suggest ten?

There is some evidence that a factor of ten is sufficient to reward real differences and to provide sufficient incentive so that all necessary jobs are filled voluntarily. In the U.S. military, for example, the highest-paid general makes ten times the wages of the lowest private. Probably the general has extra fringe benefits that may result in a factor of eleven or twelve. The same range is found in the Civil Service — a GS-18 makes about ten times the salary of a GS-1. In the university a distinguished professor is paid about ten times more than a graduate student instructor. In corporations the range is much greater, but this is largely because the top officers have the privilege of setting their own salaries, unlike generals, senior civil servants, and distinguished professors.

I take a factor of ten, then, as a benchmark. The important thing is the change from unlimited to limited inequality. The exact limits are arbitrary and can be adjusted on the basis of experience. Maybe the factor should be five, maybe twenty. After all, seven is a rather arbitrary number, also. Would it matter so much if the "sabbatical" were the sixth or the eighth year, or if the jubilee were every forty-five years?

What is the actual range of inequality? What does the actual distribution of income look like? Economists use Lorenz curves, Gini coefficients, Pareto distributions, log-normal distributions, and the like to describe income distribution. But the most graphic and imaginative description I have seen comes from Dutch economist Jan Pen, who organizes a parade of dwarfs and giants. All income recipients will be shrunk or stretched so that their height is proportional to their income. They will then pass by in a parade, shortest first, tallest last. The parade will last exactly one hour and will be observed by you and me, persons of presumed average height. What would we see? At first, there are a few people of negative height, their heads may be as much as ten yards underground. These are people who made losses that year — not necessarily poor, but they soon will be if they keep that up. Then come lots of gnomes, about the size of a matchstick. Many are part-time workers, students, or housewives who earn very little, but share in a family income, so they are not as badly off as one might think. The gnomes file by for about five minutes. Then people become noticeably larger, about three feet tall — old-age pensioners, divorced women without alimony, many handicapped, some artists. They take another five minutes. The parade has been going on for fifteen minutes before we see people four feet tall, unskilled workers. Quite a few are women, many are dark skinned. And now we continue seeing dwarfs for a long time. Then come some office workers, educated folks; not dwarfs, but definitely short from our perspective. Only after the parade has been going for forty-eight minutes, twelve minutes before the end, do we see people our own height, the average-income people. We see teachers, civil servants, insurance agents, farmers, some skilled workers. Six minutes later we see the first of the top 10 percent, people about six feet, six inches tall, mostly university graduates. In the last few minutes the giants very suddenly emerge. A lawyer, a doctor, and some accountants about eighteen feet tall, other doctors, judges, and executives around sixty feet tall. Then comes Prince Philip, one hundred and eighty feet tall, and the director of Shell Oil, more than double that. Then, at the very end of the parade come a few people whose height has to be measured in miles, like rock singer Tom Jones. At the very end comes John Paul Getty, some ten miles tall, at least.

As you can guess, Professor Pen's parade took place in Britain around 1970. Such a parade in the United States in 1990 would show greater inequality. A similar parade in our proposed limited-inequality world might begin with three- or four-footers and end with thirty- or forty-footers. The great majority falls between these limits, in any case, so the number of people affected would be relatively few; a very few at the top, more at the bottom, but fewer than the number in the first ten minutes of the parade, since many of them were dependents with adequate family income but very low part-time personal earnings.

We should adopt a range-based, rather than a variance-based, concept of inequality. Even though the variance-based concept is more usual in statistics, it is an average measure that does not correspond to particular individuals. The range concept is more in the biblical spirit of focusing on the concrete situation of particular individuals — too poor, too rich. It is these extremes that we wish to avoid. The average of deviations from the mean is not so relevant. Hence the emphasis on maximum and minimum limits.

But should the maximum and minimum limits be applied to income or wealth, or, as Scripture seems to suggest, a minimum income coupled with a maximum wealth? Let us consider the possibilities. The minimum limit clearly cannot be placed on wealth, since one always has the option of consuming one's wealth and can hardly expect to have it restored year after year. So the minimum limit must be placed on income. The maximum limit could be placed on income, or wealth, or on both. A maximum on wealth, with no maximum on income, would lead to very lavish consumption of all income for one who has reached the wealth maximum. This would simply channel increasing inequality into larger consumption disparities once wealth disparities were limited and, by encouraging consumption, would work against the larger conservation ideals of a sustainable society. Putting a maximum on income avoids that problem, but may be thought to give rise to the opposite problem of fostering excessive wealth inequality.

But this symmetry does not hold on closer analysis. Limiting income directly will also indirectly limit wealth in two ways. First, wealth would be accumulated out of income less rapidly if income were limited. Second, previously accumulated wealth would be devalued for those whose income from other wealth or work had reached the maximum income limit. They would have an incentive to consume or divest themselves of wealth the return of which they were not allowed to keep. Thus, it would seem that direct limits, both maximum and minimum, are most effectively applied to income rather than to wealth, although an additional maximum on wealth may be worth further consideration. The simplest and most obvious institution for limiting inequality is, therefore, also the best one — namely, maximum and minimum limits on income.

IMPLEMENTATION OF THE PRINCIPLE

The minimum has been much discussed, and economists have worked out negative income tax plans designed to give a positive work incentive to anyone receiving a subsidy (negative tax). Suppose the guaranteed income is set at $8,000. An individual who earns nothing would get this amount from the government. Then, an income is fixed at which no tax is paid, either positive or negative, a break-even point (say $15,000). A person who earns less than the break-even level would get a subsidy, calculated as a fixed percentage (say 50%) of the difference between the break-even level and earnings. Suppose, for example, that someone earns $3,000. The person's negative income tax (subsidy) would be ($15,000 − 3,000) × 1/2 = $6,000. That subsidy plus the $3,000 earnings yields a total income of $9,000, which is greater than the $8,000 minimum income, thus providing an incentive to work.

Other numbers, of course, can be chosen for the minimum, the break-even, and the percentage, but the principle remains the same. After an individual's earnings exceed the break-even level, then a regular proportional or progressive income-tax rate would go into effect. Since we are saying that a factor of ten is a proper range of inequality, to avoid further compression we would presumably elect a proportional income-tax within the limits. I would advocate a fairly low income-tax rate, supplemented by a high severance tax on basic resources in order to induce conservation and resource-saving modes of production and consumption, in harmony with the larger ideal of a steady-state economy. Also, a low proportional income tax within the limits would keep work incentives high for incomes below the minimum.

Such a minimum-income scheme has considerable support, although less than a majority at present. The idea of a maximum limit, however, has surprisingly little support, and, in fact, encounters strong opposition not only from the rich but also from many who have little chance of ever getting near the maximum. Perhaps many good people feel that it is basically unmagnanimous to set limits on how much someone may earn and that it reflects more a mean-spirited envy than a real concern for justice and community. Others, like some lottery players, may be attracted to big prizes, no matter how small the probability of winning. Also, since many people see no limit to the growth of aggregate wealth, they regard it as a matter of small concern if some should get rich faster than others, as long as everyone is getting richer.

The first objection (mean-spirited envy) can be reduced by remembering that we are not claiming all human differences should be confined to a factor-of-ten range. Luciano Pavarotti is more than ten times better a singer than most of us, and John McEnroe plays tennis about a thousand times better than I do. We need not gag Pavarotti or hobble McEnroe and make him play with a broken racket so that he is only ten times better than I am. Let him be a thousand times better and honor him for it with unlimited admiration. But, unlimited admiration need not imply unlimited income. Indeed, why should it?

The second objection, that as long as we are all getting richer it does not matter that some get rich faster, is based on an implicit assumption of limitless aggregate growth and will be dealt with in the next section.

Back to the institution of a maximum limit. In our example, that would occur at $80,000 (ten times the minimum of $8,000). Income beyond $80,000 would be taxed at a 100 percent marginal rate. Suppose you have reached the limit. What will you do? Your material incentive to work further ends when your earnings hit $80,000. Beyond that amount of work, moral incentives take over. If you love your work and feel that it is your contribution to the world or your duty to God, then you will keep doing it even for zero marginal gain. Leisure would coincide with work. If you are not that committed to your work, then you will devote your leisure to something more satisfying once your income hits the maximum. Incidentally, counting leisure as a part of real income effectively expands the range of inequality. We are limiting total money income, not the price of one's services or hours of leisure. If your hourly earnings increase because your services are much in demand, then you arrive at the maximum sooner and have more leisure. So, counting leisure, you will be more than ten times richer than the minimum. The way you spend your leisure is up to you, determined by your ethical choice and uninfluenced by material incentives. You may continue teaching, writing, or practicing law or medicine because you love it and are happy to donate your earnings above the limit to help bring others up to the minimum. Or, you may look for something more satisfying than your usual job. Once the maximum is reached, there is a switch at the margin to intrinsic motivation for further work. I do not think we can rely exclusively on intrinsic or moral incentives to work, as the Chinese and the Cubans attempted to do for a time, but there can be, and I think should be, some point beyond which material incentives end and moral incentives become the directing force. It just may be that most people upon reaching the maximum would experience not so much a sense of restriction as a sense of liberation.

Many details require more thought and discussion, such as eligibility for the minimum income (does it require some form of public-service work?), definition of family dependents, and so on. But one major objection sure to be raised is the issue of incentives. Many people seem to believe that all effort would immediately cease under such a system. I think this consensus is more the result of brainwashing than of clear thinking. Material incentives would be even stronger at below-maximum levels because of the substitution of a proportional income tax for a progressive one. Near the minimum, the negative income tax provides positive work incentives. A requirement for some public-service work from able-bodied recipients of the minimum income could be imposed. At the maximum there is still the "real income" incentive of extra leisure, even though marginal monetary incentives are zero. The fear seems to be that these very able people will desist from all invention or innovation. I doubt it. Many people are motivated, at least in part, by a search for truth or a desire to reduce suffering. To the extent that the powerful force of innovation would henceforth spring more from these motives and less from greed, I think we should count it as an improvement.

THE PRINCIPLE AND THE STEADY-STATE ECONOMY

So far, the principle of limited inequality has been discussed in terms of a single time period. But does not the principle also apply over time? Present people collectively should not be too rich if that implies that future people will be too poor. Or, conversely, present people should not be made too poor for the purpose of making future people richer than they need to be. In an era dominated by the idea of economic growth with its necessary squeezing of present consumption for the sake of investment, the second error has occasionally been recognized. We wonder if the costs of accumulation borne by the early generations in the Soviet Union's industrialization drive are worth the benefits to today's Soviet citizens, or if the cost to the generation living in Britain during the Industrial Revolution was really recompensed by the subsequent higher consumption of their grandchildren. But it is the former question that concerns us here—are we producing and consuming on a scale that the biosphere cannot sustain and that will impoverish the future? The principle of justice as limited inequality, when extended into the future, implies sustainability—justice extended to future people. Closely related to sustainability is the question of the scale of economic activity (involving depletion and pollution) relative to the natural rates of assimilation and replenishment in the ecosystem.

To the extent that economic growth is based on qualitative improvement, squeezing more welfare out of the same resource flow, then there is no apparent limit to its growth. But neither is there any reason not to share that kind of growth equally. If knowledge is the ultimate resource, then by all means let knowledge grow forever. Shared knowledge is multiplied rather than divided! But before getting carried away with the idea that the human mind is an ultimate resource that can guarantee endless economic growth, let us remember that, while certainly not reducible to physical terms, the mind is not independent of the body and the body is physical. "No phosphorus, no thought," Frederick Soddy reminds us. As Loren Eisley puts it, "The human mind, so frail, so perishable, so full of inexhaustible dreams and hungers, burns by the power of a leaf." Minds capable of such insight ought to be able to show more restraint toward leaves and phosphorus than is usually exhibited by our growth-bound economy. The economist Kenneth Boulding reminds us that capital is knowledge imposed on the physical world in the form of improbable arrangements. But knowledge cannot be imprinted on any kind of matter by any kind of energy — it must be low-entropy matter-energy. Otherwise, we could harness the sea breeze with windmills made of sand and use the energy to extract gold from the ocean.

Suppose that an economy stayed within the ten-to-one limits to inequality, but was growing in absolute scale: more people and higher per capita consumption. Although at every point in time the limits to inequality would be respected, over time these limits would not be maintained. Either growth would eventually make the future vastly richer, or ecological collapse would make it vastly poorer — or, likely, the first, followed by the second. Since the issues of overpopulation and ecological destruction were not important in biblical times, we have little specific guidance. As mentioned earlier, sustainability was more or less taken for granted. Ancient Israel's economy was pastoral or agricultural, small scale, and solar based — almost automatically sustainable. I say "almost" because the laws mandating fallow for the land, not taking the bird that is hatching eggs, not destroying trees in war, for instance, indicate a concern for sustainability that suggests it was not totally automatic. High death rates naturally kept the population from growing very rapidly, so that overall the economy was in a near steady state, as it would have to be in order to return to the initial historical circumstances of the jubilee. Under these conditions it could not be argued that no maximum was needed as long as everyone was getting richer and that it mattered little if the rich got richer faster than the poor got richer. In a steady state, if the rich get richer the poor must get poorer, not only relatively but absolutely. If the total is limited, there must be a maximum limit on individual income. If there is also a minimum, then, by and large, the higher the minimum the lower must be the maximum.

Many would argue that a steady-state economy among the covenant people was a fortuitous circumstance of history having nothing to do with divine revelation. Science and technology have since removed the natural limits that necessitated the steady state and in particular the need for a maximum income. Keep the minimum income, they say, but once poverty is abolished we need not worry about inequality. Furthermore, increasing inequality may be necessary to stimulate growth, which can be used to raise the minimum.

There are two points to make in reply. First, it really does matter how far apart the rich and the poor are from the point of view of community. Unlimited inequality is inconsistent with community, no matter how well off the poorest are. Even relative poverty breeds resentment, and riches insulate and harden the heart. Conviviality, solidarity, and brotherhood weaken with economic distance. Political power tends to follow relative income and cannot be allowed to concentrate too far in either a theocracy or a democracy without becoming a plutocracy. Second, the idea that science and technology, because they have greatly increased our power, have removed all limits comes close to being the opposite of the truth. Indeed, it is precisely because science and technology have given us such power that the scale of our economy has been able to grow to the point where we now must consciously face the fundamental limits of creaturehood: finitude, entropy, and ecological dependence. Science can help us adjust to these limits in the best manner, but to think that we will overcome them is to claim authority to remake God's creation on our blueprint, rather than to maintain and care for it according to God's. That we are actively engaged in building this new Tower of Babel is beyond doubt. How could it be otherwise when most of our generation rejects the very idea of the world as a creation, and even of a Creator who has made considerable use of random mutation and natural selection as a process design principle? My point is not antiscience, since if we are to maintain and care for God's creation we must surely learn how it works. The first and second laws of thermodynamics, joined by finitude and ecological interdependence, make nonsense of the notion that the economy can continue to grow forever, or even for very long, in its physical dimensions. It is unscientific not to take seriously the most basic laws of science, most of which are statements of impossibility: it is impossible to travel faster than the speed of light, or to create or destroy matter-energy, or to have perpetual motion, spontaneous generation of life, and the like.

Long before we have reached ultimate biophysical limits to growth in the scale of our economy, we will have passed the economic limit: the point beyond which the marginal costs of growth exceed the marginal benefits. No one can be sure that we have not already passed that point, since we do not even bother to count costs and benefits of growth. We just count economic activity in GNP and presume that its beneficial aspects outweigh its regrettable aspects.

The limits-to-growth debate that started in the late sixties and disappeared with the election of Ronald Reagan needs to be rekindled. It stopped precisely when people realized that limits to growth imply limits to inequality (if poverty is to be reduced) and, specifically, a maximum limit. But, the thinking went, that is clearly impossible, so there must have been a mistake in our reasoning or our premises. Let us therefore reject the premise of finitude and entropy and return to the unlimited-growth vision that does not call for political impossibilities. That it calls for physical impossibilities instead can be overlooked, since most voters have never heard of the laws of thermodynamics, and, with the advent of the space age, we all know that finitude has been abolished by the "high frontier." There is no limit to how many Towers of Babel we can build; economic growth remains the summum bonum.

But this is a pipe dream. Historically, the steady state is the normal condition; growth is an aberration. A steady-state economy aims for a scale and quality of economic activity that is ecologically sustainable for a long future at a level of per capita resource use sufficient to provide a good life for whatever population size can be accommodated under those conditions. *Sufficiency* and *sustainability* are its key characteristics. Sufficiency means enough for a good life within a range of acceptable inequality. Sustainability means a long time, but not forever, because both Christianity and science tell us that the world will end. But we affirm that life and longevity are good gifts of God to be passed on, not squandered. In addition to limiting inequality, a modern steady-state economy must institute curbs on population growth and limits to the rate of conversion of low-entropy raw materials into high-entropy wastes. These two limits were more or less automatic in ancient Israel, but are no more.

I certainly want to stop short of arguing that the ideal of a steady-state economy is a part of divine revelation. I would argue only that the principle of limited inequality has biblical authority and that when we try to institute the principle in the modern world (especially if we extend it to include future generations) we will find the concept of a steady-state economy increasingly more relevant than that of the existing growth economy. It is meaningful as a way to keep the rich from leaning too heavily on the poor and the present generations from leaning too heavily on future generations. It is also relevant in keeping human beings from leaning too heavily on other creatures whose habitats must disappear as we convert more and more of the finite ecosystem into a source for raw materials, a sink for wastes, or living space for humans and warehouses for artifacts. Stewardship requires that we move off the unsustainable growth path to which we cling precisely in order to avoid limiting inequality. And we will not be able to shift from growth to the steady state without instituting limits to inequality.

NOTES

1. C. J. H. Wright, *An Eye for an Eye: The Place of Old Testament Ethics Today* (Downers Grove, Ill.: InterVarsity Press, 1983), p. 112.

2. A. B. Cramp, *Economics in Christian Perspective*, mimeo, p. IX/26.

3. Robert B. Coote and Mary P. Coote, *Power, Politics, and the Making of the Bible: An Introduction* (Minneapolis, Minn.: Fortress, 1990).

2

Genetic Engineering: Science for People or Science for Profit?

ALAN S. MILLER

Who should have ownership rights to fundamental aspects of the life process? Dr. Miller warns that if we do not develop a social apparatus or public policy to control the big business in biotechnology, the benefits of genetic science will go primarily to those who can afford high-cost services. The poor will not only lose the benefits; their own ability to care for themselves will be restricted further.

When James Watson and Francis Crick discovered the helical structure of the DNA molecule in 1953, scientists entered a new wonderland of biological possibility. For the first time in human history, the dream of intentional alteration in the genetic makeup of our species was no longer in the realm of science fiction. Although the vision of designer genes was still clouded in mystery, molecular biologists began to think about the possibility of creating new life forms and of how they might improve the quality of life for human beings. Questions also began to be raised, however, about whether or not we were moving into forbidden genetic territory. Ordinary people and experts alike began discussing the genetic "Frankenstein" factor. Should we be permitted to tinker with evolution—in ourselves, in other animals, in plants? As the science and technology of recombinant DNA developed in succeeding decades, the question of intentionality was raised more frequently. As our ability to create unique forms of life by recombining the cells of higher and lower organisms or the genetic material of plants and animals developed, enormous problems and exciting possibilities were raised.

The recombinant process, of course, was actually quite simple once the keys to unlock the mystery were discovered. It had long been known that chromosomes control the heredity of plants and animals and that inside each chromosome was a long string of DNA (deoxyribonucleic acid) wrapped inside a protein sheath. Each chromosome is essentially divided into a number of segments (genes), and the particular sequence of certain chemical messengers within the gene codes specific instructions to each cell to perform a particular function. The detailed genetic message encoded in the DNA determines all of the heritable characteristics of the plant or animal. The trick of recombining genetic materials, however, had to wait until researchers discovered the first of more than 150 restriction enzymes that enabled them to cut the DNA within a cell at a very precise point. A segment of DNA from another organism could then be similarly cut by another restriction enzyme and the original cellular DNA inserted into the bacterial loop of DNA (the plasmid). Attached by its chemically "sticky ends," the fragments could then be reinserted into a bacterium and grow together with the new genetic characteristics incorporated into the original material. This recombinant DNA (rDNA) would then copy itself and be reproduced as the material replicated.

As we enter the last decade of the century, the progress in biotechnology and genetic engineering has surprised even its early advocates. Cells and genetic material from totally separate species have been fused in amazing fashion. Recombinant organisms now carry the mixed characteristics of rabbits and mice, humans and plants, the blood cells of chickens and the genetic stuff of yeast, of cancer and carrots and a host of other common and uncommon organisms. Once the natural barriers preventing the transfer of genetic material between lower life forms like bacteria with that of plants and animals were breached, a new and qualitatively different chapter was required to record the evolutionary process. Writing in the *New England Journal of Medicine*, medical philosopher Lewis Thomas stated:

> The recombinant line of research is already upsetting, not because of the dangers now being argued about but because it is disturbing, in a fundamental way, to face the fact that genetic machinery in control of the planet's life can be fooled around with so easily. We do not like the idea that anything so fixed and stable as species line can be changed. The notion that genes can be taken out of one genome and inserted in another is unnerving.[1]

In the same vein, religious leaders have warned that

> We are rapidly moving into a new era of fundamental danger triggered by the rapid growth of genetic engineering. Albeit, there may be opportunity for doing good, the very term suggests the danger.[2]

The real issue, however, is not between Frankenstein and Einstein — between evil science and good science — but between those who hope to use the new science and technology in an appropriate fashion (to actually help those in the world who are most needful of good people-oriented science) and those who will focus on providing high-cost services to the already overprivileged of the world's population in order to maximize market returns. As speakers at the 1987 conference on "The Socioeconomic Impact of New Biotechnologies in the Third World" in Bogeve, France, suggested, when big capital is combined with the very best in biological science and technology, remarkable things can happen very fast. If within a decade or two, aspects of the life process continue to become the private property of big business — as happens now when new organisms are patented and become simply additional possessions of great corporations — the ordinary people of the world will inevitably end up as losers. Whether we — as individuals, groups, or nation-states — are prepared to handle the economic consequences of such a coalition of powerful forces is doubtful. Our social apparatus for the development of sound and protective public policy in science has never been very good; and biological innovations from the new biotech industries seem to be moving much more quickly than our cultural understandings of the implications of the technologies. Although many dimensions of biotechnology are socially benign — new medical machinery, research on diseases like AIDS and cancer, efforts to strengthen plant resistance to certain diseases — our focus in this essay will be on genetic engineering and whether or not this new science and technology is still subject to control by other than the experts in the think tanks of government and industry who create the production orders for the scientific community.

THE ORGANIZATION OF SCIENCE

It should come as no surprise to any sensitive social observer that science has always been under the control and guidance of nonscientists. Science has always been subject to political motivation and social manipulation. Even Galileo in the early seventeenth century had to continually justify his work on military matters by saying that he could finally only work for the ruling classes, for they alone had the money to fund scientific research and development. Noting that "I can only serve princes; for it is they alone who ... make those great expenditures which neither I nor other private persons may," Galileo anticipated the dilemma that would be faced by generations of scientists in the future.[3] At a recent conference for nuclear technologists on the Berkeley campus of the University of California, I queried the director of one of our leading energy laboratories about the role of ethics in science. His response was, "Ethics is not our business in governmentally funded research. We do what we get paid to do." Not many scientists would be either so candid or so indifferent to questions about intentionality in science. But given that 75 percent of all federally funded research and development (R&D) today is related to military matters, and that all industrial R&D is geared toward the bottom line of making money rather than furthering social well-being, the imperatives within the communities of science and technology today require increased attention and surveillance.

Similarly we tend to ignore the manner in which science is functionally organized in the modern industrial world. It is too easy for zealous critics simply to blame individuals for some of the misdirections within scientific research and development. They forget that it is much more the organization of science than the attitudes of the individual practitioners that cause the problems. Like any other apparatus of production, science is constrained by the norms and goals of industry. Science in the West is large scale, centralized, hierarchically organized, and, with only rare exceptions, absolutely and inevitably dedicated to solving the kind of problems put to it by government and industry. The rough and tumble of the marketplace imprints its priorities quite as much on science as on any other dimension of production. Indeed, the only possibility of invoking social control over the direction of science today rests in the establishment and implementation of public policy that has as its goal the welfare of people rather than the profits of industry. This appears today to be the only possible arena for "solving" the problem of the direction of scientific research; it will be considered at the end of this chapter.

As we have noted, the social dilemmas posed by the new science and its related technologies are quite as great as the potentialities. We do live in a world characterized by growing disparity between the rich and the poor, the haves and the have-nots, the overdeveloped and the developing nations. A long view of the history of science suggests that new technologies tend always to favor the powerful in their relationships with the less powerful. New elitist sciences—like those that led to recombinant biology—do little if anything to address the dilemmas of survival for ordinary people whose biggest daily concerns are inequality and injustice. As one speaker at the Bogeve seminar on biotechnology noted:

> For the poor, struggling to keep their young alive and reduce the fertility of those who feel they have enough children, biotechnology is helping the rich keep the old alive and make the infertile fertile. A world which needs clean water and tropical vaccines is being offered new cosmetics and organ transplants. While the poor search for solutions to malaria and diarrhoea, biobusiness plumbs the yuppie market for genetic screening and human growth hormones so that every girl can be a Barbie doll and every boy can look like Ken.[4]

RECOMBINANT RESEARCH: FROM THE LABORATORY TO THE FIELD

A great deal of controversy surrounded the new science of recombinant DNA from the very beginning. When Herbert Boyer and Stanley Cohen of the University of California first rearranged DNA molecules in the laboratory in 1973, criticism was not long in arriving. Efforts were then under way to combine tumor viruses with the *E. coli* bacterium that lives in the gut of every human being. What if a recombinant virus infused with cancer genes escaped from the lab and infected the populace? The possibility of the development of a virulent cancer germ had to be seriously considered and scientists convened a major conference at the Asilomar Conference Center in California in 1975 to debate the question of controls over recombinant R&D. From the conference arose a number of suggestions for laboratory safeguards that were subsequently incorporated into guidelines by the National Institutes of Health (NIH) in 1976. Soon considered by the scientific community to be unnecessary, the guidelines were effectively discontinued in 1982. James Watson, Nobel laureate for his work in discovering the structure of DNA, reflected upon the Asilomar conference and the NIH guidelines:

> Although some fringe groups ... thought this was a matter to be debated by all and sundry, it was never the intention of those who might be called the molecular biology establishment to take the issue to the general public to decide. We did not want our experiments to be blocked by overconfident lawyers, much less by self-appointed bioethicists with no inherent knowledge of, or interest in, our work. Their decisions could only be arbitrary.[5]

Watson later boasted that "I, for one, have never given a moment's thought to whether my passion about the nature of the gene might be misplaced, much less a major danger to mankind itself."[6] As critics from the Hastings Center for Bioethics later stated, however:

> What irked scientists the most ... was neither scientific nor philosophical disagreements, but the insolence of their colleagues in "going public" with their anxieties. While the non-scientific community viewed these public doubters as responsible professionals, many in the ranks of the scientists saw them as apostates to the hallowed tradition of scientific self-determination. Who were they to cast the pearls of scientific inquiry before untutored masses who were incompetent to make judgments about such abstruse matters.[7]

As always, the policy matters continued to be determined by scientific self-regulation. Laboratory restrictions were dropped and researchers were essentially free to move in whatever directions they felt were both necessary and safe. Rather quickly, however, the debate moved from safety in the laboratory to safety in the actual environmental testing of genetically altered organisms. Anxious to make some quick profits from their already costly research, both university researchers and the new biotech companies sought to develop commercial applications—products—from their work. Researchers at Berkeley were finally permitted to conduct the first-ever field test of a new recombinant organism in 1988. Having removed the ice-nucleating gene from a common bacterium, the university researchers sought to prove that through dissemination of this new "ice-minus" bacterium in the environment crops could be saved that otherwise would have frozen. Enormous controversy surrounded the experiment, not so much because of its actual danger but because it would open the door to dozens of other similar field releases around the country that now await only government approval.

Indeed, the problem of how to regulate the laboratory research and the field testing of genetically altered organisms is the hot topic now in the recombinant field. Under the "Coordinated Framework" for regulating recombinant research and testing, the U.S. government has established administrative guidelines for the eighteen separate agencies now having some jurisdiction over recombinant work. Genuinely concerned about the need for such a regulatory apparatus, the U.S. government increasingly gives signals that it does not intend to interfere overmuch with the freedom of the new biotech industries in their research and testing programs.[8] With enormous investments already in place, biotech companies are massively involved today in industrial boosterism, proclaiming the wonders and minimizing the risks of the new technologies.

The expectation that increasingly there will be only perfunctory review of the research has led the industry to exaggerate the benefits and downplay the hazards of recombinant technologies. As one industry spokesman recently told this writer, "The issue of public acceptance is now critical. Our industry could die if we don't overcome public fears of environmental releases."

Greatly assisting the genetic engineering industry have been a variety of court decisions upholding the right of private companies to patent both life processes and living animals and plants. On June 16, 1980, the Supreme Court of the United States in the *Chakrabarty* decision stated that new, laboratory-modified microorganisms are subject to patent under federal law. Since plant, animal, and microbial life forms have provided the biological foundation for all ecosystem development, it is ethically clear that patents are inappropriate when applied to life itself. Because so many different patents may be involved in the future in developing new recombinant products, it is now assumed that because of the royalties demanded by companies in such "patent stacking" many otherwise beneficial products may simply be priced out of the acquisition range of most people. Since most advances in genetic engineering have been pioneered by university researchers, increasingly important questions are being posed to those who use the fruits of taxpayer-supported research to produce private profits. Many university researchers today basically skim the cream off years of taxpayer-supported work by quickly taking their research and knowledge (developed through taxpayer dollars) to the private sector. The combination of new patent laws and private appropriation of taxpayer-produced research guarantee enormous profits to private industry, with absolute corporate control of bioscience just around the corner.

> In fact, what is now emerging throughout the corporate sector in the United States, Europe and Japan is a new, unprecedented institution of economic and political power: the multi-faceted, transnational life sciences conglomerate—a huge company that will use genes to fashion life-necessity products just as earlier corporate powers used land, minerals, or oil.[9]

The corporate passion for quick profits may well be leading genetic-engineering companies to try to adapt the environment to the needs of industry rather than to help industry meet the needs of people. One of my colleagues at the University of California is investigating how to increase the resistance of corn and wheat to pesticides so that more and more of the latter can be used in agriculture. The same researcher has accepted funds from a major U.S. chemical company to guarantee that corporation's future involvement in marketing products based on his research, and as a guarantee of his own future profits. European researchers are attempting to gene-manipulate trees to withstand ever-higher doses of acid rain. Social disruptions can also occur from good science being used in a culturally disruptive fashion. U.S. biotech companies are now producing a natural vanilla flavor that in time will eliminate the need for vanilla-bean production—currently the sole source of income for seventy thousand vanilla growers in Madagascar. Many other ventures of this type are now under way, which will surely produce corporate profits but that will place increasing numbers of people in the developing world at risk.[10]

Generally, the new technologies exacerbate the survival problems of the have-not populations. Table 2.1 on page 68 suggests how the new biotechnologies actually stack up against the real needs of people in the Third World. Again, the basic requirements of people have rather little connection with the dominant biotech research under way. Faced with basic problems of conservation, crop improvement, elimination of poverty, and preventive health care, biotechnology essentially focuses on developed-world needs—pesticide resistance, developing products to substitute for traditional raw materials, and medical therapies for the chronic degenerative diseases.[11]

Often contrasted with the "Green Revolution" (the post–World War II attempt to increase global cereal grain production with new plant varieties and technologies), which was itself criticized for concentrating agricultural production in the hands of those who could afford the new technologies and dislocating the marginal peasant, the "Gene Revolution" in agriculture seems even more potentially threatening to small farmers. Table 2.2 on

Table 2.1
Third-World Needs and the New Biotechnologies

Basic need	Potential contribution of new biotechnologies	Dominant research of biotech industry
	Crop production	
Conservation and improvement of diverse poor people's crops, emphasizing hardiness, nutrition, and yield.	Tissue-culture technology could support conservation and breeding objectives.	Rather than pest resistance, the focus is on gene transfer for pesticide resistance, encapsulated embryos, and yield improvement for major crops only.
	Food processing	
Key concerns are durability, nutrition, and cost. Product and production should be culturally and environmentally sensitive, making the best use of local resources.	Improvement of traditional fermentation methods and development of new possibilities.	Focus is on reducing or substituting raw materials and the factory production of agricultural products.
	Animal husbandry	
Conserve diversity and broaden breeding efforts for foraging animals to develop healthier, more efficient livestock. Develop multipurpose domesticates.	Vaccines and diagnostics can support these efforts, and embryo transfer can help preserve diversity.	Attention is on complete control over fertility and reproduction to develop high-yielding uniform, but highly vulnerable, breeds and also on veterinarial packages and on use of livestock as bioreactors for drugs.
	Health Care	
Best way to improve health is to eliminate poverty. Following that, preventive health care focusing on improved sanitation, nutrition, and drinking water. Next, new vaccines for tropical diseases and AIDS.	Biotechnologies could help with monoclonal antibodies for water testing and gene technology for vaccine research and production.	Emphasis is on diagnostics and clinical assays, help against infertility, production of hormones and drugs related to aging, cancer, AIDS, heart disease, organ transplants, and gene therapy.

page 70 reviews the relative impacts of these two "revolutions," and suggests that in terms of overall effect the gene revolution may meet the needs of the agricultural industry but will only complicate the already difficult task of small sector agriculture. In spite of its overall social impact, the green revolution was essentially based in the public sector and had a clear, humanitarian intent: to feed the hungry people in the world by increasing grain production. No greater contrast could be found than the gene revolution, which, although largely grounded in tax-supported research, is otherwise solely based in the private sector, with a primary goal of making money for the researchers and the industries involved.[12]

GENETIC ENGINEERING IN THE MEDICAL ARENA

While commercial-sector genetic engineers are brimming with confidence about their abilities to solve a number of agricultural, industrial, and environmental problems, the application of molecular biology to medicine is at once more necessary and more frightening. Genetic screening, for example, a technique enabling medical specialists to identify a number of genetic diseases and hopefully, in time, to cure them, suggests the dilemma. Such diagnostic programs attempt to identify carriers of such heritable diseases as sickle-cell anemia, Tay-Sachs disease, and phenylketonuria (PKU); to determine whether an unborn child has been affected by negative genetic characteristics carried by the parents; to provide counseling services to prospective parents to review the possibility of their being carriers of genetic disease; and, in time, to eradicate all abnormal genetic illness.

Relatively uncontroversial in the short run, long-term aspects of genetic counseling may well include medical advice to actively intervene in cell alteration to erase the possibility of the transference of heritable disorders. With the discovery of a number of "marker genes" (genes identifiable through chromosomal DNA testing that pinpoint specific health problems), certain diseases can now be located and attempts made at medical correction. But caution must be exercised in initiating programs to reduce the appearance of "bad" genes.

> The time can already be envisioned when all information about a person's abnormal genes and chromosomes will be readily accessible. ... Mandatory screening is not justified as part of a program to produce a genetically healthy society or other politically vague and politically abusive social ideals. In the hands of repressive and exploitative political movements, such notions could be used to justify extreme eugenic measures.[13]

We already know about some of the potential abuses of even such medically benign tests as amniocentesis (the withdrawal of a small amount of amniotic fluid for chromosomal testing of the fetus) and chorionic villus testing (removal of placental cells) to determine certain genetic diseases in utero. There appear to be no major ethical problems from such fetal testing programs until the complicated issue of abortion is raised. Where are limits

Table 2.2

Green Revolution	*Gene Revolution*

Summary

• Based in public sector	• Based in private sector
• Humanitarian intent	• Profit motive
• Centralized R&D	• Centralized R&D
• Focus on yield	• Focus on inputs/processing
• Relatively gradual	• Relatively immediate
• Emphasis on major cereals	• Affects all species

Objective

–To feed the hungry and cool third-world political tensions by increasing food yields with fertilizers and seeds	–To contribute to profit by increasing input and/or processor efficiencies

For Whom

–The poor	–The shareholder and management

By Whom

–830 scientists working in 8 institutes reporting to U.S. foundations	–In the United States alone, 1,127 scientists working for 30 agbiotech companies
–Industrialized countries	
–Quasi-U.N. bodies	

How

–Plant breeding in wheat, maize, rice	–Genetic manipulation of all plants, all animals, microorganisms

Primary Targets

–Semidwarf capacity in cereals	–Herbicide tolerance
–Response to fertilizers	–Natural substitution
	–Factory production

Investment

–$108 million for agricultural R&D	–Agbiotech R&D investment of $144 million in United States (1988) by 30 companies

General Impact

–Substantial but gradual	–Enormous—sometimes immediate
–52.9 percent of third-world wheat and rice in HRVs (123 million hectares)	–$20 billion in medicinal and flavor/fragrance crops at risk
–"500 million would not otherwise be fed"	–Multibillion-dollar beverage, confectionery, sugar, and vegetable-oils trade could be lost

to be drawn? Should public policy enter the arena at all? Many doctors criticize fetal sex identification since prospective parents may decide on an abortion simply because they desire a child of the opposite sex. Happily, 90 percent of the almost two million annual abortions in the United States are performed before the twelfth week of pregnancy. Since prenatal screening tests are rarely completed before the pregnancy is well along (as late as the twenty-second week for amniocentesis), the unpleasant possibility of late abortion provides dilemmas for both patient and physician. As one physician has stated, "It makes us all schizophrenic. Nowadays we are asked to terminate a pregnancy that in two weeks doctors on the same floor are fighting to save."[14]

Not as yet true issues in genetic engineering, prenatal testing and in vitro fertilization may soon be so distinguished. Already, research on gene therapy is well under way, where an in vitro fertilized egg (the external mixing of egg and sperm, with subsequent reintroduction into the uterus) may be genetically engineered. By introducing normal genes into an in vitro fertilized egg from a couple carrying a heritable disease, the child resulting from such therapy could be born healthy. But any kind of gene pool alteration is a form of eugenics, a term coined by Francis Galton in the last century and defined by him as ". . . the improvement of the human race by better breeding." Our twentieth-century experience with such efforts (master-race eugenics in Hitler's Third Reich and the many efforts of the Social Darwinists at home and abroad) suggest that extreme care should be exercised in either allowing or supporting such efforts. As the Council of Europe recently declared, there should be

> explicit recognition in the Human Rights Convention of the human right to a genetic inheritance which has not been interfered with . . . except in accordance with principles which are recognized as fully compatible with respect for human rights.[15]

It is also understandable that every prospective parent hopes for a healthy child. The specter of genetic abnormality haunts every pregnancy. Because of a combination of environmental factors — chemically-laden air, agricultural biocides, polluted drinking water, radioactive contamination, pesticide residue on food, and smoking and other unhealthy life-style practices — and natural genetic mutation, about one of every twenty babies born today has some form of abnormality. Responsible efforts to minimize the possibilities of such abnormal births must be supported. Most medical authorities agree that here again prevention — through efforts to control the environmental contaminants of an industrial society, providing prenatal health care to all women regardless of race or class, and adopting personally responsible, self-reliant, healthy living styles — will do far more to prevent unhappy births than all the gene-therapy efforts currently dreamed about by the genetic engineers. But it is well to remember that our personal and collective striving for absolute perfection may similarly not always be well placed. Biochemist David Lygre notes:

> We should not presume that "normality," a term none of us can define adequately, is a prerequisite to a full and meaningful life. People are born with an enormous range of abilities and disabilities, and many "defective" people have not only experienced rich lives, but they have made life richer for the rest of us.
>
> Perhaps physical perfection is incompatible with mental and spiritual perfection. We lose a sense of compassion, caring, and love if we exercise these qualities only when it comes easy. Indeed, if we come to view defective people as unwanted intrusions who diminish the quality of our lives, the greatest pity may not be what is happening to them. It will be what is happening to us.[16]

Ironically, many of the so-called advances in the science and technology of reproductive-system research have provided more constraint than freedom for modern women. Harvard biologist Ruth Hubbard's cautionary note about the power exercised by the practitioners of the new technologies — that the more sophisticated a technology becomes, "the more likely it is to be controlled by elites, to increase inequalities, to reinforce hierarchies . . . and to have power over the people on whom it is used" — has direct application to the struggle of women today to control their own reproductive destinies.[17] Apart from the occasional panegyric by women who have successfully undergone such procedures as in vitro fertilization (and who seem to have often been manipulated into becoming marketing agents for a medical technique of doubtful social value), many women are aware that the distance between these procedures and even more sophisticated research is narrowing daily. Much of modern reproductive-system research seems almost geared toward the virtual removal of women from the reproductive process. Already, extensive research has been conducted on the development of an artificial placenta (using in its earlier research phase aborted but still temporarily viable fetuses) and on the possibility of full-term gestation within an artificial uterus. Germ-line therapy, the actual genetic tinkering with heredity as part of the in vitro process, is, of course, the most exciting frontier of all to the reproductive-system research community. That there is a continuum of sorts — the pleas of the eugenicists, the artificial hormonal stimulation of previously infertile women, the promises of in vitro fertilization, germ-line therapies, artificial birthing environments — that leads from one unique scientific venture to another and that places women less and less in control of their own reproductive destinies is becoming increasingly apparent.

Ironically, most of the women who have become candidates for in vitro fertilization have suffered a kind of double jeopardy from the medical profession in their attempts to control their own reproductive cycles. Most in vitro candidates have initially requested treatment due to earlier damage done to their fallopian tubes through the use of intrauterine devices originally prescribed to prevent pregnancy. Having already suffered once, they are then subjected to the physically invasive and costly testing procedures of the in vitro process—regimes that often have to be repeated several times. Adding insult to injury is that the process only occasionally works! First subjected to hormonal stimulation to prepare the uterine wall, several eggs are commonly removed from the ovary by laparoscopy (a surgical procedure requiring a small incision in the abdominal wall), placed in an atmosphere conducive to biological growth (commonly contained within a glass dish or test tube), and mixed with sperm. If the egg is fertilized and undergoes cleavage, the zygote is then reintroduced into the uterus (not necessarily that of the woman who produced the egg in the first place), where, all things being equal, a normal pregnancy results.

But not all things are equal in in vitro fertilization. Although the statistical odds of success are regularly improving, the possibility of a normal in vitro pregnancy is not good. In one early study of seventy-nine women who entered treatment, sixty-eight successfully underwent laparoscopy, forty-four yielded properly mature eggs, and thirty-two eggs were actually fertilized. Of the four women out of the original seventy-nine who actually became pregnant, there were two miscarriages and two normal births. As the procedures and success ratios improve, it seems clear that only a very select group of women will ever have the means to choose such a therapeutic option. Highly sophisticated medicine is normally accessible only to a very limited group of patients. In this case, that may not be a bad thing; but the history of reproductive-system research provides a reminder of the unequal treatment structured into our health-care delivery systems.

PUBLIC-POLICY IMPERATIVES

The history of scientific development suggests a tendency for those in power to control information either beneficial to them or of possible future use in their attempts to maintain or extend power. As our abilities to manipulate genetic material increase, so will the pressure to use the new technologies for purposes deemed appropriate for the reinforcement of the existing class structure of the society. As we learn how to bioengineer new products considered necessary for profits by corporate hierarchies, or to increase human intelligence via gene therapy, it will become difficult indeed to constrain these powers. None of this is to suggest that all genetic research should be discontinued. Even if we wished that to occur, the enormous forces within government, the university, and the corporate structure would make it impossible. Biotechnology is also an international priority, and even if we should determine to slow things down here other countries would not necessarily be so constrained. The issue, then, and the only one capable of providing any kind of long-range solution, rests in the public-policy arena.

What now seems incontrovertible is the need to provide increasingly effective means of public involvement in determining the priorities for and the control of the research task in the United States. Scientists fall prey to the temptation to "generalize their expertise," feeling that since they know what to do in the laboratory they should also be free to establish all of the policies to guide their work and to evaluate it. Historically, this has been true. To the extent that science has been regulated, it has clearly been self-regulating. Working on the questions posed by government and industry, the science industry has brooked no interference in fulfilling those mandates. While honest efforts have been made to regulate biotechnology and recombinant research in the United States by the Recombinant Advisory Committee of the federal government and the seventeen other agencies involved, very little effective control has resulted. Technically illegal recombinant research has been performed for years on my own campus with impunity. Genetic-engineering companies in the San Francisco Bay area have been found guilty of deliberate field releases of new genetically altered organisms, fined, and then told to continue with their research. The University of California, Berkeley, in conjunction with the Naval Biosciences Laboratory has long been involved in biological-warfare research subject to no public control or review. Cases of this kind are commonplace within the research communities of the United States. So it is that public-policy objectives regulating the industry and incorporating the lay community into the decision-making process must be formulated.

The following policy guidelines of the Bogeve seminar seem to sum up well the conclusions of those people—lay and professional—who are concerned about the prospects for more adequate regulation of genetic engineering:

- Biotechnology shall always be regarded as a tool, not an aim in itself.
- If the potential impact of a biotechnological innovation turns out to be detrimental to society or to the environment, other measures should be sought.
- If the impact assessment of an innovation seems benign, society must still determine if the innovation will divert resources or expertise from more important tasks.
- The release of genetically altered organisms into the environment should be undertaken only after the most careful environmental impact assessment.
- Genetic manipulations of higher organisms should not be regarded as methods of first choice.
- Genetic manipulations involving human beings should be subject to broad public debate and probably regulation and restriction.
- Reproductive technologies in human beings must also undergo broad public debate, keeping in mind cultural and religious feelings

and the necessity of not exploiting women.
- Biotechnological diagnostic and screening techniques should be monitored to avoid abuse, discrimination, and racist application.
- The conservation, utilization and improvement of genetic resources and genetic diversity must not be hindered or endangered by biotechnological innovation.
- Biotechnological research that results in significant or unnecessary torment of animals should not be allowed.
- Research projects imported from another country shall not be carried out if banned in the country of origin.
- Research projects using public monies must prove that the aim is to benefit the majority of the people, and that the project will harm neither the people nor the environment in the vicinity.
- Researchers must abide by all relevant laboratory and experimentation safety regulations, e.g., the recommendations of the Office of Economic Cooperation and Development (OECD) of the United Nations.
- The socioeconomic impact of biotechnology on poor people, small farmers, and small business should be given special consideration.
- Whenever government establishes agencies to regulate any dimension of the genetic engineering process, it must include on such agencies equal numbers of experts and lay representatives to insure that both the perspectives of science and the public welfare are protected.[18]

The difficulty, of course, rests not in defining such principles but in actually formulating the policy-making mechanisms to enforce them. The history of policy making and the correlative development of regulatory agencies in the United States has essentially been one of asking those institutions that society says need to be regulated to establish the guidelines themselves under which they are to be regulated. The decentralization of most environmental regulation in the United States (wherein the federal government essentially delegates to the states the implementation and enforcement of federal law and policy) will be ineffective in managing either laboratory or environmental research in the recombinant fields. Altered and genetically modified life forms are simply too different from other kinds of pollution to be so similarly regulated. Unhappily, the federal government has no intention at this time of establishing any separate or superagency to monitor such research and development. Unlike most items subject to governmental regulation, the issue is not so much control over products to be developed as control over the techniques to be employed in production.

The Environmental Protection Agency (EPA) has now asserted jurisdiction over all microorganisms that are not pesticides (which remain under the regulatory supervision of other agencies) under the Toxic Substances

Control Act (TSCA). EPA's assumption is that genetically modified organisms fall within the definition of a chemical under the TSCA and that the EPA is thus best equipped to monitor and regulate such organisms. Recognizing that genetically modified organisms are at least to some degree unique, the EPA has proposed a new decentralized structure to assess risk/benefit factors in regulating field releases of new organisms, much like the existing local Industrial Biosafety Committees that regulate research. To be called Environmental Biosafety Committees (EBCs), each institution to be regulated—companies or universities—would again form its own EBC to regulate itself. The history of all such previous efforts at self-regulation in research suggests that such groupings basically become rubber stamps for their own institution.

Realistically, it is now certain that the federal government does not intend to create a special agency or agencies to monitor and regulate either the research and development or the environmental releases of new genetically altered organisms. This does not mean, however, that it should be constrained in developing special mechanisms within existing agencies to accomplish these tasks. Certainly the lead agency in regulation will be the EPA. But the EPA should not have its hands tied by having to treat biotechnological research and field testing under antiquated and inappropriate toxic-substance regulation. The minimum demand from a skeptical public must be for the formulation of new policy mechanisms—rules and regulations—to guide both research and releases of genetically altered organisms by private biotechnology companies and universities.

Neither recombinant science nor the social implications of the science can be confined within traditional categories of policy or ethics. Recombinant organisms are qualitatively different from products developed in earlier historical periods. Production techniques are absolutely unique and thus require special regulatory oversight and care. And as genetically engineered changes become more and more commonplace, people in power will inevitably tend to identify social problems as genetic deficiencies of certain individuals or groups. The only guarantees that society has to control the new science and technology are continued commitments to individual rights, the further institution of federal and local controls on research and development, and renewed vigor to alert the public to the promises and the perils of genetic engineering. As the President's Commission for the Study of Ethical Problems has forcefully noted:

Like the tale of the Sorcerer's apprentice, or the myth of the Golem created from lifeless dust, . . . the story of Dr. Frankenstein's monster serves as a reminder of the difficulty of restoring order if a creation intended to be helpful proves harmful instead. Indeed, each of these tales conveys a painful irony: in seeking to extend their control over the world, people may lessen it. The artifices they create to do their bidding may rebound destructively against them—the slave may become the master.[19]

NOTES

1. Lewis Thomas, "The Hazards of Medicine," *New England Journal of Medicine* (1977), pp. 324–25.

2. President's Commission for the Study of Ethical Problems in Medicine and Biomedical and Behavioral Research, *Splicing Life*, November 1982, p. 1.

3. Stillman Drake, ed., *Discoveries and Opinions of Galileo* (New York: Doubleday/Anchor Press, 1957), p. 64.

4. Cary Fowler, Eva Lachkovics, Pat Mooney, and Hope Shand, "The Laws of Life: Another Development and the New Biotechnologies," *Development Dialogue*, 1, no. 2 (1988), p. 49.

5. J. D. Watson and J. Tooze, *The DNA Story* (San Francisco: W. H. Freeman, 1981), p. 49.

6. C. K. Boone, "When Scientists Go Public with Their Doubts," *Hastings Journal* 12, no. 6 (December 1982), p. 13.

7. Ibid., p. 13.

8. Governmental reluctance to attempt to develop new regulatory procedures for recombinant technologies or to intrude overly in attempting to oversee industrial biotechnology is clearly revealed in *New Developments in Biotechnology—Field Testing Engineered Organisms: Genetic and Ecological Issues* (Washington, D.C.: U. S. Congress, Office of Technology Assessment [OTA-BA-350], May 1988).

9. Fowler et al., p. 179.

10. Ibid., pp. 6–7.

11. Ibid., p. 51.

12. Ibid., pp. 62–63.

13. P. M. Boffey, "Panel Urges Preparation To Meet Big Demand for Genetic Screening," *New York Times*, February 27, 1983, p. 14.

14. Dena Kleiman, "When Abortion Becomes Birth," *New York Times*, February 15, 1984, p. 14.

15. Council of Europe, *Parliamentary Proceedings*, Recommendation 934 (Strasbourg, 1982).

16. David G. Lygre, *Life Manipulation* (New York: Walker, 1979), p. 69.

17. Ruth Hubbard, *Science for the People* 15, no. 3 (May-June 1983), p. 24.

18. In addition to these summary comments as expressed in the Bogeve Conference declaration and recorded in Fowler et al., pp. 226–28, note also the Draft Model Law, "The Biotechnology Safety and Environmental Protection Act," ibid., pp. 233–36.

19. President's Commission for the Study of Ethical Problems, III-9.

3

The Ecology-Economy-Ethic Connection in Land Use

FREDERICK KIRSCHENMANN

If there are inherent ambiguities in social policies regulating the use of land, it is because our history contains deeply conflicting values regarding land: progress on the one hand and preservation on the other. In addition, there have been two philosophies of land tenure: land is private property, or land is a trust from God, who retains ownership. Resolution of these ambiguities is possible in sustainable economic modes, particularly in agriculture, as Dr. Kirschenmann documents with reference to his own experience in farming.

There appears to be a growing consensus among environmental scientists that if citizens of the earth do not make some major changes in the way we use the planet within the next ten years then we will find ourselves on an irreversible course leading to global disaster. In the meantime annual global soil loss, largely attributed to our current farming and forestry practices, is now set at twenty-five billion tons. Rampant deforestation caused by acid rain and clear-cut harvesting, plus the loss of wetlands because of agricultural drainage, threaten to irrevocably damage complex ecosystems that have been in place for thousands of years. Food, groundwater, and air are all being poisoned with alarming speed. We continue to pour carbon dioxide into the atmosphere at rates that assure global warming, which, in turn, threatens to produce enormous global destruction. Yet despite these grim realities we seem to continue on our present course. As the World Watch Institute concluded in its annual report for 1986, "We live for today as though there were no tomorrow, as though we had no children."[1]

Why are we so hell-bent on destroying our nest? Why do we insist on ruining the very land that sustains us? Aldo Leopold, one of the inspirations behind the environmental movement, suggested that "we abuse the land because we regard it as a commodity belonging to us." Not until we start seeing the "land as a community to which *we* belong," he warned, will we begin to "use it with love and respect."[2] Leopold's insight is powerful. Once we have concluded that *we* own the land, we determine to use it any way we see fit and discard it when we have finished with it. That is an observation that seems to ring true. Furthermore, it is based on perceptions of human behavior that are deeply rooted in our culture. Erich Fromm reminds us, for example, that much of our irrational behavior in the modern world can be traced to our delusion that the more we *have* the more we can achieve well-being.[3]

But there is a problem with Leopold's land ethic. It lends itself too easily to a good/evil dichotomy that often derails our efforts to adopt common, sustainable land-use policies. So long as I can convince myself that the world is in a mess because the "bad guys" are despoiling it, I am relieved of personal responsibility. All I have to do is continue pointing my morally indignant finger at the perpetrators. The only task to which I need commit myself is to convert, cajole, or coerce the bad guys into becoming good guys. That approach may be not only ineffective but even counterproductive. It leads the accused to entrench themselves into a defensive posture that impedes change. The end result of this dichotomy is that the "bad guys" resist change, while the "good guys" believe they have transcended the need to change. It is a classic demonstration of the proposition that "goodness without ambiguity tends to become entropic."[4]

CONFLICTING LAND-USE VALUES IN AMERICAN HISTORY

There is, in fact, probably no good/evil dichotomy with respect to the land. We do have genuine disagreements, however, concerning its proper use. There is an inherent ambiguity in our land-use policies that can be traced to a conflict of values regarding land that is deeply embedded in our history. I believe it is important to understand the tension caused by this value conflict in order to arrive at an effective, communally shared land-use policy.

Many people of European descent who came to this new world brought with them a "dream of destiny." They believed they had been chosen by God to carry out a special mission. They regarded themselves to have been specifically selected to build a new "kingdom of God" in this new land.

From the very beginning, this mandate was understood in two different ways. Cotton Mather, for example, records his displeasure over a "well-known" pilgrim's pronouncement that while some of the Bay Puritans may have come to the new land primarily for religious motives, at Plymouth "the main end was to catch fish."[5]

In other words, on the one hand the first settlers considered it their moral obligation to prosper. Destiny had called them here to mine the natural resources, clear the trees, tame the wilderness, and make the land productive. Transforming the land from a wild, untamed, unused wasteland into a controlled, profitable enterprise was a moral obligation — the reason God had put them here.

The extent to which they were able to demonstrate progress toward such land transformation was even considered a "sign" that they were fulfilling their destiny. In fact, one reason the early settlers were able to justify appropriating the land from Native Americans was largely because, in their view, the natives had abdicated their duty to God to "improve" the land they inhabited.[6]

On the other hand, early settlers also considered it their destiny to protect and preserve the land. God had given them the land as a gift, entrusted it to their care as a place of freedom. Here they could safeguard their liberty to worship, to develop their moral character in accordance with God's word as they understood it, and to create a government that was fashioned according to the "rule of God."

Once again, the extent to which they were able to protect and preserve the land and to create a body politic that resembled the kingdom of God on earth was a sign that they were fulfilling their destiny. Failure to do so was a sign that they had aborted their true destiny. John Winthrop had already clearly articulated this view before the first Puritan ever set foot on the shores of the new land.[7]

It is not surprising, then, that this two-pronged dream of destiny should give birth to conflicts over land use. The tension between "progress" and "preservation" was there from the beginning. The disagreements, moreover, were based on the same moral grounds. It was not that those who opted for progress were evil, while those who opted for preservation were good. Both saw themselves on equal moral footing. To a large extent open conflict over land use was minimized during the first three centuries of European habitation as a result of the availability of space. When one disagreed with the policies of one's neighbors there was always a new "place" to which one could move.

This dual land ethic rooted in progress and preservation is still with us. Honest, responsible people still disagree about how the land should be used. In fact, many of us have conflicting feelings within ourselves about land use. On the one hand, we can be motivated to preserve and protect the land, to plant trees, to prevent erosion, to restrict the mining of natural resources. On the other hand, we can be motivated to make the land productive, to maximize its economic potential, to make fragile land available for logging, cropping, or grazing.

However, when conflicts over land use arise each side tends to regard the other as immoral. Environmentalists who want to save the forests of the Northwest consider the logging companies that want to harvest the trees as greedy, grubby commercialists who have no ethical commitment to higher ideals. Loggers, who want to see their communities prosper, regard the environmentalists as meddling outsiders who have no concern for the economic well-being of the people affected. Those who employ moral arguments on one side seem incapable of seeing the moral grounds of the other.

As a practicing farmer I am aware of these conflicts in myself. A part of me is motivated to be the most productive farmer I can be. I consider it a moral obligation to "improve" the land as much as I can. If my land produces best by draining sloughs, breaking up prairie, and moldboard plowing, then that is what I am motivated to do. Another part of me is motivated to protect the land. And if protecting the land means preserving wetlands, conserving fragile acreage, and leaving stubble on soil surfaces, then that is what I am obligated to do.

These moral ambiguities in no way dismiss greed as a motivating factor in the way we use land. No doubt we all have a degree of greed embedded in our characters and are sometimes motivated to use land to satisfy our desire for material gain. After all, we are probably all infected with the delusion that the more we *have* the happier we will be. But it is doubtful that this is the *major* motivating factor in our conflicts over land use. It is the need to demonstrate progress, to show improvement, to have the finest cornfield in the county, that motivates us on the one hand. And, on the other hand, it is the need to preserve and protect the land so that future generations can be free to aspire to a quality life of their own choosing that motivates us.

Another issue, also on the minds of the first settlers, further contributed to our conflicting values over land use. That was the question of how land ownership should be viewed. The right to hold private property (including land) was of great concern to the framers of our Constitution. The Sixth Amendment made it clear that land belongs first and foremost to individuals. The rights attending such ownership were not to be infringed on easily by the state. In other words, from the beginning Americans felt a moral obligation to protect the right of individuals to use their own land as they saw fit.

However, the first settlers were also keenly aware that since God had especially chosen them to come here and build a new kingdom of God on earth, the land was entrusted to them by God and never really belonged to them at all. That made them not so much owners as stewards of the land.

Once again we can clearly see the influence that these two philosophies of land tenure have on our land ethic today. On the one hand, I view my land as *my* property—the place where I do what I think is best without outside interference. On the other hand, I view my land as a trust, something that never really belonged to me at all, something that was only given into my care for a brief time.

This conflict can be observed readily in farm landowner organizations that are appearing in various parts of the country today. Landowners feel compelled to protect themselves against outside interference from government and environmental groups. Environmentalists take the position that they need to act in behalf of society to protect wetlands, native prairie, and other natural resources for future generations. Landowners, many of whom share the goals of the environmentalists, take the position that environmentalists have no business interfering with *their* operations. Landowners want to remind us that it is, after all, *their* land, land *they* purchased and on which *they* pay taxes. Neither the state nor other outside organizations has any right to interfere with their land "improvements."

In the course of human events, of course, some of us are inevitably drawn to an ethic of developing a virtuous life and practicing stewardship, while others are drawn to the values of progress and the protection of private-property rights. Consequently, conflicts over land use will arise inevitably. And it is important to remember that these conflicts do not spring from a simple good/evil dichotomy. Until we make our peace with the fact that this ambiguity is deeply embedded in our heritage, we are not likely to develop a comprehensive land-use policy that will protect the environment and preserve our resource base, at least not one that the majority of citizens will support over the long term.

THE CONNECTION BETWEEN ECONOMY AND ECOLOGY

Fortunately, there are practical opportunities to reconcile these land-use conflicts. The greatest opportunities lie in our growing awareness that there are apparent connections between ecology and economy.

We have probably always been aware that when we destroy the resource base of any economic activity that activity itself will be jeopardized. Perhaps we have even been aware that we cannot continue indefinitely to degrade the environment within which an economic activity takes place. As early as 1953, the USDA published a bulletin that clearly established the connection between land abuse and economic demise in past civilizations.[8] So the long-term connections between ecology and economy are not a new revelation.

More recently, however, we have also gradually become aware of the connections between economy and ecology in the short term. We now know, for example, that the rain forests are more valuable to us economically for the fruits they yield when we preserve them than they are when we destroy them for their logging and cattle-grazing value. Many communities are discovering that it costs less to recycle garbage in an ecologically responsible way than it does to bury it in landfills. Some economists are even beginning to suggest that it is in our own economic interest to assist underdeveloped nations, like China, to develop clean energy resources, since their reliance on cheap coal reserves so intensifies further carbon dioxide emissions that it will destroy our own economy through global warming.

At the first levels of economic activity (farming, forestry, mining, and fishing) the ecology/economy connection is beginning to become apparent from direct observation. Fishermen on the East Coast are beginning to experience the immediate economic impact of pollution and overfishing. Logging communities are beginning to understand the economic ramifications of clear-cut tree harvesting. At least a few farmers are beginning to realize the economic consequences of soil erosion and polluted groundwater.

Perhaps the reason that more farmers have not yet become aware of the ecology/economy connection in agriculture is because the economic consequences of ecologically destructive practices have been masked, to some extent, by the use of cheap, subsidized petroleum technologies. The economic consequences of soil loss from erosion, for example, can be deferred through the application of synthetic fertilizers.

Another reason that farmers often do not see the economy/ecology connection is because of the narrow, reductionistic way in which we have calculated the economic value of farm practices. The economic health of farms is often determined by year-end bottom lines rather than by overall farm prosperity. The economic value of specific management strategies is often measured on a field by field basis, rather than by determining cost-benefit ratios for the whole farm system.

The "economic threshold" of an insecticide application, for example, is generally determined by comparing the cost of crop loss from insect infestation in a specific field with the cost of the insecticide application. Farmers are never encouraged to consider the economic impact on the farm caused by secondary effects of the insecticide application, such as the loss of beneficial insects or the development of more resistant strains of insects.

Reductionistic approaches to economics have also prevented farmers from making cost-benefit analyses on the effectiveness of certain practices over a given period. Crop losses because of insects, disease, and weeds since 1940 have actually *increased* from 32 percent to 37 percent, despite the application of billions of pounds of pesticides,[9] yet this fact is seldom considered in planning effective, economically viable strategies for dealing with farm pest problems. Were "economic thresholds" calculated from a whole-systems approach, the connection between ecology and economy would become much more apparent.

Another reason that farmers have not been fully cognizant of ecology/economy connections is that not all the costs of current farming practices have been factored in. Expenditures for decontaminating groundwater, restoring eroded soil, cleaning silt from ditches and drainages, or restoring lakes and streams contaminated by synthetic fertilizers and pesticides have been ignored in calculating the economics of conventional agriculture.

In addition, we have also not factored in the taxes used to subsidize the oil and water required to produce crops by conventional means. We have not calculated the cost of restoring water reserves depleted by raising irrigated corn in Arizona or grazing cattle on irrigated pastures in California. Nor have we added in the costs of social destabilization caused by the huge migration of farmers to urban centers. These are all effects that have been precipitated largely by the structures of conventional agriculture, effects that have serious environmental impacts but whose costs have not been considered.

Furthermore, there are problems associated with present farming practices that we resist even thinking about, such as the increased health-care expenditures attributable to the hazardous materials that are part and parcel of conventional agriculture. And certainly we have not wanted to face up to the agricultural costs associated with global warming, due largely to carbon dioxide buildup, caused, to some extent, by agriculture's heavy reliance on petroleum-based technologies.[10]

Were we to factor in all of *these* costs, the connections between ecology and economy in agriculture would become painfully clear.

CLUES FOR DETERMINING THE ADVANTAGES OF SUSTAINABLE AGRICULTURE

Recently, farmers, researchers, politicians, and environmentalists have been encouraged to consider more sustainable systems of agriculture. It has been suggested that such systems would have both ecologic and economic advantages.[11]

Determining the benefits of sustainable agriculture will be difficult and time consuming. In the first place, we cannot yet be certain which farming practices will prove to be sustainable. Second, the economic and environmental impact of such systems has to be calculated based on whole-systems analyses, and we have not yet determined the best methodologies for conducting such research. Third, owing to the complex interrelationships of whole systems, multiple-year analysis becomes inevitable.

In the Northwest, however, that process has begun. Universities and farm groups are cooperating in a regionwide, whole-systems, multiyear study, funded by the Northwest Area Foundation, to determine some of the economic, environmental, and social impacts of a variety of farming systems.

In the meantime, it may be worthwhile to consider some clues, derived from on-farm observations, that appear to point to economic and ecologic advantages inherent in alternative farming practices.

During the past thirteen years, we have been evolving some alternative farming practices on our 3,100-acre grain and cattle farm in North Dakota that we think are somewhat more sustainable than the conventional methods we had used previously.

This assessment is based on several observations. With the exception of diesel fuel and electricity, our biodynamic farm relies totally on internal, renewable resources for inputs. For the past nine years, we have not needed to borrow any operating funds. We have evolved a diverse crop rotation system that appears to be keeping pests in check, as well as maintaining an adequate level of soil fertility without purchasing off-farm inputs. The diverse crop and livestock system enables us to utilize by-products (such as manure and crop residues) from both parts of the system to make the whole system more profitable. The diverse crop-rotation and regenerative-management practices appear to reduce soil erosion and to improve soil organic matter and biological activity. This soil health, combined with an absence of toxic materials, appears to be establishing a base of relative ecological stability.

Assuming that these observations are correct and that such practices can lead to a degree of sustainability, there are several factors that point to economic and ecologic advantages.

First, our observations indicate that the alternative practices we have put in place improve the farm's survivability. This is due largely to the diversity inherent in the system. Under adverse weather conditions (hail, drought, flooding, temperature extremes) diverse systems simply fare better than specialized ones. Some crops are more drought resistant, while others are more frost hardy. Some crops are susceptible to certain insects and diseases but resistant to others. And, although crops do not, livestock do survive hailstorms. All of this means that diverse systems are much less vulnerable to extensive losses from the natural adversities that come to any farm. That is an important economic advantage.

The alternative practices we use may not be less costly than conventional ones. While removing the chemical line-item from the budget represents a considerable saving, building sustainability into the system adds other costs. Our soil-building and conservation programs, as well as our cultural pest-control practices, represent sizable investments. However, there are still considerable economic advantages, even if bottom-line costs turn out to be comparable. Our expenditures are spread over a longer time, which reduces our risks. We can also avoid large periodic cash outlays, since we do not rely on external inputs that have to be applied within specific periods. Our inputs are part of the overall, interconnected system and can be incorporated over a longer time span. That saves interest costs and reduces risk, an economic advantage.

Since our farm relies mostly on internal inputs, it is also not as vulnerable to sharp price increases. The costs of green manuring, composting, and crop rotations remain relatively stable, while the costs of petroleum-based inputs can rise sharply over brief periods. That, too, is an economic advantage.

We have also noted that our crop and livestock system seems to be more stress tolerant. Livestock that are allowed to grow, feed, roam, and reproduce naturally seem to be less prone to stress than livestock that are forced to grow under hormone growth regulators, fed high-powered rations, and confined in artificial environments. All of that means lower health-care costs, lower infertility rates, and prolonged productivity. Similarly, crops produced under natural management systems with improved organic matter and increased biological activity appear to survive weather-related stress more effectively. We find these results provide economic advantages despite slower growth rates.

Our cropping system also appears to have self-accumulating benefits. Fertility derived from green manure and animal wastes builds organic matter and restores soil structure, which, in turn, supports future soil-building efforts. Crop rotations that break weed and insect cycles, creating environments that inhibit pest expansion, make future control less difficult. That is also an economic advantage. In conventional systems, where synthetic fertilizers are applied in monocropping practices, soil structure breaks down, causing compaction and fertility loss and requiring increasing amounts of fertilizers to maintain yield levels. Similarly, because of the evolution of resistant strains of pests and the destruction of beneficial species, greater use of pesticides is needed to maintain the same level of control.

Our system also provides us with some market advantages. Our practices qualify us for organic and biodynamic market niches, where we generally receive premiums for our crops. Furthermore, our diverse system gives us greater market flexibility. With eight different crops in our rotation, plus the livestock, we escape confinement to the market fortunes of a narrow band of commodities. That is also an economic advantage.

Ecological strengths of our farming practices seem rather apparent. Since we use no toxic off-farm inputs for fertility or pest control, we drastically reduce the potential for agriculture-related pollution. While livestock manure can also be a source of pollution, proper handling (such as composting) can reduce that risk to near zero. By increasing organic matter and improving soil structure with the use of green manuring and livestock manure, together with proper crop rotations, we are finding our soil losses reduced to T levels or less.[12]

The practices we use also have the potential to improve wildlife habitat. Since we apply no toxic materials to the land, there is less risk for creatures in the wild to ingest poison. Diverse crop rotations provide more opportunities for nesting habitat of a wider range of birds.

The system also provides for a healthier environment for humans by lessening exposure to hazardous materials and by reducing the amount of carcinogenic and mutanogenic substances released into the environment.

SOME POLICY IMPLICATIONS

Developing an agriculture that is both ecologically and economically responsible is not something that farmers can do by themselves. Switching to a sustainable agriculture is not just a matter of changing some on-farm practices. We cannot create an island of sustainability for agriculture in the midst of economic and social policies that promote nonsustainable lifestyles and nonsustainable economic growth. Consequently, developing an agriculture that provides a stable, steady supply of safe, nutritious food to customers at a reasonable price with a reasonable return to family-farm producers, while using production practices that enhance agriculture's resource base and protect the environment, requires a web of social and economic policies that support a wide range of changes.

We need legislation that will no longer *inhibit* the adoption of more sustainable practices on farms. Legislation on the order of that introduced by Representative Jim Jontz (HR 3552), in the 101st Congress, would go a long way toward achieving that objective. Such legislation would encourage alternative farming practices by introducing various changes in federal farm policies. The modifications are designed to support, rather than penalize, farmers for introducing soil building and conserving crop rotations and other "low-input" practices. But making such proposed changes in the 1990 farm legislation will not by itself give us a sustainable agriculture.

As long as we have trade policies that encourage cropping systems that cause soil erosion, energy policies that encourage the use of fossil fuels, economic policies that squeeze farmers between two highly leveraged and organized enterprises (farm-supply manufacturers and commodity trade industries), and investment policies that allow farmland to be traded as an investment commodity, then we cannot have agricultural sustainability. These are the policies that place farmers under the kind of economic pressures that lead them to squeeze every pound of grain out of every square inch of soil and every pound of gain out of every animal without regard for the preservation of the resource base or protection of the environment.

Accordingly, we need to engage citizens in public debate on a wide range of policy initiatives designed to attract broad citizen support for new economic and ecologic ways of behaving. The debates need to be structured so that all participants are encouraged to speak freely out of their own convictions, fully recognizing that, based on their own moral sense, citizens genuinely disagree over how the land should be used. Proposals for the debate will need to be stated so that the economy/ecology connections can be clearly understood and argued.

Following are a few proposals relating to the restructuring of agricultural land use that might be included in such debate:

RESOLVED: That publicly funded research be shifted to study alternative agriculture systems and to develop appropriate markets for the crops and livestock produced in those systems. Such research should focus on sound ecological and economical farming practices.

RESOLVED: That federal farm legislation be established to prohibit the purchase of farmland for investment purposes, establish farmland trusts or other mechanisms that would enable beginning farmers to gain easier access to farmland, and require a basic level of skill in land care and environmental protection as a prerequisite to acquiring such lands. (Model legislation for such land-use policies is available in Taiwan, Sweden, South Korea, and France.)

RESOLVED: That a new system of tax incentives and disincentives be established to discourage the use of fossil fuels and to encourage the use of alternative sources of energy.

RESOLVED: That a federal tax be applied to all farm input products that are potentially damaging to the environment. Every purchased input should produce sufficient revenue to pay the full price of its use. Revenues from this source should be used to fund research on farming practices that enhance the environment, preserve the resource base, and promote the economic health of the family farm.

A LAND-ETHIC EPILOGUE: SOME NOTES ON ECONOMY, IDEALISM AND POVERTY

Underlying all of the above deliberations is a fundamental ethical question. What do we really want? As a society we may in fact be divided on the issue, just as we were in the days of Cotton Mather. But Studs Terkel, based on his most recent trek across America, finds among us a fragile, new change of attitude that could unite us in a common cause that may bode well for the planet.

Terkel says, "What we profess to believe in this drifting decade may be something wholly different from what we really believe. Or want."[13] He finds a kind of "baby-faced Gideon's army" in our society who cheer Rambo in public but privately admire compassion and hope. Could it be that they also secretly cherish other values that have been unpopular for some time?

Clearly if we are going to alter our life-styles sufficiently during the next decade to save the planet by our changed behavior, then we have to dream some bold new dreams, dreams that dare to challenge some of our most fundamental "wish lists." And if Terkel is right, we may just be ready, as a society, to entertain such bold rethinking.

Some of the proposals that I have initiated in this paper have been branded "idealistic." That may mean that they are not grounded in reality, or that no one is ready to take them seriously. But surely it is more realistic to propose that we stop destroying the planet than it is to propose that we stay on our present course. After all, to continue as we are is to annihilate the very things we say we "want." And is it not realistic to suspect that what most Americans really want is a stable and sustainable society, rather than one that simply gives them "more" for the moment?

Of course, there are many citizens of the planet who do not have what is required to meet basic necessities. But Frances Moore Lappé and others have offered cogent arguments which suggest that the problem of world hunger is *not* tightly linked to any nation's food production, but rather to world political and social structures that use food for purposes other than keeping the world fed.[14]

At issue here, among other things, is our need to abandon the narrow, reductionistic way in which we have defined, and used, "economics." We have come to think of economic well-being purely through things that are countable, and we have failed to evaluate our needs from a more comprehensive perspective that allows us to ask whether or not we are really getting what we want.

Almost seventy years ago, Rudolf Steiner warned that the great trouble with the science of economics was that it was altogether too narrowly and too rigidly constructed. "The conceptions of Economics," he wrote, "are the very ones which you can never evolve by reference to the mere external reality. No, you must always evolve them by reference to the economic process as a whole."[15]

Wendell Berry reports that he and Wes Jackson came to this same conclusion as they labored to define the causes of the ruination of the land. They decided that only an economy based on "the kingdom of God" would be comprehensive enough to move us toward a more realistic foundation. The problem with our present industrial economy, wrote Berry, is that "it is not comprehensive enough, that, moreover, it tends to destroy what it does not comprehend, and that it is *dependent* upon much that it does not comprehend."[16] The "kingdom of God" economy is useful for our time, according to Berry, because it rests on three principles. It includes everything, everything is joined to it and to everything else, and in it humans are not in control since they can never know everything. Beginning to think about economics from those three principles could get us well on the way to seeing the ultimate connections between economy and ecology in our everyday lives.

That fundamental shift in the way we view economics could lead us toward rethinking our relationship to "things" and "ownership." Ever since the dawn of the industrial age, we have centered our lives around things, believing that unlimited progress would fulfill our every wish and, therefore, our *beings*. But as Erich Fromm reminds us, that notion is contrary to everything we know about ourselves, from ancient wisdom to modern psychology.

In some of his recent speeches, Wes Jackson has proposed the idea that we take a closer look at Francis of Assisi's relationship to nature. He suggests that trying to understand Francis's bond with nature, a bond that enabled him to obtain what he needed from nature without dominating and destroying it, may give us some clues for discovering sound ecological and economical ways to live on our planet.

Interestingly enough, Wes suggests that perhaps the only thing that is fundamentally different between us and Francis is his vow of poverty. Accepting a vow of poverty does not necessarily mean accepting deprivation. It does mean, however, accepting "well-being," rather than "having," as the foundation for human fulfillment. Such a shift in consciousness could be exactly what is needed to restore the balance between economy and ecology.

NOTES

1. World Watch Institute, "The Fate of Children," *Natural History Magazine* (April 1986).

2. Aldo Leopold, *A Sand County Almanac* (New York: Oxford University Press, 1949), p. viii. (Italics mine)

3. Erich Fromm, *To Have or To Be?* (New York: Harper & Row, 1976).

4. Bernard Loomer, "A Process-Relational Conception of Creation," in *Cry of the Environment,* ed. P. N. Joranson and K. Butigan (Santa Fe, N.M.: Bear, 1984), p. 325.

5. Cotton Mather, *Magnalia Christi Americana*, 2 vols. (Hartford, Conn.: Siles Andres and Sons, 1855), Bk. I, pt. I, ch. iv, sec. 2.

6. William Cronin, *Changes in the Land* (New York: Hill and Wang, 1983).

7. John Winthrop, "A Modell of Christian Charity," in *The Puritans*, ed. P. Miller and T. Johnson, 2 vols., rev. (New York: Harper & Row, 1963), I, 197–199.

8. W. C. Lowdermilk, *Conquest of the Land through 7,000 Years* (Washington, D.C.: U.S. Government Printing Office, USDA, SCS, Agriculture Information Bulletin No. 99).

9. *New York Times,* 6 March 1986, citing U.S. Department of Agriculture study.

10. Center for Rural Affairs, "It's Not All Sunshine and Fresh Air" (Walthill, Nebr., 1984). I am indebted to this excellent bulletin for some of the references to hidden costs in conventional agricultural production.

11. See, for example, Board on Agriculture, *Alternative Agriculture* (Washington, D.C.: National Academy Press, 1989).

12. *T* level refers to a rate of soil loss that does not exceed the capacity of the soil to restore itself.

13. Studs Terkel, *The Great Divide* (New York: Pantheon Books, 1988), p. 19.

14. Frances Moore Lappé and Joseph Collins, *World Hunger: Twelve Myths* (New York: Grove Press, 1986).

15. Rudolf Steiner, *World Economy*, trans. A. O. Barfield and T. Gordon-Jones, 3d rev. ed. (London: Rudolf Steiner Press, 1972), p. 21.

16. Wendell Berry, *Home Economics* (San Francisco: North Point Press, 1987), p. 54f. (Italics his).

4

God's Family and Flocks: Remarks on Ownership in the Fourth Gospel

ANN MARIE B. BAHR

Covenantal responsibility is not the only way the Bible challenges the norms of ownership that characterize the practices of advanced industrial societies. Dr. Bahr looks to the Fourth Gospel, John, for a challenge to the privatization of ownership characteristic of contemporary culture that undermines environmental responsibility. John's model of ownership is a position of caring for what is owned and one of responsibility to the wider community. "Caring for" involves exercising ownership rights, but with the good of the community in mind and being ultimately responsible to God for the care of what is owned.

For the purposes of this essay, I define ownership as being in the position of having made something or someone one's own. Because of the difference in nuance between the adjective and the verb, I expressly do not wish to begin with the assumption that ownership means being in the position of owning something or someone. According to *Webster*, the adjective refers to the taking of a special interest in something, and it can be used to indicate a close relationship.[1] The verb, on the other hand, carries as one of its primary meanings "to have power over, control."[2]

The Fourth Gospel presents us with a concept of ownership that does not include the elements of power or control. There are persons in the Fourth Gospel whom Jesus calls "his own" (e.g., John 13:1). In John 10, they are metaphorically likened to sheep owned by a shepherd. Although the Fourth Gospel does speak, at least in this metaphorical sense, of people being owned, it means by that only the "my own" of a close relationship.

If ownership meant the same thing in the Fourth Gospel as it does in contemporary usage, it would be highly inappropriate to speak, even metaphorically, of owning persons. Therefore, if the difference between the biblical and contemporary usage of "to own" is not kept in mind, the Fourth Gospel will appear to condone oppressive elements in our relationship to other persons and things, whereas in reality it is radically opposed to ownership as a relationship of domination and oppression.

A COMPARISON OF OWNERSHIP IN CONTEMPORARY CULTURE AND IN THE BIBLE

"And what good does it do you to own the stars?"

"It does me the good of making me rich."

"And what good does it do you to be rich?"

"It makes it possible for me to buy more stars, if any are discovered. . . ."

"I myself own a flower," he [the little prince] continued his conversation with the businessman, "which I water every day. I own three volcanoes, which I clean out every week (for I also clean out the one that is extinct; one never knows). It is of some use to my volcanoes, and it is of some use to my flower, that I own them. But you are of no use to the stars. . . ."[3]

The notion of ownership in contemporary culture stresses the rights of the owner. It does not stress the owner's responsibility to care for that which is owned. People own things because they expect to benefit from having them. There is no equal and corresponding expectation that what is owned will benefit from the arrangement. In contemporary usage, one is properly referred to as an owner whether one depletes the resources one owns or maintains their productivity and integrity. This is because ownership is a matter of legal rights in contemporary culture.[4] It is not a matter of assuming responsibility for the good or the life of that which is owned.

In contrast, if the followers of Jesus are God's sheep (or Jesus' sheep), they are so to their own benefit, not to the benefit of God or Jesus. Unlike contemporary usage, the Fourth Gospel's notion of ownership stresses the care of that which is owned, and the owner's responsibility for its life: I came that they may have life, and have it abundantly (John 10:10).

We notice also that ownership is not a reciprocal or mutual relationship in contemporary culture. I may own my land or my dog, but neither one owns me. Ownership need not be perceived as a unilateral relationship, however. If Yahweh calls Israel "*my* people," the people of Israel likewise call Yahweh "the Lord *our* God." If Jesus in the Fourth Gospel calls his followers "*my* sheep," his followers likewise have the right to address him as "*my* Lord and *my* God."

It may be protested that an equal right to use of the possessive pronoun does not necessarily indicate any equality in the relationship. Especially in the patriarchal society of biblical times, it might be thought that the parent-child relationship would strip a person of her or his autonomy, not bequeath equality.

It would be impossible to argue that the Fourth Gospel is not in some sense a patriarchal text. Its very language, replete with the terms "father" and "son," marks it as such. Nonetheless, we should not assume that all the elements of patriarchy are represented in this document simply because some are. More specifically, we should not assume that the designation of the father as the head of the household precludes any equality with him on the part of the other members of the household. Nor should we assume that it precludes their acting as autonomous agents. We will return later to the patriarchal nature of the Fourth Gospel and the problems it raises for our use of its concept of ownership. For now, however, I would like to make a few comments regarding equality and autonomy.

Although *we* might assume that the parent-child relationship does not allow for any equality between the two parties involved, this is most assuredly not the assumption of the Fourth Gospel. In John 5:18, "the Jews," who presumably understand the linguistic usage of their own culture as well as we might hope to, seem to feel that Jesus has made himself equal to God by calling God his own father. Although Jesus answers in terms that indicate that he does nothing on his own accord but rather does his father's will, the Christian tradition has not opted to strip Jesus of his equality to God for that reason.

In a later passage in the same gospel, when the question of Jesus' equality with God arises once more, his reply extends equality to all who have received the word of God. Jesus answered them, "Is it not written in your law, 'I said, you are gods'? . . . he called them gods to whom the word of god came . . ." (John 10:34–35).[5]

Given the usage of the Hebrew Bible, those who have received the word of God have the right to be called children of God. They have been adopted into God's family and received God's name. I believe that the meaning of this verse is obscured when the capitalization is inserted, as it is in modern English translations. For the capitalization provides a visual barrier to the drawing of the metaphorical linkages between the human family and God's family that I believe the evangelist fully intended to be drawn. He wishes to make the point that the children taken into God's family inherit what God owns and God's authority regarding it, just as children adopted by human parents and given their name become their heirs. To be a child of God is thus to be graciously raised up to God's level. It is not to be labeled "inferior."

Nor should we assume that since the followers of Jesus are metaphorically referred to as sheep or children it necessarily indicates a lack of autonomy on their part. I will argue in a later section of this essay that the Jesus of the Fourth Gospel addresses all human beings, whether male or female, as autonomous decision-making agents. Unaccustomed as we may be to such a view of ownership, the evidence of the Fourth Gospel is that ownership is a mutual relationship in which the two parties involved are equal and autonomous.

A third difference between the biblical and contemporary ideas of ownership lies in their degree of concern for the interests of the wider community. Owners in contemporary society own things because they expect they will benefit. For the most part, they do not own things in the hope of benefiting their community. They may *assume* that what benefits the individual will also benefit the community. But such an assumption does not encourage owners to adopt responsible policies; on the contrary, it assumes that there is no need for conscious choices in this regard.

As we shall see, the notion of ownership in the Fourth Gospel resides in the context of a different priority of interests. In this gospel, ownership is familial, not individual. And, since God's family is certainly not a nuclear family but rather a *very extended* family, we may say that ownership resides in the community (of believers) or perhaps even in the world as a whole (since all are at least created to be children of God, no matter what their later choices in that regard might lead to).

Even in those instances when contemporary culture does take account of the interests of the wider community, it may calculate those interests in market value to the detriment of other kinds of value. I am the owner of forty acres of land. Its value to me has nothing to do with the money I paid for it. "Valuing" it is something I do as I become creatively and personally involved in its life. It is of value to me because of the time I have spent there, nurturing it. To reduce the assessment of either individual or community interests to market value is to impoverish the rich multiplicity of meanings of the term "value" and potentially to cheat ourselves of the enjoyment of many values.

Society is linguistically structured. The ways in which the terms "my," "my own," and "our" are used in contemporary culture are part of the social setting in which and through which issues of environmental ethics are debated. This contemporary understanding of ownership is not environmentally neutral, however. It is in conceptual complicity with our failure to act as ecologically responsible persons. Our very understanding of what it means to say that something is "mine," or "my own," encourages self-interest. It does not encourage concern for what is owned. It divides the world into "owners" and "owned," rather than seeing ownership as a mutual relationship. It does little to encourage the owner to look toward the good of the entire community. In short, "owning" in contemporary culture is a matter of power and control rather than of love, service, and responsibility. For these reasons alone, it is appropriate to consider another paradigm of ownership that could serve to broaden the conceptual base supporting discussions of environmental ethics.

"BELONGING" IN THE FOURTH GOSPEL

The Gospel of John is one of the richest of the New Testament writings with respect to its language concerning ownership.[6] In pursuing this richness, however, we immediately face a semantic difficulty. The Fourth Gospel does not distinguish between two senses of "belonging": "belonging" to a corporate body (a household or a family) and "belonging" to a person as a result of legal entitlement. Ownership is never distinct from the idea of being part of a household or a family. This is true even in cases where the modern person would see only legal entitlement, as in the ownership of sheep or land.

We retain the double meaning of "belonging" in our language, though it has become for us an ambiguity. When I speak of an animal, such as a dog, "belonging" to a certain family, I may mean either that the family has legal title to the dog or that the dog has become so important to the family that it is as if the dog were one of the members of the family. For the householder of antiquity, anything that the family owned "belonged" to it in the second sense as well as the first. The recovery of the link between the two senses of "belonging" (legal and familial) would be of ecological value. Although on a larger scale than that of the ancient household, it is once again important to view persons, animals, vegetation, and land as a single life-unit that belongs together and makes up a kind of extended "family."

GOD'S HOUSEHOLD

The central relationship in the Fourth Gospel is the one between Jesus and God, wherein Jesus is described as "son" and God as "father."[7] We misunderstand this gospel entirely if we think that the relationship between God and God's "son" Jesus refers solely to the relationship between God and a single historical individual known as Jesus of Nazareth. For the gospel invites everyone to stand within the parent-child relationship that Jesus enjoys with his father. This is an invitation to become a member of God's household: "In my father's house are many rooms; if it were not so, would I have told you that I go to prepare a place for you?" (John 14:2).

The fourth evangelist did not invent the concept of God's household. It was already a significant part of Israelite self-understanding. When the God of the Hebrew Bible offered to dwell with Israel, and to let Israel be known by his name, God was offering to make Israel part of his own family. In effect, God was telling Israel that Israel could become a "god" because it was now a part of God's family, just as we might say that a child becomes a "Danielson," for example, because she was adopted by the Danielsons and became a member of their family. Israel had been chosen as God's heir.

This image of God as householder, with Israel as the child, expressed a wonderful sense of intimacy between Israel and its God. It was not one of the images used to indicate God's sovereign majesty. Rather, it expressed a closeness to the people. It told not of power but of love. Similarly, when the fourth evangelist describes Jesus as God's son, he means to emphasize not God's power over Jesus, but God's love for Jesus and closeness to him. The same is to be said about all of those who come to be children of God.

In a traditional society, the son inherits the father's work. Since Jesus' father is the creator God, Jesus inherits the work of creation from his father. It is clear from John 5 that this creative activity continues in the narrative present. Jesus' answer to those who wish to refuse him the right to heal on the Sabbath is "My father is working still, and I am working." (John 5:17). Needless to say, "work" in this context is not laboring in order to receive a paycheck. It is laboring to bring to life the work of creation itself.

It is the case, then, that Jesus, like his father, owns because he creates. Not only Jesus of Nazareth, however, but also all who believe in him are called to inherit their father's work of creation, for they also are children of God. If God owns both persons and land because God created them, human householders and parents, made in God's image, also own both children and land because they are co-creators, life-givers with God. What I want to stress here is that one criterion of ownership that we can take from the Fourth Gospel is that ownership must include treating what is owned in a way that is creative, not in the sense of "novel" but in the sense of "life-giving." According to the Fourth Gospel, one owns because one creates—that is, one is expected to increase the life of that which one owns.

Does this mean that parents are free to do whatever they like with their children, because they "own" them? No! To draw that conclusion would be to take the contemporary notion of ownership and apply it to children. It is to fail to understand the concept of ownership found in the Fourth Gospel. Recall what has just been said. If the parents decrease rather than enhance the life of the child, there is, at least by the standards of the Fourth Gospel, no ownership.

This does not mean that parents do not have the right to correct their children. It does mean that whenever such correction is necessary it must be carried out in love, with an intention to guide toward a greater good for the child, rather than with the intention (conscious or unconscious) to hurt or to retaliate.

Of course, there are those who will abuse their children (or their partners), physically or psychologically, and offer the hypocritical excuse that they are doing this for the good of the child (or partner). The person suffering the abuse may not even be aware that this is *not* "for their own good." By what means are we to protect people from such abuse? The gospel presumes free choice on the part of those who come to be owned by Jesus. Actual children have little free choice, however, and many spouses have not much more. Furthermore, control, deceit, and manipulation can masquerade as love. The gospel knows this. It speaks of the false shepherds who are in reality thieves who come to steal and kill and destroy (John 10:10). They have no real intention of leading their flocks to more abundant life.

The question of how to discern true from false religious authority is a central issue here. The Fourth Gospel was written to strengthen and encourage those who found it necessary to leave their families and their religious origins once they came to understand two things: first, that the authority given to people by God was the authority to carry out God's will, and, second, that God's will was in reality nothing but the love displayed in Jesus. God's ownership of God's people, as displayed in the life and death of Jesus, is a servant ownership.

The story narrated by the fourth evangelist is one of an authority based on love. It invites us to look, learn, and come to know what real love is. It is aware that many will not find such love in their families. It knows that the world is full of those who selfishly hurt and destroy the ones that they claim to love, and of those who claim to be leading people to God while in reality leading them to hell because they have no love for them. But it also knows that the love of God is in the world in Jesus and in his followers. It is by coming to know such love that people can be freed of those who abuse them "for their own good." Such is the mission of evangelism; given the number of dysfunctional families in contemporary society, the fields are ripe for the harvest. Far from encouraging us to submit to abusive authorities, the Fourth Gospel tells us of the struggle between false and true religious authorities, and it encourages us to confront and when necessary leave the false and follow the true. For the followers of Jesus in the community of the beloved disciple, this often meant leaving their families. The Fourth Gospel does not discourage leaving one's family or spouse when the genuine servant love of God as shown by Jesus is not only not found there, but actively driven out.

Before concluding our discussion of God's household, I would like to show that this image points to the family-oriented nature of ownership in the Fourth Gospel. Those who have been given to Jesus by God do not cease to belong to God simply because they belong to Jesus. The Fourth Gospel reflects a society in which ownership is centered in the family, not in the individual. There is inheritance, but there is no transfer of ownership from the father to Jesus: "All mine are thine, and thine are mine . . ." (John 17:10).

The flock continues to belong to the father, even though it belongs as fully to Jesus. Likewise, when Jesus commissions Peter to watch over his flock, the sheep continue to be designated as Jesus' sheep (John 21:15–17).

The interests involved in familial ownership extend through time as well as space. The interests of the next generation must be cared for. The person currently in authority (the current "owner") identifies with the interests of the entire family, not simply with his or her own individual self-interest. And, ultimately, every owner remains responsible to God, the head of the family. Human owners own only as God's children and heirs.

JESUS AS OWNER: THE SHEPHERD AND THE SHEEP

In John 10, Jesus is portrayed as the Good Shepherd. He owns a flock of sheep who know his voice and follow it. Jesus' sheep follow his voice, not because he coerces or threatens them but because he dwells with them and tends them. Because of his constant association with them, the sheep have discovered that they have no reason to fear Jesus. They have discovered him to be different from other authority figures. The sheep have come to trust him, and to trust his care for them.

Jesus does not claim the right to do with his "own" as he wills. Indeed, Jesus never does his own will; he always does the will of his father. There is no place in the Fourth Gospel's concept of ownership for domination and control, or for the imposition of one's own will upon what one owns.

The Good Shepherd discourse turns upon the contrast between the shepherd who owns the sheep and several other categories of persons who might interact with the sheep. These other persons are thieves and robbers, strangers, and hirelings.

The owner is the person who is able to enter by the door because he is recognized. The gatekeeper knows him and opens the door for him. The sheep recognize him because they know his voice. He knows every one of his sheep by name. The sheep follow him, not because he has power over them, but because they know him and trust him. This alone tells us much about the degree of familiarity that exists in the Fourth Gospel's concept of ownership.

The thief or the robber is different from the owner in that he comes to steal, kill, and destroy, rather than to give life. He who steals life from the land kills and destroys it and is not an owner no matter what the status of his legal claim to the land. According to this gospel, only those who nurture the life of what they own are genuine owners.

The stranger is different from the owner in that the sheep do not know him. Again, legal title alone does not confer ownership. The Fourth Gospel's concept of ownership always includes personal and intimate knowledge of that which is owned.

The hireling is different from the owner in that he flees when he sees the wolf coming.

> He who is a hireling and not a shepherd, whose own the sheep are not, sees the wolf coming and leaves the sheep and flees; and the wolf snatches them and scatters them. He flees because he is a hireling and cares nothing for the sheep. I am the good shepherd; I know my

own and my own know me, as the father knows me and I know the father; and I lay down my life for the sheep (John 10:12–15).

It is not clear that this passage makes dying for the sheep a criterion of ownership. It may be a matter of recognition. One can recognize an owner by his or her care for what is owned. If that care extends to a willingness to lay down one's life, we can be very sure that this person is the real owner, not someone hired to care for the sheep.

It is important not to think that the owner can "buy" the sheep's loyalty by protestations of willingness to die for them. The gospel itself recognizes that most such ardent claims are immature and therefore inaccurate:

Peter said to him, "Lord, why cannot I follow you now? I will lay down my life for you." Jesus answered, "Will you lay down your life for me? Truly, truly, I say to you, the cock will not crow, till you have denied me three times" (John 13:37–38).

Further, it is not a self-sacrificing demeanor that validates one's ownership. Rather, the owner is one who has enough personal investment in and identification with what is owned to be able to sacrifice at the appropriate time. The gospel does not attempt to make the self-denial involved in sacrifice into a way of life. It is not an attitude but an action. A sacrifice is a particular act that reveals the heart.

Sacrifice has become such a confused concept in contemporary culture that two further remarks need to be made in this regard. First, the idea that women are to be singled out as the practitioners of sacrifice has no biblical warrant. The Fourth Gospel does not indicate that sacrifice is a feminine rather than a masculine virtue. It is the owner, Jesus, who provides the example of sacrifice that is to be emulated. In this gospel, sacrifice is clearly *not* described as the sacrifice of the woman for the good of the whole family. It is rather described as the sacrifice of the owner, the head, for the good of one or more of those for whom he has assumed responsibility.

Second, these remarks on sacrifice are in no way intended to endorse addictive consumerism. By addictive consumerism I mean the willingness to assume risks to one's own health or even life for the purpose of coming to own more and more. The addictive consumer may be willing to put his or her own life in danger for the sake of owning things, but that is a far different attitude than the one recommended by the Fourth Gospel. To put one's life in danger for the sake of *that which* one owns is not at all the same thing as putting one's life in danger for the sake of the owning itself. The first impulse can arise only in a truly loving and generous heart, while the second can arise only in a heart set on its own self-interest.

THE PROBLEM OF THE PATRIARCHAL NATURE
OF THE FOURTH GOSPEL

In Israelite culture, the father was the head of the household. He owned
the women and children, as well as the land, and decided what was best
for the household. I would not want to encourage a return to such a social
arrangement. Certainly women, and to a great extent even children, have
autonomous decision-making powers. No one person can or need decide
what is best for the entire household. But the recognition that no one
individual ought to make decisions for another autonomous individual need
not result in a retreat from caring to a position of atomistic individualism.
We need not end up asserting that every individual is in a position to care
only for herself or himself, and that therefore each is to be concerned only
with his or her own benefit.

The notion of ownership in the Fourth Gospel describes ownership as
a position of caring for what is owned and a position of responsibility to
the wider community, rather than as a position from which one seeks to
maximize one's individual interests. Although this does entail the necessity
of making decisions for the land and the animals and sometimes for the
children, it should not entail the making of decisions for other autonomous
individuals. "Caring for" can also mean exercising ownership rights with
the good of the other(s) in mind, and this is the meaning that I believe
supplies a corrective to the emphasis on owner rights and benefits in the
notion of ownership in contemporary culture. I do not believe "caring for"
need hold the additional meaning of "taking care of," and it certainly need
not include the making of decisions for other autonomous individuals.
Again, Jesus' interaction with his own is the model of ownership offered
by the Fourth Gospel. Although Jesus cares for his followers, he does not
take care of them in any way that might inhibit their own growth toward
maturity and autonomy. While he certainly calls people to the need for a
decision, he makes the decisions for no one else. Jesus treats all those who
hear him, including those who choose to follow him, as autonomous agents.
He forces no one to do either his own will or his father's will.

So what can we say about the patriarchal nature of the Fourth Gospel?
We can say, first, that the fourth evangelist clearly portrays all human
beings, whether male or female, as having a choice of whom they will allow
to call them their "own." It is clear that the sheep choose which shepherd
to follow, and that they even choose which shepherd to crucify (John 18:39–
40). Being "owned" is far from being in a position of powerlessness in this
gospel.

The Fourth Gospel portrays a world replete with would-be authorities,
but which authority people choose to obey is up to them. No one is forced
to be the servant of God or of Jesus. Of course people can be enslaved by
those who wish to enslave them, but the work of Jesus and of his father is

to free those who are so bound. The Fourth Gospel portrays the father of Jesus as a God of freedom.

The entire Bible is based on a radical sense of the freedom necessary to a true love relationship between God and people. The cultural patriarchy, which is admittedly not removed from the Fourth Gospel, is nonetheless deeply colored by this biblical commitment to freedom. In the Fourth Gospel the bride (Israel? the world?) is left free to choose whether or not to follow Jesus. There is no coerciveness in Jesus' authority as husband or in God's authority as father of all.

Second, the fact that the cultural system was patriarchal at the time of the writing of the Fourth Gospel does not mean that the Fourth Gospel must subscribe to all that the system of patriarchy implied. In every culture there is a counterculture. Although of necessity part of the culture it opposes, a counterculture is capable of undermining key aspects of that culture from within. The Fourth Gospel is a countercultural patriarchal document. It retains the idea that the authority figures are male. But it makes the authority figures servants rather than dominators. The word of command that is passed on through the chain of authority stemming back to Jesus himself is a word of love, not of control.

There is, of course, no reason why Christians of today should emulate the patriarchal aspects of the society that produced the Fourth Gospel. There is every reason, however, why they should take to heart the message of the Fourth Gospel regarding ownership. This message is that one has a right to call one's own only that which one is willing to love, serve, and care for so that it may have more abundant life. The ecological implications of such a commitment should be clear.

We certainly do not want to return to any talk of owning people. We should, however, want to show to what we *do* own the love and care called for by the Fourth Gospel's concept of ownership. And we do want to remember that our acts of ownership are part of the ongoing life of a wider "family."

CONCLUDING REMARKS

Many of the common contemporary conceptions regarding ownership are ecologically unsound. Anything that an individual purchases legally belongs to that individual, and becomes, in the fullest sense of the term, *private* property. The purchaser has power and control over the use of the resources purchased and can impose his or her will on the use of those resources. The primary motivations for ownership are the self-enrichment and the benefits that may be derived by the owner. Except in the hope of satisfying these expectations, there is no particular responsibility to care for what is owned.

The key features of the Fourth Gospel's concept of ownership derive from its sense of God's family and household. Ownership is a matter of

belonging to God's household. Human owners are stewards who are ultimately responsible to God for the care of what they own. Ownership is
family- or community-oriented, not just self-oriented. Ownership involves
caring about what is owned, and it may sometimes involve sacrifice on the
part of the owner. Insofar as the relationship between God and Jesus, or
between Jesus and his disciples, is a relation of ownership, this gospel
portrays ownership as a mutual and intimate relationship of love, caring
and dwelling with. It is clearly *not* portrayed as a relationship in which one
party exercises power and control over the other. Ownership on the Fourth
Gospel's terms is a creative activity, life giving rather than destructive.

I would hope that the practical consequences of this essay would include
both attitude changes and changes in public policy. The Fourth Gospel's
concept of ownership ought to encourage all of us who are owners to focus
on more than our own self-interest. The gospel encourages us to see ownership as a relationship between ourselves on the one hand and the earth
and its life-forms on the other hand. This relationship should involve caring
for and dwelling with. It also encourages us to see ownership as ultimately
belonging to God. We are stewards entrusted with the care of the resources
that will provide for God's household not only while we own them but also
in the future.

Public-policy questions raised by this essay include the following. Can
owners be made responsible for the enhancement of the life of the
resources that they own, or at least for not depleting them? Can owners
be expected to make sacrifices for the welfare of succeeding generations as
they use the resources that they own? Can owners be encouraged to live
in the midst of what they own, so that ownership becomes a matter of
personal care as well as a matter of legal and financial responsibility?

NOTES

1. *Webster's Third New International Dictionary* (1981), s.v. "own," adjective.
2. *Webster's Ninth New Collegiate Dictionary* (1983), s.v. "own," verb.
3. Antoine de Saint-Exupéry, *The Little Prince*, trans. Katherine Woods (New
York: Harcourt, Brace & World, 1943), pp. 46–47.
4. I contend that contemporary culture worries primarily about the rights of
owners, not about the owner's responsibility toward what is owned. There *is*, however, a certain sort of legal responsibility that goes along with contemporary ownership. I am held legally responsible if anything that I own is injurious to the health
or the property of anyone else. Note, however, that this sort of legal responsibility
is not a responsibility toward what is owned. It is a responsibility to someone
standing outside the relation of ownership.

Further, the sense of responsibility captured by this notion of legal responsibility
for what is owned (but not *toward* what is owned) has little to do, despite superficial
appearances, with the Fourth Gospel's sense of ownership as a community affair.
This is for several reasons. First, the modern sense of legal responsibility presumes
that I control what I own. Since the Fourth Gospel's concept of ownership does

not include the element of control, its sense of the relation between owner and community does not rest upon any presumption of control. Second, the sense of "belonging" conveyed by our understanding of legal responsibility for what is owned remains that of "belonging to an individual," or, even more explicitly, "being legally owned by private citizens." The sense of "belonging" conveyed by the Fourth Gospel's notion of ownership is that of "belonging to a household."

In a nutshell, the modern sense of legal responsibility *toward* the community *for* what one owns is rooted in an individualistic and legalistic concept of ownership. The Fourth Gospel holds the owner responsible toward what is owned. It has little to say about the individual owner's responsibility toward the community because it does not think about ownership in individual terms. The Fourth Gospel's sense of ownership is neither individualistic nor legalistic, but familial.

5. I have followed the Revised Standard Version here, except that I have deleted the capitalization of "father," "son" and "god." It is impossible to determine capitalization from the earliest Greek manuscripts, since they are written entirely in capital letters.

6. A simple word study establishes the significance of this concept in the Fourth Gospel. The Greek possessive adjectives and pronouns with which we are concerned are *idios*, *mou*, and *emos*.

Idios (one's own) occurs fifteen times in the Fourth Gospel, more often than in any other gospel. (Matthew has ten occurrences of *idios*, Mark eight, and Luke six.) The maximum number of times *idios* occurs in any New Testament writing is fifteen times. In addition to the Fourth Gospel, only Acts and 1 Corinthians contain fifteen occurrences. If we consider only those occurrences in which *idios* means specifically "one's own" (rather than "privately," "apart," etc.), the Gospel of John clearly contains more such occurrences than any other New Testament writing. Thirteen such occurrences are found in the Gospel of John, nine in 1 Corinthians, seven in Acts, and three or less in all the other New Testament writings.

The Fourth Gospel also contains more occurrences of the possessive pronoun *mou* ("my," "mine," "my own") than any other New Testament writing. There are ninety-eight such occurrences in the Gospel of John. The only other New Testament writings that contain close to that number of occurrences of *mou* are Luke with eighty-two and Matthew with eighty-one. All the other books of the New Testament contain fewer than forty occurrences of *mou*.

There are forty-one occurrences of *emos* ("my," "mine," "my own") in the Gospel of John, more by far than in any other New Testament writing. Next in order of frequency of occurrence is 1 Corinthians, with eight such occurrences.

If we turn from the adjective/pronoun form to the noun form, the situation becomes a bit more complex. The Greek term for "owner" is *"kurios,"* but this is also the Greek term for "lord," "master," and "sir." The term *"kurios"* is found more often in Luke, Matthew, Acts, Romans, and 1 Corinthians than in the Gospel of John. I have made no attempt to distinguish references to ownership of property from more general uses of the noun *"kurios."*

The above comparisons are derived from information contained in J. B. Smith's *Greek-English Concordance to the New Testament* (Scottdale, Pa.: Mennonite Publishing House, 1955), p. 178 #2398 (*idios*), p. 236 #3350 (*mou*), p. 122 #1699 (*emos*), and p. 210 #2962 (*kurios*).

7. Capitalization of "son" and "father" is a modern convention. Neither is capitalized in Nestle's Greek text of the New Testament. Although it is contrary to standard confessional usage, I have chosen to use lower-case letters throughout. My purpose is to emphasize our participation in Jesus' relation to God.

PART II

RE-VISIONING RELATIONSHIP WITH THE REST OF NATURE

5

Genesis and John Muir

J. BAIRD CALLICOTT

Dr. Callicott believes that the biblical creation stories are deeply embedded in all the cultures for which they are scripture. While some read the creation accounts to say that human beings are created to subdue the rest of creation, or to exercise benign dominion, there is also a third powerful reading: Yahweh's concern is for the whole of nature and for each of its parts equally, not for people alone or even for people especially. John Muir, familiar with the Bible from childhood, conceived of the rightful role of humankind not as dominator or steward, but as citizen of the world garden. The human task, individually and collectively, is to transcend our self-centeredness, or anthropocentrism, and learn how to live as a part of, not set apart from, the rest of nature.

THE INFLUENCE OF LYNN WHITE, JR., ON ENVIRONMENTAL ETHICS

In "The Historical Roots of Our Ecologic Crisis," published in *Science* in 1967, Lynn White, Jr., laid the blame for the "environmental crisis" — which had dawned on public awareness earlier in the same decade — at the door of Judaism and Christianity.[1] White is a distinguished, authoritative professor of church history and his infamous diatribe first appeared in the organ of the American Association for the Advancement of Science, the most prestigious scientific journal published in the United States. Hence "The Historical Roots of Our Ecologic Crisis" was widely read and broadly influential. It was subsequently reprinted in practically every one of the umpteen thousand anthologies on the environmental crisis published in the decade following its appearance in *Science*, thus multiplying its already large audience and magnifying its already considerable influence.

White focused on the environmental attitudes and values set out in

Genesis and how they might have fostered ill-treatment of nature in Chris-
tendom through the ages. He argued, in effect, that since it is written in
Genesis that human beings alone among creatures were created in the
image of God and given dominion over nature and charged to subdue it,
that Jews and Christians, taking this message to heart, attempted to live by
its light. They regarded themselves as beings apart from the rest of nature,
licensed by God to rule over it and bend it to their purposes. After two
thousand years of putting this vision of the human-nature relationship into
practice with increasing success, the twentieth century's technological wonders *and* the twentieth century's environmental crisis are the end results.
Thus, White concluded, we must either jettison Judaism and Christianity
or substantially rethink the fundamental God-humanity-nature relationship
common to them if we hope to solve our environmental problems.

Of course Scripture has a wonderful quality that I would characterize
as creative ambiguity. Its words mean different things to different people
in different circumstances. White's interpretation of what Genesis has to
say about the proper relationsip between people and nature is just that —
an interpretation. It has subsequently come to be known as the "mastery"
or "despotic" interpretation. Other contemporary professors of religion and
theology, no less distinguished and authoritative than White, read the environmental message of Genesis in quite another way. In their view, the
unique status of human beings among all God's creatures confers unique
responsibilities, as well as unique rights, upon people. Among these responsibilities is to care for the rest of God's creation and to pass it on, in as
good or better condition than it was received, to future generations. In
giving us dominion over nature, God did not intend for us to enslave it or
to do with it what we pleased. Rather, God intended for us wisely to manage
or govern the creation, which remains God's, not ours. We are God's "stewards" of creation — the caretakers of nature — not nature's new owners.

The reaction to White's despotic interpretation was so swift and came
from so many quarters that no one person can be credited with formulating
this alternative reading, which is now known as the "stewardship" interpretation. Since the late sixties and early seventies there have emerged no
essentially new interpretations of the environmental attitudes and values
in Genesis. One could either adopt the mastery interpretation or the stewardship interpretation, both of which put human beings in a dominant
relationship to nature. Here I offer a third interpretation of the controversial texts that was suggested to me by some remarks of John Muir, the
great nineteenth-century advocate of wilderness preservation. In the citizenship reading of Genesis that I here propose, human beings are intended
to be neither its tyrannical masters nor benign, managerial stewards. God,
rather, created us to be "plain members and citizens" of nature — as the
celebrated twentieth-century American conservationist Aldo Leopold
argued that we are in fact and ought to be in our actions.

Whatever the merits of White's manifest argument (which I take up in due course), the subtext of his notorious article implicitly set the theoretical agenda for a future environmental philosophy.[2] Broad patterns of human behavior do not arise in an intellectual vacuum, he reminded us. To understand the environmental crisis adequately, we must first dig up and critically evaluate the ideas of nature, human nature, and the proper relationship between people and nature embedded in our inherited worldview. They provide a theater for our actions, an archetypal image or ideal of what it means to be human, and the associated values that we human beings aspire to realize.[3]

The dire exigencies of the environmental crisis mandate, moreover, radical change in broad patterns of human behavior in respect to nature. But again, the way we act is not unrelated to the way we think. What ideas of nature, human nature, and the relationship between the two might we postulate to facilitate a lasting rapprochement between people and the natural environment?

So stated, the dual *problematique* — critical and speculative — of environmental philosophy seems clear and direct. But such a simple statement of the enterprise skates blithely over not a few patches of thin ice. Though certainly ideas influence behavior, obviously they do not determine it. People do, after all, behave in ways that run contrary to their professed beliefs, ideals, and values. And, given the inertia of habit, can changed beliefs, ideals, and values actually bring about changed patterns of behavior?[4]

Supposing these queries may be favorably resolved, how does one create new ideas of nature and human nature, and envision a more harmonious relationship between the two? May we philosophers just dream them up out of the blue, or must we somehow distill an eco-philosophy and -ethic from the relevant sciences? Once formulated, how does a new paradigm trickle down into the popular worldview? Is there, indeed, a collective mind, a Zeitgeist?[5]

Not only is the forward-looking, speculative phase of environmental philosophy fraught with problems, so is the backward-looking, critical phase. Lynn White, Jr., seized upon the most visible, the most evident, of our intellectual legacies. The cognitive complex common to Judaism and Christianity is publicly confessed, literally, by a significant proportion of Western peoples in institutional settings — churches, synagogues, and temples. But a powerful secular cognitive complex is also ambient in our midst, the modern scientific worldview, as it might be called, that is rarely publicly confessed, but is routinely publicly *pro*fessed also in institutional settings — schools and universities. Moreover, technological manifestations of the scientific worldview are ubiquitous in our day-to-day lives.

White suggested that the latter is a product of the former, that science and technology grew, historically, out of Judaism and Christianity. I have no quarrel with his historical argument, as far as it goes, but what he fails to note is that the cognitive stock-in-trade of modern science, as opposed to the warrant for undertaking it, is of Greek philosophical, not biblical religious, provenance. Newton and other seventeenth-century scientists may have been inspired by belief in a transcendent creative deity and the *imago dei* to try to "think God's thoughts after Him," but the details of the Creator's supposed thoughts were inspired by Pythagoras and Democritus, not Moses and Paul.[6] In my opinion, the more culpable conceptual roots of our ecologic crisis are traceable to the intellectual legacy of Greek natural philosophy—which may have insidiously influenced the environmentally controversial parts of Genesis (as I explain below) no less than the New Testament, and which certainly inspired modern philosophy and science—rather than to the un-Hellenized intellectual tradition of the ancient Hebrews.[7]

In any case, Lynn White, Jr.'s, seminal article provoked a veritable tidal wave of apologetic literature defending the environmental attitudes and values of the Judaic and Christian worldview that he so casually and carelessly excoriated.[8] In a short essay such as mine, the principal purpose of which is to fill a small empty niche in this apologia, I cannot begin to survey the resulting flood. I hazard to say, however, that by far the main stream of this literature has followed the channel White first cut, and focused on the Big Picture found in the first two chapters of Genesis relating God, humanity, and nature. And by far the greatest volume of this literature develops, in one way or another, the stewardship alternative to the despotic interpretation that Lynn White, Jr., constructed of those crucial passages.[9]

THE STEWARDSHIP ENVIRONMENTAL ETHIC OF JUDAISM AND CHRISTIANITY—ITS VIRTUES EXTOLLED

I think that those who have argued that the stewardship interpretation is better supported by the text than White's despotic interpretation have entirely won their case. And as one who has struggled for two decades to formulate a persuasive and adequate secular environmental ethic, I would like further to say that the stewardship environmental ethic of Judaism and Christianity is especially elegant and powerful.

As Tom Regan forcefully put it, we environmental philosophers have sought to formulate "an ethic *of* the environment," not "an ethic for the *use* of the environment," a genuinely "environmental ethic," not "a 'management' ethic." And, as Regan also forcefully argued, the sine qua non of such an ethic is some plausible theory of intrinsic value or inherent worth for nonhuman natural entities and for nature as a whole—value or worth that they own in and of themselves as opposed to the value or worth that we human valuers ascribe to them.[10]

Little unambiguous progress has been made on that problem in the secular arena. On the other hand, the stewardship environmental ethic of Judaism and Christianity provides for the intrinsic value of nonhuman natural entities and nature as a whole simply and directly. Either by the act of creation or by a secondary fiat—surveying the result, as Genesis reports, and declaring it to be "good" — God conferred intrinsic value on the world and all its creatures. Technically put, in the stewardship environmental ethic God represents an objective axiological point of reference independent of human consciousness.

Those secular environmental ethicists who have managed theoretically to broker — how plausibly is another matter — intrinsic value or inherent worth for nonhuman natural entities and for nature as a whole then face the opposite problem of having too broadly distributed too much of a good thing. If every living being, as some have argued, is intrinsically valuable, then how can we human beings legitimately consume nonhuman natural entities in pursuit of our own interests?[11] After all, we must eat something. People cannot live like the lilies of the field, on sunshine, water, air, and soil. And people must have houses, and clothes, and books, and other things — all of which have to be appropriated either directly from other living things or mined at the expense of their resources and habitats.

These same secular environmental ethicists have met this problem with an elaborate set of hedges, designed consistently to rescue the practicability of their theories.[12] But it all seems forced and ad hoc. The stewardship environmental ethic of Judaism and Christianity, on the other hand, addresses this problem with the same simplicity and directness as it addresses the first. In the initial chapter of Genesis, it is clear that God is creating species, not specimens:

> And God made the beast of the earth *after his kind*, and cattle *after their kind*, and everything that creepeth upon the earth *after his kind*: and God saw that it was good.[13]

Moreover, the creation, as portrayed in the first chapter of Genesis, is replete and teeming with life:

> And God said, Let the waters bring forth abundantly the moving creature that hath life, and fowl that may fly above the earth in the open firmament of heaven.
> And God created great whales, and every moving creature that moveth, which the waters brought forth abundantly, after their kind, and every winged fowl after his kind: and God saw that it was good.
> And God blessed them, saying, Be fruitful and multiply, and fill the waters in the seas, and let fowl multiply in the earth.[14]

People have the right to harvest the surplus. Being created in the image of God burdens us human beings with certain responsibilities, to be sure. That is the essence of the stewardship reading. But let us not forget that the *imago dei* also confers on us certain complementary privileges. Hence we are entitled to the usufruct of our dominion so long as we rule it benignly and do not draw on its capital reserves. Humanity has an asymmetrical relationship with other creatures. They have no obligations in respect to us as we do in respect to them, but then we have rights in respect to them that they do not have in respect to us.

During its first two decades, environmental philosophy has been somewhat bellicose, each thinker proclaiming the superiority of her particular line of criticism and speculative reconstruction over all the others. I think such internecine conflict was a natural concomitant of the exuberance and sense of purpose characteristic of a new, morally charged field of study. More important, I think it was necessary to define clearly a variety of points of view and approach. But as we enter the 1990s and the field has matured and settled, such truculence, once both natural and necessary, now appears increasingly unbecoming and counterproductive. I think we need to rebuild burned bridges better to serve our common and very serious practical purpose.

The stewardship environmental ethic of Judaism and Christianity, accordingly, should get the intellectual respect it so very properly deserves. It has much greater potential than so far tapped to enlist the support and energies of a sizable segment of the public on behalf of environmental concerns. For the very large community of people who accept its premises — who believe in God, divine creation, a preeminent place and role for human beings in the world, and so on — it represents, in my opinion, the most coherent, powerful, and practicable environmental ethic available.

That having been said, I turn now to my main business here — which is to sketch a third, far more radical reading of the environmental implications of Genesis. This interpretation of the third kind was suggested to me by some remarks of John Muir.

MUIR'S CITIZENSHIP READING OF GENESIS

Muir's nascent environmental ethic rests, according to received intellectual history, on a refined Romantic aesthetic, and a mannerized Transcendental theology, ontology, and axiology borrowed from Henry David Thoreau and especially from Ralph Waldo Emerson via Jeanne Carr.[15] The bulk of Muir's writings supports such a framing of his ideas, but it leaves out of account a more thoroughly nonanthropocentric (or even antianthropocentric) dimension of his thought, which was rooted, surprisingly — and, some may think, paradoxically — in his youthful Christian tutelage.

As it seems to me, Transcendentalism is in the last analysis a kind of ethereal humanism. And Stephen Fox insists that after his exposure to Eastern-influenced Transcendentalism, Muir "stepped, unequivocally and permanently, outside the Christian tradition."[16] More recently, Donald Worster has gainsaid this overly neat reading of Muir's mind. "Some writers," whom Worster does not name, "have seen in this emergent Muir . . . a repudiation of . . . his Scotch Presbyterian background. [But] there was a harshly negative side to Muir's vision, a disgust for human pretensions and pride that ran very close to misanthropy."[17]

If so, Muir's misanthropy was always tempered by humor and good taste. But in any event, Muir's father, Daniel, was a religious psychopath, a Bible-reading, child-beating sadist, who forced Muir to commit to memory all of the New Testament and most of the Old.[18] Therefore, we may be confident that Muir knew his Scripture and was well acquainted with the biblical worldview. However thorough and complete was Muir's eventual conversion from fundamental Christianity to mystical Transcendentalism, Muir at age thirty—before he had ever set foot in the Range of Light—cast his first sustained thoughts about the human-nature relationship in the more conservative and pedestrian concepts of Judaism and Christianity. "The earliest product of his pen," in the words of his editor, William Frederic Badè, was a journal posthumously published under the title *A Thousand-Mile Walk to the Gulf*.[19] As Muir was addressing no one but himself, we have, in this work, a most intimate and candid record of his earlier ideas.

Muir himself gave no rubric to his eccentric interpretation of Genesis and his corollary radical environmental ethic forged from the ideas common to Judaism and Christianity. In deference to Aldo Leopold, whose secular "land ethic" would similarly exchange *Homo sapiens*'s "conqueror role" in respect to the "biotic community," not for the role of viceroy or steward, but for that of "plain member and citizen," I call it the "citizenship" interpretation.[20]

Aldo Leopold himself, incidentally, has very little to say directly on the subject of biblical attitudes and values respecting nature, but what he does say anticipates White's despotic reading: in the foreword to *A Sand County Almanac* Leopold comments that "conservation is getting nowhere because it is incompatible with our Abrahamic concept of land. We abuse land because we regard it as a commodity belonging to us." Such was the patriarch Abraham's view, he unmistakably implies. "When we see land as a community to which we belong," Leopold goes on to say, turning the despotic view inside out, "we may begin to use it with love and respect."[21] In "The Land Ethic," Leopold refers to Abraham again, this time in terms even more explicitly foreshadowing White's despotic reading: "Abraham knew what the land was for: it was to drip milk and honey into Abraham's mouth. At the present moment the assurance with which we regard this assumption is inverse to the degree of our education."[22] This remark follows right on the heels of Leopold's envisioning the ecology driven shift, just noted, from *Homo sapiens*'s traditional conqueror role in the land community to that of plain member and citizen.

Muir, similarly, was well aware that a despotic attitude toward the environment was generally assumed to be supported by Scripture. But rather than concur with such a reading, abandon the tradition, and look for other metaphysical grounds to support an environmental ethic, as Leopold does, Muir takes the argument straight to the despotarians' turf and argues for human citizenship in nature squarely on biblical principles.

He begins with an aggressive send-up of the conventional popular despotic reading:

> The world we are told was made especially for man — a presumption not supported by all the facts. A numerous class of men are painfully astonished whenever they find anything living or dead, in all God's universe, which they cannot render in some way what they call useful to themselves. They have precise and dogmatic insight into the intentions of the Creator. ... He is regarded as a civilized, law-abiding gentleman in favor of either a republican form of government or of a limited monarchy; believes in the literature and language of England; is a warm supporter of ... Sunday schools and missionary societies; and is as purely a manufactured article as any puppet of a half penny theater.
>
> With such views of the Creator it is, of course, not surprising that erroneous views should be entertained of the creation. To such properly trimmed people, the sheep, for example, is an easy problem — food and clothing "for us," ...[23]

Muir goes on to indulge his irritation at popular anthropocentrism by running through a random list of alleged God-given natural utilities. For example, "in the same pleasant plan, whales are store houses of oil for us, in lighting our dark ways until the discovery of the Pennsylvania oil wells." Most amusing, "hemp," he writes, "to say nothing of the cereals, is a case of evident destination for ships rigging, wrapping packages, and hanging the wicked." He finishes his miscellany of divine provisions for man with mention of cotton, iron, and lead, "all intended for us."[24]

Muir then returns to "the facts," and rhetorically poses the following countercases to these "closet researches of clergy":

> How about those man-eating animals — lions, tigers, alligators — which smack their lips over raw man? Or about those myriads of noxious insects that destroy labor and drink his blood? Doubtless man was intended for food and drink for all these?[25]

In this masterpiece of theological satire, Muir imagines the horrified reply of the unnamed "profound expositors of God's intentions": "Oh, no these are unresolvable difficulties connected with Eden's apple and the Devil."[26] After rehearsing a few more countercases — poisonous minerals, plants, and fishes — and pointing out that "the lord [with a small *l*] of creation," that is, humanity, is "subjected to the same laws of life as his subjects," Muir expounds an alternative environmental theology — but it is not by any stretch of the imagination a variation on the stewardship theme:

Now, it never seems to occur to these far-seeing teachers that Nature's object in making animals and plants might possibly be first of all the happiness of each one of them, not the creation of all for the happiness of one. Why should man value himself as more than a small part of the one great unit of creation? And what creature of all that the Lord has taken the pains to make is not essential to the completeness of that unit—the cosmos? The universe would be incomplete without man; but it would also be incomplete without the smallest transmicroscopic creature that dwells beyond our conceitful eyes and knowledge.[27]

Notice that Muir here seems intentionally to mix his worldviews. He writes "Nature's object" not "God's object," but in the same sentence he also writes "the creation of all" not "the evolution of all." In the next sentence he names "the Lord" as maker of "the cosmos," which then immediately becomes "the universe." He appears, in other words, to be deliberately rereading Genesis in the light of modern science. This impression is certainly confirmed as his exposition continues:

This star, our own good earth, made many a journey around the heavens ere man was made, and whole kingdoms of creatures enjoyed existence and returned to dust ere man appeared to claim them. After human beings have also played their part in Creation's plan, they too may disappear without any general burning or extraordinary commotion whatever.[28]

Muir wrote this, we should remind ourselves, less than a decade after the publication of *The Origin of Species*. Equally remarkable, twenty years before ecology had a name and separate identity as a science, he also wrote, "the antipathies [predator-prey relationships] existing in the Lord's great animal family must be wisely planned, like balanced repulsion and attraction in the mineral kingdom."[29] However, informed by a whole other way of comprehending the facts, Muir cements his citizenship reading of the place God intended for humankind in nature with a more specific and direct allusion to particulars of the creative events in Genesis:

From the dust of the earth, from the common elementary fund, the Creator has made *Homo sapiens*. From the same material he has made every other creature, however noxious and insignificant to us. They are earth-born companions and our fellow mortals. ... Doubtless these creatures are happy and fill the place assigned them by the great Creator of us all. ... They, also, are his children, for He hears their cries, cares for them tenderly, and provides their daily bread. ... How narrow we selfish, conceited creatures are in our sympathies! How blind to the rights of all the rest of creation! With what dismal irreverence do we speak of our fellow mortals! They ... are part of God's family, unfallen, undepraved and cared for with the same species of tenderness and love as is bestowed on angels in heaven and saints on earth.[30]

In comparison with Muir's citizenship rendering of the biblically ordained relationship of human beings to the rest of creation, the despotic and stewardship interpretations seem to differ only on the character of the archonship that God granted to humanity. Did God intend for us to be tyrant or regent? That we are lord and master of creation is never at issue. Muir, on the other hand, often writes "lord of creation" and "lord man" with evident contempt for the attitude to which such phrases allude. How, the question thus naturally arises, could Muir, a close, albeit forced, student of Scripture, have arrived at such a singular reading? I proceed to an examination of the text to see if it can support the spin Muir gives it.

THERE ARE ACTUALLY TWO GENESISES IN THE BIBLE

Lynn White, Jr., not only set the agenda for subsequent environmental philosophy, he also set, it seems, a low standard of biblical scholarship for critically glossing the environmental message of Genesis. Writes White,

By gradual stages a loving and all powerful God had created light and darkness, the heavenly bodies, the earth and all its plants, animals, birds, and fishes. Finally, God had created Adam and, as an afterthought, Eve to keep man from being lonely. Man named all the animals, thus establishing his dominance over them. God planned all of this explicitly for man's benefit and rule: no item in the physical creation had any purpose save to serve man's purposes. And although man's body is made of clay, he is not simply part of nature: He is made in God's image.[31]

I have by no means attempted to read systematically through all the apologetic literature amassed to counter this, the hard core of White's despotic reading, but most of what has casually scrolled across my screen conflates, with the same alacrity as White does here, the two very different genesises, Genesis-P and Genesis-J, that lie head to foot in the first pages of the Holy Bible.

White here begins with unmistakable allusions to P (the creation of light and darkness, the earth and all its furnishings, and so on), then jumps over to allude to J (the creation of Adam and Eve and the naming of the animals), then jumps back to another allusion to P (humanity's dominion), then jumps once again over to allude to J (Yahweh's forming Adam from dust), and comes to rest with a final allusion to P (the *imago dei*).

With only slightly less redactive agility, most of the stewardship counterinterpreters begin by reminding us that the *imago dei* is a double-edged sword, and point out that God finds the creation to be "good" right off the mint. Then they go on to insist that the initial ambiguity of the term "dominion," to define our God-given position in nature, is later unmistakably clarified by God's express declaration that Adam was put "into the garden of Eden to dress it and to keep it."[32] We are created to be God's gardener, so to speak. This seems to be as clear an expression of stewardship as one could hope to find, they say. (Indeed it is the horticultural equivalent — eminently appropriate to a garden setting — of the pastoral metaphor etymologically built into the very term "stewardship" itself, which comes from the Old English word *stïweard*, i.e., sty-ward.) As the coup de grace, they argue that it was far from God's intention, in commanding us to have dominion and to "subdue" — a less ambiguous, more ominously tendentious term — the earth (and all its creatures), that we pollute, degrade, and destroy it (and them).[33] Just as the vulgar despotarians mocked by Muir make convenient use of "Eden's apple" to explain the existence of natural evils, so the stewardarians point out that environmental pollution, degradation, and destruction came to pass only after the "fall."[34] Our environmental crisis is the eventual outcome of "original sin," the disobedience of Adam and Eve in tasting the fruit of the tree of the knowledge of good and evil, they argue.[35] Fallen and cursed, we have perverted this, God's "first," unnumbered commandment as we have all the ones in the Decalogue and elsewhere.[36]

But even upon the most casual reading, one may notice that there are two entirely distinct — and entirely inconsistent — accounts of creation back and forth between which indiscriminately jump Genesis's despotic and stewardship interpreters alike. Chapter 1, verse 1, of Genesis begins with the famous first words "In the beginning God created the heaven and the earth."[37] There follows an account of creation consuming six days in which the order of the creation proceeds rationally — from a modern point of view, at any rate — even in a sense scientifically. First, light was created.[38] (As in contemporary Big Bang cosmology, at first it was all flash and no substance.) Then the watery void was divided by a firmament.[39] On the third day, the dry land was gathered together and the plants created.[40] On the fourth, the sun, the moon, and the stars were hung in the firmament.[41] On the fifth and sixth, animals and people were created, respectively (in the case of the latter, please note, both male and female together).[42] Then there follow the passages — the *imago dei*, dominion, subduction, and the like — that have so exercised environmentalists.[43] Penultimately — and of special interest to animal liberationists, who have also latterly gotten into the Genesis-interpretation act — God prescribes a vegetarian diet for both people and beasts, suggesting a divine intent to ordain a world not only without environmental pollution, degradation, and destruction, but a world without any interspecies bloodletting at all, on however sustainable a basis.[44] Finally, on the seventh day God rested and commemorated the cessation of labor by establishing every subsequent seventh day as a sabbath.[45]

However, with chapter 2, verse 4, everything seems to begin again, thereupon to follow an entirely different scenario: "These are the generations of the heaven and the earth in the *day* [singular] that the Lord God made the earth and the heavens."[46] Now comes a story in which first a particular man, Adam, is created.[47] Then an arboreal garden—an agroforest permaculture, as it were—is planted for him to tend.[48] Next come the animals.[49] Then, lastly, a woman, Eve, is created—a mere "afterthought" as White provocatively (and irreverently) puts it.[50]

Nearly three centuries of scholarly reflection and research have revealed that Genesis, as we have received it, is woven from three narrative strands, conventionally labeled J, P, and E, for the Yahwist, Priestly, and Elohist sources, respectively. The Priestly narrative comes first in the order of presentation, but is last in order of composition—composed, most scholars agree, during the fifth century B.C. The Yahwist narrative—of which the Garden of Eden account of creation is a part—is half a millennium or so older, composed in the ninth or tenth century B.C. (The Elohist source does not figure in to the central texts with which environmentalists have been principally concerned and so for my purposes here can be passed over without further comment.)[51]

SIMILARITIES BETWEEN GENESIS-P AND PRE-SOCRATIC GREEK NATURAL PHILOSOPHY

The great Cambridge classicist F. M. Cornford has pointed out the remarkable similarity between the fifth-century Genesis-P and sixth- and fifth-century pre-Socratic Greek natural philosophy. According to Cornford, in the most recent biblical version of creation, "the action of Elohim has become extremely abstract and remote. . . . The whole account becomes a quasi-scientific evolution of the cosmos. The process is the same as in the Greek cosmogonies—separation or differentiation out of primitive confusion."[52]

Like the Milesians, the author of P represents the cosmos to have arisen from a primordial lawless unity, and like Thales more especially he identifies that unity with water. And just as Anaximander has the world order come into being by a process of division, a "separating out," of opposites contained in the urstuff, so the author of P represents Elohim to have effected creation first by a division of opposites: "God divided the light from the darkness"; God called the "firmament"—corresponding to Hesiod's "chaos" (which means "gap" in Greek, not "confusion")—into being to "divide the waters from the waters"; and finally, from the sweet waters of heaven, that had been divided by the firmament from the salt waters of the sea, God separated off the dry land.[53] Then, in the order, more or less, that Darwin (anticipated by Anaximander of Miletos and Empedocles of Acragas in the sixth and fifth centuries B.C.) represents organic beings actually to have arisen, God creates plants, animals, and *Homo sapiens*.

Read as a rational cosmology, Genesis-P resembles contemporaneous Greek cosmologies virtually point for point. Heaven is a star-studded leaky vault made of fresh water, held up by an airy bubble or "firmament." It arches over a disc-shaped Earth, which is surrounded by a "river" (as the contemporaneous Greeks thought of it) of salty Ocean. Even three of the four Greek elements, water, air, and earth, are unmistakably present in Genesis-P, expressly represented by the characteristic fauna that move in or on each—swimming whales and fish, flying birds, and creeping beasts and cattle, respectively.[54] And the simultaneous tendency of Greek philosophy toward humanism—"man is the measure of all things," and so forth—is also clearly evident in Genesis-P. Indeed, P's Hebrew analogue of Hellenic humanism—the *imago dei*, dominion, and subduction—is precisely what all the environmental fuss has been about.

There is something impertinent, I dare say, in the compiler(s) of the Old Testament putting the more modern account of creation before the more ancient one. Uncritical readers, by far the majority of readers, piously believe that the whole Bible proceeds from one divine source—that it is all literally the Word of God. And, moreover, most readers also piously believe that the Pentateuch, the first five books of the Bible, was transcribed by one human secretary, as tradition alleges, namely, Moses. Naturally, therefore, most readers strive consciously or unconsciously for consistency in what they read. Thus, given the dyschronological order in which the two Genesises are arranged, the more ancient is read in the light of the more modern. To get a fresh reading, therefore, of the original, the more venerable Yahwist version of creation—and the Genesis, moreover, to which Muir alludes exclusively—I suggest that we set aside the Hellenized upstart, the Johnny-come-lately Priestly version of creation, try to forget all about it, and see what the older Yahwist text has to say standing alone.

NATURE AND HUMAN NATURE IN GENESIS-J

First, as Artur Weiser comments, in J "the primeval condition of the world before the creation ... is pictured ... as a desert"—a far more appropriate image of primal homogeneity for the Sinai-sobered Hebrews than the watery *apeiron*, an image natural and appropriate to the coastal Ionian philosophers, from whom the author of P seems to have borrowed heavily.[55] A mist watered the whole face of this barren ground, and Yahweh formed a man from the mud thus made and breathed into his nostrils the breath of life.[56] As Weiser also comments, in sharp contrast to the formal style of P, "Gen. 2:4ff. ... tells the story in a lively and vivid fashion."[57]

The "breath of life" is a divine essence and may prefigure the *imago dei* of the more philosophical version that will have come along in another four or five hundred years. It is also true that when, later in the day, the animals are created—though God also forms them, working with mud, in the same lunch-bucket style—no mention is made of God's breathing into them the breath of life.[58] In his brief gloss, Muir ignores this difference and stresses instead the "dust of the earth, ... the common elementary fund" from which "the Creator has made Homo sapiens" and "every other creature." Still, I think Muir is right to insist that in this text, at least, one finds a much closer communion between us and the earth and the animals than the despotarians (and stewardarians as well) admit. Certainly one finds in J a much greater commonality among all creatures than in the canonically earlier, but temporally later, account.

Apparently thinking of Genesis as a composite whole, White remarks that "man shares, in great measure, God's transcendence over nature." That is certainly a fair inference from P, but the measure is inverted in J. In Hebrew, the word *adamah* means "earth." Thus, the man's very name, "Adam," assimilates him to the earth. John S. Kselman comments that "a number of scholars have proposed that the noun *adam*, 'man,' does not only indicate 'humankind' but, in a number of instances, is a masculine variant ... of the feminine form of *adamah*."[59] But in any case, as E. A. Speiser comments,

> in *adam* "man" and *adama* "soil, ground" there is an obvious play on words, a practice which the Bible shares with other ancient literatures. This should not be mistaken for mere punning. Names were regarded not only as labels but also as symbols, magical keys as it were to the nature and essence of the given being or thing. ... The writer or speaker who resorted to "popular etymologies" was not interested in derivation as such. The closest approach in English to the juxtaposition of the Hebrew nouns before us might be "earthling: earth."[60]

Phyllis Trible also stresses the verbal association between Adam and the earth: "A play on words already establishes relationship between earth creature (*adam*) and the earth (*ha adama*)."[61] Lexically speaking, the common Hebrew noun *adam* does mean "man," as Kselman and Speiser here report.[62] Acknowledging the masculine grammatical gender of the name (though not its lexical meaning), Trible insists that "grammatical gender (*adam* is a masculine word) is not sexual identification. ... In other words the earth creature is not the male; it [instead of 'he,' despite grammatical gender] is not the 'the first man.' "[63]

Adam may, in fact, involve a triple word play, adding another layer of earthy association to the name. According to geographer Jeanne Kay, "the Hebrew cognate *adom* also means the color red, strongly suggesting a visual relationship [with] ... the Mediterranean region's terra rosa soils."[64]

After making a man—an "earthling" (à la Speiser) or a neuter "earth creature" (à la Trible)—God planted the Garden of Eden. Is Eden a special place in the world or is it meant to signify the whole living, green earth?

J's geography of Eden is as tantalizingly ambiguous as its anthropology, but the whole-of-nature reading is powerfully suggested. Eden lies in an "eastward" direction, but east of what we are not told.[65] Other clues are more definite, however. Of the four rivers draining Eden the first seems to be the north-flowing Nile, "that compasseth the whole land of Ethiopia" (or "Cush"); the fourth bears the name in the King James translation of J that it bears on maps today, the south-flowing Euphrates; and the third, Hiddikel, is the Tigris.[66] Eden thus seems to encompass the face of the earth from the Nile Valley in the southwest to the region north of the Persian Gulf on the east—the entire known universe in the experience of tenth- or ninth-century Israelites. Eden, clearly (or at least as clearly as myth will allow), is nature primeval.

As Yahweh's breathing into Adam the breath of life in J may prefigure the *imago dei* in P, so the fact that in J Yahweh also "put him into the garden to dress and keep it" may prefigure humanity's dominion over nature—later expressly developed in P. Dominion over nature in P may be further prefigured in J by the privilege God grants Adam to name the animals, "thus establishing his dominance over them," as White puts it, assuming the same primitive logomancy just explained by Speiser.[67]

But, as in the case of our transcendence over nature, so, in the case of our dominance, the measure is far less in J than in P. To be sure, Adam may name the animals and thus control them, but why were they created? "And the Lord God said, 'It is not good that the man should be alone; I will make an help meet for him.' "[68] They were created, as Muir somewhat recklessly put it, to be our "earth-born companions and our fellow mortals." Actually, they were created as *candidates* for companion-to-Adam, a niche that Eve was finally to fill. Though Muir exaggerates, his point is, nevertheless, essentially well taken. Even though no proper companion for the man was found among the animals, the mere idea that Yahweh and Adam might look among them for one suggests once more that people were intended to share a common lot with other creatures rather than to share "in large measure" God's transcendence over creation.

There follows then the account of how Yahweh made a woman from one of Adam's ribs, having caused a deep sleep to fall upon the first earth creature. Of course, this account does go out of its way to reverse the ordinary birth relationship in which the male is born from the female. Woman in J is born from Adam, thus establishing, according to White and other traditionalist readers, the dominance of the male over the female— just as in the immediately preceding episode the dominance of people generally over the animals was established. I shall not comment further on that unnatural first human birth, nor steer attention away from the central environmental theme of this discussion by going any further into the controversy presently swirling around it. Instead, I move straight on to the fulcrum of Muir's citizenship interpretation, the meaning of the knowledge of good and evil.

THE KNOWLEDGE OF GOOD AND EVIL—WHAT IT IS NOT

The mysterious tree of the knowledge of good and evil is first mentioned along with the all-too-symbolically transparent tree of life as being among the other good and pleasant trees in the midst of the garden.[69] It is mentioned again, just before the creation of the animals, and the man is expressly forbidden to eat of it, on pain of death.[70] As soon as the woman has been created, married off, and settled in, it returns to center stage.[71]

We need not tarry over the familiar story of the temptation. The subtle serpent beguiled the woman, who ate of the fruit of the tree of the knowledge of good and evil. She did not die—not forthwith at any rate. And she found the woeful tree to be as good for food and pleasant to the eyes as the other trees of the garden and desirable to boot to make one wise. So she also gave some unto her husband and he too did eat of it.[72] Exactly as the serpent promised, "the eyes of them both were opened."[73]

And just what wisdom dawned on them?

"They knew that they were naked."[74] That's it. That's the only noetic datum the text says that they acquired. No other specific knowledge or wisdom is mentioned. We are left to wonder how this particular bit of knowledge is related to something so fundamental and so general as the knowledge of good and evil. What's the connection?

In the popular mind, the knowledge of good and evil is inevitably equated with the knowledge of sexual congress. Certainly this hypothesis can be linked simply and directly with nakedness. Exposed genitalia arouse sexual desire. Immediately the man and the woman sewed aprons of fig leaves to cover themselves, adding credence to the vulgar view.[75] The whole story, moreover, is erotically charged—we are given to imagine a perpetually youthful adult couple, both nude, who spend days without number in a lush, tropical garden with nothing to do but eat the mangoes, bananas, figs, pomegranates, and whatnot everywhere surrounding them, chat with Yahweh during walks through the garden in the cool of the evening, . . . and entertain one another. Since Freud and Jung have made us so keenly aware that the serpent, who tempts the woman, is a patent phallic symbol in dream and in myth, the coital gloss even seems "scientifically" supported by modern psychology.

But, despite all of this, knowledge of sexual congress cannot be the correct understanding of the knowledge of good and evil in Genesis-J, because the man and the woman have already lawfully known one another—in the biblical sense of the term. For what else could be meant when it is earlier said, *before* they ate of the fruit of the tree of the knowledge of good and evil, that "therefore shall a man leave his father and mother, and shall cleave unto his wife: and they shall be one flesh"?[76]

Having disposed of the vulgar interpretation, which equates good and evil with sex—as if chastity were all there is to morality, or as if sex and not money were the root of all evil—let us consider a more general, if equally simple, reading. Before eating of the fruit of the tree of the knowledge of good and evil, we might suppose that the first man and woman simply had no knowledge whatever of good and evil. That is, they were unable to distinguish right from wrong. If acquaintance with the distinction between good and evil, *simpliciter*, is what we are given to understand that the man and the woman acquired upon eating of the fruit of the tree of the knowledge of good and evil, then Yahweh is slandered by implication. For not having eaten of the fruit of the tree of the knowledge of good and evil, the man and the woman could not *know* that it was wrong, evil, to disobey Yahweh and eat of the fruit of the tree of the knowledge of good and evil. They would be caught in a double bind, a "Catch 22," and Yahweh would be guilty of cruelly toying with them . . . planting (literally) a deadly trap for them . . . setting them up for a fall.

So, let us go back to the drawing board, and work with the scant—but, as we shall see, entirely sufficient—information that we are given to discover the true and profound meaning of this mysterious knowledge.

ANTHROPOCENTRISM AND THE KNOWLEDGE OF GOOD AND EVIL

The serpent says that the knowledge of good and evil is a divine perquisite: "and ye shall be as gods, knowing good and evil."[77] As it turns out, the serpent did not lie about that either. Yahweh confirms it. Apparently addressing other gods in the neighborhood, Yahweh says, "Behold, the man is become one of us, to know good and evil."[78] And so that man not become a god in fact, as well as in pretense to an exclusively divine wisdom, that is, "lest he put forth his hand and take also of the tree of life, and eat, and live forever," Yahweh "sent him forth from the garden of Eden to till the ground from which he was taken."[79]

Putting the two clues together—the phenomenological discovery that the first couple made upon eating the fruit of the tree of the knowledge of good and evil, namely, *that* they were naked, and, second that the knowledge of good and evil is properly a divine not a human knowledge—I suggest that the knowledge of good and evil means neither knowledge of sexual congress, certainly, nor the simple knowledge of the difference between right and wrong, but the power to *judge*, to *decide*, to *determine* what is right and what is wrong *in relation to self*. When the author of J says "they knew that they were naked," we may understand that to be just a graphic way of saying that they became *self*-conscious, *self*-aware. That information, which a moment ago seemed so particular and trivial, *is* just the knowledge of good and evil—if not the whole of the knowledge of good and evil, then the foundation for all the rest. For once aware of themselves, they may treat themselves as an axiological point of reference. Indeed, the text suggests by its very silence on any alternative to Yahweh's banishment, or any compromise, and by the finality of that banishment, that once aware of themselves they *will* inevitably treat themselves as an intrinsically valuable hub to which other creatures and the creation as a whole may be referred for appraisal. Self-consciousness is a necessary condition for self-centeredness, self-interestedness.

Yahweh, it seems, cares for the creation as a whole. J's idyllic description of Eden, the delight that Yahweh evidently takes in the garden, the fact that it was created not for us, but us for it, "to dress it and to keep it," all subliminally indicate that Yahweh's concern is for the whole of nature and for each of its parts equally, not for people alone or even for people especially. At any rate, that is exactly how Muir reads this text. Once again:

> Why should man regard himself as more than a small part of the one great unit of creation? And what creature of all that the Lord has taken the pains to make is not essential to that unit—the cosmos. The universe would be incomplete without man; but it would also be incomplete without the smallest transmicroscopic creature that dwells beyond our conceitful eyes and knowledge.

Taking courage from Muir's insight, we may fill in explicitly what he finds unmistakably implied. Once human beings became self-aware and therefore self-centered, they began to size up the creation in relation to themselves. Some of the things that Yahweh had created people declared "evil" weeds and vermin—nettles and poison ivy; mosquitoes, wolves, bears, and the like—and put them on an agenda for extermination. In Muir's inimitable prose, "all uneatable and uncivilizable animals, and all plants which carry prickles, are deplorable evils which ... require the cleansing chemistry of universal planetary combustion."[80] On the other hand, the edible plants and tamable animals are pronounced "good," and they are cultivated and encouraged.

The gnarly curses that Yahweh imposes upon Adam and Eve, it seems so harshly and remorselessly, represent and epitomize, in the powerful and subliminal symbolism typical of mythopoeia, the inevitable alienation from nature that necessarily attends anthropocentrism. If the part would separate itself from the whole, and parse the whole into good and evil categories in relation to self-interest, then the part, by that very act, disrupts the harmonious life of the whole.

ANTHROPOCENTRISM AND YAHWEH'S CURSES

First, there will be enmity between human beings and the lower animals, represented by the serpent.[81] What could be a clearer indication of the rupture of a harmonious world?

Second, for women, childbirth—natural and easy for all other species—shall be unnaturally labored and painful.[82]

Third, for men, work becomes necessary. Animals live, as Adam and Eve once did, on what nature freely provides. With the emergence of anthropocentrism, agriculture comes into being, and with it thorns, thistles, and sweat.[83] As agro-ecologist Wes Jackson remarks:

The Fall, at least as Christians have understood it from Hebrew mythology, can be understood in a modern sense as an event that moved us from our original hunting-gathering state, in which nature provided for us exclusively, to an agricultural state, in which we took a larger measure of control over our food production, changing the face of the earth along the way. . . .
I suspect that agriculture is at the core of the Fall."[84]

Agriculture is indeed a central and ambivalent preoccupation of J.[85] In the beginning, the dusty chaos was barren for two reasons: because "the Lord God had not caused it to rain upon the earth and there was not a man to till the ground."[86] Yahweh put the earthling "into the garden of Eden to dress it and to keep it"—a further allusion to cultivation of a kind. But upon being banished from the fruity forest, people afterward must eat "the herb of the field."[87] The light pruning and raking implied in dressing and keeping God's permaculture is, accordingly, exchanged for heavy and coercive field work. Genesis-J thus insightfully unites labor-intensive agriculture and anthropocentrism. The connection is this: Farming begins precisely when the "good" plants are favored and cultivated. The ordinary course of nature must be opposed. One gets one's bread thereby, but it takes work. You have to plow the ground, hoe the "weeds," and battle the "pests." It also insightfully unites agriculture and an increase in human fertility: Yahweh says to Eve, "I will greatly multiply thy sorrow *and thy conception.*"[88]

And if all that were not a clear enough indication that original sin is just anthropocentrism itself and the inevitable alienation from nature that it brings in its train, the author of J represents Yahweh to expel Adam and Eve from Eden, from nature altogether. From the point of view of my earlier geographical interpretation, this expulsion is not literally to another locale; it represents, rather, the abandonment of *Homo sapiens*'s intended ecological "place" in nature.

Finally, God imposes the death sentence upon Adam and Eve for their disobedience. Death, I think, is clearly but subtly connected to self-consciousness—as a matter of logic. A conscious, but not *self*-conscious being lives in the eternal present. She remembers no personal past, and dreads no future end to her personal existence. No self-consciousness, no experiential identity as a continuous being, no personal death.

Of course, I do not mean to suggest that other animals, if indeed they lack self-consciousness, and the ancestors of *Homo sapiens* do not and did not die, organically speaking. I mean that they do not and did not die phenomenologically speaking. Before eating the fruit of the tree of the knowledge of good and evil, man and woman were naked, but did not *know* that they were naked. Similarly, before eating the fruit of the tree of the knowledge of good and evil, they died, but they did not *know* that they died.

Eventually, "men began to multiply on the face of the earth."[89] Yahweh remarks, "My spirit shall not always strive with man. . . ."[90] Indeed, so out of hand had become anthropocentric, agricultural humanity that "it repented the Lord that he had made man on the earth, and it grieved him at his heart. And the Lord said, " 'I will destroy man whom I have created from the face of the earth,' "[91] Fortunately for us, however, "Noah found grace in the eyes of the Lord."[92] Yahweh did not destroy us altogether, but seems to have hoped, after cleansing everything by means of the Flood, to make a new beginning with the righteous Noah and his seed. Apparently, however, there was no way to restore us to our previous animal-like innocence and integration with the rest of creation. Once we had tasted the fruit of the tree of the knowledge of good and evil, there was no possibility of a return to Eden.

THE ATAVISM OF GENESIS-J

Stepping back from the details of this most remarkable narrative, one may sense here deep racial memories and a nostalgia for a past that, by the time J was composed three thousand years ago, is only dimly visible — as through a glass darkly. J seems openly to lament the neolithic revolution, the shift from foraging to agriculture that had befallen evolving *Homo sapiens* some seven millennia beforehand. If the Nile is not the modern name of the River Gihon, if Cush has been misrendered "Ethiopia" by King James's scholars, and if, therefore, Eden is to be understood as a place in nature, not nature as a whole, a place eastward of Palestine, then J even seems also to have pinpointed the exact location of the baleful origins of agriculture — Mesopotamia, the Tigris and Euphrates valleys.[93] It regards an agricultural modus vivendi as a cursed way of life and marks the dawn of the neolithic as the point of departure for an upwardly spiraling human population and a multitude of human evils. It accurately, if in a foreshortened fashion, suggests that *Homo sapiens*'s earliest ancestors dwelt in a tropical forest and fed on fruit. It yearns for a return to that simian life of unself-conscious, guiltless ease and absorption. Then, there was no death, in a sense, because there was no self-awareness. And, in a sense, there were not many people, only two, a generic, earthy everyman and everywoman, for the same reason. Perhaps this latter point warrants a brief explanation.

As a philosopher I have always had a problem understanding the Hindu doctrine of reincarnation. For if one does not remember one's former life (or lives) then how is one's present self any more identical with one's former self (or selves) than with other past centers of consciousness? "I" live for a while, let us say during the eighteenth century, and die. Then, I am born (again?) during the twentieth, the person who is the author of this essay. One continuous series of phenomenological events ends and, two hundred years later, another begins. Absent self-consciousness uniting "my" past life and my present one, then how am *I* identical with one eighteenth-century person rather than another? Ah, but absent self-awareness how am I identical with my "own" (as I can say only because I am self-conscious) immediate past, present, and future; or different from the past, present, and future of some other conscious being? No self-consciousness, no experienced identity as a continuous being, no phenomenological difference between me and you.

However that may be, J is, in a word, atavistic. It suggests that salvation lies in an evolutionary reversal—but bars the way back with cherubims and a flaming sword. It urges a return to innocence, to immersion in nature—but provides no recipe for fulfilling that longing. The environmental ethic that it seems to suggest, given how far we have "progressed," appears impractical to all except a few scattered earth-hippies stuck in the 1960s. It seems to recommend that we lose our*selves*; quit work; go back to the jungle; take off our clothes; get naked; don't worry; be happy; don't hassle the animals; live on fruit and other forage; have fewer children (as a consequence perhaps of a low-fat diet); and just do what comes naturally. One may notice, I think, in Muir's accounts of his wilderness adventures a striving for just this style of life.

In addition to the sheer impracticability of the apparent retrogressive orientation of the citizenship environmental ethic, one might argue that there lurks a glaring formal contradiction at its core. We have tasted the forbidden fruit. The effects of its esters are irreversible. Try as we may, we cannot return to Eden. After all, even Muir came down from the mountains, married, farmed, raised children, and wrote books.

But perhaps, invoking a helical historical image borrowed from W. B. Yeats, we can return to Eden at a higher level of consciousness, a level of consciousness that does not negate but transcends self-consciousness. Arne Naess and his followers have propounded just this idea—albeit without reference to the fruit of the tree of the knowledge of good and evil—in their concept of the "ecological self" or "Self- [with a capital *S*] realization." Writes Naess,

> It seems to me that in the future more emphasis has to be given to the conditions under which we most naturally widen and deepen our "self." With a sufficiently wide and deep "self," ego and alter as opposites are stage by stage eliminated. The distinction is in a way transcended.[94]

Thus our damned self-consciousness, lamented by J, might be less overcome by self-abnegation, by a return to simple consciousness, than transcended by Self-realization, *sensu* Naess. Naess's idea is captured concretely and graphically by Australian environmental activist and deep ecologist John Seed in respect to an appropriately Edenic setting. After quoting the passage from P, quoted here three paragraphs below, Seed writes,

> As the implications of evolution and ecology are internalized . . . there is an identification with all life. . . . Alienation subsides. . . . "I am protecting the rainforest" develops to "I am a part of the rainforest protecting myself."[95]

Seed goes on to say, "I am that part of the rainforest recently emerged into thinking." But in light of these investigations here we might want to say rather, "I am that part of the rainforest recently emerged into thinking . . . and more recently still that part of the rainforest gone beyond egoistic thinking to a wider sense of self."

In any case, we can well imagine that literate, progressive, fifth-century Hebrew priests were mortified by the melancholy primitivism and atavism in J and—with the alternative to its hopeless nostalgia offered by deep ecology some two and a half millennia off in the future—deliberately constructed P to amplify the slightest distinctions between *Homo sapiens* and the other creatures drawn in J.[96] Thus the author of P might make it seem to be God's intent all along that people be a case apart from the rest of nature, and that people were in fact given dominion over and charged to subdue the earth and fill it from pole to pole and ocean to ocean with our own species.

Evidence of such deliberate tampering comes in chapter 9 of Genesis when, after the Flood abates, the anthropocentrism of the author of P appears again, this time more militant than ever: "And the fear of you and the dread of you shall be upon every beast of the earth, and upon every fowl of the air, upon all that moveth upon the earth, and upon all the fishes of the sea."[97] Exploiting the new deal that God cuts with humanity after the watery decimation, the author of P seems quite consciously to recall and then to countermand the God-given, pre-Fall and pre-Flood human dietary regime: "Every moving thing that liveth shall be meat for you; even as the green herb have I given you all things."[98] Thus he justifies carnivory. In sum, P, one might say, makes a virtue of anthropocentrism, the very thing that J condemns as original sin.

One might also better understand the militant anthropocentrism of modern Despotarians. As Muir remarks, "the fearfully good, the orthodox, of this laborious patchwork of modern civilization cry 'Heresy' on every one whose sympathies reach a single hair's breadth beyond the boundary epidermis of our own species."[99] Perhaps they sense that a tide of antianthropocentrism wells just beneath the surface of Scripture and must be diked up lest it spill out and run riot. Now perhaps we can better understand why, moreover, the Priestly compiler of the Old Testament did not simply slip the progressive and humanistically oriented version of creation in after—but put it instead in front of—J.[100] Doubtless he wanted P to blunt J's atavism and craftily redirect its original nostalgic sentiment and primitivistic passion toward something that he regarded as more progressive and forward looking—agriculturally based civilization.

A CONTEMPORARY CITIZENSHIP ENVIRONMENTAL ETHIC OF JUDAISM AND CHRISTIANITY— A GLIMPSE OVER THE MOUNTAINTOP

Impatient with both the narrow textual focus and the anachronistic odor of the whole debate provoked by Lynn White, Jr., Jeanne Kay has recently complained about the distortion we risk in "viewing Iron Age beliefs through modern environmental lenses."[101] Reviewing the relevant texts in the whole Hebrew Bible, Kay concludes that primarily

> nature is God's tool of reward and punishment and its beneficence depends upon human morality. . . .
> A society which explains destruction of pasturage as the result of God's anger over idolatry or insincerity in temple sacrifices, rather than as the outcome of climatic fluctuations or overgrazing, may have little to offer modern resource management. Few environmentalists today believe [or will be persuaded by the Bible to believe] that environmental deterioration results from oppression of widows and orphans.[102]

But Kay's excellent Old Testament historiography misses the point. Contemporary Jews and Christians, searching for meaningful advice about how to live in the world in which they find themselves, will consult the Bible and will inevitably ponder what they read (in translation) in light of their contemporary concerns, their personal experience, and their own locale. And as to the disproportionate attention lavished on Genesis at the expense of the rest of the Bible in the contemporary debate about biblical environmental attitudes and values, not only is Genesis more explicitly concerned with setting out the Big Picture than other passages in the Bible, that it comes at the very beginning also makes it a more important source for contemporary Jewish and Christian environmental attitudes and values than other biblical books: the slowest and least disciplined readers will have gotten through its first few chapters, even if they go no further with their sacred studies.

The despotic, stewardship, and citizenship models are all, in a sense, mythic, not scholarly, interpretations. Though the work of historians of ideas and Biblical scholars may be of use in their development, they are not intended to reveal what the Bible actually said in an archaic language to a specific people at a specific time about their relationship with a specific environment. Lynn White, Jr., rather, intended to explore how the Bible may plausibly have been read in the late medieval, early modern, and modern West to inspire and justify massive technological transformations of the environment.[103] And the proponents of the stewardship interpretation argue that however Scripture may have been used in the past to motivate and justify human tyranny over other creatures and nature as a whole — all in the name of human progress — it can very plausibly be made to say to us, here and now, that we ought to govern nature with humility, care, and responsibility.

For more radical environmentalists who feel no more comfortable with the managerial anthropocentrism of the stewardship reading, however benign, than with the defiant human chauvinism of the despotic reading — but who still relate to Scripture — I resurrect and reconstruct here Muir's hitherto unheralded and incompletely developed citizenship model.

So just how can we live in the light of the citizenship environmental ethic of Judaism and Christianity? We cannot go back to Eden — to foraging and to simple animal consciousness — as I just pointed out, but we can hope, individually and collectively, to transcend self-centeredness and achieve deep ecological Self-realization. Attempting to translate that stance toward nature into action in the world, however, may lead to contradictions of another sort. How can we resolve what seem to be the irreconcilable conflicts of interest that exist in a world in which the divine injunction of P — that people seize dominion over the earth and subdue it and that we be fruitful and multiply — has been at last fulfilled? Can we, at this late date, afford to open our eyes to "the rights of all the rest of creation," as Muir calls on us to do, while, in a global village already bursting at the seams and still growing exponentially, universal basic human rights continue to elude our efforts to vouchsafe them?

Contemporary environmentalists and contemporary proponents of human economic development share a common understanding of the global environmental problematique, though they weigh in on opposite sides of the issue. As one economist put it, notoriously, there are people and penguins and when push comes to shove human rights take precedence over penguin rights.[104] Environmentalists, on the other hand, see themselves as sticking up for the rights of penguins, mountain gorillas, timber wolves, and all the other threatened and endangered species in a swelling flood of humanity.

To resolve their conflict, environmentalists and proponents of human economic growth and development have basically agreed to zone the globe, roughly in proportion to the political clout each can command. Islands, large and small, of "habitat" in the sea of humanity and humanity's warrens, roads, and domestic plants and animals are reserved for the wild creatures. The large islands are called wilderness areas, "where the earth and its community of life are untrammeled by man, where man himself is a visitor who does not remain."[105] The smaller are called wildlife refuges, nature reserves, and national parks.

This shared understanding of conservation rests on a shared philosophical assumption, namely, that people are a case apart from the rest of nature, and an even deeper shared metaphysical assumption, namely, that the world is an aggregate, a mere collection or assortment, of separable parts.

The citizenship environmental ethic of Judaism and Christianity, however, challenges both of these assumptions. At the core of the citizenship interpretation of the Big Picture set out at the beginning of the oldest Hebrew sacred texts is the notion that people are created to be a part of, not to be set apart from, nature. The human/nature bifurcation—and, a fortiori, the bifurcation of human interests and the interests of all the rest of creation—was unintended by Yahweh. The very concept of conflicting and competing interests emerged, taking the citizenship point of view, from a presumptuous act on the part of the original human couple. As modern secular ethicists urge us to exchange narrow, shortsighted self-interest for an "enlightened" self-interest—pretty much the same thing that contemporary sociobiologists call "reciprocal altruism"—so a contemporary citizenship environmental ethicist might urge us to exchange modern enlightened self-interest for a postmodern "embedded" self-interest.

And the central insight of ecology—the contemporary myth inspiring the citizenship reading of the ancient text—is that the world's myriad living things do not exist in isolation from one another. We earth creatures are all enmeshed in a tangled web of life.

Although the web-of-life metaphor has become hackneyed, it seems, nevertheless, neither to have been well understood nor to have thoroughly percolated into the collective cultural consciousness. From an ecological point of view, as ecologist Paul Shepard so beautifully expressed it,

> the self [is] a center of organization, constantly drawing on and influencing the surroundings, whose skin and behavior are soft zones contacting the world instead of excluding it. ... Ecological thinking ... requires a vision across boundaries. The epidermis of the skin is ecologically like a pond surface or forest soil, not a shell so much as a delicate interpenetration. It reveals the self as ennobled and extended rather than threatened as part of the landscape and the ecosystem, because the beauty and complexity of nature are continuous with ourselves.[106]

Shepard goes on to endorse Alan Watts's felicitous phrase, "the world is your body."[107] And, complementarily of course, each of us is the world: the focus of a unique concatenation of relationships with all the other foci — the "knots in the biospheric web of relations," as Arne Naess puts it.[108]

Self-realization, so understood, leads us, then, to reframe our practical environmental problems. Framing our most important latter-day existential dilemma as human rights versus the rights of nature, indeed, is part of the problem, not a correct statement of the problem. To think in terms of multiple centers of sharply defined, exclusive, and competing interests in a zero-sum struggle for life is, from a deep-ecological point of view, like thinking of the parts of our bodies in a similar way. We do not pit the rights of the heart against the rights of the liver or the rights of the hands against the rights of the feet. From an ecological point of view, it makes as little sense to pit the rights of people against the rights of other creatures and of nature as a whole. Pursuing Self-realization and adopting its corollary embedded self-interest approach to problem solving leads us instinctively to avoid simply assuming a zero-sum and to look first for a win-win solution when human aspirations confront environmental and ecological exigencies.

Rather than thinking, therefore, of the planet as divided into ever-expanding human economic development zones—assumed to be inevitably environmentally destructive—and ever-shrinking wilderness areas and biological refugia, let us think instead about creating a garden planet. We can no more re-create the original Garden of Eden than we can recover our aboriginal unself-consciousness. But we can try to live harmoniously in and with nature—not by reverting to a condition of pre-agricultural savagery, but by employing all of our postindustrial technological ingenuity and ecological understanding to create an environmentally benign sustainable civilization.

Don't get me wrong. I support—with both purse and pen—wilderness zones and wildlife reserves as ardently as any environmentalist. But I think that in addition to dedicating tracts of land for the exclusive habitation of other species, both plant and animal, we might also envision and then attempt to create patterns of human development and styles of life that are adapted to the natural ecosystems in which they are enmeshed. It is possible, in principle, for human economic activities to be compatible with ecological diversity, integrity, and beauty. Not only that, it is possible, in principle, though it seems like heresy for an environmentalist to say so, for human economic activities to enhance natural ecosystems. Yea, verily I say unto thee that we can enrich nature, while enriching ourselves.

The surest proof of possibility is actuality. Here are some actual examples of mutually sustaining and enhancing human-nature symbioses.

The Desert Smells like Rain by ethnobotanist Gary Nabhan is about Papago dry farmers in the desert Southwest.[109] From time immemorial two oases some thirty miles apart, A'al Waipia and Ki:towak, had been inhabited by Papago. The former lies in the United States, in the Organ Pipe Cactus National Monument, and the latter in Mexico. The United States government designated A'al Waipia a bird sanctuary and stopped all cultivation there in 1957. Ki:towak is still being farmed in traditional style by a group of Papago. Nabhan reports visiting the two oases, accompanied by ornithologists, on back-to-back days three times during one year. At the

A'al Waipia bird sanctuary they counted thirty-two species of birds; at the Ki:towak settlement they counted sixty-five. A resident of Ki:towak explained this irony: "When the people live and work in a place, and plant their seeds and water their trees, the birds go live with them. They like those places. There's plenty to eat and that's when we are friends to them."[110]

Conservation biologist David Ehrenfeld concludes from this "parable of conservation" that "the presence of people may enhance the species richness of an area rather than exert the effect that is more familiar to us."[111] In general, the whole desert ecosystem in which they live, not just the Ki:towak oasis, is as adapted to and dependent upon the Papago as they are on it. Their little charco fields, built to catch and hold the runoff from ephemeral desert rains, are home to a wide variety of coevolved uncultivated plants (some of which the Papago eat) and unfenced animals ("field meat" as the Papago think of them). Undoubtedly the desert ecosystem is enriched rather than impoverished by millennia of Papago habitation.

Changes in the Land by historian William Cronon is an ecological history of New England.[112] Like the Papago in the desert Southwest, the Micmacs, Naragansetts, Abenaki, Mohegans, and Pequots of the northeastern United States and southeastern Canada were horticulturalists as well as gatherers and hunters, and so, in Wes Jackson's sense, they had at least nibbled at the flesh of the forbidden fruit. Actually, they had enjoyed more than just a little taste: in addition to planting and tending swidden patches of corn, beans, and other cultivars, these American Indians actively managed their forest larders, principally by pyrotechnology. Periodical deliberately set forest fires consumed accumulated detritus, thus forestalling larger, hotter, and more destructive burns and resetting plant succession on the forest floor to a stage more hospitable to deer and other browsers, thereby increasing their populations. The incredible abundance of fish, fowl, and game found and documented with wonder by the first European intruders into North America mutely testifies to the success of the land-management practices of the native inhabitants. Here again the presence of *Homo sapiens* arguably enhanced the ecosystem by objective measures of biological productivity, species diversity, and ecological integrity.

Incidentally, such considerations as these raise serious doubts about the very concept of wilderness. North America at European landfall was hardly a place "where the earth and its community of life are untrammeled by man, where man himself is a visitor who does not remain." Unless American Indians are not human beings—a view entertained by European settlers from the 1500s to the 1800s, but a view, nevertheless, that is wholly untenable—then North America was very much a settled country, thoughtfully, actively, and successfully managed by its human citizens, when "discovered" by Columbus in 1492.

So was South America. The *New York Times* reports that the National Research Council, an arm of the National Academy of Sciences, is, as I write, "rediscovering the lost crops of the Incas."[113] The Incas created a sophisticated, sustainable system of irrigated montane terraces and cultivated, according to the *Times*, "an estimated 70 species of crops, almost as many as the farmers of Europe and Asia combined."[114]

And Central America. Arturo Gomez-Pompa, on the basis of the higher incidence of fruit-bearing trees in the remnants of rainforest in southern Mexico, suggests that what appear to the untutored eye to be pristine patches of wilderness, rich in animal as well as plant life, are actually surviving fragments of an extensive lowland Maya permaculture.[115]

I cite these pre-Columbian American examples of human-nature symbiosis not to suggest that we give the New World back to the Indians or attempt somehow to recreate American Indian culture in the late twentieth century. I wish to point out, rather, that the past affords paradigms aplenty of an active, transformative, managerial relationship of people to nature in which both the human and the nonhuman parties to the relationship benefited. The human-nature relationship is an ongoing, evolving one. We can, I am confident, work out our own, postmodern, technologically sophisticated, scientifically informed, sustainable civilization, just as in times past the Minoans in the Mediterranean, the vernacular agriculturalists of western Europe, and the Incas in the Andes worked out theirs.

The symbiotic win-win philosophy of conservation is gradually replacing the bifurcated zero-sum approach as the twentieth century gives way to the twenty-first. I will cite but one example, an example, however, that epitomizes the ideal of a garden planet because it focuses on a region that has come to symbolize the original garden—a region, incidentally, that Christopher Columbus actually thought was the lost paradise described in Genesis J—the Amazon.[116] Writing in *Nature*, Charles M. Peters, Alwyn H. Gentry, and Robert O. Mendelsohn report that the nuts, fruits, oils, latex, fiber, and medicines annually harvested from a representative hectare of standing Amazon rainforest in Peru is of greater economic value than the sawlogs and pulpwood stripped from a similar hectare—greater even than if, following clear-cutting and slash-burning, the land is, in addition, converted either to a forest monoculture or to a cattle pasture. From a painstaking econometric study they conclude that "without question, the sustainable exploitation of nonwood forest resources represents the most immediately profitable method for integrating the use and conservation of the Amazonian forests."[117]

Surely we can envision and work to create an eminently livable, systemic, postindustrial technological society well adapted to and at peace and in harmony with its organic environment. Can't we come to value a plethora of useless products and needless gadgets less and natural aesthetic, intellectual, and spiritual bounty more? A civilized, technological humanity can live not merely in peaceful coexistence but in benevolent symbiosis with nature. Is our current *mechanical* technological civilization the only one imaginable? Is the nature *preserve* the only way we can effect conservation?

Aren't there alternative technologies? Can't we be good citizens of the biotic community—drawing an honest living from nature and giving back as much or more than we extract? We cannot find God's paradise lost and return to a state of innocence among its trees, but we can transform the industrial wasteland into a healthy, self-sustaining planetary garden of our own design.

NOTES

1. Lynn White, Jr., "The Historical Roots of Our Ecologic Crisis," *Science* 155 (1967): 1203–7.

2. For a discussion of the role played by Lynn White, Jr., in the development of environmental philosophy and ethics see Eugene C. Hargrove, "Religion and Environmental Ethics: Beyond the Lynn White Debate," in Eugene C. Hargrove, ed., *Religion and Environmental Crisis* (Athens: University of Georgia Press, 1986), ix–xix; and Eugene C. Hargrove, "Foreword," in J. Baird Callicott and Roger T. Ames, eds., *Nature in Asian Traditions of Thought* (Albany: State University of New York Press, 1989), xii–xxi.

3. White writes: "Unless we *think* about fundamentals, our specific measures may produce new backlashes more serious than those they are designed to remedy" ("Historical Roots," p. 1204, emphasis added); "What people do about their ecology depends on what they *think* about themselves in relation to things around them" ("Historical Roots," p. 1205, emphasis added); and "What we do about our ecology depends on our *ideas* of the man-nature relationship" ("Historical Roots," p. 1206, emphasis added). After ruminating on the complex relationship between attitudes and values, on the one hand, and behavior, on the other—a cryptotheme or subtext of "Historical Roots"—White concludes, in "Continuing the Conversation," in Ian Barbour, ed., *Western Man and Environmental Ethics* (Reading, Mass.: Addison-Wesley, 1973), p. 58: "And so one might comment indefinitely. But in the end one returns to value structures"—as providing the best insight into a culture's behavior patterns.

4. Such general doubts were raised almost immediately in response to White's seminal paper by Yi-Fu Tuan in "Discrepancies between Environmental Attitude and Behaviour: Examples from Europe and China," *The Canadian Geographer* 12 (1968): 176–91, and "Treatment of the Environment in Ideal and Actuality," *American Scientist* 58 (1970): 244–49.

5. For a general discussion and resolution of these problems see J. Baird Callicott and Roger T. Ames, "Epilogue: On the Relations of Idea and Action," in J. Baird Callicott and Roger T. Ames, eds., *Nature in Asian Traditions*: 279–289.

6. White, "Historical Roots," p. 1206: "The consistency with which scientists during the long formative centuries of Western science said that the task and the reward of the scientist was 'to think God's thoughts after him,' leads one to believe that this was their motivation."

7. More detailed attention to the contribution of the Greek natural-philosophical legacy to contemporary environmental problems is given in J. Baird Callicott, *In Defense of the Land Ethic: Essays in Environmental Philosophy* (Albany: State University of New York Press, 1989), and in Eugene C. Hargrove, *Foundations of Environmental Ethics* (Englewood Cliffs, N.J.: Prentice Hall, 1989).

8. It is well to remember that Lynn White, Jr., describes himself in "Historical Roots" as a "churchman," and that while he believes that "since the roots of our trouble are so largely religious, the remedy must also be essentially religious, whether we call it that or not," the religious remedy that he recommends is Judaic and Christian. Rejecting Zen Buddhism and other exotic alternatives fashionable in the then new, growing, and (to some) threatening American "subculture," White suggests reviving Franciscan doctrines — "recessive genes," as it were, in the Judaic and Christian pool of ideas, "which in new circumstances may become dominant genes"—as he put it in "Continuing the Conversation," p. 61.

9. My personal favorite is James Barr, "Man and Nature: The Ecological Controversy and the Old Testament," *Bulletin of the John Rylands Library* 55 (1972): 9–32. An early (post–Lynn White, Jr.) articulation of the stewardship interpretation may be found in John Black, *The Dominion of Man: The Search for Ecological Responsibility* (Edinburgh: Edinburgh University Press, 1970); a post–Lynn White, Jr., Judaic stewardship interpretation is developed by Jonathan Helfand in "Ecology and the Jewish Tradition," *Judaism* 20 (1971): 330–35; for an early partisan Protestant rendition of the stewardship theme see Francis Schaeffer, *Pollution and the Death of Man: The Christian View of Ecology* (London: Hodder and Stoughton, 1970); for a committed Catholic development of stewardship see Albert J. Fritsch, S.J., *Environmental Ethics: Choices for Concerned Citizens* (Garden City, N.Y.: Anchor Press, 1980); for a secular stewardship interpretation see Robin Attfield, *The Ethics of Environmental Concern* (New York: Columbia University Press, 1983); for a history of the stewardship interpretation in the West see Robin Attfield, "Western Traditions and Environmental Ethics," in Robert Elliot and Arran Gare, eds., *Environmental Philosophy: A Collection of Readings* (University Park: Pennsylvania State University Press, 1983), 201–27.

10. Tom Regan, "The Nature and Possibility of an Environmental Ethic," *Environmental Ethics* 3 (1981): 19–34.

11. Among the first papers in environmental philosophy to work out a clear secular theory of intrinsic value for nonhuman natural entities is Kenneth Goodpaster, "On Being Morally Considerable," *Journal of Philosophy* 75 (1978): 308–25; see Paul Taylor, *Respect for Nature: A Theory of Environmental Ethics* (Princeton, N.J.: Princeton University Press, 1986) for the most fully developed nontheistic theory of intrinsic value in nature; see also Holmes Rolston III, *Environmental Ethics: Duties to and Values in the Natural World* (Philadelphia: Temple University Press, 1988).

12. See Taylor, *Respect for Nature*, ch. 6.

13. Moses, Genesis 1:25, in King James et al., tr., *The Holy Bible* (Cleveland, Ohio: World, n.d.), p. 5 (emphasis added). I quote throughout from the King James Version because I prefer its poetic and antique qualities. Hereinafter, all references to this work will be by book, chapter, and verse.

14. Gen. 1:20–21.

15. See Roderick Nash, *Wilderness and the American Mind* (New Haven, Conn.: Yale University Press, 1967), ch. 8, "John Muir: Publicizer."

16. Stephen Fox, *John Muir and His Legacy: The American Conservation Movement* (Boston: Little, Brown, 1981), p. 51.

17. Donald Worster, review of Michael P. Cohen, *The Pathless Way*, *Environmental Ethics* 10 (1988): 268.

18. See John Muir, *The Story of My Boyhood and Youth* (Boston: Houghton

Mifflin, 1913); see also the analyses by Fox, *John Muir and His Legacy*, and Michael P. Cohen, *The Pathless Way: John Muir and the American Wilderness* (Madison: University of Wisconsin Press, 1984).

19. John Muir, *A Thousand-Mile Walk to the Gulf*, William Frederick Badè, ed. (New York: Houghton Mifflin, 1916), p. xxv. Badè prepared *A Thousand-Mile Walk*, after Muir's death, from a journal written during 1867–68.

20. Aldo Leopold, *A Sand County Almanac* (New York: Oxford University Press, 1949), p. 204.

21. Ibid., p. viii. I might note here that Leopold wrote a playful piece called "The Forestry of the Prophets," *Journal of Forestry* 18 (1920): 412–19, and though he was a nonbeliever he was a close student of the Bible. See Curt Meine, *Aldo Leopold: His Life and Work* (Madison: University of Wisconsin Press, 1988).

22. Leopold, *A Sand County Almanac*, pp. 204–5.

23. Muir, *A Thousand-Mile Walk*, pp. 136–37.

24. Ibid., pp. 137–38.

25. Ibid., p. 138.

26. Ibid.

27. Ibid., p. 139.

28. Ibid., p. 140.

29. Ibid., p. 98.

30. Ibid., pp. 98–99, 139.

31. White, "Historical Roots," p. 105.

32. Gen. 2:15.

33. Little aid and comfort is given to the stewardship interpretation by repairing to the Hebrew words translated as "dominion" and "subdue." According to Barr, "there has indeed been in the modern exegetical tradition, especially when the image of God has been identified with man's dominion over the world, a tendency to dwell with some satisfaction on the *strength* of the terms. The verb *rada* 'have dominion' is used physically of the treading or trampling down of the wine-press; and the verb *kabas* 'subdue' means 'stamp down.' According to [John] Black ([*The Dominion of Man*,] p. 37), it 'is elsewhere used for the military subjugation of conquered territory, and clearly implies reliance on force'; 'it is a very powerful expression of man's attitude toward the rest of nature, and suggests that he sees himself in a position of absolute command' " in *Ecology and Religion in History*, David and Eileen Spring, eds. (New York: Harper and Row, 1974), pp. 61–62.

34. Genesis, incidentally, nowhere identifies the fruit of the tree of the knowledge of good and evil as apples.

35. Joining the Lynn White, Jr., debate, Wendell Berry, a most eloquent stewardarian, writes in *The Gift of Good Land* (San Francisco: North Point Press, 1981), p. 268: "The instruction of Genesis 1:28 was, after all, given to Adam and Eve in the time of their innocence, and it seems certain that the word 'subdue' would have had a different intent and sense for them at that time than it could have for them, or for us, after the Fall."

36. Nash, *Wilderness and the American Mind*, p. 31, associates the explicit interpretation of Genesis 1:28 with Puritan literature.

37. Gen. 1:1.

38. Gen. 1:3.

39. Gen. 1:7.

40. Gen. 1:9–13.

41. Gen. 1:14–19.

42. Gen. 1:20–27.

43. Gen. 1:26–28.

44. Gen. 1:29–31.

45. Gen. 2:1–3.

46. Gen. 2:4 (emphasis added).

47. Gen. 2:7.

48. Gen. 2:8–9.

49. Gen. 2:19.

50. Gen. 2:21–22.

51. See Artur Weiser, *The Old Testament: Its Formation and Development* (New York: Association Press, 1961).

52. F. M. Cornford, *Principia Sapientia: The Origins of Greek Philosophical Thought* (Cambridge: Cambridge University Press, 1952), p. 200.

53. The quoted passages are found in Gen. 1:4 and 1:6. That everything might be made of water and that there are waters above as well as below may have followed "logically" from reflection on the fact that the sky and sea are both blue and that water falls from the sky.

54. Here one might fruitfully compare Plato, *Timaeus* 40: "There are four such [species]. One of them is the heavenly race of the gods; another the race of birds whose way is the air; the third, the watery species; and the fourth the pedestrian and land species. Of the heavenly and divine, he created the greater part out of fire. . . ." Benjamin Jowett, tr., in Edith Hamilton and Huntington Cairns, eds., *The Collected Dialogues of Plato* (New York: Pantheon Books, 1961), p. 1169. If we associate the God of Abraham and Moses with fire, as the burning bush vignette suggests we might, then all four classical Greek elements are represented in fifth-century B.C. Hebrew cosmology as well.

55. Weiser, *The Old Testament*, p. 73.

56. Gen. 2:6–7.

57. Weiser, *The Old Testament*, p. 73.

58. Gen. 2:19. Jeanne Kay, "Concepts of Nature in the Human Bible," *Environmental Ethics* 109 (1988): 314, comments that "The Hebrew word *nefesh* is used in the Bible both as the human spirit and also for animal spirits. . . . *Ruach,* meaning wind, spirit, or breath, is the source through which God animates *all* life (see Ps. 104:30)" — emphasis added.

59. John S. Kselman, "*adamah*" in Paul J. Achtyemeier, ed., *Harper's Bible Dictionary* (San Francisco: Harper and Row, 1985), p. 12.

60. E. A. Speiser, *Genesis: Introduction, Translation, and Notes* (Garden City, N.Y.: Doubleday, 1964), p. 16.

61. Phyllis Trible, *God and the Rhetoric of Sexuality* (Philadelphia: Fortress Press, 1978), p. 77.

62. See Ludwig Koehler and Walter Baumgartner, *Lexicon in Veteris Testamenti Libros* (Leiden: E. J. Brill, 1958), pp. 12–13.

63. Trible, *Rhetoric of Sexuality*, p. 80.

64. Jeanne Kay, "Human Dominion Over Nature in the Hebrew Bible," *Annals of the Association of Geographers* 79/2 (1989): p. 219.

65. Gen. 2:8.

66. Gen. 2:11–14.

67. Gen. 2:19–20.

68. Gen. 2:18.

69. Gen. 2:9.

70. Gen. 2:17.

71. Gen. 3:1–3.

72. Gen. 3:1–6.

73. Gen. 3:7.

74. Ibid.

75. Ibid.

76. Gen. 2:24.

77. Gen. 3:5.

78. Gen. 3:22. Of J, Weiser remarks, "individual passages still enable its original polytheistic mythology to be recognized," *The Old Testament*, p. 103.

79. Gen. 3:22–23.

80. Muir, *A Thousand-Mile Walk*, p. 141.

81. Gen. 3:14–15.

82. Gen. 3:16.

83. Gen. 3:17–19. Thorns and thistles attend disturbed, eroded, and exhausted soil.

84. Wes Jackson, *Altars of Unhewn Stone* (San Francisco: North Point Press, 1987), pp. 6, 64.

85. It is very interesting to compare Muir's reading of Genesis, as a partisan of wilderness, with Wendell Berry's reading, as a partisan of traditional agriculture. See Berry, *The Gift of Good Land*.

86. Gen. 2:5.

87. Gen. 3:18.

88. Gen. 3:16 (emphasis added).

89. Gen. 6:1.

90. Gen. 6:3.

91. Gen. 6:6–7.

92. Gen. 6:8.

93. For doubts about these particulars, see the relevant entries in *Harper's Bible Dictionary*.

94. Arne Naess, "Self-Realization: An Ecological Approach to Being in the World," *Trumpeter* 4/3 (1987): 40.

95. John Seed, "Anthropocentrism," Appendix E in Bill Devall and George Sessions, *Deep Ecology: Living as if Nature Mattered* (Salt Lake City, Utah: Peregrine Smith Books, 1985), p. 243.

96. That P was written deliberately to offset the implications of J is argued by Richard Elliott Friedman, *Who Wrote the Bible?* (New York: Summit Books, 1987).

97. Gen. 9:2.

98. Gen. 9:3.

99. Muir, *Thousand-Mile Walk*, p. 139.

100. Friedman, *Who Wrote the Bible?*, argues convincingly that "the redactor," the person who gave the Pentateuch its present shape, was Ezra, an Aaronid priest working in and on behalf of the Priestly source.

101. Jeanne Kay, "Concepts of Nature in the Hebrew Bible," *Environmental Ethics* 10 (1988): 311.

102. Ibid., pp. 317, 327.

103. Reviewing the Lynn White debate, Roderick Nash, *The Rights of Nature*

(Madison: University of Wisconsin Press, 1988), p. 89, makes a similar point: "White knew that the relevant question was not, what does [the Bible] mean but what did it mean to a particular society at a given time and place?"

104. William F. Baxter, *People or Penguins: The Case for Optimal Pollution* (New York: Columbia University Press, 1974).

105. The Wilderness Preservation Act, quoted in Nash, *Wilderness and the American Mind*, p. 5.

106. Paul Shepard, "Ecology and Man: A Viewpoint," in Paul Shepard and Daniel McKinley, eds., *The Subversive Science: Essays toward an Ecology of Man* (Boston: Houghton Mifflin, 1969), p. 2.

107. Ibid., p. 3. Shepard cites Alan Watts, *The Book on the Taboo Against Knowing Who You Are* (New York: Pantheon Books, 1966).

108. Arne Naess, "The Shallow and the Deep, Long-Range Ecology Movement: A Summary," *Inquiry* 16 (1973): 95.

109. Gary Nabhan, *The Desert Smells like Rain: A Naturalist in Papago Indian Country* (San Francisco: North Point Press, 1982).

110. Ibid., p. 96.

111. David Ehrenfeld, "Life in the Next Millennium: Who Will Be Left in the Earth's Community?," *Orion Nature Quarterly* 8/2 (Spring 1989): 9.

112. William Cronon, *Changes in the Land: Indians, Colonists, and the Ecology of New England* (New York: Hill and Wang, 1983).

113. William K. Stevens, "Rediscovering the Lost Crops of the Incas," *New York Times* (October 31, 1989), p. 17.

114. Ibid.

115. Arturo Gomez-Pompa and Andrea Kaus, "Conservation by Traditional Cultures in the Tropics" in Vance Martin, ed. *For the Conservation of the Earth* (Golden, Co.: Fulcrum, Inc., 1988).

116. For Columbus's edenic delusions see Charles L. Sanford, *The Quest for Paradise* (Urbana: University of Illinois Press, 1961) and Daniel J. Boorstin, *The Discoverers: A History of Man's Search to Know His World and Himself* (New York: Random House, 1983).

117. Charles M. Peters, Alwyn H. Gentry, and Robert O. Mendelsohn, "Valuation of an Amazonian Rainforest," *Nature: An International Weekly Journal of Science* 339 (June 1989): 656.

6

Ecofeminism and Deep Ecology: Reflections on Identity and Difference

MARTI KHEEL

There are two political and philosophical trends that share the view that the moral and spiritual condition that precipitated the current destruction of the natural world is a failure to feel connected to all life. They are ecofeminism and deep ecology. In the previous essay, Baird Callicott articulated one view related to deep ecology of how to transcend our self-centeredness. In this chapter, Marti Kheel warns that the tasks involved in reconnecting our sensibilities with the rest of nature are quite different for women than they are for men, because the self is very different for the two genders. She uses the example of sport hunting and its role in establishing male identity to illustrate this point and concludes that the crucial spiritual problem in the environmental crisis is not anthropocentrism, but androcentrism.

INTRODUCTION

It is a sad irony that the destruction of the natural world appears to be proceeding in direct ratio to the construction of moral theories for how we should behave in light of this plight. Behind the proliferation of moral theories lies a profound crisis in our feeling of connection to all life. Unable to trust or draw upon a sense of connection, most environmental theorists endorse reason as the sole guide in dealing with the natural world. The

An earlier abridged version of this essay appears in *Reweaving the World: The Emergence of Ecofeminism*, Irene Diamond and Gloria Orenstein, eds. (San Francisco: Sierra Club Books, 1990).

vast majority of theories that constitute the field of environmental ethics are thus axiological, or value theories, whose primary purpose is the rational allotment of value to the appropriate aspects of the natural world.

Both ecofeminism and deep ecology share an opposition to these value theories. The emphasis of both philosophies is not on an abstract or "rational" calculation of value, but, rather, on the development of a new consciousness for all of life. It is, perhaps, above all, this emphasis on the primacy of consciousness that underlies the mutual interest taken by eco-feminists and deep ecologists in one another's thought. But, before ecofem-inism and deep ecology consider merging their respective identities, it may be useful to determine in what ways the two philosophies diverge.

Ecofeminist philosophy is still in the process of formation. No single philosophical theory can fully represent its ideas and, undoubtedly, this will remain the case.[1] All would agree that ecofeminism entails the notion that the devaluation of women and nature has historically gone hand in hand. Most would concur, in addition, that our environmental problems have "psycho-sexual roots."[2] By this it is meant that domination of "outer nature" (the female-imaged environment) is inextricably tied to the dom-ination of "inner nature" (one's passions, emotions and desires). As one environmental writer has aptly put it, "Instead of saying that we face an environmental crisis, it might be more appropriate verbal convention to say that *WE ARE* the environmental crisis."[3] To this, ecofeminists have has-tened to add that this "inner environmental crisis" is rooted, above all, in the psychic identity of men. Men, it is argued, have sought to deny their feelings of vulnerability and dependency in relation to women and nature, and, in so doing, have sought to dominate both. Many ecofeminists have, therefore, concluded that no solution to our environmental problems will be forthcoming until sexism in all its forms is rooted out.

Outside of these overarching ideas, there seems to be little consensus as to what precisely ecofeminism is. This diversity of views undoubtedly reflects the multiplicity of paths by which women have found their way to ecofeminism. As Charlene Spretnak points out, some were drawn to eco-feminism through their exposure to nature-based goddess religions; others were drawn from the environmental movement; and, still others, from the study of political theory and history.[4] My own journey, which was via the animal-liberation movement, reflects the diversity of routes by which women have found their way to ecofeminism.

As ecofeminists attempt to weave together their common threads, it is useful to determine what is unique to the identity of ecofeminism as a philosophy. The attempt to contrast ecofeminism with what is, perhaps, its closest philosophical ally — deep ecology — can be a helpful means of fur-thering this process of identity formation. By scrutinizing the ideas of deep ecology through a feminist "lens," we can begin to discern what is unique to the identity of an ecofeminist philosophy. But before examining the differences between ecofeminism and deep ecology, it will be helpful to outline briefly the features that the two share.

Ecofeminism and deep ecology are united in their critique of an environmental ethic that is grounded in abstract principles and universal rules discoverable through reason alone. Feminists have argued that behind the preoccupation with universal principles and abstract rules lies a mistrust of nature, including nature as it is found within ourselves—namely, our instincts and feelings of connection to all of life. The quest for "truth" or "objective" knowledge is thus equated with the masculine endeavor to transcend the contingencies of the natural world.[5] In keeping with this notion, much of Western philosophy, including (ironically) environmental ethics, may be viewed as a continuation of the attempt to dominate the natural world.

In the masculine worldview, individuals are seen as discrete, atomistic beings, who must be compelled, through the use of reason, to behave in moral ways. Feminist moral theorists have contrasted this notion of morality with different ways in which women describe their ethical thought. In her book, *In a Different Voice*, Carol Gilligan argues that women speak about moral problems in a "different voice" from that of men. For women, moral problems arise from what are perceived as conflicting responsibilities, rather than from competing rights. The resolution is, thus, sought in a mode of thinking that is "contextual and narrative," rather than "formal and abstract." Gilligan argues that the emphasis on particularity and feeling is a predominantly female mode of ethical thought. In her words:

> The moral imperative that emerges repeatedly in interviews with women is an injunction to care, a responsibility to discern and alleviate the "real and recognizable trouble" of this world. For men, the moral imperative appears rather as an injunction to respect the rights of others and thus to protect from interference the rights to life and self-fulfillment.[6]

Embedded in such feminist theories is the notion that women have a sense of connection to other living beings that men need to re-create. Some have argued that this is a bodily wisdom that women have by virtue of their capacity to bring forth life. Others have argued that it stems from the differing conceptions of self that women and men develop in the process of socialization into sex roles necessary to the maintenance of patriarchy. Whatever the origin of this gender-related difference, the question, according to some feminist moral theorists, is not why people should behave in ethical ways, but when and why compassion, or moral behavior, fails. The search, then, for many ecofeminists is not for an abstract conception of appropriate value for the natural world, but, rather, for the development of a receptive consciousness that enables one to hear the "other voice."

Deep ecologists articulate a similar theme in their statement that

cultivating ecological consciousness is a process of learning to appre-
ciate silence and solitude and learning how to listen. It is learning to
be more receptive, trusting, holistic in perception, and it is grounded
in a vision of non-exploitative science and technology.[7]

Emphasizing the experiential nature of this ecological consciousness, deep
ecologist Warwick Fox refers to:

> ... the extent to which deep ecology is ultimately grounded in *sensi-
> bility* (i.e., an openness to emotions and impressions) rather than a
> *rationality* (i.e., an openness to data ("facts") and logical inference
> but an attempted closedness to empathic understanding).[8]

It is this ecological sensibility that deep ecologists view as the matrix
from which ethical conduct ultimately flows. According to Fox, "Deep ecologists agree with Birch and Cobb's insight that 'human beings are more
deeply moved by the way they experience their world than by the claims
ethics makes on them.' "[9] Similarly, Arne Naess states that, "I'm not much
interested in ethics and morals. I'm interested in how we experience the
world."[10] And as George Sessions concludes, "The search then, as I understand it, is not for environmental ethics but for ecological consciousness."[11]
Both ecofeminism and deep ecology may, therefore, be viewed as "deep"
philosophies in the sense that they call for an inward transformation in
order to attain an outward change. Deep ecologists contrast their philosophy with that of "shallow ecology" or "reform environmentalism," which
sets as its purpose the preservation of the environment for future human
needs. Deep ecologists argue that nature has inherent worth apart from
any value with which humans may imbue it. Deep ecologists thus attempt
to move beyond the prudential concerns of conservation, to the development of a deep ecological sensibility that recognizes the value of all forms
in the biosphere.

For both ecofeminists and deep ecologists, the inward transformation of
sensibility is often perceived as spiritual. Although deep ecologists criticize
the mainstream religions for their anthropocentrism and shallow ecology,
they nonetheless take inspiration from the minority traditions within these
and other religious traditions (e.g., Zen Buddhism, Taoism, Christianity,
and Native American spirituality). Ecofeminists, on the other hand, draw
especially on the ancient goddess religions and Native American spirituality. Although not all ecofeminists agree that there is a spiritual dimension
to ecofeminism, many of them concur with deep ecologists on the importance of spirituality in helping us to attain a sense of our deep interconnection with all of life. Both ecofeminists and deep ecologists also look to
the study of ecology to help reinforce spiritual insights such as the importance of diversity, as well as our interdependence with all of life.

Ecofeminists are less sanguine than deep ecologists that the major religious traditions can help promote a sense of interconnection with all of life. In fact, many claim that these traditions actually hinder development of this sensibility. My own spiritual journey has led me to reject the Judeo-Christian tradition on several accounts, foremost among which is its emphasis on (male) humanity's special relation to the divine. The exclusivity found in the notion that one species (more specifically "Man") is made in the image of God, precludes, in my mind, a true feeling of kinship with nature and sense of embeddedness in the natural world. Although I have found spiritual inspiration from knowledge of the ancient, earth-worshipping goddess religions, it can be difficult to adapt these beliefs to the contemporary world. For ecofeminists like myself, a sense of interconnection with nature must be forged, first and foremost, from personal experience and apart from the teachings of the major religions.

The two key norms of deep ecology—biospherical egalitarianism and the process of self-realization—flow from an ontological understanding of the interconnection of all of life. Self-realization, according to deep ecologists, entails a growing sense of identification with all of the natural world. As they argue, the small, ego-identified "self" expands its awareness into the larger more inclusive "Self." According to Devall and Sessions, this process

> ... begins when we cease to understand or see ourselves as isolated and narrow competing egos and begin to identify with other humans from our family and friends to, eventually, our species. But the deep ecology sense of Self requires a further maturity and growth, an identification which goes beyond humanity to include the non-human world.[12]

This widened self-identification is also tied in with biospherical egalitarianism, the second norm of deep ecology. Biocentric or biospherical egalitarianism entails the notion that all members of the biosphere have equal inherent worth, which deep ecologists argue must be interpreted in a metaphorical, rather than a literal, sense.[13] According to Devall and Sessions, "Biocentric equality is intimately related to the all-inclusive self-realization in the sense that if we harm the rest of Nature we are harming ourselves."[14]

Thus far, it might appear that ecofeminism and deep ecology have a great deal in common. Both posit a critique of abstract rationality while emphasizing the importance of feeling, experience, consciousness, and spirituality, as well as a holistic awareness of our interconnection with all of life. A superficial analysis might tempt us to dissolve the separate identities of the two bodies of thought. But let us examine more closely the differences between the two philosophies to see whether a merger between them is, in fact, warranted.

Perhaps the most significant distinction between ecofeminism and deep ecology resides in their respective understandings of the root cause of our environmental malaise. For deep ecologists, the anthropocentric worldview is foremost to blame. The two norms of deep ecology are thus designed to redress this self-centered worldview. Ecofeminists, on the other hand, argue that it is the androcentric worldview that deserves primary blame.[15] For ecofeminists, it is not just "humans" but men and the masculinist worldview that must be dislodged from their privileged place.

The key to understanding the differences between the two philosophies thus lies in the differing conceptions of self that they both presuppose. When deep ecologists write of anthropocentrism and the notion of an "expanded Self," they ostensibly refer to a gender-neutral concept of self. Implicit in the feminist analysis of the androcentric worldview, however, is the understanding that men and women experience the world, and hence their conceptions of self, in widely divergent ways. Whereas the anthropocentric worldview perceives humans as at the center or apex of the natural world, the androcentric analysis suggests this worldview is unique to men. Feminists have argued that, unlike men, women's identities have not been established through their elevation over the natural world. On the contrary, women have been identified with the devalued natural world, an identification that they have often adopted themselves as well.

Deep ecologists emphasize the importance of seeing into the nature of the real world, and then expanding one's conception of the self. However, if in this process we fail to recognize the real psychological differences in men's and women's identities, our grasp of the world must remain incomplete. If ontology is to be of any value, we must recognize the reality of not just "external" nature but of our inner drives and needs as well.[16]

In the remainder of this essay, therefore, I examine more closely the deep ecologists' concept of an expanded Self. What problems ensue from the assumption of gender neutrality in the concept of Self? Is the expanded Self a norm with which ecofeminists can identify? Or, does it express inner drives and needs that reflect a distinctly masculine point of view? In order to evaluate these questions, it is necessary to delve more deeply into the "inner ontology" or psychology of the masculine self. The second section of the paper, therefore, provides a brief review of some of the relevant philosophical and psychological theories of the self.

One of the precepts of feminism has been the importance of grounding one's theories in practical experience. In keeping with this notion, the concept of widened identification must be examined, not only for its conceptual legitimacy but for its practical implications as well. In the third section of this essay, therefore, I apply the aforementioned theories of self-hood to help explain the experiences of certain men who claim that their process of widened identification (or self-realization) takes place within the context of a concrete activity in the natural world—namely, by means of hunting.

CONSTRUCTING THE SELF

One of the most thoroughgoing analyses of the masculine and feminine conceptions of self is found in Simone de Beauvoir's monumental work,

The Second Sex. According to de Beauvoir, under patriarchal society, woman's sense of self is inextricably tied to her status as the "other":

> Now, what peculiarly signalizes the situation of woman is that she — a free and autonomous being like all human creatures — nevertheless finds herself living in a world where men compel her to assume the status of the other. They propose to stabilize her as object and to doom her to immanence since her transcendence is to be overshadowed and forever transcended by another ego (conscience) which is essential and sovereign.[17]

According to de Beauvoir, the facts of pregnancy, menstruation and childbirth have historically confined women to the world of immanence and contingency, a state of being in which life "merely" repeats itself. Authentic subjectivity is achieved to the extent that one raises oneself above biological necessity, and hence, above the animal world. Men have historically transcended the world of contingency through exploits and projects — that is, through attempts to transform the natural world. In her words: "Man's design is not to repeat himself in time: it is to take control of the instant and mold the future.[18] According to de Beauvoir, the prototypal activities of transcendence (hunting, fishing, and war) involve both risk and struggle. As she explains:

> For it is not in giving life but in risking life that man is raised above the animal; that is why superiority has been accorded in humanity not to the sex that brings forth but to that which kills.[19]

De Beauvoir claims that self-hood is an identity that emerges through an antagonistic relation to an "other." For women to achieve full human status or self-hood, they must, therefore, join with men in exploits and projects that express this opposition to the natural world.

De Beauvoir developed her concept of the "other" from the writings of Hegel and Sartre.[20] Both of these philosophers considered antagonistic consciousness to be necessary for the establishment of the self. For Hegel, consciousness could only be achieved through recognition from an "other." If the truth of self-certainty — the sustained sense of oneself as a part of the world — was to be achieved, the "other" had to be overcome. The contradictory need for both recognition from, and negation of, the "other" could result in only two possible outcomes — the death of the "other" or the subjection of the "other" in the relation of master and slave.

Sartre developed the notion of the antagonistic nature of consciousness with his concept of the "Look." The struggle between two consciousnesses thus becomes one of competing "Looks." When one is looked at, according to Sartre, one becomes objectified; one is no longer the center of infinite possibilities. Hegel's life-and-death struggle between rival consciousnesses thus becomes transformed in Sartre's thought into the struggle of competing "Looks." Each self struggles to attain transcendence by transforming the other into an object.

De Beauvoir extended Sartre's thought by showing that it was women who had been assigned the role of the looked upon "other."

While agreeing with much of de Beauvoir's analysis, many contemporary feminists reject the masculine norm of autonomy that she endorsed. The notion of an autonomous (masculine) self, established through the defeat of a female-imaged "other," is viewed by many feminists as a central underpinning of the patriarchal world.[21] Feminists have shown that many of the world's most sacred traditions depict similar stories of struggle and conquest. Typically, the conquest is of Darkness or Chaos, usually symbolized by a female-imaged, animal form, frequently a dragon or a snake. Through this struggle against unruly nature, the world of Light and Order is born. As Monica Sjöö and Barbara Mor describe these struggles:

> The sun-worshipping pharaohs of later Egypt slay the dragon Apophys, Apollo slays Gaia's python. The Greek hero Perseus slays the Amazonian Medusa—who is described as three headed (the Triple Goddess) with snakes writhing from her three heads. St. George slays the dragon in England, even St. Patrick must drive the snake from the snakeless Ireland. And in Hebrew Genesis, the serpent is doomed by the War God Yahweh to be forever the enemy of the human race: to be crushed under our heels, and to give back to us only one poison. In Christian prophesy, in Revelation 12-21:1, the final extinction of the dragon is promised when a king-messiah kills the watery cosmic snake and then takes over the world unchallenged: "and there was no more sea." This event is prefigured in Psalms 74:13: "Thou breakest the heads of dragons in the waters."[22]

Similarly, in the Christian tradition, we find God, saints, and archangels enacting the same heroic struggle against the Devil, who is frequently depicted in animal form. The horned gods common to Mesopotamia, both in Babylon and Assyria, are transfigured, in the Christian tradition, into the familiar image of the horned Devil. The Devil is seen as the source of disorder or unruly nature that faith, prayer, and divine intervention must overcome.

These stories of struggle and conquest contrast sharply with the mythologies of the earliest matriarchal societies, in which the Goddess was intimately connected with the animal world. It is, in fact, the conquest of the Goddess in her animal aspect that the patriarchal mythologies record.

According to Erich Neumann,[23] the matricide of the "Terrible Mother," typically depicted in animal form, is the act of killing the "Archetypal Feminine" who represents, for both women and men, the eternal dark side that threatens to destroy ego consciousness. For Neumann and other Jungians, the heroic matricide of the mother figure was necessary for the development of consciousness. The matricidal act brings with it ambivalent feelings for the mother figure. Having sundered oneself from the mother figure, one longs to return to her as well. The heroic ego then must kill the "Terrible Mother" as an act of self-defense designed to protect the heroic consciousness against the return to an unconscious state.

According to Jung, the heroic ego establishes itself through the stolen power of the Mother Goddess. Eventually, it is a debt that must be repaid through the hero's self-sacrifice to the Mother. It is often at mid-life that the illusion of autonomy is broken down and the ego finally faces the depths of its unconscious. Thus, the spiritual journey, for Jung, requires not an outward act of aggression, but an inward sacrifice of the self.

Although the Jungian "transpersonal" journey is designed to "sacrifice" the (masculine) autonomous self, what is of interest is that the imagery of struggle and conquest is still retained. Long before such modern analyses, Plato also depicted the spiritual journey in terms that reflect the notion of struggle and conquest. In Plato's thought, the spiritual journey of the soul is achieved through its struggle with, and conquest over, the nonrational aspects of itself. According to Plato, the highest part of the soul, embodied in reason, may be likened to a winged charioteer that must assert its control over the nonrational parts of the soul. In Plato's allegory, two winged steeds represent the lower passions that must be brought under the control of the charioteer. The spiritual journey commences, for Plato, with the sight of one's "beloved." The struggle ensues when the onlooker attempts to transform the desire for one's beloved into a spiritual journey of return to an original unified state. The desired union is ultimately not with an individual being but with the forms of Truth and Beauty, situated within a "higher," spiritual realm. As Plato describes the charioteer's struggle:

> But the driver, with resentment even stronger than before, like a racer recoiling from the starting-rope, jerks back the bit in the mouth of the wanton horse with an even stronger pull, bespatters his railing tongue and his jaws with blood and forcing him down on legs and haunches delivers him over to anguish. . . . And so it happens, time and again, until the evil steed casts off his wantonness; humbled in the end, he obeys the counsel of his driver.[24]

What is significant, for our purposes, in this Platonic allegory is that the inward struggle over one's passions is depicted with the use of an image of violence towards the animal world. Furthermore, the violent struggle with internal nature (depicted as an animal) is conceived as an integral part of a spiritual journey to transcend the individual self.

Plato's allegory, thus, lends support to one of the major insights of the feminist writings on women and nature, as well as that of the Frankfurt school,[25] that is, that the domination of "external nature" is intimately

linked to the domination of "inner nature." Susan Griffin highlights this
point in her analysis of pornography. According to Griffin, the images of
pornography reflect men's attempt to subdue the knowledge of bodily feeling. As she explains:

> Yet the pornographer fears the power of nature; he cannot decide to
> admit his own feelings into his knowledge of himself. Therefore he is
> caught. And like a trapped animal, trapped by his own body, he
> becomes violent. He punishes that which he imagines holds him and
> entraps him: he punishes the female body.[26]

The psychoanalytic theory of object relations presents a modern-day
critical analysis of the establishment of the masculine self in heroic opposition to the female world. According to this theory, both boys and girls
experience their first forms of relatedness as a kind of merging with the
mother figure. The child then develops a concept of self through a process
of disengaging from this unified worldview. Unlike girls, boys have a two-
stage process of disidentification. They must not only disengage from the
mother figure, but in order to identify as male they must deny all that is
female within themselves, as well as their involvement with all of the female
world. The self-identity of the boy child is thus founded upon the negation
and objectification of an "other."[27]

According to Chodorow, since the girl child is not faced with the same
need to differentiate her self-identity from that of the mother figure, "girls
come to experience themselves as less differentiated than boys, as more
continuous with and related to the external object world and as differently
oriented to their inner object-world as well."[28] Girls, therefore, emerge from
this period with a basis for "empathy" built into their primary definition of
self in a way that boys do not. Thus, girls emerge with a stronger basis for
experiencing another's needs or feelings as one's own, or of thinking that
one is so experiencing another's needs and feelings.

Dorothy Dinnerstein extends this analysis to the masculine mode of
interacting not only with women but with all of the natural world. For
Dinnerstein, since a child's self-identity is originally viewed as indistinct
from the surrounding world, later self-identity comes to be founded not
only upon the notion of not being female, but upon the notion of not being
nature as well.

For Dinnerstein, the process of developing a separate self brings with it
the ambivalent feelings of rage and a fear and longing to return to the
original coextensive self. Dinnerstein argues that it is the current sexual
arrangement of women as the sole nurturers of children that results in
women becoming the scapegoat for the repressed rage that the child feels.
The rage is, in reality, a rage against the "knowledge of fleshly transience."
In her words:

We hold this knowledge at bay by rejecting what is hardest to endure in the immediate sense of our own vulnerable animal existence, by demeaning it, splitting it off from our humanity. And we keep this knowledge nearby by embodying that immediate sense, disowned and degraded, in our pre-rational image of women.[29]

It is not necessary to concur with Dinnerstein's conclusion that the current sexual arrangements of childbearing are the sole cause of the contemporary conceptions of masculine and feminine self[30] in order to perceive the valuable insights of object-relations theory. Object-relations theory sheds important light on the long tradition that views the masculine self as a product of the negation of both women and all of the natural world.

EXPANDING THE SELF

This brief excursion into psychoanalytic and philosophical theories of the self should underline some of the problems entailed in assuming a gender-neutral concept of self. If men in our society are socialized to perceive their identity in opposition to a devalued, female-imaged world, we might expect that the process of reinstituting this forbidden identification will be fraught with problems along the way. At the very least, we might expect that the process of identification would be experienced in different ways by women and men. As we have seen, women's sense of identity is characterized by the maintenance of ties and connection; there is no felt need to establish their self-hood in opposition to others, or to the natural world.

In order to understand how these differences in women's and men's self-identities affect their process of self-realization, it is therefore helpful to consider concrete examples of the self-realization process. The works of three prominent male writers and philosophers, who claim that their process of self-realization occurs through the act of hunting and killing animals, are suggestive in this regard. Two of the three writers are cited with approval by deep ecologists. Although the third, Randall Eaton, is not, to my knowledge, mentioned in their writings, the personal insights he provides into his own process of self-expansion are still relevant to the argument being developed here.

My criticism is directed not merely at the support that (at least some) deep ecologists have given to hunting; it is, rather, a critique of the limitations of a gender-neutral concept of self, which uses hunting to *illustrate* my point. Indeed, I would go so far as to say that the cogency of my argument would still hold even if deep ecologists never endorsed hunting as a means of expanding the self. The criticism, moreover, is not confined to deep ecologists but applies equally to all ecophilosophies that endorse the notion of identification with nature by means of expanding the self. My purpose in employing the example of hunting is to bring the discussion of identification and expansion of self down from the heights of abstraction, so characteristic of philosophical theory, to the level of concrete example. I feel that only in this way is it possible to assess the tangible results of the differences in women's and men's concepts of self as they find expression in identification with the natural world.

According to the philosopher/biologist Randall Eaton, "To hunt is to experience extreme oneness with nature. . . . The hunter imitates his prey to the point of identity."[31] As he explains:

> . . . hunting connects a man completely with the earth more deeply and profoundly than any other human enterprise. Paradoxical as it may appear at first glimpse, the hunter's feeling for his prey is one of deep passion, ecstacy and respect. . . . The hunter loves the animal he kills. . . .[32]

Let us recall that according to psychoanalytic theory the boy's yearning to identify with the mother figure is fueled by his feelings of alienation and the consequent urge to re-experience the original state of union. Randall Eaton's view conveys such a longing, which may be seen as a longing for the original self. In his words,

> What do I mean at the deepest level when I say I want to know the behavior of the tiger? I really mean that I have affection for tigers and that I want to know the essential nature or being of the tiger. If the truth be known, I want to *be* a tiger, to walk in his skin, hear with his ears, flex my tiger body and feel as a tiger feels.[33]

The writings of a well-known Spanish philosopher, José Ortega y Gassett,[34] reflect a similar urge toward union with the animal, which he sees as a unification with the animal within himself. In his words,

> Man cannot re-enter Nature except by temporarily rehabilitating that part of himself which is still an animal. And this, in turn, can be achieved only by placing himself in relation to another animal.[35]

For such men as Eaton and Ortega y Gassett, the ultimate purpose of the hunt would appear to be this reversion to an earlier, more primitive, state of being in which one's separation, not from women, but from animals, has not yet occurred. Ortega y Gassett, in fact, refers to hunting as a kind of "vacation from the human condition through an authentic 'immersion in nature.' "[36] He explains, "In that mystical union with the beast a contagion is immediately generated and the hunter begins to behave like the game."[37]

Hunting is portrayed by all three authors as a pleasurable activity to which one is continually drawn. The erotic undertones of this pleasure can be found in their sensuous descriptions of the hunt.[38] Thus, the prominent environmental writer Aldo Leopold, much endorsed by deep ecologists, notes that he "tingled" at the recollection of the big gander that sailed honking into his decoys[39] and Ortega y Gassett writes of the "exquisite" feel of the air that "glides over the skin and enters the lungs."[40] At other times, both write of hunting in more heated terms, using such words as "hunting fever" and the "drama" and "contagion" of the hunt. Indeed, Ortega y Gassett goes so far as to assert the "unequaled orgiastic power" of blood,[41] contending that wildlife photography is to hunting what Platonic love is to the real thing.[42]

According to both object-relations and Jungian theory, it is the ongoing denial of the original union with the mother figure that creates the lifelong yearning to experience this original state. Hunting is, in fact, described by all three writers as a permanent or instinctive longing. According to Ortega y Gassett, sport hunting is "however strangely a deep and permanent yearning in the human condition."[43] And in the words of Aldo Leopold, "The instinct that finds delight in the sight and pursuit of game is bred into the very fiber of the human race."[44] Desire for hunting, according to Leopold, lies deeper than that of other outdoor sports. In his words, "Its source is a matter of instinct as well as competition." He elaborates, "A son of Robinson Crusoe, having never seen a racket, might get along nicely without one, but he would be pretty sure to hunt or fish whether or not he were taught to do so."[45] In other words, for Leopold, a boy instinctively learns to shoot a gun, and moreover instinctively wants to hunt and kill! It must be emphasized that all three writers describe hunting not as a necessary means of subsistence, but rather as a *desire* that fulfills a deep psychological need.[46] At times Leopold is unclear as to whether this instinct is universally held by all humans or only men and boys. Leopold writes, ambiguously:

> A man may not care for gold and still be human but the man who does not like to see, hunt, photograph or otherwise outwit birds and animals is hardly normal. He is supercivilized, and I for one do not know how to deal with him.[47]

To understand how the act of identification can coexist with the desire to kill the being with whom one identifies, it is important to understand the ambivalent nature of the hunt. Ortega y Gassett refers to this "ambivalence" felt by every hunter that results from "the equivocal nature of man's relationship with animals." As he explains:

> Nor can it be otherwise, because man has never really known what an animal is. Before and beyond all science, humanity sees itself as something emerging from animality, but it cannot be sure of having transcended that state completely.[48]

The hunter is thus driven by the conflicting desires to both identify with the animal and to deny that he is an animal himself. The "drama" of the hunt enables the hunter to experience the yearning for a return to unity while ensuring, through the death of the animal, that such a unification is never attained. Nancy Hartsock provides an insight into this phenomenon through her analysis of the psychology of the masculine self.[49]

In words reminiscent of Hegel, she states:

> As a consequence of this experience of discontinuity and aloneness, penetration of ego-boundaries or fusion with an other is experienced as violent. Thus, the desire for fusion with another can take the form of domination of the other. In this form it leads to the only possible fusion with a threatening other: when the other ceases to exist as a separate, and, for that reason, threatening being. Insisting that another submit to one's will is simply a milder form of the destruction of discontinuity in the death of the other since in this case one is no longer confronting a discontinuous embodiment. This is perhaps one source of the links between sexual activity, domination and death.[50]

Deep ecologists caution that identification must entail a recognition of the "relative autonomy" of the other being, but it is precisely this autonomous existence that the above writers have failed to convey. According to object-relations theory, the mother is transformed and incorporated by the boy child into an object from which his identity can then be forged. In a similar way, animals have become objects in the eyes of these men. In fact, Aldo Leopold openly expresses this urge to reduce animals to the status of objects. He states that "critics write and hunters outwit their animals for one and the same reason—to reduce that beauty to possession."[51] Interestingly, the original title of his famous *A Sand County Almanac* was "Great Possessions."[52]

The significance of the reduction of the animal to object status is that the *relationship* to the animal becomes more important than the animal itself. The feelings of yearning for union, the urge to "outwit"—all these take precedence over the living being that is killed. The animal is swallowed up in the act of merging. Even the death of the animal is considered incidental—a by-product of the more important desire that finds its expression in the hunt. As Ortega y Gassett explains:

> To the sportsman the death of the game is not what interests him; that is not his purpose. What interests him is everything he had to do to achieve that death—that is, the hunt. Therefore, what was before only a means to an end is now an end in itself. Death is essential because without it there is no authentic hunting. . . . To sum up, one does not hunt in order to kill; on the contrary, one kills in order to have hunted.[53]

Hunters express multiple reasons for their desire to hunt, often downplaying their desire to kill. Many contend that they hunt in order to be in nature, to experience a sense of camaraderie with their fellow hunters, to obtain the meat of the animal, and so on. What is significant about this complex of motives, however, is how inextricably they are intertwined. As Ortega y Gassett points out, the killing of the animal is not an incidental event that can be eliminated while leaving the other experiences intact. Rather, the killing of the animal is the one ingredient in the hunting experience that cannot be removed. It is the climax of the "drama" — that which gives meaning to all the other experiences that have led up to that point. This is not to deny the social aspects of the hunting experience. Clearly, hunting is a powerful experience of male bonding, often between fathers and sons. Male bonding acts not only as a powerful social reinforcement of the hunting experience but as a strong inducement as well. Men often feel pressured into hunting by fathers and friends, succumbing to such pressure to avoid the accusation that they are not "real men." It would seem that not all men adapt with equal facility to the social construction of masculinity and to the acts of aggression typically entailed in this norm.

Deep ecologists argue that a widened identification will ensure that one will want to minimize harm to individual beings in that they will be viewed as part of the all-inclusive Self. However, it is clear from the above examples of self-realization, that for these men this was not the case. For all three men, the killing of animals is an *integral part* of the process of self-realization. The mind-set that they reveal is that of a psychological instrumentalism in which the animal is seen, not as a unique, living being, but rather, as a means of achieving a desired psychological (or psycho-biological) state. The animal is thus reduced to the status of object or symbol.

What first appears to be a transpersonal or beyond-the-ego experience upon further examination is merely the familiar, heroic struggle to establish the masculine self. The animal still functions in the role of the "other," a necessary prop for establishing the heroic, trans-egoic state. The ego is seemingly transcended by vanquishing the "other," but, in reality, the ego has merely assumed another form.

For all three writers, the desire to hunt is clearly of greater importance than the life of the animal that they kill. For Leopold, the urge to hunt is strong enough to merit its enshrinement as an inalienable right.

> Some can live without the opportunity for the exercise and control of the hunting instinct, just as I suppose some can live without work, play, love, business or other vital adventure. But in these days we regard such deprivation as unsocial. Opportunity for the exercise of all the normal instincts has come to be regarded more and more as an inalienable right.[54]

Aldo Leopold is considered by many to be a pioneer of deep ecology and ecophilosophy. He is perhaps best known as an early promulgator of

an ethic of nonanthropocentrism and biocentric equality. What is not widely
recognized, however, is how paramount the hunting instinct was to Leopold's philosophy, and to the "land ethic" for which he is so well known.
Just after Leopold discusses the inalienable right for the free exercise of
the "normal" instinct to hunt, he goes on to deplore that, "the men who
are destroying our wildlife are alienating one of these rights and doing a
good job of it."[55] Wildlife must be conserved not because of the animals'
inalienable right to life but rather because of "man's" inalienable right to
hunt and kill! As Leopold elaborates:

> His instincts prompt him to compete for his place in the community
> but his ethics prompt him also to cooperate (perhaps in order that
> there may be a place *to compete for*) [emphasis added].[56]

Leopold expands on this notion of ethics as a form of restraint when he
argues,

> An ethic ecologically is a limitation on freedom of action in the strug-
> gle for existence. An ethic philosophically is a differentiation of social
> from anti-social conduct. These are two definitions of one thing. Good
> social conduct involves a limitation of freedom.[57]

Leopold's land ethic is thus conceived as a necessary restraint for a self
that is motivated by an inherently aggressive drive. All three authors see
such aggression and struggle as a fundamental fact of life. In Ortega y
Gassett's words, "Life is a terrible conflict, a grandiose and atrocious con-
fluence."[58] This notion of life's inherent conflict can be understood, with
reference to object-relations theory, as the result of the male's ongoing
internal struggle to maintain his self-identity as distinct from the female-
imaged natural world. This internal conflict then becomes projected onto
the "outside" world. The deep ecological concept of a widened identification of self fails to account for the fact that, contrary to what all three
authors would have us believe, not everyone's concept of self entails such
an aggressive drive. For many women this is clearly not the case. Such
women's process of identification and widening of the self finds expression
in different ways.
    For many women, identification with animals entails not the simulta-
neous urge to express an aggressive drive but, rather, the desire to avoid
causing them harm. At times, deep ecologists would seem to express this
feeling as well. Thus, Arne Naess writes,

> There is a basic intuition in deep ecology that we have no right to
> destroy other living beings without sufficient reason. Another norm is
> that, with maturity, human beings will experience joy when other life

forms experience joy, and sorrow when other life forms experience sorrow.[59]

This statement, however, would appear to be contradicted by Devall and Sessions who suggest, in *Deep Ecology*, that hunting, along with such diverse activities as surfing, sailing, sunbathing, and bicycling, is "an especially useful activity" that, with the "proper attitude," can help encourage "maturity" of the self.[60]

In order to understand this seeming contradiction, we must recall that it is the *widest* sense of identification that deep ecologists ultimately call for, namely, an identification not with individual beings but rather with the larger biotic community or whole. Warwick Fox expresses this relative prioritizing when he states:

> In terms of the wider identification approach, then, it can be seen that there is a strong sense in which community (e.g., the species or the ecosystem) is even more important than the individual expressions that constitute it since the community itself constitutes an entire *dimension* of the world with which I identify, i.e., of my Self.[61]

Robinson Jeffers, whom deep ecologists cite with approval, expresses this relative prioritizing in even stronger terms:

> I believe the universe is one being, all its parts are different expressions of the same energy, and they are all in communication with each other, therefore parts of an organic whole. ... It seems to me that this whole *alone* is worthy of the deeper sort of love. [Emphasis added][62]

Deep ecologists maintain that this primary identification with the "whole" is not at the expense of individual beings, since they too must be seen as part of the same all-inclusive self. But, as we have seen, the danger with widening one's identification to the "whole" or biotic community (as in the case of Leopold) is that one may widen it beyond the reach of individual beings.[63] This preference for identification with the larger "whole" may be seen to reflect the familiar masculine urge to transcend the concrete world of particularity in search for something more enduring and abstract.

FORMING AN ECOFEMINIST IDENTITY

Deep ecologists would have us believe that self-realization is a simple process of expanding one's identity to all of the natural world. We have seen, however, what problems this process may entail. When, in the name of self-realization, sunbathing can be equated with killing a living being, we must question the value of this abstract norm. The foregoing analysis can, thus, be helpful in pointing to the ways in which ecofeminist philosophy might distinguish itself from deep ecology. Ecofeminists must continue to question the value of all gender-neutral generalizations. They must probe beneath such generalities to see what activities and motives they might conceal. When deep ecologists write of expanding the self, ecofeminists must be prepared to examine more deeply the unconscious drives that fuel the self that one seeks to expand.

We have seen that women and animals have been used as psychological instruments for the establishment of the masculine self. The conquest of the snake, the dragon, and other female-imaged monsters reflects the inner drives and needs of the masculine self. What we witness, in the experiences of the above-mentioned hunters, is the same conquest mentality now operating on an allegedly "higher" plane. Nonetheless, animals are still used as instruments of self-definition; they are killed not in the name of an individual, masculine ego but instead in the name of a higher, abstract self. But whether one is establishing the "self" writ small or the larger "Self," the experience of the animal — the loss of her or his life — remains the same.

As we have seen, the danger of an abstract identification with a larger "whole" is that it fails to recognize or respect the existence of independent, living beings. This has been one of the major failings of both environmental philosophy and the environmental movement. By alternately raising the ecosystem or an aggrandized Self to the level of supreme value, they have created a holism that risks obliterating the uniqueness and importance of individual beings. The disillusionment of many animal liberationists with both the environmental movement and environmental philosophy is a consequence of this fact.[64]

Ecofeminist philosophy must be wary of a holist philosophy that transcends the realm of individual beings. Our deep, holistic awareness of the interconnectedness of all of life must be a *lived* awareness that we experience in relation to *particular* beings *as well as* the larger "whole." As Carol Gilligan's research suggests, women's moral conduct is grounded in "contextual particularity," and the feelings of care and responsibility that such situations bring forth.[65] The emphasis is more on the image of an interconnected web than on that of an expanded self.[66]

If, as object-relations theory argues, women's self-identity, unlike that of men, is not bound up with the urge to negate one's dependence on the natural world, we should not be surprised to find that women's experiences with nature may differ from those of men. Although it cannot be claimed that no women hunt or experience their sense of nature in the ways described by the hunters above, most people, I believe, will recognize such behavior as primarily characteristic of men.[67] Throughout history, hunting has been, in fact, an activity that has been pursued by and large by men.

Many women have found other ways to experience their oneness or identification with nature. Charlene Spretnak writes that women often have such experiences through the "body parables," that is, "re-claimed menstruation, orgasm, pregnancy, natural childbirth and motherhood." She goes on to comment:

> Men, too, experience moments of heightened awareness when everything seems different, more vividly alive. They have often written that such instances occur during the hunting of large animals, the landing/ killing of a large fish, the moments just before and during combat. Not feeling intrinsically involved in the process of birthing and nature, nor strongly predisposed toward empathic communion, men may have turned their attention, for many eras, toward the other aspect of the cycle, death.[68]

We have seen that women's self-identity, unlike men's, is not established through violent opposition to the natural world. The guiding motive in women's self-identity is not the attainment of an autonomous self, but rather the preservation of a sense of connection to other living beings. This is not to say that women have not also been alienated from nature. A woman who buys or wears a fur coat has clearly accepted male standards of beauty, and hence the violence toward nature that such fashion entails.[69] The task for women, however, in contrast to that of men, may be to develop a *stronger* sense of separate identity while *simultaneously* recognizing their interconnection with other living beings.[70] Perhaps only in this way can women break free from male norms of violence and alienation, and reclaim their deep-felt connection to the natural world. As Alice Walker's character, Shug, observes, in the context of describing her experience of "being part of everything, not separate at all. . . . Before you can see anything at all . . . you have to git man off your eyeball."[71]

The development of an ecofeminist philosophy is analogous, in many ways, to this process of self-realization for women. Just as women must begin to develop a sense of our separate identities, so, too, must ecofeminism develop its own unique sense of "self." Ecofeminism, however, need not develop its "selfhood" by means of the masculine model of opposition. Indeed, ecofeminists need not oppose the philosophy of ecofeminism to that of deep ecology; on the contrary, we would do well to affirm those aspects of value in deep ecology and related philosophies. At the same time, ecofeminists would also do well to recognize the benefits to be gained for the identity of ecofeminism by contrasting its unique philosophy with other schools of thought. In the end, however, the foundation of ecofeminism and the source of its greatest strength lies in women's shared personal experiences vis-à-vis the natural world.

It is out of women's felt sense of connection to the natural world that an ecofeminist philosophy must be forged. Identification may, in fact, enter into this philosophy, but only to the extent that it flows from an *existing* connection with individual lives. Individual beings must not be used in a kind of psychological instrumentalism to help establish a *feeling* of connection that in reality does not exist. Our sense of union with nature must be connected with concrete, loving actions rather than being born from an "aggressive drive" to "fuse" an "alienated self."[72] The *quality* of connection is more important than the mere *existence* of a connection of any kind.

A holistic, ecofeminist ethic, as I conceive it, is a way of perceiving the world that invites us to affirm our interconnection with all of life, while at the same time acknowledging the distinction between ourselves and other living beings. It is an invocation to become "responsible" to nature, not in the sense of obligations and rights, but in the literal sense of our "ability for response." It is an appeal to attend to nature in order to detect, not what we might want from her, but rather, what she might want from us. It is, in short, an invitation to re-spect nature, literally to "look again."

Both ecofeminism and deep ecology have suggested, at times, that the new consciousness that each refers to is a consciousness of love. In this, and many other ways, ecofeminism and deep ecology concur. Love, however, can mean many things, and can be expressed in a variety of ways. As ecofeminism develops in relation to other philosophies, ecofeminists must carefully examine the practical consequences of all abstract ideals. Only then will ecofeminists know how far our own identification with these philosophies can go. But this is only one step in our journey toward self-identity. Our personal experiences and unfettered imaginations must take us the rest of the way.

NOTES

1. Some of the major works on ecofeminism include Leonie Caldecott and Stephanie Leland, eds., *Reclaim the Earth: Women Speak Out for Life on Earth* (London: Women's Press, 1983); Mary Daly, *Gyn/Ecology: The Meta-Ethics of Radical Feminism* (Boston: Beacon Press, 1978); Irene Diamond and Gloria Orenstein, eds., *Reweaving the World: The Emergence of Ecofeminism* (San Francisco: Sierra Club, 1990); Susan Griffin, *Woman and Nature: The Roaring Inside Her* (New York: Harper and Row, 1978); Carolyn Merchant, *The Death of Nature: Women, Ecology and the Scientific Revolution* (New York: Harper and Row, 1983); Judith Plant, ed., *Healing the Wounds: The Promise of Ecofeminism* (Philadelphia: New Society, 1989); Elizabeth Dodson Gray, *Green Paradise Lost* (Wellesley, Mass.: Roundtable Press, 1981); and *Heresies #13: Feminism and Ecology* 4 (1981); Andrée Collard with Joyce Contrucci, *Rape of the Wild: Men's Violence against Nature and the Earth* (Bloomington, Ind.: Indiana University Press, 1989).

2. Gray, *Green Paradise Lost.*

3. Neil Evernden, "The Environmentalist Dilemma," *Trumpeter: Journal of Ecophilosophy*, vol. 5, no. 1 (Winter 1988): 5.

4. Charlene Spretnak, "Our Roots and Flowering," in Diamond and Orenstein, eds., *Reweaving the World.*

5. The status of truth claims is a much debated topic in feminist theory. Although not all feminists (or ecofeminists) are willing to relinquish all claims to "objectivity" and "truth," most are agreed that the current definitions are derived

from men. For an in-depth analysis of how the quest for "objectivity" reflects masculine drives and needs, see Evelyn Fox Keller, *Gender and Science* (New Haven, Conn.: Yale University Press, 1985).

6. Carol Gilligan, *In a Different Voice* (Cambridge, Mass.: Harvard University Press, 1982), p. 100.

7. Bill Devall and George Sessions, *Deep Ecology: Living as if Nature Mattered* (Salt Lake City, Utah: Peregrine Smith Books, 1985), p. 8.

8. George Sessions, *Ecophilosophy* VI (May 1984): 12

9. Warwick Fox, "On the Guiding Stars to Deep Ecology: A Reply to Naess," *The Ecologist* 14 (1984): 203–4.

10. Quoted in Bill Devall, "Greenies: Observations on the Deep, Long-Range Ecology Movement in Australia," ms., 1984, p. 17.

11. George Sessions, *Ecophilosophy* III (April 1981): 5a.

12. Devall and Sessions, p. 67.

13. George Sessions, *Ecophilosophy* III, (April 1981): 5–5a.

14. Devall and Sessions, p. 68.

15. For a sustained critique of deep ecology for its emphasis on anthropocentrism as opposed to androcentrism, see Ariel Kay Salleh, "Deeper than Deep Ecology: The Ecofeminist Connection," *Environmental Ethics* 6 (1984): 339–345.

16. One of the significant trends within current feminist philosophy has been the recognition of the role of unconscious drives in the production of apparently abstract and universal knowledge. According to Jane Flax, feminist philosophy thus represents the "return of the repressed." See "The Patriarchal Unconscious," in *Discovering Reality: Feminist Perspectives on Epistemology, Methodology, and Philosophy of Science*, ed. Sandra Harding and Merrill B. Hintikka (Boston: D. Reidel, 1983), p. 249.

17. Simone de Beauvoir, *The Second Sex*, trans. H. M. Parshley (New York: Vintage Books, 1974), p. xxxiii.

18. Ibid., p. 74.

19. Ibid., p. 72.

20. For further feminist critique of the notion of transcendence in the thought of Hegel, Sartre and de Beauvoir, see Genevieve Lloyd, "Masters, Slaves and Others," in *Radical Philosophy*, ed. Ray Edley and Richard Osborn (Thetford, Norfolk: Thetford Press, 1985), pp. 291–309.

21. The masculine ideal of autonomy is not always depicted as a story of conquest. For a brilliant analysis of the multiple manifestations of the masculine "separative self," see Catherine Keller, *From a Broken Web: Separation, Sexism, and Self* (Boston: Beacon Press, 1986). According to Keller, the serene, rational, single God depicted by Aristotle as the Unmoved Mover achieves the same ideal of autonomy. As she states, "No wonder both the Greek and the Hebrew deities achieve an image of absolute independence from their worlds. They fulfill the heroic ego's impossible wish for an inpenetrable dominion and for the final conquest of the too penetrable, permeating force-field of femaleness (p. 87). Similarly, the Christian concept of an omnipotent, transcendent, and eternal God reflects the masculine ideal of the autonomous self. Also see Evelyn Fox Keller, *Gender and Science*.

22. *The Great Cosmic Mother: Rediscovering the Religion of the Earth* (San Francisco: Harper and Row, 1987), pp. 250–251.

23. Erich Neumann, *The Origins and History of Consciousness*, trans. R. F. C. Hull (Princeton, N.J.: Bollingen Series XLII/Princeton University Press, 1974).

24. In Reginald E. Allen, *Greek Philosophy: Thales to Aristotle*, rev. and enl. ed. (New York: Macmillan Free Press, 1966), p. 254.

25. See Max Horkheimer and Theodor W. Adorno, *Dialectic of Enlightenment*, trans. John Cumming (New York: Herder and Herder, 1972). See also Herbert Marcuse, *An Essay on Liberation* (Boston: Beacon Press, 1969).

26. Susan Griffin, *Pornography and Silence: Culture's Revenge against Nature* (New York: Harper and Row, 1981), p. 97.

27. Nancy Chodorow, *The Reproduction of Mothering* (Berkeley: University of California Press, 1978).

28. Ibid., p. 167.

29. Dorothy Dinnerstein, *The Mermaid and the Minotaur: Sexual Arrangements and Human Malaise* (New York: Harper and Row, 1976), p. 246.

30. For femininist critiques of both Chodorow and Dinnerstein for their emphasis on the primacy of sexual arrangements in determining gender identity, see Pauline Bart, "Review of Chodorow's *The Reproduction of Mothering*," in *Mothering: Essays in Feminist Theory*, ed. Joyce Trebilcot (Totowa, N.J.: Rowman and Allanheld, 1984), pp. 147–152. See also, in the same volume, Iris Young's "Is Male Gender Identity the Cause of Male Dominance?," pp. 129–146.

31. "The Hunter as Alert Man: An Overview of the Origin of the Human/Animal Connection," in *The Human/Animal Connection*, ed. Randall L. Eaton (Incline Village, Nev: Carnivore Journal and Sierra Nevada College Press, 1985), p. 9.

32. Ibid., pp. 9–10.

33. Ibid., p. 47.

34. Ortega y Gassett was cited with approval by deep ecologist Bill Devall in a recent Elmwood Institute dialogue. According to Devall, Ortega's reflections exemplify the proper attitude toward hunting. "Whose Ecology: The Deep, the Socialist, or the Feminist?" (San Francisco, August, 1989).

35. *Meditations on Hunting*, trans. Howard B. Wescott, with a Foreword by Paul Shepard (New York: Charles Scribner's, 1985), p. 121.

36. Ibid.

37. Ibid., p. 124.

38. The erotic aspect of the hunting experience is also tellingly revealed by language. Thus, the word "venery" means both the "art of hunting" and "the pursuit of sexual pleasure," and the word "venison" is derived from the name of the Roman goddess of love.

39. Aldo Leopold, *A Sand County Almanac with essays on Conservation from Round River* (Oxford: Oxford University Press, 1966), p. 229.

40. Ortega y Gasset, p. 123.

41. Ibid., p. 92.

42. Ibid., p. 121.

43. Ibid., p. 29.

44. Leopold, p. 227.

45. Ibid., p. 232.

46. I have omitted discussion of subsistence hunting in this essay since it presents a far more complex situation. Although hunting, in most tribal cultures, was (and is) typically associated with rituals and norms of masculine identity, the situation is complicated by the fact that some hunting may have been (or still may be) necessary for survival in such societies because of climatic and other environmental factors. Deep ecologists and other environmentalists often justify their support of

hunting by pointing to the example of native cultures. This ignores, however, the very real differences in killing for reasons of survival and killing in order to achieve a particular psychological state.

47. Leopold, p. 227.

48. Ortega y Gassett, p. 88.

49. For more on Western culture's coupling of love and death, see Denis de Rougement, trans. Montgomery Belgion, *Love in the Western World* (New York: Pantheon, 1956). See also Georges Bataille, *Death and Sensuality* (New York: Ballantine Books, 1969).

50. "The Feminist Standpoint," in *Discovering Reality*, ed. Sandra Harding and Merrill B. Hintikka, p. 300.

51. Leopold, p. 230.

52. The parallel attitude toward women is not difficult to discern. Men are "lured" by women's "beauty." Women are possessed by such acts of violence as pornography and rape.

53. Ortega y Gasset, pp. 96–97.

54. Leopold, p. 227.

55. Ibid.

56. Ibid., p. 239.

57. Ibid., p. 238.

58. Ortega y Gassett, p. 98.

59. Quoted in Devall and Sessions, p. 75.

60. Ibid., p. 188.

61. "Approaching Deep Ecology: A Response to Richard Sylvan's Critique of Deep Ecology," *Environmental Studies Occasional Paper* 20, University of Tasmania, 1986.

62. Quoted in Devall and Sessions, p. 101.

63. An example of this danger may be found in the philosophy of Spinoza, which provides an important inspiration for deep ecologists. Spinoza argued that the attainment of a higher self was to be achieved through a correct understanding of God/Nature—that is, through a unification of Mind and Nature. This understanding, however, did not include a respect for animals, for whom Spinoza felt deep contempt. In his words: "It is plain that the law against the slaughtering of animals is founded rather on vain superstition and womanish pity than sound reason." (Note I to Prop. xxxvii, pt. IV of the *Ethics*; in R. H. M. Elwes, trans., *The Chief Works of Benedict de Spinoze*, vol. 2 (New York: Dover, 1955), p. 213. Although deep ecologists dismiss Spinoza's speciesism as an "anomaly" (Devall and Sessions, p. 240), this disparity should underline some of the perils of grounding one's morality in an abstract conception of unity, rather than in a felt sense of connection to individual beings.

64. For a feminist critique of the dualistic mentality that underlies the current divisions between animal-liberation and environmental philosophies, see Marti Kheel, "The Liberation of Nature: A Circular Affair," *Environmental Ethics* 7 (Summer 1985): 135–149.

65. Gilligan, p. 182.

66. For an in-depth critique of deep ecology for its adherence to an abstract vision of unity, in contrast to the development of an ethical voice that emerges from the contextual particularities of one's human community or niche, see Jim Cheney,

"The Neo-Stoicism of Radical Environmentalism," *Environmental Ethics*, vol. 2, no. 4 (Winter 1989): 293–325.

67. A study by Stephen Kellert and Joyce Berry confirms that there are, in fact, "dramatic" differences in men's and women's attitudes toward animals. According to their study: "The strength and consistency of male vs. female differences were so pronounced as to suggest gender is among the most important influences on attitudes toward animals in our society." ("Attitudes, Knowledge and Behaviors Toward Wildlife as Affected by Gender," *Wildlife Society Bulletin*, vol. 15, no. 3 [Fall 1987]: 365).

In discussing these differences, the authors point to the consistency of their findings with Carol Gilligan's research. In their words: "The postulate of a female moral emphasis on caring for intimates, nonaggressiveness, and compassion is consistent with our findings that women tend to assert strong emotional attachments to individual domestic animals and object to a wide variety of activities involving the possible infliction of cruelty, harm and suffering on animals. . . . Also consistent with Gilligan's (1982) model, males were characterized by a more cognitive and logically abstract perception of animals, reflected in substantially greater knowledge of animals and ecological concern for the relationship of wildlife to natural habitats. A further consistency was the tendency of males to derive greater satisfaction than females from competition and mastery over animals, as well as from their own exploitation. (Ibid., p. 369).

68. Charlene Spretnak, ed. *The Politics of Women's Spirituality* (New York: Anchor Books, 1982), p. xvii.

69. Clearly, some of the alienation from nature that women experience is facilitated by a physical alienation from the actuality of violence. The women who wear fur coats have been carefully shielded from the violence that the manufacture of furs entail. In order to break free from such alienation, it is, therefore, necessary for women to break through the mystification that surrounds so much of the violence of the modern world.

70. A similar point is made by Valerie Saivings, who critiques religious and theological traditions that posit a gender-neutral notion of sin as pride or self-aggrandizement. She argues that sin, for women, is more apt to take the form of "underdevelopment or negation of the self." Saivings, thus, concludes that "the feminine dilemma is, in fact, precisely the opposite of the masculine." "The Human Situation: A Feminine View," in *Womanspirit Rising: A Feminist Reader in Religion*, ed. Carol Christ and Judith Plaskow (San Francisco: Harper and Row, 1979), pp. 24–42. See also Susan Nelson Dunfee, "The Sin of Hiding: A Feminist Critique of Reinhold Niebuhr's Account of Sin," *Soundings*, vol. LXV, no. 3 (Fall 1982): 317–327, and Ann Carolyn Klein, "Finding A Self: Buddhist and Feminist Perspectives," in *Shaping New Visions: Gender and Values in American Culture*, ed. Clarissa W. Atkinson, Constance H. Buchanan, and Margaret R. Miles (Ann Arbor, Mich.: UMI Research Press, 1987), pp. 191–218.

71. Alice Walker, *The Color Purple* (New York: Pocket Books, 1982), p. 178.

72. For a discussion of the drive toward fusion with an aggrandized Self as a manifestation of the atomistically defined (primary male) self's attempt to overcome alienation, see Jim Cheney, "Ecofeminism and Deep Ecology," *Environmental Ethics*, vol. 9, no. 2 (Summer 1987): 115–145. See also Cheney, "Neo-Stoicism of Radical Environmentalism."

7

Reflections on the Exploitation of the Amazon in Light of Liberation Theology

JAMES LOCKMAN, O.F.M.

Brother Jim Lockman uses the demise of the Amazon rain forest to illustrate the major thesis of this book: the unsustainable exploitation of an ecosystem through a politics of domination is inseparable in its history from the exploitative domination of the people in that ecosystem. Unsustainable efforts at exploiting other rain forests, including the Hawaiian and Northwest temperate rain forests in the United States, are resulting in similar politics of domination. Liberation theology, particularly as it has been developed in Central and South America, contains a theological method for reflecting on the lives of dominated peoples toward the end of overcoming that domination. An awareness and inclusion of the ecological factor in the socioanalytical method of liberation theology will deepen that method and make it appropriate for ecological theology.

INTRODUCTION

I can remember from childhood the *National Geographic* photographic essays of the Amazon, picturing the dense, mysterious jungle, with its lush, tropical vegetation, its mighty rivers, and its primitive people. Those were the days, now some thirty years ago, when schemes for development of the isolated and roadless wilderness of the Amazon were, for the most part, only dreams. It was thought then that the rain forest would provide endless resources and rich agricultural yields, though those projections themselves were not based on knowledge or experience of that environment.

165

Since that time, Brazil has plunged headlong into "development" of its portion of the Amazon (65 percent of the total rain forest of the basin is in Brazil). In recent years, assessments of these activities have made headline stories in the media. For instance, in its March 1987 issue, *Smithsonian* featured an article on rain forest destruction, especially in the Amazon Basin. In June of that year, the *Los Angeles Times* ran a series of front-page articles on deforestation, focusing again on recent activity in the Amazon. In January 1988, the *New York Times Magazine* featured a cover article on the mysteries of the rain forest, emphasizing just what the human community may lose in the wake of its demise. The April 30, 1988, edition of *The Nation* featured an article entitled "Financing Ecocide," which discussed the financing of rain forest destruction, particularly in Brazil, by first-world capitalist development organizations. The September 18, 1989 edition of *Time* featured a cover article, complete with dramatic full-color pictures, describing the destruction of the Amazon rain forest as "one of the great tragedies of history." Brazil's plunge into the development of the Amazon, as the range of these popular articles indicates, presents a complex, multidimensional problem.

The debate on current activity in the Amazon has not been limited, of course, to the popular press. Major academic disciplines, especially in the natural and social sciences, have studied pieces of the problem of current rain forest exploitation. Most of the experts, from Latin America to North America and Europe, warn that development should proceed cautiously, or not at all, until more is known about both sustainable potential and long-range consequences of development. Yet we are told that the forest is disappearing at such a fast rate that within a few decades it will be gone. Moreover, the experts say, the demise of the rain forest is irreversible and will have profound global consequences.

"Ecocide" and the ensuing environmental ramifications are not the only potential problems. The human community of the Amazon is one of the poorest on earth. Development promised economic relief for these people and economic opportunity for many of Brazil's poor from other parts of the country. Nevertheless, the current state of most of the population of the Amazon region is one of profound misery. Patterns of unemployment, poverty, and violence in the Amazon resemble the worst of conditions in Brazil's poverty-stricken northeast and its southern urban centers.

Many today approach the demise of the Amazon rain forest with both a sense of urgency and one of frustration. The historical interconnection between the exploitation of the environment and the human community in the Amazon Basin presents a multidimensional problem of analysis for those seeking to promote systemic change responsive to both the ecological and the human needs of the area. We cannot consider the ecological issues without considering the socioeconomic and political issues and vice versa. Nor can we to the north dictate to the Brazilians what they alone should do to resolve the current crisis in the Amazon. Yet, as shall be discussed in this essay, all of us are affected now, and will be to a much greater degree in the future, by the current trend in destructive exploitation now taking place in the world's largest remaining rain forest.

The core of the approach taken here is to locate ourselves in the current crisis of exploitation in the Amazon Basin. Is it enough simply to become familiar with the facts, both about ecology and the social conditions of the region? I think not. I will propose a theological context derived from liberation theology from which to view the exploitation of the Amazon, one that will help us to locate ourselves in this crisis. I will begin by surveying the ecology of the rain forest, the consequences of its destruction, and the history of its exploitation. This will provide us with data to which we can apply a form of social analysis used in liberation theology. I will conclude with some considerations for a theology of the rain forest.

THE RAIN FOREST OF THE AMAZON

Biologists consider tropical rain forests worldwide to be among the most extensive, diverse, and least well known of all the ecosystems on earth. The rain forest of the Amazon Basin is by far the largest remaining representative of this fascinating biome (see Table 7.1 on p. 168). Occurring mostly within the national boundaries of Brazil, portions of the Amazon rain forest also occur in Bolivia, Colombia, Ecuador, Peru, Venezuela, and Guyana (see map, p. 168).[1] Given the former and even the present extent of this biome, it may seem at first incomprehensible that it could ever be threatened, yet biologists and geographers tell us that this biome may cease to exist by the middle of the next century. Indeed, some suggest that the end may be only a few years away.[2]

Ecologists describe the threatened tropical rain forest as a dense, evergreen forest structured in layers of under-story, middle-story, and upper-story zones. The tallest trees reach 200–250 feet, and often are festooned with vines and epiphytic plants (those growing nonparasitically on the branches of trees), the most noticeable being orchids and bromeliads (plants of the pineapple family). The seeming homogeneity and vastness of the green expanse belie the incredible diversity of plant life. The nearly even year-round climate can lull the casual observer into thinking that one patch of forest is the same as any other. No doubt, these characteristics have contributed to the idea that the rain forest could give way, when cleared, to a similarly productive agricultural system of high-yielding crops year round, land for the landless, and much-needed revenue for the developing nations in which the rain forests of the world are located. However, the ecological issues are far more complex. Scientists worldwide are warning that development for any purpose may have disastrous consequences for the biome itself, for global meteorological conditions, and even the future well-being of the human race.

The enormous ecological complexity of tropical rain forests is only begin-

Table 7.1
Location and Size of Rain Forests World-Wide

Location of Rain Forests	Area in Millions of Square Miles
Amazon Basin	2.1
Asia	0.5
Africa	0.3
Worldwide Total	2.9
Brazilian Amazon	1.4

Source: Adapted from UNESCO, *Tropical Forest Ecosystems: A State-of-Knowledge Report* (Paris: UNESCO, 1979), p. 22.

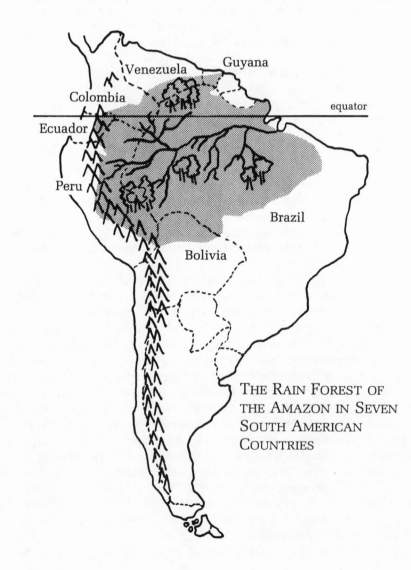

THE RAIN FOREST OF
THE AMAZON IN SEVEN
SOUTH AMERICAN
COUNTRIES

ning to be understood. In the absence of a thorough knowledge of its ecology, scientific literature abounds with seemingly contradictory claims of its fragility and resiliency, its stability and complexity, and its general and site-specific characteristics. Moreover, the study of tropical rain forest ecology has, in many ways, upset assumptions about ecosystems arrived at by the study of various relatively simple temperate biomes. Six major elements of rain forest ecology discussed below illustrate some of the unique features of this biome as well as point the way toward areas of environmental concern regarding development of the Amazon Basin.[3]

1. *Limited Seasonality.* Given its equatorial location and relative lack of elevational change, there is little seasonal change in the rain forest of the Amazon. Mean daily temperature, day length, and relative humidity are nearly the same throughout the year. Variation in rainfall is somewhat more significant, with most of the rain falling between October and May. The range of rainfall during these months is from 4 to 20 inches per month. The driest months occur from July to September, with rainfall ranging from 0.5 to 5 inches per month. Total rainfall in the Amazon Basin ranges from 78 to 108 inches annually, allowing for local variation in rainfall patterns. Ecologically, these variations are most notable in the treetops and on bare ground or heavily disturbed sites. The forest itself acts as a protective, self-regulating blanket so that seasonal fluctuations in solar radiation (higher during the drier months) and rainfall are minimized beneath the canopy.

2. *Species diversity.* About half of the 4.5 million species of plants and animals thought to occur worldwide are found only in the rain forest biome. Of these rain forest inhabitants, fewer than 25 percent have been catalogued by biologists, let alone studied in depth. By comparison, some two-thirds of temperate climate species have been identified and studied. Furthermore, some 5,000 species of fish are thought to occur in the Amazon Basin, about the same number as occur in the entire Atlantic Ocean. Some 30,000 species of flowering plants are thought to exist in the Amazon rain forest, as compared to 10,000 in all of temperate South America, or 50,000 for all of the North Temperate Zone. The Amazon supports some 10 percent of all plant species, most of which await *possible* discovery. Even more significant for biologists is the diversity and number of insect species. Four out of five rain forest species are insects, most of which occur in highly localized distributions and specialized relationships with the ecosystem, living in association with only one particular plant or animal species. As such, minor localized disruptions in the ecosystem could eliminate entire species.

The diversity of plants and animals found in rain forests represents an evolutionary process of millions of years. The rain forest itself is thought to be the oldest land-based ecosystem on earth. The biological richness of the rain forest is not only significant in what it may contain today, but it is also a sort of biological archive, a source of both species diversity and species evolution.[4]

3. *Vegetation types.* There are three major vegetation types in the Amazon Basin: the *terra firme*, the *varzea*, and the *igapó*. The *terra firme* forest is the nonflooded higher ground and occupies 94 percent of the Amazon Basin. It occurs on gently undulating terrain and has very poor soils. The typical species diversity of trees in this type of forest is 40–60 species per hectare (1 hectare = 2.5 acres), as compared to 10–15 per hectare in "rich" temperate forests. A five-hectare plot may have several hundred species of trees, whereas a temperate forest plot of similar size would top out at 20 species. The *varzea* is the floodplain along the Amazon River and its tributaries, and it supports both grassland and forest. It comprises about 2 percent of the Brazilian rain forest area, and its soils are periodically renewed by deposited silt. The *igapó*, or swamp forest, is permanently flooded, and takes up less than 1 percent of the Brazilian rain forest.

4. *Three-story structure.* Flying over the forest, one would notice occasional giants, the upper story, reaching high above the foliage mass to 200–250 feet. The dense continuous canopy of the middle story forms the roof of the forest at 125–175 feet. The upper part of this second story, together with the crowns of the emerging giant trees, comprise the richest life zone of the forest. Here, numerous epiphytic plants, insects, and arboreal vertebrates and birds live out their entire lives. This is also the least documented part of the forest, for clearly logistical reasons. The lower story is dominated by the dense, leafy canopy of the middle story. In some areas, the forest floor is relatively open because of the lack of light penetration. Also typical at the ground level is the constant environmental condition of high humidity and little air circulation.

5. *Soils and nutrient cycling.* The luxuriant growth of the rain forest would, at first glance, seem to indicate the presence of extremely rich soils. With the exception of the *varzea* (2 percent of the Brazilian Amazon) nothing could be further from the truth. According to Fearnside,[5] most of the *terra firme* soils are very old and highly leached. These soils, because of deep weathering, are nearly devoid of plant nutrients, but remain high in aluminum and iron oxides, making them extremely acidic. Phosphorus, a major essential plant nutrient, is rendered totally unavailable to plant roots by the usual acidity of rain forest soils. Organic litter generated by the forest is quickly mineralized. Loam-type soils so familiar in fertile areas of the Temperate Zone are nonexistent in the *terra firme* areas. The entire nutrient reserves required by the forest are contained in the living and dead biomass.[6] Since forest litter is mineralized so rapidly, and since the roots are never really dormant, nutrients present in decaying organic matter are released into the soil and immediately taken up by the dense root mass near the surface of the forest floor. Virtually nothing is lost to leaching. Indeed, the mineral content of water in streams is close to that of distilled water. This sort of nutrient cycling is the opposite of the modern agricultural ecosystem, which depends on high annual inputs of nutrients in order to be sustained. Because of the rapid cycling of nutrients, the rain forest

can grow on the same site for thousands, even millions, of years, despite the very poor condition of the soil.

6. *Succession and primary/secondary growth.* Ecologists recognize the rain forest as a primary, or ancient, forest community.[7] In the Amazon rain forest, a primary forest can be sufficiently disturbed by the lightest logging practices; that is, with the removal of as few as five trees per hectare, the forest degrades to a secondary forest, with significant losses in structure and floristic composition.[8] This in turn dramatically affects animal life. The tropical rain forest is held together by such a complex web of ecological interactions that disturbances on one hectare may have effects for several kilometers. Natural causes, such as storm damage or fire (which is usually brought about in the primary rain forest by humans) can also trigger primary to secondary degradation. Following the disruption/destruction of primary forest, the resulting secondary succession produces a vegetation fundamentally different from that of the primary forest. In the rain forest biome, the secondary forest is dramatically less diverse. Depending on the size of the disruption, extinctions may have occurred. Still, initial regrowth is fast. Many more years are required, though, before the secondary forest develops into primary forest. Indeed, biologists estimate that, following destruction, rain forests may need a successional process of a thousand years or more before primary forest is reestablished, provided that significant reduction in the seed source has not occurred.[9] The degree to which primary tropical rain forest in the Amazon can be disturbed and still allow for even long-term secondary succession is now a matter of utmost concern to biologists studying that ecosystem.

ENVIRONMENTAL CONCERNS AND CONSEQUENCES OF RAIN FOREST USE

Widespread development, always involving deforestation, has already dramatically altered the rain forest biome worldwide. The threatened total destruction of the remaining stands of primary forest looms as a real possibility. The consequences of such activity are currently being hotly debated among scientists, land-use planners, developers, and politicians. Yet the ever-increasing rate of deforestation in the tropical rain forest biome may bring an end to the debate before significant, long-term questions are intelligently discussed. Clear-cut answers, however, may only be available to humanity in the form of an unimaginable and irreversible environmental disaster. Some of the major questions, concerns, and possible consequences are raised here to shed light on the true cost of current rain forest use.

First among these is the contribution of rain forest clearing to the *greenhouse effect*. The effect of increases in atmospheric carbon dioxide (CO_2) has been debated in scientific circles for some time, and the scientific community has come to a general agreement that increased amounts of CO_2 in the atmosphere could lead to a global warming trend over the next 100 years[10]. Early on, the debate centered on the release of CO_2 as part of industrial pollutants or from the burning of fossil fuels. But more recently, concern about accelerated CO_2 generation has been raised because of the practice of burning as the method of clearing tropical forestlands for agricultural or road-building purposes. Such extensive burning, and the extrapolation of the effects of future burning, based on the estimated amount of carbon in the rain forest biomass (thought to be about 50 percent of the total world carbon stored in plants), have led to projections of a much more rapid "greenhouse effect" than was earlier thought.[11]

Atmospheric doubling of CO_2 from preindustrial levels (1850) is now expected, based on these projections, to occur by 2030. Scientists estimate that by 2050, global temperatures will have risen by 2° to 3° C. As the oceans warm, the polar ice caps will almost certainly melt. Sea levels will rise and flood coastal cities. In all, at least a 15-foot increase in ocean levels is expected.[12] More ominous, and as yet less publicized, are the associated meteorological effects of polar warming. An open Arctic Ocean would result in a major shift of all climatic zones a hundred or more miles to the north. Major agricultural areas in the temperate zone could become arid; Mediterranean climates could also become significantly drier, reducing the west coast of North America, for example, to the hot, dry desert now typical of northern Mexico.[13] According to Nigel Smith, "a paradoxical situation could develop when more forest is cleared in the tropics to produce food and rainfall decreases in the maize- and wheat-growing belt of North America, thus producing a net loss of food for the world."[14] Though firm conclusions may come only with such catastrophic changes, Fearnside suggests that "the simple doubt that major and irreparable meteorological changes could occur should give pause to planners intent on promoting massive deforestation."[15]

Another anticipated consequence of deforestation is an increase in atmospheric nitrous oxide (N_2O), which is known to catalyze the breakdown of ozone (O_3) molecules. Ozone in the stratosphere is credited with absorbing solar ultraviolet radiation, thus shielding the earth's surface. Such radiation is known to cause, among other things, skin cancer in humans. It is also thought that even slightly increased levels of ultraviolet radiation could cause deleterious mutations in the agricultural gene pool, especially in grains, possibly resulting in a disastrous negative impact on food production.[16] The ozone layer and the holes now developing in it have, consequently, become a major global concern.

Rain forest clearing, according to Fearnside, appears to be one of the significant contributors to atmospheric N_2O.[17] Most other sources are also anthropogenic, with significant amounts being generated by fossil fuel combustion.[18] Deforestation is thought to be another major contributor for two reasons. The first is, again, burning of the biomass. The other is the tendency for bare soil, especially in recently cleared areas, to give off greater amounts of N_2O (chiefly from decaying organic matter) than the same areas when forested.[19] Once again, the long-term impact of deforestation on N_2O levels is unclear. Still, given the indications available today and the consequences of a depleted ozone shield tomorrow, the likely contributions of rain forest felling to N_2O levels cannot be ignored.

One of the great ironies in the debate on the future of the Amazon Basin is that a rain forest area can become a desert. The hydrologic cycle (the cycle of water through the environment) is a dynamic one, and this is especially apparent in the Amazon. Applying information discussed earlier about evapotranspiration (the combination of water vapor given off by physiological processes within the leaf and evaporation of water from the usually large leaf surface) in the rain forest, it becomes possible to imagine how the rain forest ecosystem produces its own weather, especially in terms of rainfall.

The contribution of evapotranspiration to rainfall in the Amazon Basin is estimated at about 55 percent of the total rainfall.[20] It is thought that rainfall on the eastern Andean foothills (the western edge of the Amazon Basin and the ultimate destination of weather systems moving through the basin) has been recycled four or five times between the mouth of the Amazon River and its precipitation in that area. Since evapotranspiration rates are directly related to leaf area, reducing leaf area by deforestation significantly reduces this process. Furthermore, evapotranspiration contributes significantly to the normally high relative humidity of the basin, during which the physiological processes within the leaf that generate water vapor are more active. Indeed, one of the main defenses against dry conditions is for the plant to shut down these processes by closing the stomatal pores in the leaf through which water vapor escapes as transpiration. Consequently, reducing leaf area reduces rainfall in the region. A significant loss of forest cover could lead to a significant decrease in the frequency of rainfall, as well as to an overall reduction in yearly precipitation.

An immediate secondary effect of reduced rainfall would be the demise of any remnant stands of rain forest growth. As pointed out earlier, even slight declines in precipitation could cause fatal water stress to the forest. As the climate of the basin becomes significantly drier, the vegetation would degrade to scrubland, and eventually to desert. Once again, when the complex and highly tuned balance of the rain forest ecosystem is tampered with, major dynamic changes can occur.

One of the predicted long-term effects of deforestation in the Amazon Basin related to the hydrologic cycle is increased albedo (ratio of reflected light to incident light). Such increases would be caused by a reduction of the evergreen forest cover. Increased albedo in the equatorial zones could significantly upset global rainfall patterns, with the likely result of decreased rainfall in the temperate zones (perhaps much sooner than a similar reduction caused by the "greenhouse effect"). The global climatic effects of Amazonian deforestation, summarized in Table 7.2, cannot be overstated.

The environmental consequences of deforestation in the Amazon rain

Table 7.2
Possible Macroclimatic Effects of Amazonian Deforestation

Item	Change	Effect
Carbon Dioxide	Increase	Global temperature increase
Nitrous Oxide	Increase	Global temperature increase; ultraviolet-radiation increase at ground level
Albedo	Increase	Decreased rainfall in temperate zones
Evapotranspiration	Decrease	Decreased rainfall in the Amazon Basin and neighboring regions; temperature increase due to decrease of heat-absorbing function of evapotranspiration
Rainfall	1. Decrease in total 2. Increase in length of dry season	Vegetation changes: climatic regime becomes unfavorable for rain forest; reinforces trend toward still dryer climate

Source: Adapted from Philip M. Fearnside, "Environmental Change and Deforestation in the Brazilian Amazon," in *Changes in the Amazon Basin: Man's Impact on Forest and Rivers*, ed. John Hemming (Manchester, U.K.: Manchester University Press, 1985), pp. 71–89.

forest discussed here are overwhelming. However, these horrors pale in the face of what is described by Brazilian ecologist José Lutzenberger:

> What we see today in Brazil and in much of Latin America is the biggest biological holocaust in the history of life. Never in the course of three and a half billion years, since the first stirrings of life on this planet, has there been such wholesale, accelerated, violent demolition of all living systems as today. We have passed the point where we only desecrate this or that scenic landscape, this or that ecosystem. We are now in the process of demolishing whole biomes.[21]

The genetic diversity of the Amazon rain forest is staggering. The loss of this ecosystem and its gene pool would have short-term and long-term negative consequences for humanity and for the very nature of life on this planet. Short-range effects include the loss of potentially new sources of food, both among plants and animals. The majority of Amazonian species have yet to be discovered, named, and studied. Of these, scientists surmise that there are potentially many new forms of food, fiber, oil, and fuel sources not yet known to the human community.[22] Such genetic diversity also offers the possibility of varietal improvement of current crops of tropical origin,[23] especially in yield and pest and disease resistance. In addition, the rain forest is a source of pharmaceutical chemicals. According to Myers,

> Tropical forests represent nature's main storehouse of raw materials for modern medicine. Plants alone offer a host of analgesics, antibiotics, heart drugs, enzymes, hormones, diuretics, anti-parasite compounds, ulcer treatments, dentifrices, laxatives, dysentery treatments, and anti-coagulants, among many others. The total number of plant-derived products in modern pharmacopoeias amounts to several thousand, including such well known trade products as emetine, scopolamine, and pilocarpine.[24]

He sees the tropical forest as a vast pharmaceutical factory, containing the largest number of medicinal plants of any biome. One could say without hyperbole that the array of potentially useful products obtainable from the rain forest is unimaginable.

The long-term effects of the obliteration of the rain forest gene pool may influence the very course of biological evolution. The thousands, perhaps millions, of species will wipe out millions and millions of years of evolution, not only of plants and animals, but also of the most complex biotic community in the world.[25] In the short term and in the long term, the degradation of the rain forest biome will impoverish both the human community and the whole rich and continually evolving array of plant and animal species in a way unknown before our time.

HUMAN ACTIVITY IN THE BRAZILIAN RAIN FOREST

Prior to the arrival of Europeans in the Amazon Basin in the early sixteenth century, most of the indigenous population lived in concentrated settlements in the *varzea*. The population estimate generally accepted today for the region at the time compares with the rural population figure for 1980, about 2.5 million.[26] For several thousand years, the indigenous peoples of the Amazon Basin applied a wide spectrum resource use, which generally allowed for renewal of their resources. Patterns of resource use allowed for long-term support of a relatively large population. Since this population was virtually isolated from the rest of the world until the sixteenth century, the peoples of the Amazon relied entirely on the resources of the forest. Their site-specific uses of resources reflected the ecological diversity of the Amazon. Their approach to the use of the forest relied on extensive knowledge of plants and animals, a cultural knowledge of the forest that allowed for sustained use of its resources without causing severe environmental destruction. This knowledge was highly specific according to the diversity of the ecosystem as a whole. Thus, local patterns of resource use reflected long-term accumulation of the experience of living with the rain forest environment, which contrasted sharply with developments after 1500.

The turning point in the ecological history of the Amazon Basin occurred with the arrival of the first Europeans in the early sixteenth century. If the history of human activity in the Amazon prior to 1500 could be characterized as one of a subsistence economy with limited resource exploitation and minimal ecological impact, then the post-Columbian period up to the present might be characterized as one of extractive resource exploitation accompanied by social impoverishment, violence, and irreversible cultural and ecological destruction. This section will examine the continuing and widening patterns of destructive exploitation since the early European penetration of the Amazon Basin.

The colonial conquest of the Amazon during the sixteenth and seventeenth centuries was gradual. Spanish, Portuguese, Dutch, French, and English naval forces fought for control of the delta region to secure new sugar-producing areas. In the process, indigenous settlements along the lower river were destroyed, pushing the forest peoples upriver and/or away from it into the *terra firme*. As the power of the Portuguese increased in the region, their plantations needed workers, and the indigenous peoples became victims of a local slave trade. When these populations scattered or were enslaved, the highly successful and ecologically stable adaptation of the first inhabitants to the *varzea* and the site-specific knowledge needed for the maintenance of this system were lost.[27] Local populations not displaced by military activity or the slave trade were subjected to new and decimating diseases, including smallpox, influenza, and measles. By the early eighteenth century, many of the indigenous settlements on or near the riverways of the lower Amazon Basin were entirely lost.

As colonial power became established in the Amazon, the economy of the area moved from subsistence-level self-sufficiency to an ever-more-dependent export-oriented, or extractive, economy. In the larger picture, the Amazon became a vast resource base for distant centers of consumption and production. Colonial powers extracted what was profitable from the land with little concern for sustained yields, or, more importantly, internal development. As local labor power was siphoned away from subsistence activities, a spiraling system of credit indebtedness was forced on the inhabitants, making them extremely vulnerable to exploitive overlords. The exorbitant costs of imported basic food and of fiber no longer produced locally, as well as the price of necessary equipment for the extractive work, were higher than the remuneration for gathered forest products. Moreover, market fluctuations, together with dwindling resources made the local population even more susceptible to cyclical impoverishment, while the few who profited from the extractive economy were able to move from place to place in search of new, rapidly exploitable exports.

Value was concentrated at the other end of this raw-material export trade. According to Steven Bunker,

> When natural resources are extracted from one regional ecosystem to be transformed and consumed in another, the resource-exporting region loses values that occur in its physical environment. These losses eventually decelerate the extractive region's economy, while the resource-consuming communities gain value and their economies accelerate.[28]

As the extractive process proceeded, the area of concentration of materials, manufacturing, consumption, and profits became the (usually urban) core of the economic system, while the area exploited and depleted of resources became the periphery.

The local economy of the Amazon periphery was dictated by the ephemeral nature of extractive economies, characterized not only by dependence on the core for vital necessities but also by destabilization and dislocation of populations and their infrastructure. As the urban core areas became enriched and more highly organized economically and socially (that is, developed), the Amazon periphery collapsed into stagnation and poverty, becoming progressively underdeveloped. As local systems of political and social organization crumbled, its people became increasingly vulnerable, powerless, and voiceless.

Short-term profits and unsustainable economies, together with the decimation of indigenous populations and culture, were characteristics of colonial activity in the Amazon. Though profits ultimately enriched the colonial power in this period, the pattern of extractivism did not change with Brazil's independence from Portugal in 1822, since production, development, and profits in the core necessitated extraction from the periphery. Local elites simply took over a colonial economic system, with its core remaining in the areas of economic concentration. In economic relationships, the Amazon Basin continued to be peripheral in both the Brazilian and international economies and thus subject to spiraling impoverishment and underdevelopment. It should not be surprising, then, that the postcolonial history of the Amazon continued to be characterized by waves of extractivism.

A major example of this is the rubber boom of 1850 to 1910. The Amazon Basin was the world's major source of rubber latex, since the rubber tree is a native species of that region. Demand for the product soared in the mid-1800s with the discovery of vulcanization and the subsequent manufacturing of rubber tires. With the development of the automobile, increased demand led to increased exploitation of a new wave of immigrant laborers, because the local indigenous population had been virtually depleted as a labor source during colonial times.[29]

The basic economic structure of colonial extractivism remained in place during this period. Profits from rubber exports accumulated in the centers of economic activity far from the Amazon Basin. Labor practices resembled slavery. Local populations continued to be decimated. Local knowledge of the forest continued to be lost. When the rubber boom collapsed shortly after the turn of the century, it failed to leave behind any lasting economic or social development. It repeated past extractive patterns in the Amazon: the rapid enrichment of a few followed by sudden collapse and enduring poverty for most of the population. And, without any local structures among the poor capable of spurring internal development, and because of the isolation of the population groups from each other and the outside world, there was little hope for the alleviation of their misery.

Brazilian interests, following the collapse of the rubber boom, were focused on the more temperate south, with its established agricultural and industrial bases and its large population centers. Only a few individual attempts were made in the Amazon, and each typically ended in failure. With the military coup of 1964, however, government interest in developing the region rapidly emerged and inaugurated the present-day rush to development in the rain forest region.

Since then, Brazil's national government has promoted rapid industrialization following a model of capitalist development. International capital has supplied the money to fuel this development, but at the cost of the now-infamous foreign debt of $100 billion. While a few in Brazil have prospered, and Brazil as a nation has entered into the circle of modern developing states, the vast majority of Brazil's population remains poor or destitute.[30] In his sharp critique of his government's development policy, Brazilian ecologist José Lutzenberger says, "Their definition of development was a technocratic one—an economic model geared to making the strong ever stronger and the poor ever weaker."[31] As Brazil has entered into the modern capitalistic world, private capital accumulation has accelerated. In addition, ownership of much of the best agricultural land, whose purpose and production are subordinate to the requirements of industrialization, has become highly concentrated. And as development in Brazil has occurred mostly in the southern part of the country, the Amazon Basin has continued to be on the periphery, and is thus seen primarily in the light of extractable resources, with little or no consideration given to their protection, conservation, or sustainability. This is the context of Brazil's present-day colonization of that region.

Soon after it came to power, the military government of Brazil began a campaign to improve access to the Amazon region, which comprises 59 percent of the nation's territory. Road-building and colonization projects became the responsibility of a newly created bureaucracy, the Superintendency for Development of the Amazon (SUDAM), in 1966. Four years later, President Medici, in a widely publicized emotional speech to drought victims of the northeast, promised to provide "land for men without land in a land without men."[32] Central to this promise was the National Integration Program for incorporating the territory of the Amazon Basin into the rest of the nation, requiring the construction of the Transamazon Highway, which would stretch from Recife on the Atlantic coast to the Peruvian border, a total of 5,400 kilometers, 60 percent of which is in the rain forest. With its connecting roads, this new highway system would provide access to Brazil's Amazon frontier.

In light of the government's official emphasis on social factors and economic benefit to the country, some observers suggest a third, and even more compelling, reason for Brazil's push to integrate the Amazon into the rest of the nation. According to Smith, Fearnside, and Bunker, geopolitical considerations, though not publicly acknowledged, were paramount in the decision to build the highway system and integrate the Amazon Basin.[33] Fear of foreign interference in, or even accession of, the Amazon, a view promoted by the prominent Brazilian historian A. F. Reis, has been recurrent in Brazil for years.[34] Even the rhetoric of the National Integration Plan reveals this fear: "mark, by the presence of Brazilian men in Amazonian lands, the conquest for themselves and for their country, of that which belonged to them, so that no one would ever dare to contest them on this objective."[35] The government, preoccupied with this extensive unsecured territory, was determined to colonize and exploit its resources, especially in light of its need for foreign exchange to finance development, before anyone else moved in. Together with the road-building project, the installation of several army garrisons along the highway in the early 1970s further emphasized the national security motivation for developing and defending the vast Amazon territory for Brazilian interests.

The highly touted social objectives of Amazon development were rooted in the very serious problems of poverty, unemployment, and landlessness in both the drought-stricken northeast and the industrialized south. Resettlement of the country's disenfranchised into the Amazon Basin was seen as the solution, though the real problem of extreme inequality of land-tenure distribution was not addressed.[36] The government bureaucracy developed its own series of plans to settle the newly opened rain forest lands (all *terra firme*), though these were most often developed without any site inspection, let alone understanding of ecological factors. Furthermore, none of these plans was ever conceivably adequate to serve as a substitute for real land reform. Landless peasants, only a small number of whom were part of the government resettlement program, rushed to the area as new roads opened up unoccupied territory. Clearing land to which they held no legal title and farming land incapable of supporting crops for more than three to five years, this latest wave of immigrants quickly became victims of crop failure and, according to Bunker, large ranching, mining, and lumbering concerns, which moved in quickly behind the peasants. These large companies had access to force, fraud, legal services, and government subsidies that enabled them to drive those peasants who did not leave their land voluntarily.[37] Thus, in this early phase, while the initial land clearing was done by small farmers hoping to settle, it was the large corporate interests that ultimately benefited, while the poor became part of a migratory labor force or the swelling ranks of unemployed already congregating in the few Amazonian cities. "Recent peasant migrants," says Bunker, "displaced by the advance of large, government subsidized extractive industries into the jungle lands they have cleared, constitute the majority population of many new towns."[38]

Within a few years, the government officially gave up any attempt at small-scale colonization and began to openly encourage large-scale capitalist enterprises. Its attempts to exert any real control on this type of development while at the same time stimulating it have suffered setback after setback. The contradiction and infighting of the government bureaucracy made up of agencies at cross purposes to each other have led, once again, to a free reign of corporate interests bent on short-term gain.

While small-scale farm colonization occurred to some degree during the initial phase of the current wave of development, large-scale cattle ranching has been the predominant agricultural enterprise in the Amazon Basin. The destruction of forests for cattle ranches has been the principal cause of widespread "conversion," or the replacement of the original ecosystem with another. According to Susanna Hecht, as much as 95 percent of all land cleared in the Brazilian Amazon is now used for cattle ranching.[39] Unlike earlier, small-scale farms, which usually averaged about 100 hectares per family, these mostly corporate ranch lands average 10,000 hectares. Some of the largest, owned by such multinational corporations as Volkswagen and Armour-Swift, exceed 100,000 hectares.[40] To these corporate interests, SUDAM offers fiscal incentives of up to 50 percent of annual corporate taxes to encourage cattle ranching. Because these fiscal incentives are extended only to corporate interests, and require rapid forest clearance, the Amazon's natural and human resources are subordinated to corporate concerns with large profits and government interest in "settling" the frontier and eventually exploiting the international beef market.[41]

Most of the land presently being cleared for pasture is being converted directly from forest rather than from the consolidation of small peasant farms, since the process of dislocating small-scale colonizers is now largely completed, and, with the demise of weak government support, land is no longer available for new small-scale farmers. The heavy machinery and herbicides, including Agent Orange, used in this type of land clearing, together with the huge segments of land cleared at one time, virtually guarantee the irreversibility of the deforestation process.[42] Furthermore, little effort is made to harvest the wood once it is felled since, according to Bunker, neither the government nor the ranchers have been willing to invest the time or money necessary to cut and transport the vast timber resources.[43] Instead, the land is burned and the lumber wasted.

Of the 280 million hectares of rain forest in the Brazilian Amazon, about

11.3 million acres had been cleared, almost entirely for pasture, by 1975, at the rate of 1 million hectares per year.[44] By 1979, according to Myers, about 10 percent of the forest had been cleared, totaling about 26 million hectares.[45] Fearnside notes that the rate of clearing is not linear but, rather, exponential, and is closely tied to government road building in the region, financed largely by World Bank funds.[46] He estimates that at present exponential rates of *increase* in deforestation, some territories, such as Rondonia, once completely forested, may be totally cleared within a few years.[47] Again, most of this land is being used for export-beef production.

Establishment of these cattle ranches has not only destroyed a huge area of forest. As noted earlier, soils in the area are very poor, shallow, and mostly sandy. With the loss of forest cover, the soils quickly erode. The introduction of cattle brings the danger, especially in wet weather, of soil compaction. These two factors, erosion and compaction, severely damage the already fragile, poor soils. Introduced grasses thrive for only a few years on the nutrients left by the burning of the forest. After that, with soil nutrients either leached by the rains or exported in animal carcasses, the grasses deteriorate, and within five to ten years the land can no longer be used for pasture, having become choked with weeds and brush usually toxic to livestock. Areas cleared are too large and too damaged to be recolonized by plant species capable of beginning a successionary process. Thus, for the sake of quick profits and geopolitical claims, vast tracts of the Amazon rain forest may be permanently lost to future human use or biological recovery.[48]

Brazilian interest in cattle ranching in the Amazon has been fed, in part, by the expectation of a world shortage of beef predicted by the Food and Agricultural Organization of the United Nations by the 1990s. According to Myers, Brazil is determined to become the major beef-exporting country.[49] Ironically, because of the lack of sustainability of such an enterprise in the Amazon Basin, Brazil's goal will never be reached. A few will become rich, but many more local people will be further impoverished, not to mention the global and long-range biological catastrophe such activity will bring on us all. Furthermore, if the ecosystem were managed effectively, a far greater yield in fish protein could be realized from the rivers of the basin than could ever be produced by cattle.[50] According to Myers, estimates suggest that Amazonian fish could supply Brazil's entire requirements for animal protein and produce a surplus for export.[51] Moreover, fishing has historically been a local, small-scale, broad-based activity, and, with proper management, could not only be sustainable in the long term but offer employment and the means to local development for a far greater number of people than capital-intensive ranching. Cattle ranching in the Amazon, then, may be seen as another example in a historic trend of the economics of extractivism, with little interest shown in long-term sustainability or local development. Brazil's current development scheme, with its heavy emphasis on beef production for export by large-scale enterprises, says Bunker,

... promises to repeat the history of colonial conquest and of the rubber boom. By sacrificing the social and the natural environments to immediate political and economic demands for the rapid transformation of natural resources into exportable commodities, government and business threaten an even more profound impoverishment of the Amazon as soon as these natural resources are exhausted.[52]

The future of development in the Amazon, barring a major turnaround in government policy, is not promising. The current large-scale and rapidly increasing exploitation of resources in the Amazon, without concern for sustainability or social development, promises to reinforce the colonial-periphery status of the region and to subordinate any interest in meaningful development to short-term profits and their concentration in core areas. In the absence of environmentally balanced strategies designed to sustain and empower a local population with minimal ecological impact, the social and ecological future of that naturally rich but tragically abused region promises further impoverishment of the land, its people, and future possibilities beneficial to the global human community.

CONSIDERATIONS FOR A THEOLOGY OF THE RAIN FOREST

We have entered into the rain forest of the Amazon and marveled at this, the most complex and expansive of ecosystems. We have observed that the rain forest is a fundamentally different ecosystem from those in the temperate climates, rendering development schemes, which are at best based on temperate-zone ecology, counterproductive and dangerously destructive. We have also explored some of the likely local and global consequences of its destruction in the name of development. No doubt, our response to the enormity and urgency of the problem of rain forest demolition was a sense of being overwhelmed and powerless and, at the same time, outraged.

We then shifted our perspective from the ecosystem itself to its human inhabitants and their activities. An indigenous population roughly equal in number to the present-day rural population occupied the forest at the time of its discovery by Europeans. These indigenous people, organized into small tribal units, had learned how to live in the forest as a part of that natural community, and their activities in the forest, subsistence and otherwise, seemed to have had minimal ecological impact. Such activity sharply contrasted with the colonial activity of the Europeans.

Moreover, the domination of the Amazon by outsiders produced several waves of extractivism, each one further diminishing the indigenous culture and the delicate ecological balance of the forest. Each wave was characterized by an economics of accumulation and enrichment of a few and a corresponding impoverishment of many others. Extractivism not only typified European colonial activity in the rain forest, but also that of the modern, capitalist Brazilian state. The current wave of development in the Amazon, characterized by massive destruction, exploitation, and impoverishment of both the land and the people, is not only rooted in the colonial past but also intensified by modern, multinational capitalism. The Amazon, since the beginning of colonial activity there, has had the status of a periphery region in a permanently dependent relationship to a highly developed core. In that sense, the Amazon is being progressively underdeveloped.

This case study presents us with the opportunity to assess the exploitation of the Amazon in light of liberation theology. It provides the concrete experience from which to propose the place of ecological concerns in the method of that theology. Specifically, I intend to demonstrate, using the example of the exploitation of the Brazilian rain forest region and its inhabitants, that an awareness and inclusion of the ecological factor in the socioanalytical method of liberation theology both deepens and broadens the impact of that analysis. What I propose here is to use liberation theology's method to analyze the exploitation of the Amazon, which will highlight the considerations involved in theological reflection, taking the rain forest as the point of departure.

Liberation theology begins with the reality of misery in the world today.[53] Most of its forms — hunger, homelessness, unemployment, a lack of basic human needs — are widespread and clearly documented. Christian faith, a faith informed by love, demands a response on the part of Christians to the scandalous reality of poverty. That response begins by entering into the world of the poor and viewing reality from their perspective. It is a world located at the impoverished periphery of society; to view reality from this location is to view it from the underside of history.

The first task, then, is to view the reality of the "misery" of the Brazilian Amazon from the point of view of the poor. The complexity of the problem, though, is made manifest in any attempt to determine the scope of impoverishment. Among liberation theologians, the poor are those who, in contrast to the rich, are denied access to the essentials needed to maintain a dignified human life. They are dehumanized, or made less than human; they are the objects of exploitation, impoverishment, and marginalization.[54] This case study shows that the whole ecosystem is an object of destructive exploitation, impoverishment, and marginalization. The ecological complication, I propose, demands a broadening of the usual anthropocentric perspective of liberation theology, since both the poor and the ecosystem of the Amazon have been objectified and made poor. I make this proposition not for the sake of developing a theology with a special focus solely on the rain forest. Rather, the exploitation of the rain forest is inextricably linked, as our case study shows, to the exploitation of much of the human community there, where each wave of the exploitation of the resources of the land and the people of the Amazon has led to further impoverishment of the land, its inhabitants, and their progeny. Therefore, our perspective in doing a theology of the rain forest is that of the exploited and of the impoverished, that is, both ecosystem and people.

By choosing to perceive reality from the viewpoint of the poor, liberation theology has reversed the historical tendency of seeing reality from the viewpoint of the dominant class in society. This case study challenges us to view the reality of the rain forest from the perspective of the exploited and objectified forest itself. The opposite of such a view would be that of an exploiter who would see the rain forest as an exploitable and profitable resource base, especially for short-term gain or private enrichment.

Furthermore, this case study challenges us to view the forest as something of value in and of itself. As Christians, we can see the forest as one of the great crowning achievements of God's creation and, as noted earlier, a place where God's creative process continues to unfold. As members of a global community, we can view the intact forest as a primary source of biological and ecological knowledge, as a natural laboratory of biological evolution, and as a vast gene pool powering the continual diversification of life on the planet. Perceiving the rain forest in such a way is, I propose, analogous to viewing human reality from the underside of history, from the standpoint of the exploited and impoverished poor.

Thus, perceiving the reality of the exploitation of the rain forest from below produces a sense of indignation and protest. It moves us to look for the deeper, structural causes of its destruction and the resulting misery to the human community caused by its loss. Since the destructive exploitation of the rain forest has profound local effects — desertification, displacement of people, impoverishment caused by the destruction of renewable resources (for example, fishing, hunting, and gathering, all of which are more productive for local people than anything offered by development schemes) — viewing its destruction from the underside deepens the impact of a resulting analysis, as we shall soon see.

A view of the exploitation of the rain forest from the underside would recognize the breadth of the resulting consequences of rain forest destruction. The impact of destruction of the rain forest on those of us who are not forest dwellers and who may never fully develop an appreciation of the forest itself as something of worth is nevertheless devastating because of the likely global consequences of the deforestation of the Amazon and the widespread human suffering they will cause. All of us become objects of exploitation and victims of impoverishment. In this sense, the ecological factor broadens the scope of those who are the exploited and impoverished ones. What is, on one hand, a localized experience of oppression is unveiled as one of global oppression. The ecological factor shows that all people are oppressed and impoverished by social structures that promote destructive exploitation of the environment. It provides the means by which all people may become conscienticized about their own impoverishment, and therefore linked in solidarity with the poor and oppressed who are directly and immediately affected by exploitation in the Amazon. This solidarity could take on the form of liberative action on a global scale.

Finally, our perspective is that of the poor themselves. The exploitation and impoverishment of the vast majority of the human inhabitants of the Amazon have been discussed in our case study. Looking at reality from their perspective brings into full view the misery, indignity, and violence with which they live.[55] By doing this, we begin to make an option for the poor. An option for the poor necessarily leads one to participation in the struggle for their liberation. It means joining directly with them not only in overcoming their oppression but in building a qualitatively new society.[56] In an analogous way, a simultaneous move toward the liberation of the earth from domination, exploitation, and impoverishment accompanies an option for the poor. Leonardo Boff already opens the door for this insight in his articulation of different understandings of poverty and their corresponding option for the poor, where he discusses an ecological mentality as one of five ways to make an option for the poor (see Table 7.3 on p. 186).[57] Making this option leads us to consider the ecological factor and the liberation of the earth as a part of the process of an integral human liberation.

Here, we come up against a major challenge in our liberative work toward a qualitatively new society. Lynn White, Jr., in his seminal essay on the ecological crisis, implicates the dominant Jewish and Christian understanding of the relationship between humans and nature as the religious matrix from which the exploitive and dominating human attitude toward nature sprung.[58] Rather than viewing ourselves as part of nature, White points out, we have viewed ourselves as superior to it and contemptuous of it. White claims that without a new religious view of the relationship between humans and nature, we will never find our way out of the "ecologic crisis." He suggests that we appropriate the ecological attitude of Francis of Assisi, who considered all of nature in terms of brother and sister. His humility, expressed as an equality with the rest of creation, was not merely a personal, private, or pietistic virtue. It was to be an attribute of the human community in right relationship with the rest of God's creation, and ultimately with God.[59] The ecological mentality that Boff speaks of as part of the option for the poor, then, would recognize the human person as one among equals in God's creation rather than as dominating ruler and exploiter over it.

The ecological mentality, furthermore, broadens our perspective of who the poor are. As noted earlier, the poor are those who are made less than human by exploitation, impoverishment, and marginalization. They are less than equal to the rest of the human community. The ecological mentality, as an expression of option for the poor, would recognize poverty wherever there is inequality anywhere in God's creation. In this sense, we recognize and can make an option for the poor wherever, in all of creation, there is inequality marked by or brought about by exploitation, impoverishment, and marginalization. In the context of our case study, the rain forest eco-

Table 7.3
For the Poor against Poverty: Schema of Boff's Five
Dialectical Understandings

Form of Poverty	Its Opposite	Option for the Poor
A lack of means for production and reproduction of life and society	A wealth of, or accumulation of, means of production and reproduction of life and society	Opting to struggle with the poor against their poverty; a conscious and organized effort to create technical and social development that promotes the growth of life beyond the struggle for survival
Injustice characterized by exploitation, producing impoverishment	Social justice	Opting to work for the necessary social transformations that will promote justice and equity for all
An evangelical way of life (poverty of spirit): total availability	Pharisaism: bragging, arrogance, self-promotion	Opting for a radical conversion of heart toward simplicity, detachment, availability in the face of a culture of power and domination of others
The life of poverty as an ascetic way of liberating the spirit from possessiveness and materialism	Prodigality and irresponsible waste	Opting for an ecological mentality, responsible for all the goods of nature and culture, for a sober and anticonsumeristic life-style
Solidarity and identification with the poor and a protest against their poverty	Selfishness and insensitivity	Opting to live with and as the poor, participating in their struggle for survival and fighting for the cause of their liberation

system of the Amazon can, in this way, be seen as part of "the poor." This recognition, then, legitimates the introduction of an ecological factor into the socioanalytical method of liberation theology.

Before moving on to a social analysis of this case study, I find it necessary to raise the issue of participation. Liberation theology stresses the prerequisite of participation for those who are to engage themselves in doing liberation theology. I cannot claim that I am actively engaged in the struggle for liberation among the poor of the Amazon. Indeed, a theology of the rain forest would most appropriately arise from the people of the Amazon engaged in the liberation struggle. What I contribute here must be seen, therefore, as a resource to those who are actively involved in the local process there of doing liberation theology by their participation in the concrete reality of the poor. Nevertheless, in light of our case study, I have opened up an avenue by which the scope of those who are exploited and impoverished is broadened to include all of us. From our sense of indignation and protest, we can use the resources available to us to contribute to the theological process. All of us can become involved, in solidarity with their struggle, and contribute from our own areas of expertise. In the context of our case study, resource contributions from several fields are particularly appropriate, as any theology of the rain forest will necessarily be a multidisciplinary work.

By now, the necessity of a clear analysis of our complex case study has become apparent. The misery already caused by exploitation in the Amazon demands it. A critical knowledge of the roots of exploitation and impoverishment is needed in order to practice an efficacious love, a love that will produce real and significant change. The task here is to uncover the mechanisms that exploit and impoverish the people and the land of the Amazon, and ultimately all of us.

At the heart of the use of social analysis as a tool of liberation theology is the discussion of development and dependence. Gutiérrez notes that in Latin American thinking, particularly in the 1950s and 1960s, the idea of development, as primarily economic growth and modernization, stirred much hope among the poor majority of those countries. However, in more recent times, the ideology of developmentalism has come under fire. Gutiérrez says that developmentalism failed because it did not attack the root causes of poverty.[60]

The failure of development is linked with a fundamental flaw in its design. International organizations, including multinational corporations, that promoted developmentalism were close to the centers of power. Changes promoted by developmentalism were not structural, as these would undermine the influence of international powers and their local elites. Rather, according to Gutiérrez, apparent changes were often nothing more than new and underhanded ways of increasing the power of strong economic groups.[61] Developmentalism proved to be counterproductive to achieving a real transformation.[62]

Moreover, development in a meaningful sense, the growth of economic, social, political, and cultural values as a total process, would only occur when the domination of rich countries was broken. Thus, underdeveloped countries are, more accurately, dependent countries. They are kept on the periphery of economic, social, political, and cultural centers and maintained in a dependent status, guaranteeing the continued dominance of the powers at the center. Developmentalism is now seen, by its critics, to be an ideology used by local elites in their countries, in conjunction with international capital, to mask an array of arrangements that keeps their countries, on the whole, dependent, while benefiting an elite handful.

The masses of poor people are relegated to the status of a cheap labor reserve, especially for multinational corporations, with the government, army, and police maintaining this arrangement by force.[63] It should not be surprising, then, that the language of liberation, which recognizes that the problem of dependence is basic and calls for deep structural transformations, has replaced the language of developmentalism among those whose cause is the end of poverty and oppression in Latin America.

Returning to the case study, I noted that the environmental and social disruptions in the Amazon over the past 400 years have been clearly linked to an extractive export economy. My description of the human activity in the rain forest since 1492, moreover, was a description of the reality of colonialism. As commodity extraction increased, environmental and social destruction increased. We saw that no lasting benefit has been realized for most of the inhabitants of the Amazon, indigenous or immigrant. Rather, environmental plunder for the economic benefit of a few and for consumption by far-removed populations at the centers of wealth and power destabilized, displaced, or literally destroyed local populations.

I discussed three major waves of extractive activity, each producing progressive underdevelopment of the region for the benefit of world-market demands. The decimation of indigenous societies, the forced dispersion of imported forest laborers, the undermining and eventual forceful destruction of more recent peasant communities, and the devastation of key plant and animal resources have characterized colonial and neocolonial exploitation of the Amazon. Both the human communities and the environment were so exploited that neither was able to fully reproduce themselves. The quality of human life has been progressively degraded, as has the complexity and balance of the ecosystem.

The case study clearly shows that the exploitation of natural and human communities in the Amazon has been one and the same action. The enslavement and decimation of indigenous cultures has been directly linked with exploitation of river and forest "products," which in turn greatly upsets natural systems of ecological reproduction. Survivors in the indigenous and natural communities experienced destabilization, degradation, and impoverishment.

I noted also that similar patterns of clearly linked social and environmental disruption and degradation occurred during the rubber boom of the late nineteenth century. In the wake of its collapse, local labor was abandoned to enduring poverty and misery, even though vast fortunes were made by a few *suringalistas* as a result of years of labor by tappers.

Finally, I noted the current wave of devastating activity now taking place in the rain forest. Similar, though far more massive, structures underlie the current form of extractivism. The forest is viewed solely as a resource for short-term gain. It is fuel for development in the industrial south of Brazil, and a resource base for international capitalism. Little effective concern is being shown for lasting, sustainable development. Rather, in the name of growth, the rain forest and the human community there are being plunged toward their final demise.

Exploitation in the Amazon is one movement with two victims: the human community and the rain forest ecosystem. The structures of exploitation are exogenous to the region, and have demonstrated, both historically and presently, little if any concern for the human or environmental impact of their activities. We see, rather, a primary concern for profits from extractable resources accumulated in centers far from the Amazon and a geopolitical concern reminiscent of the "tragedy of the commons."[64] Consequently, the Amazon has been progressively impoverished economically, socially, politically, culturally, and environmentally. It has been forced into a peripheral, dependent status. The violence to both the human and the natural communities indicates a conflictual relationship between center and periphery. Indeed, as indicated in note 55, the church in São Felix has recognized the conflictual nature of the relationship between exploiter and exploited in that region. Bishop Casaldáliga's condemnation of the exploiters of the poor, I suggest, could be equally applied to the same exploiters for the environmental devastation for which they are responsible.

In summary, an analysis of the exploitation of the Amazon has revealed an underlying structure of external domination, producing economic benefit for a few while causing widespread suffering and progressive impoverishment for many others. The linkage of environmental destruction to social exploitation has deepened the historical impact of exploitation by reinforcing progressively diminishing future possibilities for a development based on justice, equality, and sustainability. Moreover, it has revealed a historical conflict between exploiter and exploited, aimed at maintaining and reinforcing the domination of forces outside the Amazon over the rain forest region. Far from being developed, either by colonial powers or by the modern Brazilian state in conjunction with international development organizations, the Amazon has been systematically and rapaciously exploited, degraded, and impoverished. The environmental, social, economic, political, and cultural degradation within the Amazon, moreover, threatens to repeat itself globally as a direct consequence of exploitation. It now becomes clear just what the fundamental structures in need of transformation in our case study are. A liberative theology of the rain forest must be aware of these in order for it to be truly efficacious.

Liberation theology is primarily concerned with transforming the oppressive reality of the poor in an efficacious way, and that this work is demanded by the Gospel and by the church's theological tradition of social teaching, especially as it has been articulated at the Latin American bishops' meetings at Medellín and Puebla. Yet liberation theologians from the periphery tell us at the center that our role in solidarity with the poor is to work for transformative changes here at the center of the world's oppressive structures. In that sense, we can engage ourselves in the liberation process by identifying specific aspects of our lives that contribute to or benefit from the oppression of the people and the environment of the Amazon. For instance, we could analyze both the corporate and personal benefits we may enjoy from cattle ranching in the rain forest, clearly the most destructive and oppressive of activities in the region today.[65] We can also identify specific funding sources contributing to "development" in the Amazon and pressure them into taking social and ecological responsibility for the projects financed by their institutions.[66] We can identify and align ourselves with political organizations that promote an agenda of ecologically appropriate and socially responsive changes.[67]

We in the United States also must continue to work toward greater environmental protection in our own backyard. Policies that move toward curbing our consumption of fossil fuels and contributions to the greenhouse effect would not only make us more responsible stewards, but would give us a more credible footing with the Brazilian government in any international discussion about the environment. In a similar vein, managing our own tracts of ancient forestland in the Pacific Northwest and Alaska in a more responsible manner would make our concern about deforestation in the Amazon Basin less hypocritical. Finally, environmentally concerned people anywhere in the First World could work toward a more just solution to the foreign debt situation faced by developing countries, including Brazil, whose lands encompass the remnant stands of primary-growth rain forest and other ecologically sensitive environments that invite exploitation for quick gain.

Our own liberative action could be seen in the context of liberation theology's method as a conversation develops between our actions and our analysis and reflection in light of an option for the poor. Our deeds begin to inform what we see and how we see it, and our analysis and reflection informs our continued activity and engagement. In this sense, we begin to do liberation theology, and, specifically, contribute toward the liberation of the people and the environment of the Amazon. We begin to do a theology of the rain forest.

NOTES

1. By 1978, according to UNESCO's *Tropical Forest Ecosystems: A State-of-Knowledge Report* (Paris: UNESCO, 1979) 20 percent of the Amazon rain forest had already been destroyed, and far more extensive inroads had been made into the African and Asian rain forests.

2. For example, see the work of William M. Denevan, "Development and the Imminent Demise of the Amazon Rain Forest," *Professional Geographer* 25 (May 1973):130–35, or A. Gomez-Pompa et al., "The Tropical Rain Forest: A Nonre-

newable Resource," *Science* 177 (September 1, 1972): 762–65

3. For more detailed discussions of rain forest ecology, see Heinrich Walter, *Vegetation of the Earth* (London: English Universities Press, 1973); Emilio F. Moran, *Developing the Amazon* (Bloomington: Indiana University Press, 1981); Nigel J. H. Smith, *Rainforest Corridors* (Berkeley: University of California Press, 1982); Norman Myers, *Conversion of Tropical Moist Forests* (Washington, D. C.: National Academy of Sciences, 1986) and *The Primary Source: Tropical Forests and Our Future* (New York: W. W. Norton, 1984); Philip Fearnside, *Human Carrying Capacity of the Brazilian Rainforest* (New York: Columbia University Press, 1986); and John C. Kricher, *A Neotropical Companion* (Princeton, N.J.: Princeton University Press, 1989).

4. The idea of the tropical rain forest as both remnant and active gene pool is prominent in the writing of Norman Myers, particularly *The Primary Source*. Myers is concerned with the threatened degradation of a largely untapped gene pool that he regards as enormously valuable for the future welfare of humanity.

5. Fearnside, *Human Carrying Capacity*, p. 38.

6. Walter, *Vegetation*, p. 41.

7. The concept of *succession and primary /secondary growth* in plant ecology has been prominent since the late nineteenth century. A detailed discussion of succession and climax plant communities appears in Henry J. Oosting, *The Study of Plant Communities* (San Francisco: W. H. Freeman, 1956), pp. 236–337. The basic idea is that each habitat has a particular climax form of plant community that is reached over time by a series of successionary changes. Beginning with bare rock, various organisms begin to interact with the habitat. For example, lichens accumulating over time begin to form organic matter, which, as it breaks down, releases organic acids that contribute to the weathering of the rock. The resulting mineral and organic substrate becomes a habitat for more and more complex plants. Eventually, together with climatic influences, a complex plant community evolves as each successional wave modifies the habitat and produces a vegetational change. This process, of course, can take thousands of years, and in temperate climates, with greater extremes in weather patterns, can proceed in fits and starts. Eventually, a relatively stabilized and diversified community forms that is known as the climax community. In forested areas, it may sometimes be called "virgin forest," referring to its seemingly untouched and pristine character. This term, though, has not been one favored by ecologists, since even a climax community is one in dynamic equilibrium with its environment. Ecologists prefer to use the term *primary growth*. Thus, a primary forest, such as rain forest undisturbed by exploitive human activity or widespread natural destructive processes, is one in which successionary stages are no longer recognizable.

8. Myers, *Conversion*, p. 19.

9. Gomez-Pompa et al., "The Tropical Rain Forest," pp. 762–65.

10. G. Woodwell, "The Carbon Dioxide Question," *Scientific American* 238 (January 1978): 34–43.

11. R. J. Goodland and H. S. Irwin, *Amazon Jungle: Green Hell or Red Desert?* (Amsterdam: Elsevier, 1976), p. 25.

12. E. Marshall, "By Flood, If Not By Fire, C.E.Q. Says," *Science* 211 January 30, 1981): 463.

13. R. Revelle, "Carbon Dioxide and World Climate," *Scientific American* 247 (August 1982): 33–41.

14. Smith, *Rainforest Corridors* p. 58.

15. Fearnside, *Human Carrying Capacity*, p. 44.

16. J. Eigner, "Unshielding the Sun: Environmental Effects," *Environment* 17 (April 1975): 15–25.

17. Fearnside, *Human Carrying Capacity*, p. 46.

18. R. F. Weiss and H. Craig, "Production of Atmospheric Nitrous Oxide from Combustion," *Geophysical Research Letters* 3 (1976): 751–63.

19. Fearnside, *Human Carrying Capacity*, p. 47.

20. G. L. Potter et al., "Possible Climatic Impact of Tropical Deforestation," *Nature* 258 (December 25, 1976): 697–98.

21. J. A. Lutzenberger, "Systematic Demolition of the Tropical Rain Forest in the Amazon," *Ecologist* 12 (November-December 1982): 248.

22. Norman Myers, *The Sinking Ark: A New Look at the Problem of Disappearing Species* (New York: Pergamon, 1979), pp. 122–127.

23. Margery L. Oldfield, "Tropical Deforestation and Genetic Resource Conservation," in *Blowing in the Wind: Deforestation and Long-Range Implications*, Studies in Third World Societies, no. 14, ed. Vinson H. Sutlive, Nathan Altshuler, and Mario D. Zamora (Williamsburg, Va.: Department of Anthropology, College of William and Mary, 1981), pp. 277–346.

24. Myers, *The Primary Source*, p. 210.

25. Gomez-Pompa et al., "Tropical Rain Forest," p. 766.

26. William M. Denevan, "The Aboriginal Population of Amazonia," in *The Native Population of the Americas in 1492*, ed. William M. Denevan (Madison: University of Wisconsin Press, 1976), pp. 206–31. According to Brazilian government statistics, the 1980 rural population of the Amazon basin was 2.8 million. See *Anuário Estatístico Do Brasil 1986* (Rio de Janeiro: Fundação Instituto Brasiliero de Geografia & Estatística, 1987), pp. 66–69.

27. Steven G. Bunker, "Forces of Destruction in Amazonia," *Environment* 22 (September 1980): 14–46.

28. Steven G. Bunker, *Underdeveloping the Amazon: Extraction, Unequal Exchange, and the Failure of the Modern State* (Urbana: University of Illinois Press, 1986), p. 22. Bunker, in this book, has provided an extensive analysis of the economic exploitation of the Amazon region. His description of extractivism has been used by other prominent authors, including Moran, Smith, and Fearnside.

29. Goodland and Irwin, *Amazon Jungle*, p. 18. Indigenous survivors of the colonial period had, by this time, moved deep into the interior of the forest, where they were less vulnerable to exploitation and/or forced labor.

30. José Alimiro, a Franciscan friar who lives in São Paulo, Brazil's largest and most industrialized city, visited California in 1984 and talked about the plight of the poor in Brazil. At that time, he gave the approximate figures typical to much of the developing Third World: 1 percent very rich, 4 percent rich, 25 percent middle-class professionals, government bureaucrats, or medium-size business proprietors, 40 percent poor working class, and 30 percent destitute, landless, and unemployed.

31. Lutzenberger, "Systematic Demolition," p. 248.

32. It is now known that major droughts lasting a number of years are a cyclical pattern in the northeast, and, as a result, starving peasants have been driven to supplying labor for more than one major development scheme in the Amazon.

33. Smith, *Rainforest Corridors*, pp. 12–15; Fearnside, *Human Carrying Capacity*, p. 17; Bunker, "Forces of Destruction," p. 36.

34. Fearnside, *Human Carrying Capacity*, p. 17. Fearnside refers to Arturo César Ferreira Reis's *A Amazonica e a Cobica Internacional (Amazonia and International Covetousness)*, 4th ed. (Rio de Janeiro: Companhia Editora Americana, 1972).

35. Fearnside, *Human Carrying Capacity*, p. 17, quoting from INCRA (Ministry of Agriculture and Land Reform), *Projeto Integrado de Colonização Altamiro-I* (Brasilia: INCRA, 1972), p. 1.

36. Sue Bradford and Oriel Glock, *The Last Frontier: Fighting over Land in the Amazon* (London: Zed Books, 1986), p. 28. According to a Brazilian government survey taken in 1975, 0.8 percent of all Brazilian farms covered one thousand hectares or more, but they accounted for 43 percent of arable land. Fifty-two percent of farms were one hundred hectares or less, accounting for only 3 percent of the land.

37. Bunker, "Forces of Destruction," p. 35.

38. Bunker, *Underdeveloping the Amazon*, p. 83.

39. Susanna Hecht, "Deforestation in the Amazon Basin: Magnitude, Dynamics, and Soil Resource Effects," in *Where Have All the Flowers Gone?: Deforestation in the Third World*, Studies in Third World Societies, no. 13, ed. Vinson H. Sutlive, Nathan Altshuler, and Mario D. Zamora (Williamsburg, Va.: Department of Anthropology, College of William and Mary, 1981), p. 62.

40. Fearnside, *Human Carrying Capacity*, pp. 26–27; Moran, *Developing the Amazon*, p. 76; Bunker, "Forces of Destruction," p. 36; Bradford and Glock, *The Last Frontier*, pp. 106–9.

41. Bunker, "Forces of Destruction," p. 36.

42. William M. Denevan, "Swiddens and Cattle versus Forest: The Imminent Demise of the Amazon Rain Forest Reexamined," in *Where Have All the Flowers Gone?*, p. 33.

43. Bunker, "Forces of Destruction," p. 36.

44. Hecht, "Deforestation in the Amazon Basin," p. 68.

45. Myers, *Conversion*, p. 128.

46. Philip M. Fearnside, "Deforestation in the Brazilian Amazon: How Fast Is It Occurring?," *Interciencia* 7 (March-April 1982): 82–88.

47. Rondonia is a central Amazonian territory of Brazil, covering 230,104 square kilometers (100 ha = 1 km2). Some 1,200 square kilometers had been cleared as of 1976; by 1978, 4,000 square kilometers had been cleared, an increase of 41 percent per year.

48. Goodland and Irwin, *Amazon Jungle*, pp. 110–11; Bunker, *Underdeveloping the Amazon*, pp. 91–92; and Fearnside, *Human Carrying Capacity*, pp. 26–28. I have been unable to find any recent studies that support cattle ranching in the Amazon basin as a sustainable form of agriculture for that region.

49. Myers, *Conversion*, pp. 123–25.

50. Ibid.; see also Nigel J. H. Smith, *Man, Fishes, and the Amazon* (New York: Columbia University Press, 1981), pp. 83–98, 121–32.

51. Myers, *Conversion*, p. 125.

52. Bunker, "Forces of Destruction," p. 40.

53. I presume here a familiarity with the basic articulation of liberation theology. See Gustavo Gutiérrez, *A Theology of Liberation*, trans. Sister Caridad Inda and John Eagleson (Maryknoll, N.Y.: Orbis Books, 1988); Leonardo Boff and Clodovis

Boff, *Introducing Liberation Theology*, trans. Robert R. Barr (Maryknoll, N.Y.: Orbis Books, 1987) and *Salvation and Liberation: In Search of a Balance between Faith and Politics*, trans. Robert R. Barr (Maryknoll, N.Y.: Orbis Books, 1984); and Juan Luis Segundo, *The Liberation of Theology*, trans. John Drury (Maryknoll, N.Y.: Orbis Books, 1976).

54. The specific focus and perspective of liberation theology is the poor. It is, purposefully, an anthropocentric theology. The poor are its subjects, its doers, and, on the popular level, its formulators.

55. The church itself has become deeply involved in the reality of the poor of the Amazon. For example, Dom Pedro Casaldáliga, bishop of the diocese of São Felix in the heart of the Amazon, is one of the outspoken members of the hierarchy clearly on the side of the poor. In a pamphlet he wrote several years ago for peasants in his diocese, he stated: "Our Church is against the *latifúndio* [large landowner] and against slavery, and for this reason it is persecuted by the Masters of Money, Land, and Politics. Neither sharks [landowners] nor exploiters, nor traitors to the people have a place in our Church. For no one belongs to the People of God if he crushes the Sons of God. No one belongs to the Church of Christ if he does not carry out the Commandments of Christ." (See Bradford and Glock, *The Last Frontier*, p. 141.)

56. Boff and Boff, *Salvation and Liberation*, p. 12.

57. The preferential option for the poor has become a guiding pastoral strategy in the church in Latin America, first presented by the Latin American Bishops' Conference (CELAM) at their meeting in Puebla in 1979. Boff articulates five forms this option may take in *St. Francis: A Model for Human Liberation*, trans. John W. Diercksmeier (New York: Crossroads, 1982), pp. 58–63.

58. Lynn White, Jr., "The Historical Roots of Our Ecologic Crisis," *Science* 155 (March 10, 1967): 1206.

59. Francis's insights into this relationship are uniquely expressed in his "Canticle of Brother Sun." For the critical edition of the "Canticle" in English, see *Francis and Clare: The Complete Works*, ed. Richard J. Payne (New York: Paulist Press, 1982), pp. 38–39.

Francis used the familial language of brother and sister for the first time in the Christian tradition to express a human equality with creation rather than a dominance over it. In his writings, Francis did not elaborate on his idea of all of nature as brother and sister to the human being. The context, however, is one of praise of the Creator, and, hence, is one of prayerful attitude rather than ethical category. For us today, however, Francis's thirteenth-century insight raises important and complex questions about the ethical standing of the rest of nature in relation to human beings. These are beginning to be addressed, for instance, in the debates about the rights of nature, animal rights, and the "deep ecology" argument for the value of wilderness in and of itself.

60. Gutiérrez, *A Theology of Liberation*, pp. 25–26.

61. Ibid.

62. See also Hugo Assman, *Theology for a Nomad Church*, trans. Paul Burns (Maryknoll, N.Y.: Orbis Books, 1976), p. 49.

63. Arthur F. McGovern, *Marxism: An American Christian Perspective* (Maryknoll, N.Y.: Orbis Books, 1984), p. 183.

64. Garret Hardin, "The Tragedy of the Commons," *Science* 162 (December 13, 1968): 1243–48. The tragedy of the commons refers to a situation in which a

resource base is available to a community for common use, and is presumably equally accessible and beneficial to all the members of the community. The tragedy, according to Hardin, is that one member of the community may decide to maximize his or her benefit over the short term to the detriment of the benefit of others over the long term. The resource base is misused, depleted, and ruined. The geopolitical concerns described earlier include not only national-border issues but also the question of who can use the rain forest's resources, and the fear that if Brazil does not use them up now covetous foreign economic and political powers will.

65. Catherine Caulfield, "How Hamburgers Destroy Tropical Forests: A Tale of Big Mac, the Whopper, and the Delicate Forests Destroyed To Create Them," *Business and Society Review* 39 (Fall, 1981): 29–32

66. Robert J. A. Goodland, "Environmental Ranking of Amazonian Development Projects in Brazil," *Environmental Conservation* 7 (Spring 1980): 9–21

67. Ynestra King, "Coming of Age with the Greens," *Zeta Magazine*, February 1988: 16–19.

8

Ethics, Conservation, and Theology in Ecological Perspective

MARTHA ELLEN STORTZ

Constructive changes are possible in ethics, conservation, and theology when there is a move away from human centeredness in all these fields. As they expand to include care for the rest of the natural world, the dominant focus on reason and history is also growing to acknowledge the importance of space in how we reason and participate in history and the importance of stretching our reason and expanding history to include the existence and history of nonhumans. Hence, ethics is being affected by a movement from rights-in-conflict resolution to an ethic of relation-with-caring as the norm. Conservationists are correcting their view of nature solely as resources to an appreciation of nature for its own sake. Christian theologians are grappling with a hierarchical conception of the cosmos that puts humankind at the center of the created world. Dr. Stortz proposes a theological perspective on Christ as the one who heals all alienation, whether between humanity and God or humanity and the rest of creation.

Words that are cited frequently when people speak of the emerging ecological crisis are words that come, oddly enough, neither from the Club of Rome, nor from former President Carter's study on the year 2000, nor from any of the emerging classics on the environment, but words that come from the mouth of a two-dimensional cartoon figure. It's Pogo, and he cries with great fear: "We have met the enemy, and it is us!"

Put more abstractly, the problem to which Pogo points is speciesism: placing the human species at the center of one's attention. With the dawning realization that humans may be more a part of the problem creating the ecological crisis than the solution addressing it, speciesism seems more and more inadequate as a presumption embedded in our thinking about ethics, about conservation, and about theology. What is needed is nothing less than a Copernican revolution in each of these areas. Copernicus challenged the old Ptolemaic conception of the universe: the earth at the center of the solar system, with sun and planets whirling around the earth in their courses. Copernicus suggested that the sun was the center of the solar system, with the earth merely one among many other planets orbiting around it.

Perhaps a similar revolution is upon us. Where the human species had been the central consideration in the fields of ethics, conservation, and theology, the ecological crisis has challenged such an emphasis. Are humans really at the center of the natural world? And, given our preference to control rather than to care, to dominate rather than to preserve, should we indeed be the center of the natural world? Many ethicists, environmentalists, and even a few theologians are responding resoundingly in the negative. Biocentrism and ecocentrism are proffered as viable alternatives. Both would remove the crown of creation from the human race and suggest other centerpieces for the natural world.

But what might ethics, conservation, and theology look like in this move beyond speciesism? The task of this essay is to address that question, examining moves beyond speciesism in each of these fields and making some specific suggestions for the task of contemporary Christian theology in an age of ecological crisis.

Perhaps something needs to be said at the outset about method. The operative experiential category here needs to be space rather than time. Because the move is beyond speciesism, there is a coordinate challenge to extend beyond categories of analysis that exist only for humans: reason and history. These have been touted as marks of distinction bestowed upon humans by their creator; these have been cited as validating the privileged place humans hold in the natural world, with reason separating us from the beasts and all organic and nonorganic life and with history being a category limited to human experience. Moving beyond speciesism requires that we stretch our reason to understand our place in the universe, that we expand history to include nonhumans' history. Moving beyond speciesism requires that we use more holistic, less sequential thinking, that we attend to our place in the whole. Moving beyond speciesism challenges us to expand our categories of thought, to stretch our faculties of comprehension, and, most important, to develop the less-practiced discipline of attention. Attention involves watching, touching, smelling, tasting, listening – all dimensions of being in a place.

An author who lyrically describes the discipline of attention is Annie Dillard, particularly in her early books. In *Holy the Firm* she chronicles her pilgrimage to British Columbia:

I came here to study hard things — rock mountain and salt sea — and to temper my spirit on their edges. "Teach me thy ways, O Lord" is, like all prayers, a rash one, and one that I cannot but recommend. These mountains — Mount Baker and the Sisters and the Shuksan, the Canadian Coastal Range and the Olympics on the peninsula — are surely the edge of the known and comprehended world. They are high. That they bear their own unimaginable masses and weathers aloft, holding them up in the sky for anyone to see plain, makes them, as Chesterton said of the Eucharist, only the more mysterious by their very visibility and absence of secrecy.[1]

These remarks, particularly as they suggest extrapolations into territory not yet fully mapped out, are probably something not to think about too much, but to follow, to watch, and to attend to.

BEYOND ETHICS

Moving beyond speciesism entails that we move beyond traditional definitions of ethics. I'd like to argue that, but first I'd like to illustrate it. Each year I teach a required course that always concludes by teaching me new things. It is an introduction to ethics, and I structure the course around several questions: What is ethics? What is religious ethics? What is Christian ethics? The only examination is administered in the first ten minutes of the first day of the course, when students are required to submit an answer to the first question. The exercise defies grading, but the responses are always quite illuminating. Year after year, I observe that these first-day-of-class, off-the-cuff, utterly unpremeditated answers are largely framed and phrased in terms of ethics as something that has to do with relationship among people. It is, to a definition, species centered.

Of course there is great variation within the definitions. Some focus primarily on ethics as having to do with one's relationship to one's self, to one's God, to one's community of memory or some other aggregate of human beings. Moreover, the definitions variously describe the ways in which these relationships are conducted: by the rules and principles of a deontological ethic, by the goals and ends of action of a teleological ethic, or by the virtues and vices of an aretaic ethic. Intuitively, my students easily exhaust the regnant philosophical options in ethics, which are also dominantly species centered.

But neither students nor philosophers have considered that there might be a moral universe that could include things human and things not human: nature, the environment, the ecosphere, animals, the solar system, the cosmos — mysterious and complex as that notion is. Could there be rules and principles that might include things not human? Congress recognized this in laws like the Animal Welfare Act (1966), the Marine Mammal Protection Act (1972), and the Endangered Species Act (1973). Could there be a goal or end that might embrace nature itself? Certainly the astronauts who first walked the moon and attended to the earth from her closest celestial neighbor thought so. They were studying what they suddenly and spontaneously named the "Spaceship Earth," and they wondered suddenly what would be its destiny. Is it possible that there are certain qualities within humans that dispose one toward living in community, not only with other humans, but with the whole of the created order? Struggling to name the effect of such harmony, early twentieth-century Scotch biologist J. Arthur Thompson stumbled upon the phrase "web of life."

Many environmental ethicists are convinced that ethics must extend to nonhuman life. In a fascinating book detailing the history of environmental ethics in the United States, Roderick Frazier Nash describes an evolution of the discipline of ethics itself. According to Nash, the earliest form of moral reflection was hedonism, a preoccupation with the self and its pleasures. Only gradually did the circle widen to include relationships to family, clan, tribe, and region. In the recent past and in the present, ethics has been broadened to encompass relationships to nation, race, and all of humanity, but Nash predicts a future in which ethics will, of necessity, move to consider relationships with animals, plants, organic life, rocks and other nonorganic life, ecosystems, the planet, and finally nothing short of the universe itself.[2] He notes landmarks in this evolutionary process of ever-expanding rights: a natural-rights theory, which was fundamental to much classical ethical theory; the Magna Carta of 1215; the Declaration of Independence of 1776; the Emancipation Proclamation of 1863; the Nineteenth Amendment of 1920, which enabled women to vote; the Indian Citizenship Act of 1924; the Civil Rights Act of 1957; and the Endangered Species Act of 1973.[3] He suggests implicitly that other legislation may be pending and may need to be considered to move beyond speciesism and extend rights to nature itself.

Many environmental ethicists have been pressing for precisely this kind of legislation. But more important, since ethics is—or should be—different from law, environmental ethicists have been pressing for the kind of human conversion that will make possible a move beyond a merely species-centered ethics. Two strategies appear to be operative at present.

The first is an attempt to extend political theory, in specific, liberal political theory, beyond the treatment of relationships among humans and into the arena of treating relationships with and within nature. The chief values of liberal political theory are the notions of liberty and freedom; these values are preserved in a series of rights with corresponding duties or obligations. Rights to life, liberty, and the pursuit of happiness are stated in our Constitution, and yet such rights were not seen to apply to blacks or women in 1789. Gradually, these rights were extended to them. This first group of environmental ethicists argues that they ought to be extended beyond human relationships to nature as well. Nature itself has certain rights, and humans have the duty and obligation to protect and defend these rights. Here liberal political theory is used to define an environmental ethic.

It is fascinating that the same political theory that is under such widespread critique from such formidable persons as Robert Bellah, Alasdair MacIntyre, Carole Pateman, William Sullivan, and Linda Nicholson[4] is proving a rich resource for environmental ethicists like Aldo Leopold, Tom Regan, Holmes Rolston, and Peter Singer.[5]

A second strategy in environmental ethics emerges from the ranks of ecofeminists, and this approach turns away from a language of rights toward a more organic and even vitalistic approach to nature. Carolyn Merchant argues forcefully against twin legacies of the Scientific Revolution: the presumption that all matter is inert and dead and the presumption that matter is moved by external forces.[6] Such presumptions and the mechanistic metaphor that undergirds them justify domination of nature and the management and manipulation of so-called natural resources. Merchant uncovers another tradition of belief in the innate vitality of all matter and tries to argue that we need to reappropriate such a belief today. The metaphor is less hierarchical and conflictual than the notion of rights and duties. Ecofeminists look more holistically and examine the interconnections, even the spiritual interconnections, between humans and the world around them.[7]

It is interesting to look at these two dominant strategies in environmental ethics and ecofeminism in terms suggested by Carol Gilligan in her work on the difference between "male" and "female" patterns of development.[8] The "male" pattern, she argues, tends to think in terms of a hierarchy of rights and duties, using justice as its norm. The "female" pattern, on the other hand, tends to think more relationally in terms of affections and loyalties, using caring as its norm. Both of Gilligan's patterns, whether one of rights with justice as the norm or one of relation with caring as the norm, are cut in a deontological mold of ethical reflection; each draws on a rule or principle—here the norms of justice or caring—to determine human action.[9] Both focus on *human* action and *human* relationships and thus share a focus on the human species.

Extending Gilligan's "male" and "female" patterns to environmental ethics and ecofeminism affords certain insights. Gilligan's "male" pattern of moral development is very much like environmental ethics, with its focus on rights extending to nature and its references to ecojustice. The comparison invites two related questions: how does one adjudicate among competing rights? And to what degree is there an implicit hierarchy of rights embedded in environmental ethics? Nash's history of ethics—moving from self to family to nation to race to species to animals to the reaches of the cosmos itself—suggests a hierarchy that moves from center to periphery. While such a hierarchy certainly includes all forms of life within its embrace, it would in situations of conflict prioritize those forms closer to the center. Interestingly, at the center of the circle in this universe of rights is the human species.

The question then becomes: Does an environmental ethics configured around "rights" really avoid charges of speciesism? The question is crucial in view of the fact that, while environmental ethicists have talked a lot about rights of nature, they have been less clear what these rights mean for the human species. These environmental ethicists fail to recognize that rights for other species entail obligations for the human species. In the absence of clearly delineated and defined obligations for humans and in the presence of a hierarchy of rights centered on the human species, environmental ethicists concerned with "rights of nature" risk positing an inclusively arranged, but dangerously ordered, universe of competing rights. When conflict occurs within such a universe, the only criterion offered for its adjudication is the implicit principle that life-forms closer to the center have priority over those more toward the periphery.

Gilligan's "female" pattern of moral development offers the necessary complement to an environmental ethics configured around "rights." Here, an ethic of relation based on caring describes the obligations that rights of other species entail for the human species. While it does not challenge the basic center-periphery structure, the ethic of relation does offer a necessary balance and complexity to rights-based environmental ethics by emphasizing that rights imply obligations. Humans remain at the center, but they are held in place not by a superior constellation of rights but by a norm of caring. It is important to note the similarity of this model to biblical notions of stewardship, which we shall discuss in the third section. At this point, however, let us consider the dissimilarity between both patterns of moral development and ecofeminism.

The chief difference between Gilligan's patterns of moral development and ecofeminism is the latter's consistent challenge to speciesism. That challenge would disallow any form of center-periphery structure regardless of whether rights or relation held it together. Ecofeminists gravitate toward another conceptual metaphor. Oddly, it is one familar to Gilligan. Although her presentation of moral development centers on humans and suggests a center-periphery structure, Gilligan speaks throughout her book of a web of relationships. For her, the web is constituted by human relationships and held in place by caring. The norm of caring offers a rule that directs one's actions in each relationship; its focus is temporal—the cause-effect relationship between rule and response.

Ecofeminists draw the web and the ethic it delineates differently. Focusing on the whole and examining the order, proportion, and harmony within a whole, the emerging ethic could be called a cathekontic ethic. Its focus is spatial—the place each part occupies within a whole. Energy is directed, not toward application of a rule or principle or norm, whether caring or justice, but toward attending to the whole. Ecofeminists attempt to frame an ethic that defines a whole larger than the human species and that demands attention.

Thus, ecofeminists, with their attention to the whole of nature, frame a challenge to the discipline of ethics: How will the discipline move beyond its preoccupation with humans as the center of the moral universe? How will ethics move beyond its species-centered biases?

BEYOND CONSERVATION

Just as the discipline of ethics is moving gradually, like some ancient beast, into a universe in which not the human species, but rather the whole of creation is at the center of the moral universe, so the discipline devoted to the care and nurture of the earth has been evolving as well. Conservation itself has been moving away from a human-centered appropriation of natural "resources" to an appreciation of nature for its own sake. A brief chronology of terms describing the relationship between the human and the nonhuman creation over the past few decades should illustrate this shift: the human society, the conservation movement, management of natural—some would even add "human"—resources, environmentalism as the concern for a microhabitat or for our immediate physical surroundings, ecology as the concern for our macrohabitat or many and various environments, deep ecology or biocentrism, ecofeminism. If you have followed in your imagination this recent history of talk about the place of humans in the natural world, you see that we have moved a long way from a conceptual universe with humans at its center to a universe that might conceive of someone or something else at its center. Shifts in language are simultaneously shifts in conceptualities.

Take the shift from the title of an institution labeled "the Humane Society" to a "Society for the Prevention of Cruelty to Animals." The initial title never really made sense to me as a child. Why would a word that, on the face of it, referred to something that was of the best part of human nature have anything whatsoever to do with climbing into trees and rescuing frightened cats or clearing dead opossums from the side of the road? It seemed so abundantly and consistently clear to the child that cats did not need to be in trees and that dead animals needed to be given decent burials. What did not occur to me is that such abundant and insistent clarity would evaporate with time and maturity, that as adults we would need to be called back to some higher human nature in order to care for animals. There would be little hope in appealing to any respect we might have for the animals themselves.

A group that calls itself a Society for the Prevention of Cruelty to Animals suggests that it is wrong to inflict pain on animals, not because it will morally damage or erode our finest human selves and our sense of being "humane," but because animals should not be abused by humans. The shift in language reflects a shift in conceptualities as well: one acts, but not because of the merits or demerits that the human agent of action will earn. Rather, animals have some inherent rights that any potential agent ought not to violate, but ought rather to respect—perhaps even actively to ensure.

Other words are fraught with conceptual assumptions. Look at "resources" or "raw material." This is language from an eighth-grade geography class. One learns what these are for any country under consideration. The natural resources of South Carolina are sand, gravel, lumber, granite, peat. The natural resources of California are oil, fish, and, again, lumber. But such thought never asks questions like: resources for what? to whom? to whom for what? The unquestioned assumption is that resources are generously stashed away in land and in sea for the express purpose of human management, development, and final consumption. A "raw material" is similarly ripe for refinement and rich for utilization straight up to the time when it suddenly becomes the rare material, the endangered species, the last in the line.

Such an attitude is the legacy of a political philosophy born of and in the Industrial Revolution — a liberal political philosophy. Perhaps its chief proponents, John Locke and John Stuart Mill had a sense of foreboding. There are two limits on an individual's relentless pursuit of life, liberty, and property. The first is another liberal individual; one's rights extend only as far as the rights of the next person. The second limit is that imposed by limited resources, for which all liberal individuals compete.[10] Thus, the attitude toward natural resources is one of competition, as people struggle to secure the necessities for survival and, beyond that, gain.

The portrait of the human person that emerges here is the portrait of the manager.[11] One must manage all the conflicting and highly volatile desires that storm around in one's soul; one must manage one's relationships with others, so as to further accommodate accumulation; one must carefully manage one's natural resources, so as to be able to continue accumulation. The end of all this management is unclear. All talk of a common good has vanished, because the common good is subordinated to the goods and goals of each individual. The manager decides for herself what is her own good. If she is quite clever, she can perhaps manage to convince others that her good is also theirs, thereby organizing people around pursuit of something that they are convinced would profit each of them individually.

This managerial ethos suffused early conservation movements in this country. Governed by a desire to "manage" natural resources and frightened by the prospect of scarcity, early conservation movements were largely utilitarian in motivation and economic in aim. Roderick Nash sums up these attempts laconically:

> Timber-producing forests and useful game species of animals, birds, and fish attracted the most attention. Progressive conservation became the showpiece of a philosophy of efficient progress.[12]

At base was a glaring speciesism: if we don't do this now, we are going to be in Big Trouble later on!

The appeal is a strong one with the U.S. public. Nash points out that even such ecologists as Aldo Leopold and Rachel Carson, who believed in the intrinsic worth of everything alive, had public sides that looked conservationist. Both pitched a large portion of their public rhetoric, not toward elaborating a whole that could not possibly have humans at the center, but toward making a simple and compelling point—if we don't do this now, we are going to be in Big Trouble later on![13]

Yet there is another strand in Leopold and Carson that runs counter to the surface conservationist rhetoric and presents a view quite opposed to speciesism. The sentence that embodies the argument of Leopold's formative essay, "The Land Ethic," has a message that is quite different. Land-use decisions should stem from "the integrity, stability, and beauty of the biotic community"[14] rather than from human needs or human futures. At the center of Leopold's land ethic is nothing less than the whole of the biotic community, of which humans are a part, but only a part. The focus of such an ethic is spatial: Leopold's emphasis on integrity and stability recalls the metaphor of a web. He demands a rigorous attention to the whole. In its esthetic dimension, the ethic is mindful of "beauty" and symbolizes the shift in environmental thinking beyond the speciesism of various conservation movements and toward a biocentrism, or a focus on the whole of life.

BEYOND SPECIESISM IN THEOLOGY

When Christian theologians address the ecological crisis, they turn to the book of Genesis, specifically to the blessings of Genesis 1:28—"And God blessed them, and God said to them, 'Be fruitful and multiply, and fill the earth and subdue it; and have dominion over the fish of the sea and over the birds of the air and over every living thing that moves upon the earth' " (RSV). The passage focuses on the commands to "be fruitful and multiply and fill the earth" and to "subdue and have dominion."

Such imperatives are points of particular neuralgia today. As the threat of overpopulation looms larger on the ecological horizon, theologians and scientists alike are ready to defy any command to "be fruitful and multiply." Outright renunciation is not too bold a reaction to the first command. The second command provokes an apologetic and even penitential response. The operative verbs *kabash* ("to subdue, to bring into bondage") and *radah* ("to rule over, to exercise dominion") are hard to soften and their historical impact is hard to ignore.[15] Men and women of faith throughout the centuries have been content to take these words quite literally.

Lynn White, Jr., in a provocative and widely read article appearing in 1967, charges such religious values with underlying what was then emerging as "the environmental crisis."[16] As a historian, he was interested more in the history of an idea, notably the idea of dominion. Interpreted literally, dominion had justified human domination of nature. This scripturally based domination then fed into a mechanistic view of nature and aligned itself all too easily with the scientific and industrial revolutions. According to White, the fallout of such an interpretation has been nothing short of disastrous — outright exploitation of nature and onerous oppression by humans of nature.

Interestingly, White is not urging his audience to abandon such oppressive traditions. "Since the roots of our trouble are so largely religious, the remedy must also be essentially religious, whether we call it that or not."[17] White moves to reappropriate strands within Christianity that cut against the dominant interpretation. He finds a particularly sympathetic spirit in Saint Francis of Assisi:

> With [Francis] the ant is no longer simply a homily for the lazy, flames a sign of the thrust of the soul toward union with God; now they are Brother Ant and Sister Fire, praising the Creator in their own ways as Brother Man does in his. . . . I propose Francis as a patron saint for ecologists.[18]

Other theologians concerned with the environment have proposed other saints — and other sinners, for that matter — but all concur that the apparent biblical injunction "to have dominion" must be wrestled with.

A significant revisionist attempt has been to understand dominion as stewardship. A 1966 essay in the *Christian Century* by Richard Baer articulates an understanding of dominion as a kind of stewardship that moves decisively away from exploitation and instrumentality.[19] Baer regards the fact of human "dominion" over nature as inescapable; it is the command of God. What is critical, however, is the quality of human rule, and Baer defines that as an obligation to preserve the balance and beauty of what God has created and called "good." Failure to do so amounts to disobedience and violation of a special trust. A more recent treatment deals even more directly with dominion as stewardship. Douglas John Hall focuses on the *imago dei* as a way of understanding stewardship in terms of "being-with" nature and not against it.[20] Both Baer and Hall favor a revisionist reading of dominion as stewardship.

Theological discussions of stewardship recall Carol Gilligan's "female" pattern of moral development. The steward has been given oversight over the possessions of another; obligations attend these special responsibilities. Protection and caring define the bearing of a steward toward the possessions of another. Unchallenged within the model of stewardship is the whole center-periphery structure of such obligation. Speciesism seems implicit in biblical models of stewardship.

This has not escaped the attention of other theologians, who challenge stewardship as an adequate concept in an age of ecological crisis. Elizabeth Dodson Gray points out that it plays into the same hierarchical conception of the cosmos as dominion:

Many theologians today remind us that "dominion" can mean responsible stewardship. But it is clear that — however "dominion" is interpreted — it always means "above" and implies a right to exercise power over others.[21]

Others rebelled against a perceived species centeredness in stewardship. An Eleventh Commandment Fellowship eschewed such centering on humans, proposing an amendment to the Decalogue: "The earth is the Lord's and the fullness thereof; thou shalt not despoil the earth nor destroy the life thereon."[22] For these people, an implicit speciesism and hierarchicalism in stewardship disqualifies it for use in any theological discussion about the environment.

If one were to draw a trajectory of the interpretations of Genesis 1:28, one could plot a line beginning with domination, moving through dominion and through stewardship, and now ending in uncertainty as theologians and ethicists attempt to wrestle with biblical texts at the heart of their tradition. It is at this point of uncertainty and possibility that I would like to interject another possible interpretation of the biblical material, one that might offer a new perspective on how humans might interface with the rest of creation.

Theological attention to the biblical material has focused on the blessings in Genesis 1 and the commands they contain to "be fruitful and multiply" and to "subdue and have dominion" over the earth. As noted above, these blessings have been variously interpreted, from domination to dominion to stewardship and beyond. What has received almost no attention is what happens in subsequent chapters of Genesis: Adam and Eve, the serpent, the fruit of the forbidden tree, God's anger, and, most important, the curses that God places upon Adam and Eve, upon the serpent, and upon the earth. Following shortly after the bestowal of these blessings in Genesis 1 are the curses of Genesis 3, and these are flung upon all of creation as a result of an event generally referred to as the Fall. Whether the Fall was an act of disobedience or of freedom is not my concern here; what does concern me are the curses it precipitates.

God's anger sears the ear, and we read with distress:

> The Lord God said to the serpent,
> "Because you have done this,
>   cursed are you above all cattle,
>   and above all wild animals;
> upon your belly you shall go,
>   and dust you shall eat
>   all the days of your life.
> I will put enmity between you and the woman,
>   and between your seed and her seed;
> he shall bruise your head,
>   and you shall bruise his heel."

To the woman he said,
"I will greatly multiply your pain in childbearing;
  in pain you shall bring forth children,
yet your desire shall be for your husband,
  and he shall rule over you."
And to Adam he said,
"Because you have listened to the voice of your wife,
  and have eaten of the tree
of which I commanded you,
  'You shall not eat of it,'
cursed is the ground because of you;
  in toil you shall eat of it all the days of your life;
thorns and thistles it shall bring forth to you;
and you shall eat the plants of the field.
In the sweat of your face
  you shall eat bread
till you return to the ground,
  for out of it you were taken;
    you are dust,
    and to dust you shall return.
      (RSV, Gen. 3:14–19)

The curses are deeply disturbing—perhaps this is part of the reason none of the theologians concerned with a biblical ethic of creation has paid them any attention—but they suggest that life after the Fall is even worse than dominion. The curses illumine an aspect of creation that is now conspicuous by its absence. What happened in the mythical seven days of creation is far more than the generation of light and darkness, heaven, earth and seas and plants yielding seed and fruit trees bearing fruit, stars and sun and moon, great sea monsters and all manner of birds, cattle and creeping things, and finally humans themselves. What happened in addition to the making of the whole panoply of creation was the creation of relationships between and among its various parts and partners and pieces. Whatever happened in the Fall sundered some of these relationships.

Specifically, the following relationships have been broken:

1. animal-earth: The serpent is told that it will move on its belly and eat dust
2. animal-animal: The serpent is "cursed" above all other animals
3. animal-human: There is "enmity" between the woman and the serpent
4. human-human: Eve will have pain in childbearing; Adam will rule over her
5. human-earth: The ground is cursed, because of Adam's "disobedience" (here so named by God); he will toil "in the sweat of [his] face" and bring forth only "thorns and thistles"

6. human-God: Adam and Eve are thrown out of the Garden and
deprived of God's companionship

This litany of broken relationships describes an environmental crisis of
enormous proportions. The myriad relationships between creation and Creator are in jeopardy.

Focusing on the blessings of Genesis 1:28 raises one question: How are
the blessings to be understood—as exploitation, as dominion, as stewardship? Focusing on the curses of Genesis 3 poses another: How are the
curses to be revoked? The question is both desperate and urgent.

How then are the curses to be revoked? The Christian theologian is
driven to an answer, not of human invention, but of divine provision. Tra-
ditionally, the turn has been to the redemption embodied in Jesus Christ.
But it is interesting that the Christ presented by most Christian theologians
is able to address only one of the curses, the broken relationship between
God and humans. The salvation voiced by most Christian theologians is a
salvation that does not extend beyond humans. The christology that they
describe focuses on human salvation.

The Christian preoccupation with human salvation seems a natural
extension of Jewish soteriology. The Hebrew scriptures focus on God's
promise to God's people in the gift of the land—a specific place for a
specific people.[23] The Christian scriptures present God's promise to God's
people in a person, Jesus Christ. The import of the salvation presented in
Christ is twofold. No longer is God's promise limited to a specific place
and a specific people. It is located in a person and it is extended to all
people, Gentile and Jew, slave and free, male and female. W. D. Davies
comments:

> Salvation was not now bound to the Jewish people centered in the
> land and living according to the Law: it was "located" not in a place,
> but in persons in whom grace and faith had their writ. By personal-
> izing the promise "in Christ" Paul universalized it. For Paul Christ
> had gathered up the promise into the singularity of his own person.
> In this way, "the territory" promised was transformed into and ful-
> filled by the life "in Christ."[24]

As set out by these theologians, the salvation presented in Christ, though
extended to all peoples, does not seem to extend beyond people. It revokes
only one of the curses: the broken relationship between God and humans.
Surely God's promises embrace the entirety of God's creation.

What revokes the other curses? The Christ who revokes the curses of
Genesis 3 is the Christ depicted in the pastoral epistles of Colossians and
Ephesians. The ancient authors of these texts are concerned to present a
Christ who *is* in himself the new creation. They appear to be quite aware
of all the relationships in need of repair and of all the curses in effect. The
portrait of the cosmic Christ is boldly drawn in Colossians 1:15–20:

He is the image of the invisible God, the first-born of all creation; for in him all things were created, in heaven and on earth, visible and invisible, whether thrones or dominions or principalities or authorities — all things were created through him and for him. He is before all things, and in him all things hold together. He is the head of the body, the church; he is the beginning, the first-born from the dead, that in everything he might be preeminent. For in him all the fullness of God was pleased to dwell, and through him to reconcile to himself all things, whether on earth or in heaven, making peace by the blood of his cross. (RSV)

The language in the passage is organic; its range is cosmic. The scope of redemption recapitulates the scope of creation and encompasses "all things . . . created, in heaven and on earth, visible and invisible." The redemption pictured here extends far beyond the realm of the human species; the repairs accomplished address fractures fanning out through all of creation. The Christ who revokes the curses of Genesis 3 is none other than a Christ who takes all of the creation into Christ's own body. One could go so far as to say that the incarnation pictured here is neither androcentric,[25] in that Christ is incarnate in male flesh, nor anthropocentric, in that Christ is incarnate in human flesh, but creational — Christ is embodied finally in the new creation.

All theological tendencies toward speciesism are erased in this portrait of the cosmic Christ. Firmly established at the center of the creation is the Christ. Preeminence and priority are given only to this Christ; all other creatures "hold together in him." Our unique task as humans is to honor the whole and to discern and preserve our place in it, taking care neither to displace nor to disturb the positioning of other creatures and things within the whole. Our discernment entails a careful attention to space, as we attempt to maintain order, proportion, and harmony within the whole.

NOTES

1. Annie Dillard, *Holy the Firm* (New York: Harper and Row, 1977), pp. 19–20.

2. Roderick Frazier Nash, *The Rights of Nature: A History of Environmental Ethics* (Madison: University of Wisconsin Press, 1989), p. 5.

3. Ibid., p. 7.

4. The critics of liberal political theory are legion: for example, Anthony Arblaster, *The Rise and Decline of Western Liberalism* (Oxford: Basil Blackwell, 1984); Robert Bellah et al., *Habits of the Heart: Individualism and Commitment in American Life* (Berkeley: University of California Press, 1985); Frances Moore Lappé, *Rediscovering America's Values* (New York: Ballantine Books, 1989); Alasdair MacIntyre, *After Virtue: A Study in Moral Theory* (Notre Dame, Ind.: University of Notre Dame Press, 1981); Alasdair MacIntyre, *Whose Justice? Which Rationality?* (London: Gerald Duckworth, 1988); Linda J. Nicholson, *Gender and History: The Limits of Social*

Theory in the Age of the Family (New York: Columbia University Press, 1986); Carole Pateman, *The Problem of Political Obligation: A Critique of Liberal Theory* (Cambridge: John Wiley, 1985); and William M. Sullivan, *Reconstructing Public Philosophy* (Berkeley: University of California Press, 1986).

5. Appeals to "rights" language are found in such works as Aldo Leopold, *A Sand County Almanac* (New York: Ballantine Books, 1966); Anthony J. Povilis, "On Assigning Rights to Animals and Nature," *Environmental Ethics* 2:1 (Spring 1980): 67–71; Tom Regan, *The Case for Animals' Rights* (Berkeley: University of California Press, 1983); and Holmes Rolston III, *Philosophy Gone Wild: Environmental Ethics* (Buffalo, N.Y.: Prometheus Books, 1989). For an analysis of the language of rights in environmental ethics, see Joel Feinberg, "The Rights of Animals and Unborn Generations," in W. T. Blackstone, ed., *Philosophy and Environmental Crises* (Athens: University of Georgia Press, 1974) and Roderick Frazier Nash, especially chapters 1, "From Natural Rights to the Rights of Nature," and 2, "Ideological Origins of American Environmentalism."

6. Carolyn Merchant, *The Death of Nature: Women, Ecology and the Scientific Revolution* (New York: Harper and Row, 1980).

7. See also J. E. Lovelock, *The Ages of Gaia: A Biography of Our Living Earth* (New York: Norton, 1988); Judith Plant, ed., *Healing the Wounds: The Promise of Ecofeminism* (Philadelphia: New Society, 1989); and Elisabeth Sahtouris, *Gaia: The Human Journey from Chaos to Cosmos* (New York: Pocket Books, 1989).

8. Carol Gilligan, *In a Different Voice: Psychological Theory and Women's Development* (Cambridge, Mass.: Harvard University Press, 1982).

9. I realize that the categorization of Carol Gilligan as a deontological ethicist might be challenged — and, indeed, is challenged within the pages of this book. Such variance only attests to the significance of her work in ethics and to the richness and complexity of the work itself. Gilligan is not primarily an ethicist but a developmental psychologist. Insofar as she articulates an ethic, it is, as are most sound ethical proposals, a mixed one. I draw on a deontological moment in Gilligan, on her emphasis on choice and decision making, and on the principles of caring, nonviolence, and interconnection that guide women and men in making their decisions.

10. Alison Jaggar emphasizes this in her treatment of liberal political philosophy. See her *Feminist Politics and Human Nature* (Totowa, N. J.: Rowan and Allanheld, 1983), p. 30.

11. There is much on the manager as a contemporary cultural ideal or personality type. Alasdair MacIntyre identifies three such types: the therapist, the manager, and the aesthete. See *After Virtue,* pp. 28ff. Robert Bellah and his colleagues argue that the manager and the therapist are in fact one type: one accomplishes in the arena of feelings what the other accomplishes in the arena of interpersonal relationships. See Bellah et al., *Habits of the Heart,* p. 127. For further evidence of the presence of managerial attitudes in the realm of the affections, see Arlie Russell Hochschild, *The Managed Heart: Commercialization of Human Feeling* (Berkeley: University of California Press, 1983.)

12. Nash, p. 49.

13. Roderick Nash discusses the conservationist rhetoric of both Carson and Leopold as they addressed environmental concerns in the public realm: Leopold's "instrumentalism" and Carson's "anthropocentrism" pp. 69–70, 79–80.

14. The context of the phrase is worth repeating: ". . . quit thinking about decent land use as solely an economic problem. Examine each question in terms of what

is ethically and esthetically right, as well as what is economically expedient. A thing is right when it tends to preserve the integrity, stability, and beauty of the biotic community. It is wrong when it tends otherwise." Leopold, p. 262.

15. Perhaps the best exegetical study of Gen. 1:28 is W. Lee Humphreys's essay, "Pitfalls and Promises of Biblical Texts as a Basis for a Theology of Nature," in Glenn C. Stone, ed., *A New Ethic for a New Earth* (New York: Friendship Press, 1971), pp. 99–118.

16. Lynn White, Jr., "The Historical Roots of Our Ecologic Crisis," in Ian G. Barbour, ed., *Western Man and Environmental Ethics: Attitudes toward Nature and Technology* (Menlo Park, Calif.: Addison-Wesley, 1973).

17. Ibid., p. 30.

18. Ibid., pp. 28, 30.

19. Richard A. Baer, Jr., "Land Misuse: A Theological Concern," *Christian Century* 83 (October 12, 1966).

20. Douglas John Hall, *Imaging God: Dominion as Stewardship* (New York: Friendship Press, 1986).

21. Elizabeth Dodson Gray, *Green Paradise Lost* [formerly *Why the Green Nigger?*] (Wellesley, Mass.: Roundtable Press, 1981), p. 2.

22. Reported in Nash, *The Rights of Nature*, p. 111.

23. Walter Brueggemann, *The Land* (Philadelphia: Fortress Press, 1977).

24. W. D. Davies, *The Gospel and the Land* (Berkeley: University of California Press, 1974), p. 166.

25. For a careful appraisal of the dissimilarities between deep ecology and eco-feminism, see Marti Kheel's contribution to this collection.

9

Creation and Covenant:
A Comprehensive Vision
for Environmental Ethics

CHARLES S. McCOY

Respect for creation requires social justice and responsibility. The covenantal view of the environmental crisis emphasizes that when we violate any part of the created order it is harmful to the whole. Put socially, the breaking of community, acts of enmity, and injustice are violations of covenantal ties and result not only in social distress but also in offense to the rest of creation. Among the implications of this theological perspective is this challenge: the covenant forms the basis and bounds of creativity, but God's covenant is not static; it provides a framework for purposeful human agency. There is room for dialogue about what new covenantal relations will be.

The twentieth century opened with great optimism, bright with promise. Science and technology seemed destined to lead humanity into an enduring era of peace, plenty, and security. But as the century draws to a close, the optimism has faded, even disappeared. Humanity and the earth itself are in grave danger, caught between prosperity and poverty, between unprecedented possibilities and destructive perils. Rising demands for justice combine with the threat of nuclear holocaust and environmental catastrophe to deepen the crisis.

Faith in science has proved as illusory a dogma as earlier versions of such sectarian triumphalism. The world needs a wider vision, one with ethical sensitivity and courage as well as technological expertise, with the breadth to encompass the diversity of human perspectives. An understanding illumined by the covenant can help in developing that sense of interdependency and symbiotic relationship among all human communities and within the entire world of nature that is crucial for the well-being of every part of the world today.

COVENANT AS BASIS FOR ENVIRONMENTAL ETHICS

Covenantal relationships permeate most human communities. From tribal life and family to community bonding and the fiduciary arrangements of complex economies, human relations and actions are governed by the trust and loyalty derived from implicit or explicit covenants.

The covenant and covenantal faith are also central to the Hebrew and Christian Scriptures. In varied forms, the covenant remains an important element in the early church and in the Middle Ages. With the Reformation, the covenant emerges as a powerful motif in the modern world.

The idea of covenant is central in both the Old Testament and in the New. Indeed, the word "testament" comes from the Latin *testamentum*, which is the way the Vulgate translates the Hebrew *berith* (covenant). Walter Eichrodt focuses his *Theologie des alten Testaments* on the covenant and bases the first of the three volumes on the notion of Yahweh as the Covenant God. The covenant, Eichrodt says, is "the critical term for Israelite thought" and "the basic principle of the relationship to God."[1] Just as God in the Hebrew faith is the Covenant God, so also are other terms in the Old Testament to be understood in terms of the covenant—for example, *mishpat* as covenant justice, *hesed* as covenant loving-kindness, and so on.[2] Martin Buber asserts that it is impossible to grasp the inner coherence of the faith of Israel without understanding the covenant.[3]

God makes covenant in creation with the whole of the natural order (Jer. 33:20–25). Humanity is created within the same covenant of creation, a covenant that Adam breaks, beginning the faithlessness of humans to God (Hos. 6:7). God upholds the covenant and makes it anew with Noah (Gen. 9:8ff.), with Abraham (Gen. 15:17f; 17:7), with Isaac (Gen. 17:19), and with Jacob (Gen. 28:18ff.; 35:9ff.). Whatever humans may do, the covenant from God's side remains firm. The covenant with Israel can no more be broken from the divine side than can God's covenant with the day and with the night, that is, with the natural order (Jer. 33:20).

The covenant of God is historical and communal. Bernard Anderson writes: "The peculiar nature of the Hebrew community is expressed in the covenant relationship between Yahweh and the people of Israel, and the Laws and the institutions by which this relationship is expressed is . . . the core of the life of these people."[4] The Hebrew nation is founded on the covenant made at Sinai (Horeb) (Exod. 19:5, 24:7ff., etc.) after the liberation from Egyptian bondage. This covenant with God becomes the constitution of their life as a people, the basis of their theology and ethics, and the pattern for understanding the whole of creation and history. It is renewed repeatedly despite the faithlessness of Israel.

The covenant is projected forward from Sinai toward the consummation of God's purposes and backward from Sinai to the creation. Sinai is the place where God renews the covenant made with Abraham; the covenant with Abraham is a continuation of the covenant made with Noah; and that covenant with Noah is rooted in God's creation of the world. The core of Israel's story is summed up as follows: " 'You stand this day all of you before the Lord your God . . . that you may enter into the sworn covenant of the Lord your God, which the Lord your God makes with you this day' " (Deut. 29:10ff.).

The prophets speak from this covenantal context and call a faithless Israel back to God. Jeremiah declares a new covenant (Jer. 31:33) that Jesus affirms in saying, " 'This cup which is poured out for you is the new covenant in my blood' " (Luke 22:20), a theme taken up again and again throughout the New Testament (for example, 1 Cor. 11:25, Rom. 11:27, 2 Cor. 3:4–6, and 12–17, Gal. 4:22–26, Eph. 2:12 and 13, and virtually the entirety of Hebrews).

THE COVENANTAL VIEW OF CREATION

What resources are available in the covenantal tradition for disentangling Christian faith from exploitative forces and renewing the Christian understanding of the created order? In this tradition, covenant signifies an inclusive view of God as the Faithful One and of God's faithful will as embodied in the wholeness of creation.

The Meaning of Covenant

In biblical perspective, covenant means an unconditional agreement of community, friendship, peace, and justice. Covenant can be contrasted with what we usually call contract. A contract is a conditional agreement with the stipulation understood: the obligation to carry out the terms of a contractual agreement derives from the performance of certain contractual obligations by the other party. Contract means quid pro quo. Covenant as unconditional agreement is not dependent upon the performance or nonperformance of the parties. The commitment fundamentally is to one another and to God. Covenant, therefore, means gift. It signifies a relation based on grace. Parties in a covenant are unconditionally committed to one another. In addition to community, friendship, peace, and justice, covenant implies a means for overcoming enmity, alienation, conflict, and injustice.

In the ancient semitic world, covenants might be from a superior to an inferior or between equals. The first was a suzerainty covenant imposed by conquerors on the conquered, or extended from God to the creation (Gen. 9:13). The second was an agreement of friendship, common purpose, and peace among humans, as the covenant between Abraham and Abimelech (Gen. 21:27). Hebrew faith includes both forms, uniting their meaning and transforming them by referring the final meaning of covenant to God's covenant. God makes covenant with Israel as the continuation of the covenant God has already made with the created order, including nature and all humanity. God's covenant with Abram fits into this sequence (Gen. 15:18). But David and Jonathan also make a covenant with one another, so there is friendship between them deep enough to overcome the enmity that threatens to divide them. And "the soul of Jonathan was knit to the soul of David" (1 Sam. 18:1).

God is understood through covenant, not by any final name, but as the One who is faithful, who makes covenant and keeps covenant. Lines from what may be an early Christian hymn convey this Hebrew view: "If we are faithless, God remains faithful, for God cannot deny God's very own selfhood"(2 Tim. 2:13).

Covenant reaches back to creation and depicts the origin of the world in God's faithful action. Covenant points forward toward the consummation of the process initiated in creation. The wholeness of creation, coming to focus in the coherent pattern and responsibility of every present, is covenantal, is faithful. Nature no less than history is understood through covenant. The covenant of the rainbow after the flood reminds us of the inclusion of nature: "While earth remains, seedtime and harvest, cold and heat, summer and winter, day and night, shall not cease. . . . I set my bow in the cloud, and it shall be a sign of the covenant between me and the earth"(Gen. 8:22; 9:9, 10, 13). And Jeremiah affirms the same: "Thus says the Lord: If you can break my covenant with the day and my covenant with the night, so that day and night will not come at their appointed time, then also my covenant with David my servant may be broken" (Jer. 33:20–21).

The Symbiotic Relation of All Creation

In convenantal perspective, the entire created order is within the covenant of God—nature, history, and humanity. By creation they are in community and friendship with God and with one another. Peace and justice are constitutive elements of the world as created. All parts are joined together dependent upon the faithful will of God.

Violation of the covenant is an attack upon the created order of the world and is rebellion against God. Injustice, conflict, enmity, and alienation result from unfaithfulness to the covenant; such unfaithfulness disturbs the ordered relation and process of nature, history, and humanity. Actions that violate the covenant do harm to every part of the symbiotically related creation. When humans treat other humans unjustly or exploit nature, they are acting against God, the covenant, and themselves. Faithlessness harms the exploiter as well as the exploited. The symbiotic nature of creation means, therefore, that all action has a boomerang effect, going out toward goals intended but turning back upon the agent originating the action.

Johannes Althusius (1557–1638), author of the first federal or covenantal political philosophy, speaks of politics as the art of associating in societal life and upbuilding all within it. Thus, he says, politics is called "symbiotics."

And humans are known as "symbiotes" because of their symbiotic relation with one another, with the entire creation, and with God.[5]

Sin means faithlessness to the covenant of God. It is rebellion against and an attempt to violate the integral wholeness of creation. Sin is, therefore, unfaithfulness toward God, toward nature, toward humanity, and toward the self, for all are bound together in the symbiotic relationship of covenant.

Because of the pervasiveness of sin, it should not be a shock to find that nature has been abused and exploited, even as the human story is one of continuing inhumanity of humans to one another. The covenantal view of the environmental crisis emphasizes that when we violate any part of the created order it harms the whole. That is precisely what we are discovering painfully today: when we are unfaithful to the covenant with nature, nature snaps back at us, and we see the results in ecological disruption, that is, in the disturbance of the symbiotic relations of the covenant.

Covenant, thus, includes command, promise, and threat. God's covenant as embodied in nature and history contains the command to live in community, friendship, peace, and justice. The promise of the covenant is the enjoyment of well-being through the relations established and growing in creation.

The threat of the covenant is that violation leads to the fragmentation of community, to alienation, to conflicts, and to injustice.

Nature and History in Process toward Fulfillment

In the light of the covenant of God, we may say that nature has a history no less than that history is embedded in nature and is natural. Both are integrally related aspects of God's covenant in creation. Nature and history, therefore, are not static but are in process toward a consummation given by God and ultimately hidden in God.

Covenantal theology and ethics have a distinctive way of understanding creation as historical. The world as created by God "in the beginning" through covenant is not complete, but is created in process toward increasing fulfillment and toward final consummation. Humanity as part of this created order is also created incomplete and in process toward further growth and toward fulfillment.

This view is not to be identified with recent process theologies based on philosophical systems. Covenantal thought derives its process elements from the biblical understanding of creation within the covenantal purposes of God that contain a process of fulfillment. Indeed, it is highly probable that the process philosophies of the nineteenth and twentieth centuries emerged from contexts influenced by the covenantal tradition and thus are in part intellectual progeny of covenantal theology and ethics.

Covenantal theology and ethics stand also in contrast to the Augustinian views of creation, history, and humanity, views widely influential in Western theology. Creation, including humanity, for Augustine, is from God and is as good as can be. Only God is perfect. In the fall into sin, humanity declines from that creational goodness. As a result, humans and all their deeds are corrupt in that they seek lesser goods than God. Jesus Christ redeems humanity and the entire creation from their fallenness and restores them to their created goodness.

Covenant theology and ethics offer a different theology of history and understanding of the Fall. Creation is good but incomplete, in process toward fulfillment. Nature and humanity by creation are undergoing change, as history unfolds toward completion in God. There is a greater goodness lying ahead as creation moves toward consummation. Humans know themselves to be developing toward fulfillment, yet they do not know their full potentialities. In all human aspiration, there is a nagging "not yet" of hope and anticipation. The fall into sin is a fall from that mutability in which humans develop toward their fulfillment into immutability, into a static state that is resistant to change, that seeks to avoid the process of growth toward the fulfillment that is our covenantal destiny in God.

The "unquiet heart," the restlessness of human existence, is not the result of the Fall, as in the Augustinian view, but rather is built into humans with their creation. Humanity is created with a restless heart, a striving beyond the incompleteness of creation toward the fulfillment of the potentiality given by God. Humans do not know completely what their full potentiality is, but they look forward in hope, knowing through covenant faith that the final consummation is community and unity of the entire creation in God.

The redeeming word of Christ is twofold. First, whether humanity had fallen or not, Christ is the pioneer of this developmental, covenantal order moving toward consummation. Without the Fall, for Augustine, the work of Christ is problematical. Second, because of the fall of humanity into immutability and resistance to change, Christ restores mutability to humanity, that ability to respond to God's call to grow and change toward fulfillment.

In this meaning of covenant, in the symbiotic relations of nature and humanity, and in the incompleteness of the world as it develops toward its fulfillment, the basis for a renewal of the Christian understanding of the created order takes shape. The covenant of God in creation points to the pattern of nature and history as faithfulness. Creation relates every part to every other part. Creation is an interdependent whole, based upon and related through the covenantal will of God. By origin and nature, humans belong to one another and to nature.

Faithfulness to the covenant of God is the way of continuing development toward the fulfillment intended for the world and all its parts in creation. Faithlessness means a retreat into stasis, a resistance to change. Faithlessness violates the covenant and harms the object of the action as well as the agent.

In covenant, creation is known to be incomplete, to place nature and humanity in process toward their fulfillment. Community, friendship, peace, and justice, understood through the love of God and guaranteed in Jesus Christ, who is our covenant, provide the key to the creating, judging, and redeeming activity of the covenant God.

From the covenant tradition can come the resources for a renewal of the Christian understanding of the creation and for a new environmental ethics. It is a tradition with deep roots in the Bible and in the Western heritage of theology and ethics. Covenantal thought, though its biblical and theological background is often forgotten, remains woven into the fabric of the modern world. Drawing on this tradition thus offers a means also for renewing the relationship of Christian faith to the patterns of human community and developing a covenantal ethics comprehensive enough for the cultural, environmental problems endangering humanity today.

THE MEANING OF ETHICS

Ethics can be understood most comprehensively as reflection within a community of its interpretation on the moral significance of human action. Codes of conduct, laws, and styles of living may be regarded as related to ethics insofar as they represent the results of ethical reflection. Reflection in a more general sense or as careful reasoning takes place in particular human locations and receives its warrants of validation from specific historical, societal contexts of commitment. Ethics is not necessarily relativistic because it takes place within social locations, but ethics emerges within and depends upon a particular community of interpretation and commitment.

Though many hope otherwise, ethics does not suddenly disclose a realm of absolute right and wrong not previously visible. Instead, ethics can help us see more clearly and steer with greater precision through the environment of values, moral directives, and behavioral valences that surround us.

Morality as "Natural"

We emerge as human beings immersed in social contexts permeated by values. Moral directives are given to us from the time we are born. We internalize these directives and participate in shaping the moral climate of society. From the womb to the tomb, humans exist in relations of intense moral valence. The fabric and varying strength of the particular factors will differ somewhat from one location to another within the same society and will differ greatly from one culture to another. But the presence of values, directives, and moral valences will be a constant.

Morals and behavioral expectations are as "natural" in human social environments as physical objects and biological needs. Varied dietary practices in different cultures do not lead to the conclusion that the need for food is unreal, unnatural, or "merely" emotive. Nor do different colors and shapes of bodies persuade us that physical existence is epiphenomenal to culture. The world as experienced has a wholeness in which the parts are symbiotically related. It is a dubious practice to presuppose the priority of one part and assume the presupposing to be an adequate demonstration. Moral meaning is a pervasive and ineradicable part of the whole that constitutes human living.

Through overt directives and laws and in myriad subtle ways of approval, disapproval, and nuanced response, humans communicate values and valences of behavior to one another. From parents, peers, preachers, police, and teachers—home, school, government, and religious community—the moral directives come and the behavioral valence is enunciated. Communal and ecclesiastical rituals convey and reinforce societal values. And the patterns of intimate human relationship evoke profound impulses to internalize these values.

Plural Moralities and the Rise of Ethical Reflection

Insofar as the framework of explanation and legitimation of moral meaning and action form a coherent totality, we may speak of a religious/cultural system. But there is never complete coherence, certainly not in developed societies and probably not even in societies called "underdeveloped" or "primitive." In our own lives, we become aware early of uneven valences and conflicting moral directives. We are compelled to engage in ethical reflection in order to deal with the directives demanding contradictory actions. At first ethics takes the form of seeking a way to deal with the contrasting directives of parents and siblings, of home and community. Later we find decisively different traditions within our society grasping for our loyalty and commitment. Finding criteria and meaning to make our own as we steer through cultural crosscurrents is the process of forging our ethics and our own identity in a context of plural values and moral directives.

When the plurality of religious/cultural systems around the globe comes into view, the problems of ethics are compounded. The differing moral directives to be found within the fairly coherent heritage of Western culture are difficult enough. Finding adequate criteria for action within the cultural plurality that includes Islam, the varieties of Buddhism and Hinduism, the Marxisms of Lenin and Mao, and widely differing sectors of Christianity, varying with cultural location, may seem impossible for those who must manage policy for nations and transnational social organizations. Ethics can provide important guidance, but not a single, absolute way of "right action" in such a global context. Within particular social enclaves, adherents of Special Revelation or Tradition or Reason may claim to possess a final authority for ethics. But the diversity of moral meaning and action in the wider human community discloses the inadequacy of such absolutisms and demonstrates the extent to which ethics depends on particular historical and social locations.

Such recognition in no way entails relativism. It does involve taking account of differences in values and purposes. Only then can persons and organizations operate outside the limits of particular communities in the wider world arena where plural cultural systems meet.[6]

Ethics as Social

In this perspective, ethics is no less social than it is individual. From the context of moral directives and valent relationships that shape our lives, it is clear that ethics is a profoundly social and deeply necessary human undertaking.

As reflection on the moral significance of human action, ethics takes place on different *levels of agency*. First, there is the individual level of agency. So accustomed have some become to thinking of ethics only in individual terms that they regard this as the only level on which ethical reflection takes place. Such a limited view of ethics is inadequate.

Second, there is the organizational/institutional level of agency. Policymakers in organized groups discuss and deliberate about alternative courses of action for the organization. As diverse values are weighed and priorities set, ethical reflection is taking place. Policy ethics is a way to characterize the ethics of an organization. Illustrations of this level of agency are business corporations, governmental departments, hospitals, labor unions, churches, social service agencies, and community groups of all kinds.

Third, there is the level of agency best described as a social sector. Such professional groups as physicians, dentists, lawyers, artists, and clergy fit here, as do banking, religious groups, health services, government, agriculture, the entertainment industry, the communications media, and the like. Professionals are socialized into a social sector, taking on its values and behavioral patterns.

Fourth, there is the societal level of agency—a total society, political economy, or religious/cultural system, among other forms. On this level the development of criteria takes place gradually and changes slowly. Traditions that have become embedded in societal action represent reflection of an ethical nature. Once developed, this more encompassing level of action exercises great influence over the others. On all these levels, ethics pertains to social groups and organizations as well as to individuals.

As culture and societal interaction emerge on a world scale, a fifth level of moral agency is taking shape, giving a more comprehensive global scope to ethics.

Ethics is social in that moral agents draw criteria for action not primarily from individual reasoning but more from traditions, faiths, and communities of interpretation and commitment that permeate the society. These sources of ethical criteria are communicated as humans touch one another through story and social ritual, as morals are transmuted into law, and as social valence is transformed into internalized values by individual and organizational agents.

ENVIRONMENTAL ETHICS IN THE LIGHT OF CREATION AND COVENANT

Keeping this wider meaning of ethics in mind, we now draw explicitly on the Christian tradition for resources to recover a sense of responsibility toward the environment and for a renewed appreciation of humanity as part of the created order. We shall do this under three headings: creation, creativity, and covenant.[7]

Creation

In keeping with its biblical origins, Christian ethics is an ethics of creation, an understanding that can serve as a primary resource for environmental ethics today. A Christian ethics of creation means, first, that any criteria for human action in Christian faith derive from an understanding of the world as created and valued by God. When God looks upon the creation and declares it good (Gen. 1:31), the inseparability of reality and value is affirmed for ethics and for human action. The created order is good, and goodness is built into the reality of creation.

A Christian ethics of creation, second, does not involve the notion, however, that "nature knows best," as such environmentalists as Barry Commoner appear to be saying. The ground and judge of what is and what exists of value is God, not nature or humanity in themselves. Yet what is good, insofar as humans can understand and respond to it, is present through human experience and through nature.

Third, a Christian ethics of creation does not imply that human values eclipse the value of the natural order. Humanity is created within nature as a part of nature. No meaning of "domination" and "subdue" can make sense when it ignores God's valuation of the entire created order and the relation established in creation between the environment and humanity. Humans are enjoined to use the abundance within which they have been created but not to misuse or abuse it. Neither nature nor humanity is the center of value. God is. And in virtue of that source of value, the entire created order, including humans, shares a goodness permeating its inter-related parts.

Fourth, a Christian ethics of creation derives criteria of human action from "what is." Ethics is rooted in the reality of creation and the wholeness of that reality. On the one hand, the welfare of humanity is bound up with the welfare of the whole. On the other hand, human violation of the created order is as much a peril to the well-being of humanity as of nature. Christian ethics is axiological, that is, concerned with what is valuable. But Christian ethics is equally ontological, that is, concerned with the reality of the created order within which human life emerges and has its context of existence and action.

Christian ethics, fifth, is theocentric. This should already be clear, but it

bears emphasis and clarification. Christian ethics displaces meaning, purpose, and value away from humanity in any original or final sense. Human
life is part of the created natural order. Even more important, however,
for the biblical perspective, meaning, purpose, and value derive from God
as creator and inhere in the created order only in a secondary sense. To
say that Christian ethics is theocentric does not suggest that humans can
somehow achieve the perspective of God. Such a view, for biblical faith,
would be patently idolatrous. The meaning of "theocentric" for Christian
ethics, therefore, cannot be a meaning defined as the opposite of "anthropocentric." Any human believing, any human attempt to understand the
will of God, will inevitably take place from particular human locations and
will in that way be anthropocentric. Copernicus did not leave his human
location and earth-centered perspective when he proclaimed a heliocentric
solar system; he was using his human imagination to construct a different
way of understanding our human location. To the extent that Christians
believe themselves created by God, they know that they live by faith and
not by a certainty derived from occupying the place of God and viewing
reality and value from that center. Though aware that their reflection as
moral beings takes place within historical, social, and natural locations,
Christians believe in the deepest sense that the source of reality and value
is God. As an ethics of creation, Christian ethics points beyond human
location to God for its validation and the possibility for change and renewal.

Sixth, a Christian ethics of creation involves awareness of the wholeness
of the world and the interdependence of all its constituent parts. Christian
ethics, when faithful to the biblical teaching of creation, cannot be other
than committed to environmental integrity. This is required by the value
given the created order by God, as well as by the knowledge that the well-
being of humanity is symbiotically linked to the well-being of nature. For
policy ethics, this wholeness reminds us that tissues are closely related and
cannot be separated out and dealt with one by one as scientific rationality
would prefer. Policy in its implied wholeness corresponds well to the wholeness of a Christian ethics of creation.

Creativity

To speak of ethics and the environment in Christian perspective involves
also an ethics of creativity. Creation is not a static, once-for-all occurrence
but rather refers to the making of something that is new. Creation, as it is
understood in the Bible, is a process involving change and the continuing
emergence of the new. Creation means ongoing renewal toward a consummation hidden in God. Genesis reports God declaring the creation good,
and Revelation affirms that God is making all things new (Revelation 21:5).
It is not a contradiction but rather an illustration of the creativity of God's
activity in creation.

A Christian ethics of creativity, first, means understanding the world and
humanity as created and existing in process. Reflection about the moral

significance of action and the criteria for guiding human responses to God must take account of change. God did not create a perfect world but rather a good world in process toward a greater completeness, toward an everemerging goodness the course and end of which are shrouded in mystery. We know in bits and pieces, but as we move toward that consummation we shall know in the wholeness with which we have been known all along (1 Cor. 13:12). In this perspective, we cannot say that we know with certainty where we are headed. We make projections and we plan on the basis of imagination and information. But reality unfolds in unanticipated ways. We are aware only that we are called in faith toward a future in the hands of God the Faithful One.

A Christian ethics of creativity, second, means human seeking for the new, yet knowing renewal from God is also necessary. On the other hand, humans come into the world with compelling evidence around them of a past filled with emergence of the new. Creation exhibits creativity and calls humans to responsibility in freedom that requires participating in the creativity of the world. New problems calling for new solutions are constantly emerging on the horizons of human experience. The creativity of the Creator is reflected in the responsive creativity of the creatures. On the other hand, humanity rebels against the goodness and faithfulness of God. Humans resist the creational process and turn from the possibilities inherent in creativity. God's renewing and redeeming work through Christ is crucial if creativity is to continue and humans have the possibility of rejoining God's creative process.

Third, a Christian ethics of creativity involves also a sense of purpose, projection, and goal. Responsibility means responding not just to what is happening at the moment but to the unfolding future. Creativity means dreaming forward toward real possibilities while paying careful attention to the present. Because Christians believe that the sovereign reality as created by God is in process toward fulfillment, Christian ethics as ontological must also be teleological. Humans are called to have goals and to make plans to accomplish them. The movement from old to new in the Bible embodies the newness and renewing power of God's love and also points forward to a more encompassing consummation. Jesus speaks of the newness when he says, "You have heard it said of old ... but I say unto you" (Matt. 5:21–22, 27–28, 31–32, 33–34, 38–39, 43–44). He proclaims the new in relation to customs, by his own treatment of and relation to women, and in his dealing with the law. It is not a doing away with the past or with the law but a fulfillment of them (Matt. 5:17). Paul underscores this teleological element that Jesus represents: "For Christ is the end [telos] of the law, that every one who has faith may be justified" (Rom. 10:4).

A Christian ethics of creativity, fourth, with its teleology of nature and history, does not involve a belief in progress either as inevitable or probable. The future holds unfolding possibilities that we perceive dimly. Those possibilities insofar as we can judge them contain a mixture of good and evil.

From both natural occurrences and human action, good and evil come, and rain falls on the just and on the unjust. Jesus is crucified. Prophets and prophetic minorities are persecuted. Leaders of movements for justice are assassinated. Every human accomplishment stands forever on the razor's edge of danger, both in the possibility of being swept away and in the possibility of producing bad rather than good results. The ethics of creativity offers no historical guarantees. But such an ethic does offer guidelines helpful in understanding our creation within, submersion in, and responsibility for the created order and our environment. The ultimate hope of Christian ethics lies in the resurrection of Christ, in possibilities beyond tragedy, and in the faithful action of God bringing all things to consummation with faithfulness.

Covenant

A Christian ethics of creation and creativity requires completion in an ethics of covenant. The entire created order is within the covenant of God and therefore to be valued and respected in itself. The covenant emphasizes the bond among all parts of creation making them interdependent. The covenant provides the basis and bounds of creativity, while creativity underscores that God's covenant is not static but rather shapes a process with purpose and possibility. A Christian ethics of covenant understands humanity as social and symbiotically related to the environment, morally responsible to God for other humans and for nature, and called to act in faithfulness and fittingness.

First, Christian ethics as covenantal involves an understanding of humanity as existing in relationship to society, nature, and God. Humans can be viewed in covenantal perspective neither as separate nor as autonomous individuals. Humans are born into natural and social relationships and exist by means of a web of interdependency. To be an individual is to be in symbiotic relationship with nature and with particular human communities. The natural order and history have a dynamic quality of change, yet there are also in our experience strong elements of stability and dependability. Experience discloses a covenanted world of change within steadfast patterns. Philosophers may presuppose a static substance underlying the ordered flow of events, but nothing of that static substructure appears in human experiencing. Or scientific positivists may adhere to the dogma of static "facts" waiting to be uncovered and described, but their seeking for "objective reality" never escapes its involvement with their "subjective interpretations." A covenanted wholeness provides a more adequate rationality or metaphor for our world than do the fragmented results of critical rationality or metaphors of organism and society alone. Covenant encompasses the parts, restores the relatedness of the whole environment, and adds dimensions of commitment and loyalty to the created order and to God.

Second, Christian ethics as covenantal includes the moral responsibility of humans within and through the fabric of relationships in an environment that is at once natural, social, and divine. The covenantal call of the Hebrew prophets for justice in the political economy and for liberation from oppression, the command of Jesus that we love one another as he has loved us, and the demand flowing through all the Bible for faithful response in all our actions to the faithfulness of God—all these and the vivid narratives in which they are conveyed give content and valence to covenantal ethics.

Third, Christian ethics as covenantal reminds us that fittingness and faithfulness through Jesus Christ, who is our covenant, are central for Christian faith and action. Fittingness means that human action must correspond to the need of the context and be appropriate within the pattern of prior and subsequent action. In one sense, fittingness underscores the importance of particularity—responding to particular persons, situations, and issues. In a larger sense, fittingness requires taking account of the encompassing context of the social and natural environment, so that what is done fits in with everything else that is happening and avoids causing more problems than it solves. Faithfulness means loyalty to the cause of God, whatever the consequences. In the extreme cases, it could involve a martyr's death. In the more usual sense, however, faithfulness means loyalty to our companions on life's journey, to our world, and through these loyalty to God. In seeking justice for the downtrodden, liberation for the oppressed, food for the hungry, clothes for the naked, sound ecological policies, and ways to avoid nuclear holocaust, we are being faithful not only to our neighbors in society and the larger environment but also to God the Faithful One, who in covenant creates a symbiotic order and continually judges, redeems, and renews this bent and battered world.

Christian ethics within this vision provides a comprehensive and rigorous pattern for recovering the biblical sense of living in the light of creation as we develop a meaningful environmental ethics for today.

NOTES

1. D. Walter Eichrodt, *Theologie des alten Testaments*. Three volumes (Leipzig: J. C. Hinrichs, 1933), vol. I, p. 6.

2. See Norman H. Snaith, *The Distinctive Ideas of the Old Testament* (London: Epworth Press, 1944); and Otto J. Baab, *The Theology of the Old Testament* (New York: Abingdon-Cokesbury Press, 1949).

3. Martin Buber, *The Prophetic Faith* (New York: Macmillan, 1949), passim.

4. Bernard H. Anderson, *Understanding the Old Testament* (Englewood Cliffs: Prentice-Hall, 1958), p. 51.

5. Johannes Althusius, *Politics*, trans. by Frederick S. Carney (Boston: Beacon Press, 1964), I, 1.

6. See Charles S. McCoy, *When Gods Change: Hope for Theology* (Nashville, Tenn.: Abingdon, 1980).

7. For a somewhat different but compatible treatment, see H. Paul Santmire, *Brother Earth: Nature, God, and Ecology in Time of Crisis* (New York: Thomas Nelson, 1970).

PART III

RECONSTRUCTING JUSTICE FOR ENVIRONMENTAL ETHICS

10

A Right To Know, A Call To Act

ALEXANDRA ALLEN

It is absolutely necessary to establish strong environmental lobbying efforts to counter the efforts of industry and other factions resisting environmental legislation. No such environmental lobbying efforts can achieve anything of significance in the absence of vital grassroots movements keeping legislatures accountable. Even in the face of meaningful victories, democratic forces are well aware of the limitations of the environmental legislation that has been approved. Alexandra Allen appeals to all of us to become active in grassroots struggles for environmental controls and offers some suggestions about how to do that. One is that we become familiar with the "People's Bill of Rights" and the "Three Rights." Since rights language is justice language, these claims challenge us to consider whether we really believe citizens have a legitimate right to demand a healthy environment.

From their position off the floor of the House of Representatives, a handful of environmental lobbyists peered through the doorway to glimpse the electronic board tallying the members' votes. It looked grim. The vote on whether to require industries to publicly disclose the types and amounts of toxic chemicals they put into the environment, begun just before 7 P.M., would last only another fifteen minutes, and the "ayes" trailed by thirty votes. The most senior of the environmental lobbyists shook his head, patted a few of the hopefuls on the back, and headed out the door and down the marble steps of the Capitol. Fifteen minutes later, bill sponsors Reps. Bob Edgar of Pennsylvania and Gerry Sikorski of Minnesota, and the lobbyists left behind, began to celebrate one of the most significant environmental victories ever — passage, by a one-vote margin, of the 1986 Community Right-To-Know Act.

The right-to-know victory created an important new tool for communities, achieved through persistent, creative citizen organizing, coordinated with skillful lobbying and legislative maneuvering. It was a victory achieved in the face of well-financed adversaries in industry and powerful political opponents. Passage of the Superfund toxic-waste cleanup law (the Superfund Amendments and Reauthorization Act, or SARA), of which the Right-To-Know Act was a part, marked a step forward by vastly increasing the funding available for cleanups, and by reinforcing the principle that polluters should pay for environmental damage.

Yet, there is a long way to go. While the right-to-know law offers a dramatic example of how democratic forces can be unleashed when citizens gain access to critical information about their communities, it is just a bare beginning toward empowering citizens to hold polluting companies and governmental agencies directly accountable for their actions. Meanwhile, the failures of the Superfund toxic-waste cleanup program have been a notorious result of the federal bureaucracy's open hostility toward it. Today, the poisoning of people and places continues, a sign of the violent, unsustainable relationships that exist within the human world, and between the human world and the rest of creation. Other signs abound: strip-mined mountains and decaying mining towns; unhealthy urban air and city dwellers' scarred lungs; the condition of the earth's ozone layer, its oceans, or its old-growth forests; and on and on.

That these environmental crises are linked by their common source in a crisis of justice and democracy is not a new observation. Even in the early days of the American conservation movement, when citizens fought to save forestlands and other natural resources from pillaging by corporate raiders, their struggle for conservation became a larger fight for what President Teddy Roosevelt called "real democracy."[1] Some eighty years later, notwithstanding George Bush's claim to be the "environmental president," people who are ready to demand real democracy and environmental justice do not yet have sufficient political power to force needed changes in U.S. government and industry. While there are glimmers of hope, and some nascent victories, the time to get involved is now. And the place to get involved need not be very far away; it can be right where you live.

ORGANIZE! THE CAMPAIGN FOR A NEW SUPERFUND AND THE RIGHT TO KNOW

Every year, chemical companies, oil companies, pulp and paper mills, and other industries produce some 560 million tons of hazardous waste. For decades, these chemical poisons have been dumped and abandoned at thousands of sites across the country. The federal Environmental Protection Agency (EPA) has listed 30,000 hazardous dumpsites as possible candidates for Superfund cleanup. Out of these thousands of examples of corporate and governmental irresponsibility, a handful have become national symbols: Love Canal in Niagara Falls, New York; Times Beach, Missouri; the Stringfellow Acid Pits in Glen Avon, California.

Congress made its first legislative response to this crisis with the passage of the original Superfund law in 1980. That law allocated $1.6 billion over five years for the cleanup of abandoned hazardous-waste sites. From the start, the Superfund program was crippled by the failure of the Reagan-appointed EPA head, Anne Burford, and the Superfund program director, Rita Lavelle, to carry out the mandate of the law. In 1983, Burford left office and Ms. Lavelle was imprisoned after a series of scandals and highly publicized congressional investigations. Yet, the scandals were only part of the problem, as the Reagan EPA carried out a concerted effort to thwart Congress's intent to create a workable cleanup program.

By the middle of 1985, EPA had placed 850 locations on its "National Priorities List" of the most dangerous sites, but had completed cleanup of only six of them. With that dubious record, the original Superfund legislation expired in 1985, and grassroots groups launched a nationwide effort to press for a stronger law. In September of 1985, the National Campaign Against Toxic Hazards (NCATH), a coalition of 300 citizen, labor, and environmental groups, issued a five-year "Progress Report" on Superfund that spelled out the program's failures and called for major improvements. In case studies of 15 cleanups, NCATH demonstratd EPA's shortsighted attempts to save money through cleanups that perpetuated existing dumps and created new ones. EPA practice had become a "toxic shell game" of attempting to contain wastes at a site, or shift wastes to a new site — rather than using available means to destroy toxic substances and reduce risks on a permanent basis.

NCATH and other citizen groups called for an end to the toxic shell game, mandatory standards governing the way sites are cleaned up, strict adherence to the polluter-pays principle, a $10 billion cleanup fund, and the right to know about chemical emissions. Only with an adequately funded program would EPA have the option of either forcing polluters to do cleanups or carrying them out itself and then suing polluters to recoup expenses.

Action by the U.S. Senate was early but weak. In September of 1985, the Senate passed a $7.5 billion Superfund bill with lax cleanup requirements and a limited right-to-know program. But even as the senators were voting, the momentum for tougher action was kept alive by the timely arrival in Washington of the "Superdrive for Superfund."

Four flatbed trucks, known as the "Stringfellow Special," the "Love Canal Limited," the "Times Beach Bullet," and the "Jersey Express," made stops in 120 communities in 37 states on their way to Washington, D.C. At each stop along the NCATH-sponsored drive, local residents turned out to hand over jars, cans, and bags containing samples of contaminated soil and water, as well as posters, dead plants, and other mementos of life in the midst of chemical poisoning. Local citizen groups organized news conferences held as the samples were loaded onto the trucks. Over a million signatures were also collected on petitions urging members of Congress to enact a Superfund program with enough financial backing and legal force to get the toxic dumps cleaned up.

At a stop in Portland, Oregon, aboard the "Stringfellow Special," John O'Connor, who led NCATH and now serves as director of the National Toxics Campaign, called the Superfund program a "super failure" that had created a toxic merry-go-round. In Washington, O'Connor and others stood beside the Capitol, and beside samples of the country's toxic waste, and presented their petitions to members of Congress.

Without the citizen organizing that sustained the "Superdrive for Superfund" and many other grassroots efforts, the victories in the Superfund legislative battles would have been impossible, for the environmental lobbyists in Washington advocating a strong Superfund were thoroughly outnumbered and outspent by the industry opposition. A 1985 report by Superfund lobbyist Rick Hind of the U.S. Public Interest Research Group (U.S. PIRG) revealed that 122 corporate lobbyists identified themselves as working on Superfund. The same inspection of environmental and public-interest groups' lobbying records showed only eight Superfund lobbyists.

Environmental and consumer groups that did have lobbyists working on Superfund included the Clean Water Action Project, Public Citizen, National Audubon Society, Sierra Club, Environmental Action, and U.S. PIRG. In addition, one of the most important successes in the campaign for Superfund and the right to know was the cooperation that occurred among labor and environmental groups. Grassroots action and Washington lobbying by labor unions, including the Oil, Chemical, and Atomic Workers Union, the United Auto Workers, and the United Steelworkers, proved critical.

Aligned against the Superfund bill were more than 450 corporations, including such major multinationals as Exxon, Union Carbide, Eastman Kodak, and United Airlines, as well as such industry trade associations as the American Petroleum Institute, the Chemical Manufacturers Association, the American Insurance Association, and the National Association of Manufacturers.

Reports of lobbying expenses filed by Superfund opponents read like a directory of Washington's most expensive restaurants, including one $220 bill at the posh Le Lion D'Or to introduce a member of Congress to a corporate executive concerned about Superfund.[2] On top of their lobbying expenses, corporate opponents of Superfund were leading participants in Congress's corrupt system of campaign finance, contributing thousands of dollars in order to gain access and influence there.

A chief industry ally during the Superfund battle was Rep. John Dingell, Democrat of Michigan, the powerful chairman of the Committee on Energy and Commerce through which roughly half of all House legislation passes. Working in concert with Republican opponents of a strong Superfund, Dingell had pushed a weak bill with no right-to-know program through his committee in July of 1985.

However, Dingell's panel was just one of five committees that considered the Superfund bill, and in the Public Works and Transportation Committee environmentalists found badly needed support from the late chairman, Rep. James J. Howard, and Rep. Bob Roe, both Democrats from New Jersey — the state with the largest number of toxic waste dumps on the National Priorities List, and one with a vocal statewide network of community groups fighting toxic hazards. In November of 1985, the public-works committee produced a Superfund bill much stronger than Rep. Dingell's version.

After weeks of negotiation, the committee leaders reached an agreement that resolved some of the differences between their bills. The agreed-upon provisions were introduced as H.R. 3852 on December 4, and it was late the following day that the first, but not the final, House floor vote on the community right-to-know amendment was held. H.R. 3852 contained a limited right-to-know program requiring disclosure only for chemicals known to cause immediate dangers. A liberal Pennsylvania Democrat, Rep. Bob Edgar, took the lead on improving that program by offering a comprehensive alternative requiring disclosure of emissions of chemicals that cause health problems, such as cancer and birth defects, over a long period of exposure, as well as of those that cause immediate effects. By a vote of 183–166, the Edgar amendment was adopted.

Angry and defeated, Dingell contended that the Edgar amendment would unduly burden small business with unmanageable paperwork, and that too large a group of chemicals was covered by the disclosure requirement. During the House debate, he had ridiculed the list of covered chemicals as including "anything which could cause anything, from flat feet to falling hair, and anything else."[3]

Also stung by the defeat, Republican opponents of the right-to-know law quickly sought a second vote on the amendment. Under House rules, second votes may be permitted by the leadership where it can be shown that a switch in members' votes, or the added votes of absent members, is likely to change the outcome. Eighty-five members had been absent during the initial vote, and the margin of victory was only 17 votes. Thus, five days later, right-to-know opponents received a second chance.

Excerpts from the floor debate give some indication of how important it was to some members of Congress, and even some members of the medical and teaching professions, to keep the extent of industries' poisoning hidden from the public.

Dingell's ally, Rep. Al Swift, Democrat of Washington, argued that the Edgar amendment was unnecessary since it would be nearly impossible for "all but the most sophisticated local governments" to absorb the information. A Kentucky Republican, Rep. Gene Snyder, presented a letter from the presidents of the Association of American Medical Colleges and the American Council on Education that read, in part: "At issue here is the appropriate balance of health and environmental considerations and the operational realities facing individual institutions. Unfortunately, the Edgar amendment is heavily tilted towards inchoate fears about health risks."

An exasperated Rep. Edgar responded:

> Mr. Chairman, for the life of me, I cannot understand what we are trying to hide from the American people. We are talking about poisons. Whether the poison kills you today or tommorow or next week, we are talking about poisons. . . . Does your community have the right to know whether workers are being exposed to vinyl chloride or dioxin or toluene? Does a mother have the right to know whether her children are playing in PCB's or dioxin released from a nearby factory? Do pregnant women have the right to know the amounts of discharges which may cause birth defects in their children? I say yes, and I think it is incumbent upon this House . . . to support this amendment."[4]

Once debate concluded, the roll was called, and the right-to-know victory was preserved by the narrowest possible margin, 212 ayes to 211 nays.

However, the floor victories were not final, and grassroots groups focused their attention during the following months on the conference committee charged with reconciling the House and Senate versions of the bill. Citizens brought national attention to the fact that Rep. John Dingell, as chairman of the conference committee, was seeking to weaken the House bill for which he was ostensibly delegated to fight. However, Dingell's aim was largely thwarted by members acting under pressure to produce tough legislation. After the final version was approved by the House and Senate, veto threats from the White House hung as the last clouds of doubt. But the clouds were quietly broken when President Reagan signed the Superfund and right-to-know bill, without ceremony, on the afternoon of October 17, 1986.

The new Superfund was a big improvement over the original law of 1980. The size of the cleanup fund went from $1.6 billion over five years to $8.5 billion over the same period. A mandatory schedule was established that required the EPA to complete cleanups of at least 375 sites over six years. Cleanups were to achieve permanent destruction of contaminants whenever possible. Citizens' opportunities to participate in the selection of cleanup methods at sites was to be expanded through grants that would enable them to hire technical experts to work on their behalf. And through the Community Right-to-Know Act, citizens became able to learn what toxic chemicals were being stored and discharged at industrial plants.

Yet, the experience since 1986 is a clear illustration of the limitations of the Superfund and right-to-know victories, and of how much more organizing, educating, and challenging of political and economic institutions there is yet to be done.

A FOOT IN THE DOOR OF ENVIRONMENTAL JUSTICE

The right-to-know law requires companies to publicly disclose their annual emissions of some 300 hazardous chemicals. This information is collected at the plants and in local, state, and federal government offices; it is available to citizens in those places and, increasingly, over a computer network. (The Working Group on Community Right-To-Know can help citizens obtain and interpret emissions data. See note 17, below.) Already more than 30 organizations have exercised their right to know by collecting emissions data and producing reports that have received wide media and public attention.

In 1987, industries reported releasing 20 billion pounds of toxics into the air, land, and water of this country, or 80 pounds per person. EPA called the figure "shocking" and said the numbers "have got to come down." According to a policy analyst at the Office of Technology Assessment, "Twenty billion pounds is just the tip of the toxic tower. We estimate that as much as 400 billion pounds [of emissions] are probably being generated by American industry annually."[5]

The right-to-know information has also made plain the gross inadequacy of existing toxics-control laws, for the emissions reported under the right-to-know law are all legal. Meanwhile, voluntary efforts by companies to reduce emissions of toxics have been rare indeed. An analysis of 1987 data for the states of Maryland and Illinois by the Natural Resources Defense Council, a national environmental group, revealed that 75 percent of the toxic releases to the air were totally uncontrolled.

However, under the right-to-know spotlight some companies that produce and use toxic chemicals have proven that they can do more to reduce emissions into the air, land, and water than they had ever previously acknowledged. At Northern Telecom, redesign of steps in the electronic-circuit manufacturing process has led to vastly reduced use of chlorofluorocarbons, chemicals that destroy the earth's ozone layer.

Yet, not all claims of reduced use and emissions of toxics seem to be valid. In Santa Clara, California, for example, the Santa Clara County Manufacturing Group, which includes large semiconductor and computer manufacturers, has claimed that for 1988 two dozen companies' emissions of toxic chemicals were down 40 percent from the 1987 level. However, Ted Smith, executive director of the Silicon Valley Toxics Coalition, attributes most of the companies' reductions to changes in the way they calculate their emissions. Smith, whose organization has been a persistent watchdog over local industries, sees them at a very early stage in addressing emissions reductions.

Toxics activists have also confronted the danger that reduced emissions of toxic chemicals to the environment may simply mean greater use of toxics in products to which workers and consumers are exposed. For instance, it was reported in 1985 that Monsanto Corporation had reformulated an industrial adhesive so that hazardous wastes remained in the product, thus eliminating the waste stream. Yet, as a result, the product itself was more toxic to the consumer, and it remained a danger to the environment once the material was thrown "away."[6]

The questions that remain unanswered by right-to-know data reflect limitations in the law itself, such as its complete reliance on self-reporting by industry and the absence of any requirement that companies divulge their total *use* of toxic chemicals. Such a requirement would help reveal transfers of toxics from waste streams into products and would make right-to-know data a more effective tool in citizens' advocacy for reduced use of toxic chemicals by industry. Yet, despite its limitations, in the right-to-know law citizens have created for themselves a powerful new tool of local democracy, enabling them to press polluters and governments to cut down chemical poisoning.

Not nearly so dramatic a change has resulted from the 1986 regulatory requirements governing cleanup of Superfund sites. Since the 1986 passage of Superfund Amendments and Reauthorization Act (SARA), virtually every aspect of the Superfund program has come under criticism. While comprehensive reports have detailed the program's failures, a few general observations make the point.[7]

First of all, out of the tens of thousands of toxic dump sites identified, and the 1,200 on EPA's National Priorities List, just 26 have been cleaned up. Although cleanup is under way at more than 400 locations, to have completed the job at just over two dozen sites in the nine-year history of the program is an abysmal record indeed.

Second, permanent cleanup technologies, which were required under SARA to be used wherever possible, are not being used nearly enough. Of cleanup plans developed in 1987, technologies that could actually destroy toxic contaminants were used in only eight percent of the cases. There was some improvement in 1988, when such technologies were planned for use at half of the sites. But to a large extent EPA has ignored the requirements of the new law and continued to conduct "cleanups" by attempting to contain toxic wastes or by moving them to new sites rather than by actually destroying them.

Third, resources allocated to Superfund and management of the program are both still inadequate. EPA itself has estimated that the cleanup cost at sites currently on the National Priorities List could reach $30 billion, more than three times the size of the current fund. Accountability and consistency in Superfund cleanups are rare. A multitude of private contractors hired by EPA are supervising one another, while EPA regional offices render decisions without any oversight or coordination from headquarters to ensure that legal requirements are being met.

Finally, the Environmental Protection Agency has thwarted the objectives of the Technical Assistance Grant (TAG) program created by SARA in 1986. Grassroots groups had succeeded in convincing Congress and the EPA that if citizens were going to be full participants with government and industry in decisions on site cleanup they should have technical advisors of their own. The TAG program offers up to $50,000 to local groups to hire such experts. However, after long delays in getting the TAG program off the ground, EPA came up with a set of procedures and requirements for grant applicants so burdensome that many community groups cannot or will not apply. Perhaps the most blatant example of EPA's unwillingness to let the TAG program achieve its aim comes from Jacksonville, Arkansas, where the EPA awarded three Technical Assistance Grants, totalling $150,000, to a group that the agency knew had been formed by the very industries responsible for the three Superfund sites in Jacksonville. Meanwhile, the EPA rejected the TAG application from the most active citizens group in the community, Friends United for a Safe Environment (FUSE). The National Toxics Campaign, which has worked with FUSE for the last four years, has called for a congressional investigation of EPA's misuse of TAG funds and undermining of the Superfund program.

FROM THE CITIZENS OF TOXIC AMERICA, NEXT STEPS TOWARD ENVIRONMENTAL JUSTICE

The inadequacies of the Superfund program and the limitations of the right-to-know law are most apparent to people living in the midst of toxic-dumpsites and major chemical polluters. From their knowledge and experiences have come new goals and demands. While there is no single agenda or platform behind which every grassroots environmental group is united, strategies have emerged that reflect a refusal to wait for government to come up with solutions, a commitment to empowering local citizens to fully participate in decisions affecting their health and safety, and an insistance on the right to live free of toxic poisoning. Their demands can be summed up as a call for environmental justice.

Out of experiences in local communities across the country, the National Toxics Campaign has developed the "Three Rights" organizing model to directly empower local citizens. The "Three Rights" are:
- the *right to know* about the presence and risks of toxics that directly or indirectly affect public health and safety
- the *right to inspect* any facility, factory, landfill, or source of industrial pollution with technical experts of the citizens' choosing
- the *right to negotiate* with management a legally binding agreement requiring health and safety improvements at a facility.[8]

The Citizens Clearinghouse for Hazardous Wastes, a resource center and nationwide organizing network born out of the struggle at Love Canal, New York, has developed the "People's Bill of Rights." It reads as follows:

People in this country have the right to be safe and secure in their homes and workplaces. We have the right to bring up our children and live our lives free from harm imposed by toxic substances that have been brought into our communities, neighborhoods, workplaces, schools and farms by others, without our knowledge and without our consent. We have the right to clean air, clean water, uncontaminated food and safe places to live, work and play. We have the right to require our government to be accountable and industry to be responsible. We have the right to action and to public policy which will restore to us that which has been taken away and to stop the needless and unjustifiable attack on our lives, families, homes, jobs and future that come from the imposition of toxic substances in our environment.

Right To Be Safe From Harmful Exposure. People have the inherent right to be safe in their homes and workplaces. Our children have the right to grow up strong and healthy, not diseased, deformed or to die before they've had the chance to live, to be safe in their schools, free from cancer-causing asbestos or other hazards, and to play in their backyards free from erupting chemical pits or contaminated soils. We have the right to be free from exposures, imposed on us against our will, to poisonous substances that can cause birth defects, cancer, sterility, genetic damage, miscarriages and still births.

Right To Know. We have the right to know what poisons other people, industry, corporate polluters and government have decided to bring into our neighborhoods and workplaces and the right to know how these chemicals can adversely affect our health, our environment and exactly what they intend, if anything, to do about it.

Right To Clean Up. We have the right to safe, total cleanup of hazardous waste sites and spills, to have the cleanups take place quickly with our neighborhoods, homes and environment restored to the way it was before the polluters chose to contaminate them with chemical poisons.

Right To Participate. We have the right to participate, *as equals*, in decisions affecting our lives, children, homes and jobs on the matter of exposure to hazardous wastes. We have the right of access, without cost, to information and assistance that will make our participation meaningful and to have our needs and concerns be the major factor in *all* policy decisions.

Right To Compensation. We have the right to be compensated for damages to our health, our homes and our livelihoods. The responsible parties must compensate us for the cost of cancer treatments, care of our birth-defected children, the loss of our farms and jobs, livestock and the burial of our loved ones.

Right To Prevention. We have the right to public policy that *prevents* toxic pollution from entering our neighborhoods by using existing technology beginning with reduction at the source—a technology that will provide jobs, business opportunities and conservation of valuable resources. Our workers have the right to safety equipment and other safety measures to prevent their exposure in the workplace.

Right To Protection and Enforcement. We have the right to strong laws controlling toxic wastes and vigorous enforcement of those laws, not backroom, sweetheart deals. If a child dies from exposure to chemical poisons in the environment, someone must be arrested and prosecuted for manslaughter.[9]

While these basic environmental rights are aimed at protecting communities against toxic poisoning, they are fundamentally the same rights that are at stake in any struggle for environmental justice, whether the immediate issue is forest preservation or hazardous-waste incineration: the right to live free of dangers and deprivation created by environmental destruction, and the right of citizens to fully participate with businesses and government in decisions that affect their communities.

Achieving the new political and economic order called for by the "People's Bill of Rights" will require a change in attitudes and actions not only by corporate and governmental officials but by each of us. The changes include shifting to less consumptive life-styles and increasing community ties and political awareness and participation.

In his 1990 New Year's Day address, President Vaclav Havel of Czechoslovakia spoke to the need for ordinary Czechoslovakians who had been deprecated and victimized by the Communist regime to accept responsibility for their nation's condition. Said Havel

all of us have become accustomed to the totalitarian system, accepted it as an inalterable fact and thereby kept it running. In other words, all of us are responsible, each to a different degree, for keeping the totalitarian machine running. None of us is merely a victim of it, because all of us helped to create it together. ... If we can accept this, then we will understand that it is up to all of us to do something about it. We cannot lay all the blame on those who ruled us before, not only because this would not be true but also because it could detract from the responsibility each of us now faces—the responsibility to act on our own initiative, freely, sensibly and quickly....[10]

Havel's words ring as true for Americans' struggle to overcome corporate malfeasance and bureacratic indifference and to achieve environmental justice as they do for central and eastern Europeans' struggle to shake off forty years of totalitarianism. In some way, it is incumbent upon each of us to move into action.

OVERCOMING HURDLES TO ACTION

Rather than a specific action plan for confronting governments and industries, what follows is a discussion of some of the obstacles that can deter people from becoming educated about and involved in the environmental-justice struggle. Some ideas are offered on choosing a group that can provide information and opportunities for involvement. Through involvement with others, specific action plans will develop.

Three very frequently encountered obstacles to involvement are discussed here: the challenge of finding a starting point; reluctance to become involved in an issue fraught with conflict; and the seemingly incomprehensible maze of technical and legal issues that envelops acts of environmental destruction.

As a point to start, and maintain, one's involvement, there is no better place than one's own community. For the scope of change needed to end the environmental crisis is so great that it will affect every neighborhood in every community as environmental problems themselves now do.

In *Cry of the Environment*, Joranson and Butigan have written that

worldwide environmental abuse is rooted in a set of ideas which have become the assumptions and axioms of modern human behavior—assumptions about technological progress, about an infinitely expanding consumption of raw materials, about the primacy of humankind in the world order, and about the unceasing maximization of "development."[11]

Surely, some manifestation of these assumptions is present in every community. Thinking about the following questions, several of which are based on a questionnaire developed by Jim Dodge, a sheep rancher and bioregionalist in western Sonoma County, California, can help illuminate manifestations of misguided assumptions that are ripe for challenge in a local community or region.

1) What is the source of the water that you drink? Who owns industries or farms that pollute the water source? What treatment does the water undergo, and at whose expense?

2) Where does your garbage go? What does your garbage consist of?

3) What are some beings (nonhuman) which also inhabit the region where you live?

4) Who supplies the energy and fuel used in your area? Does the local or state government have a plan concerning future energy needs? Did your community participate in making the plan?

5) What are the costs—all the costs—of motor vehicle use in your area? Are less costly transportation alternatives available?

6) How many people live next door to you? What are their names?

7) What types of chemicals have been used to grow fruit, vegetables, cereals, and other foods sold in your neighborhood?

8) Were the stars out last night? [12]

No matter what the problem that needs to be fixed, or what new awareness needs to be cultivated, probably the most important thing about making the leap from concern to action is that few people make it alone, or are very successful when they do. The title and tenet of the first section of this chapter, "Organize!," holds true whether the institution that needs to be changed is a business down the street or an agency in Washington, D.C. Fortunately, literally thousands of groups of citizens working for environmental justice in their communities already exist. Their work is focused where they live, but through such organizations as the Citizens Clearinghouse and the National Toxics Campaign, grassroots groups have enabled themselves to share information and experiences and to plan nationwide strategies. In other words, to build a movement. In 1989, the National Toxics Campaign and three other environmental groups, the Clean Water Action Project, Greenpeace, and the U.S. Public Interest Research Group, formed a new alliance of grassroots organizations that is currently working to promote the use of safe alternatives to chemicals that destroy the earth's ozone layer. Addresses for these organizations, and information on obtaining a directory of environmental organizations, are listed in note 17, below.

There are numerous organizations with a wide variety of environmental campaigns and educational programs, and making a reasoned choice about where to get involved can take some investigating. Environmental groups vary tremendously in the extent to which they maintain accountability to their members, provide opportunities to get involved in one's own community, and recognize and respond to the environmental crisis as an issue of social justice. A recent project undertaken jointly by most of the national environmental-advocacy organizations illustrated some of the differences in outlook between them and some of the locally based groups that have been working to stop environmental destruction in their communities.

Shortly after George Bush's election in 1988, 18 national environmental and conservation groups put together an agenda for the President-elect known as the "Blueprint for the Environment." It called for policy changes from several federal agencies concerned with pollution, public lands, energy, endangered species, and other matters. However, the "Blueprint" did not link the environmental crisis to an underlying political crisis, as the following critique by Richard L. Grossman, former director of Greenpeace USA and of Environmentalists for Full Employment, points out:

> the Blueprint reinforces existing power relationships and the way decisions have been made. It does not call for citizen mobilization, for democracy in action. Indeed, it reveals that beyond "protecting" what they narrowly define as "environment," these groups are pretty satisfied with how things work. This publication does not "see" the growing disparities between producers and workers, between producers and communities — along with other symptoms of democracy gone awry — as sources of our planetary destruction. ... [The "Blueprint"

is] a brake on social action . . . [that] helps people focus their gazes anywhere but upon the poisoners and destroyers.[13]

Organize, yes. But reflect before you leap.

Once a group has been found that can provide opportunities to learn and to become involved, another hurdle, aversion to conflict, is frequently encountered. The late Chicago community organizer Saul Alinsky attributes this aversion at least in part to Madison Avenue public relations and "middle-class moral hygiene," which have made conflict something negative and undesirable, when in fact it is the essential core of a free society.[14]

There is an obvious and direct conflict between citizens struggling to protect themselves and their communities from toxic poisoning and other environmental hazards and corporate decision makers for whom short-term maximization of profit is the chief objective. However, as a Christian organizer against hunger, Kimberley Bobo, has said, "Neither the concept of empowerment nor the likelihood of conflict are foreign to Christians. . . . For Christians, seeking justice is fundamental to faith. . . . If seeking justice requires social change, we must organize to achieve social change. If that causes conflict, we must find courage to face the problem."[15]

Closely related to aversion to conflict are potentially paralyzing feelings of guilt and personal responsibility for one's contribution to the environmental crisis. How, after all, can we feel right about criticizing corporations for their actions when we drive cars, send our trash to landfills, and use plastic bags, household cleansers, polyester, and a host of other products derived from synthetic chemicals? The question, really, is about choices. And it is dangerous for the public, but beneficial to many corporations, for people to forget that large, remote governments and businesses routinely make decisions that drastically narrow the choices that individuals can make.

Who knows of anyone who decided they would rather *not* have a cleaner-running, more fuel-efficient car; less-polluting alternatives to transportation by private automobile; the opportunity to buy products in reusable, or at least recyclable, packages; or the option of purchasing cleaning supplies and other products whose manufacture does not depend on petroleum and produce toxic waste? We can make some personal choices that reduce our contribution to environmental dangers, and help rid ourselves of guilt, but it will not suffice simply to start up environmentally conscious boutiques for those who can afford them. Solutions lie in making better alternatives available to everyone, and that will not come from a citizenry paralyzed by guilt.

Finally, an often formidable barrier to citizen involvement in environmental issues is the belief that the issues are so scientific and technical that people without specialized training cannot or should not participate. This belief is a close cousin of the idea that "advanced technology" can solve any problem and will always improve the economy. To their great benefit, industrial corporations and their allies in government avidly promote these beliefs. Thus, citizens attempting to get answers from the "experts" in industry and government instead routinely get incomprehensible, jargonistic responses, which leave them thinking either that they are hopelessly handicapped because they lack the appropriate specialized background or that there was something unjust and undemocratic about their experience.

When citizens conclude the former, the winners are the polluters. But when they conclude the latter, it can lead to some interesting discoveries, and to action. It is typical, for example, in a conflict between local citizens and a corporation operating a plant in the community to find that none of the industry "experts" who assure others of the plant's safety actually live in the affected area. Nor, very often, do many government officials, who frequently do more to represent corporate interests than citizens' interests. Those who are so eager to deny local people a voice in decisions affecting them are almost always from somewhere else.

On this point, the author Wendell Berry warns that "[a] powerful class of itinerant professional vandals is now pillaging the country and laying it waste." Berry describes a class

> whose allegiance to communities and places has been dissolved by their economic motives and their educations. These are people who will go anywhere and jeopardize anything in order to assure the success of their careers.[16]

This is not to say that there is never a need for technical expertise. Many successful grassroots environmental groups have refused to be shut out of decisions filled with technical complexities. They have hired experts of their own and have acquired expertise on their own. It is the as-yet-unfulfilled goal of the Superfund Technical Assistance Grant program, discussed earlier in this chapter, to enable grassroots groups to obtain independent technical advice concerning cleanup of toxic-waste dumps. In addition, grassroots organizations are already using right-to-know data to do "waste audits" of industries, and there is a long history of citizens documenting illegal dumping into rivers and lakes under the federal Clean Water Act. Many more such projects and funding arrangements need to be developed so that technical complexity ceases to be an obstacle to democratic decision making and environmental justice.

Finally, a basic reason for overcoming the "expertise barrier" to action on environmental issues is the simple fact that, fundamentally, environmental issues are not technical issues at all, but ethical and political ones. While new technologies play a role in the solutions, solutions do not come from technology. Rather, they must come from greater political and economic democracy, and from changed attitudes and values.

Our society has a long way to go toward establishing just and sustainable relationships within the human world and between it and the rest of creation. And, as the right-to-know and Superfund experiences illustrate, despite their rhetoric about "investment in the future" neither industry experts nor government agencies will establish these new relationships. If safe, sustainable, and just communities are to be created, they must be founded by ordinary people who recognize what is valuable and organize to protect it.[17]

NOTES

I thank Bill Walsh, Gene Karpinski, Rick Hind, Paul Orum, and, especially, Timothy Carr for their very helpful contributions to this chapter.

1. Stewart L. Udall, *The Quiet Crisis* (New York: Holt, Rinehart, and Winston, 1963), p. 134.

2. Rick Hind, "Super Lobbyists: The Corporate Campaign To Stop Superfund" (Washington, D.C.: U.S. Public Interest Research Group, May 1985).

3. *Congressional Record* (December 5, 1985): 34, 761.

4. Ibid. (December 10, 1985): 11, 591–93.

5. Paul Orum, ed., *Working Notes on Community Right To Know* (Washington, D.C.: U.S. Public Interest Research Group Education Fund, June 1989), quoting Kirsten Oldenburg of the Office of Technology Assessment, U.S. Congress.

6. "From Pollution Control to Pollution Prevention" (Boston: PIRG Toxics Action and the National Toxics Campaign, Feb. 1989), p. 4, citing David Sarokin et al., "Cutting Chemical Wastes" (New York: INFORM, 1985).

7. For a thorough review of the Superfund program's implementation, see "Right Train, Wrong Track: Failed Leadership in the Superfund Cleanup Program" (Washington, D.C.: Environmental Defense Fund, Hazardous Waste Treatment Council, National Audubon Society, Natural Resources Defense Council, National Wildlife Federation, Sierra Club, and U.S. Public Interest Research Group, June 1988); and "Are We Cleaning Up?: 10 Superfund Case Studies" (Washington, D.C.: Office of Technology Assessment, Congress of the United States, June 1988).

8. Jane Nogaki, "Citizens Negotiate a Good-Neighbor Agreement in New Jersey," *Toxic Times* (Boston: National Toxics Campaign, Spring 1989).

9. "Grassroots Convention 1989, Songbook" (Arlington, Va.: Citizens Clearinghouse for Hazardous Wastes, October 1989), p. 48.

10. Vaclav Havel, "Our Freedom," *Washington Post*, January 3, 1990, p. A15.

11. Philip N. Joranson and Ken Butigan, *Cry of the Environment: Rebuilding the Christian Creation Tradition* (Santa Fe, N.M.: Bear, 1984), p. 3.

12. Bill Devall and George Sessions, *Deep Ecology* (Layton, Utah: Gibbs M. Smith, 1985), p. 22.

13. Richard L. Grossman, "Wrenching Debate Gazette," (Somerville, Mass.: Feb. 1989), pp. 6–7. The "Blueprint" and summary booklets can be obtained from the publishers, Howe Brothers, P.O. Box 6394, Salt Lake City, UT 84106, 1-800-426-5387.

14. Saul Alinsky, *Rules for Radicals: A Practical Primer for Realistic Radicals* (New York: Vintage Books, 1971), p. 62.

15. Kimberley Bobo, *Lives Matter: A Handbook for Christian Organizing* (Kansas City, MO: Sheed and Ward, 1986), pp. 3–4.

16. Wendell Berry, *Home Economics* (San Francisco: North Point Press, 1987), pp. 50, 150.

17. Sources for information and action:
Citizens Clearinghouse for Hazardous Wastes
P.O. Box 926
Arlington, VA 22216
703/276-7070

Clean Water Action Project
317 Pennsylvania Ave., S.E.
Washington, DC 20003
202/547-1196

Greenpeace USA
1436 U Street, N.W.
Washington, DC 20009
202/462-1177

National Toxics Campaign
37 Temple Place, 4th floor
Boston, MA 02111
617/482-1477

U.S. Public Interest Research Group
215 Pennsylvania Ave., S.E.
Washington, DC 20003
202/546-9707

Working Group on Community-Right-To-Know
215 Pennsylvania Ave., S.E.
Washington, DC 20003
202/546-9707

Each of these groups can provide information about its local offices and organizing staff.

Dozens more national and regional environmental groups are listed in the directory *GOODWORKS*, available from

Dembner Books
80 Eighth Avenue
New York, New York 10011
212/924-2525

A 1990 edition of this directory is currently being created. While it is aimed at readers seeking jobs in environmental organizations and other public-interest groups, it is useful for anyone interested in finding out about such organizations. Its cost is $16.50 for paperback, $25 for hardcover, plus $2 for shipping.

11

Feminist Theological Theses on Justice, Peace, and the Integrity of Creation

INA PRAETORIUS FEHLE, SUSANNE KRAMER-FRIEDRICH, MONIKA WOLGENSINGER, AND IRENE GYSEL-NEF

Analyses of our present predicament are faulty and erroneous if they disregard the fundamental relationship of domination existing between the sexes. For instance, the Ecumenical Movement for Justice, Peace, and Integrity of Creation needs to question each problem in light of the role played by sexism. Centuries of injustice toward women, marked by their being considered property of husbands and fathers, being of lesser value than males, and being underpaid for their labor, requires an acknowledgment of the sin of sexism in order to make justice possible. The use of the protection of women and children as the reason men go to war, as well as the ubiquitous violence against women by conquerors, are issues that must be dealt with to lay foundations for peace. The refusal to admit women to such fields as science has prevented their taking a role in the healing of creation. Thus, sexism is a structural sin that prevents work toward justice, peace, and the integrity of creation.

The Ecumenical Movement for Justice, Peace, and the Integrity of Creation wishes to set a worldwide commitment of Christian women and men in motion against the catastrophic developments threatening our world.

Translated from the German by Jill Waeber.

Such an initiative is both important and necessary, if based on an honest, accurate, and self-critical analysis of the historic causes and origins of the present situation.

In the course of growing feminist consciousness, women have come to realize that analyses of today's reality that disregard the fundamental relationship of domination existing between the sexes are erroneous and therefore futile as a foundation on which to base our strivings towards liberation. It is misleading to continue to talk about "mankind" as having bred injustice, plotted wars, and destroyed creation. It could be said that there have always been certain active fellow creatures who introduced historic changes and who, according to circumstances, have contributed in their different ways to the course of development that is threatening us today. Women, on account of their state of oppression, are involved in the molding of history in a way different from that of men. *For this reason, we call upon all women and men participating in the Ecumenical Movement for Justice, Peace, and the Integrity of Creation to question each problem dealt with in the light of the role played by sexism and its influence on the origins of each problem and to ask what consequences the elimination of sexism would have for the solving of the problem.*

A first step toward differentiation of the generalizing term "mankind" is to recognize that looking at things in terms of sex, and thereby clearly acknowledging the structural sins of sexism, must have its influence on the language used in church and in theology when we refer to "our guilt" and "our liberation." In the theology of the rich West, it is gradually becoming a generally accepted fact that in order to obtain a sufficiently clear view of reality we must distinguish between poor and rich. "Churches and Christians in the rich West, or in the North as the case may be, carry a *different* guilt and require a *different* kind of liberation from that of Christians and churches in the poor South." Corresponding to this distinction, we think of guilt and redemption considered specifically in terms of sex. Men must acknowledge a *different* confession of guilt from women; women have need of a *different* liberation from that of men. Guided by three fundamental concepts of the ecumenical movement, we should like to clarify our concern.

ON THE CONCEPT OF "JUSTICE"

"Women make up half of the world population, work almost two-thirds of all man-hours, receive a tenth of the world's income and own less than a hundredth part of the world's wealth" (United Nations Report, 1980). In view of such officially confirmed facts as these, it is deceptive to proceed from a concept of poverty that makes no distinction between the sexes. Poverty does not affect men, women, and children in the same way. On the contrary, women are not *systematically* driven to poverty quite by chance, but rather on account of their sex, and that is because of their ability to bear children and because of their ascribed role in society as that of an unpaid domestic worker or, as the case may be, as a subsistence worker carrying the major responsibility for the preservation of the family. The fact that poverty is preeminently a problem concerning women and children has reasons rooted in the structural sins of sexism. These reasons can be described.

Up to now, women's work has been dealt with by the current economic system in the same way as our natural resources, that is, it has been regarded as being inferior or of no value and consequently excluded from income and wealth. Women, because of the prevailing economic theory, are poor, and rightly so.

For centuries, women and children were considered to be the property of their husbands or of their fathers and, indeed, could be acquired and owned just like any other piece of property, while they themselves were not able to acquire or own anything. This far from obsolete assumption that women are to be assigned to the realm of property, an assumption that partially molds the law of today, confirms female poverty.

Human rights did not initially include women and children. Women began only in the ninteenth century to struggle against the resistance of men to gain access to the jurisdiction of human rights. Men's work, based on an accepted obligation to act as breadwinner of the family, is more highly valued than women's work, although in actual fact by no means all men support families and nothing like all women can rely on a male bread-winner.

The feminizing of poverty is therefore a direct consequence of the structural sin of sexism. A church that fails to pay close attention to such relationships suppresses an important dimension of worldwide injustice and ignores the sin of sexism. Failure to acknowledge the sin of sexism renders justice impossible.

ON THE CONCEPT OF "PEACE"

The defense of "wife and child" has at all times been considered by men as providing a legitimate reason for the waging of wars. Throughout history, women have only seldom taken an active part in war and in the preparations for war, while at the same time they were to suffer in one respect as the motive for male warmongering and, in the other, as the object of male acts of violence. Those very men who pretend to wage war in order to defend their (supposedly chaste) wives rape the wives of their enemy in *every* war and regard this conduct of sexual subjugation as being the legitimate expression of their victory over the male opponent. The soldier's dual morality, by which the woman is looked upon as being merely a creature in need of protection on one hand and as an object for violent sexuality on the other, is a manifestation of the sin of sexism, forming society right through middle-class, everyday life and language. The approach to language and the physical hostility of the military ideal of manliness adequately exposes the relationship between militarism and violence toward women. Failure to acknowledge and deal with such relationships renders peace impossible.

ON THE CONCEPT OF THE "INTEGRITY OF CREATION"

Women were refused admittance to the fields of science and technology well into this century, with the argument that they lacked intelligence and that they had other duties to perform in society. Women had, and still today have, no chance of influencing the paradigm of Western science underlying the catastrophic destruction of nature, from which we are suffering today. Of course, there are some highly qualified women scientists today, but even these women have no chance of correcting the prevailing paradigm, because this paradigm has been established firmly for a long time and access to scientific studies and to high-technology laboratories continues to be controlled by men. Admittance is only granted to over-accommodating women, who perform brilliantly in the field of a science as defined by men. All other women are still considered unintelligent; indeed, they are pushed by current scientific theory itself in the direction of nature, an area to be dominated by man. Francis Bacon, one of the key figures in the history of Western science, describes the relationship of the scientist to nature as corresponding to that between man and woman in the patriarchal marriage: the husband dominates and penetrates her in the same way as the scientist subdues nature, invades and takes advantage of it. On the level of social and scientific theory, there exists a connection between the controlling of nature and the oppression of women. The exclusion of women from the fields of science and technology is a metaphoric identification of woman and nature. Failure to acknowledge and deal with these relationships renders the integrity of creation impossible.

When we women call for an analysis of all the problems to be discussed, specifically in terms of sex distinctions, then what we are demanding is a fair, differentiated way of looking at the question of guilt. For this reason, we demand that different forms of responsibility and participation, different forms of the acknowledgment and treatment of guilt be evolved.

It is, for us, not a question of assuming the innocence of women and saddling the "hostile image of man" with entire responsibility for the catastrophe. We women, however, are no longer willing to be charged with the lust for power, the direct destruction of nature, and the belligerent perpetration of violence. Our guilt rests rather in having calmly and idly witnessed how men "wanted to be like God," having failed to become aware of our responsibility, and having supported men's activities by putting our everyday services at their disposal. We do not regard ourselves as being innocent victims, but as participating partners, who have made our particular contribution to the catastrophe. We are prepared to assume responsibility for this—and for nothing else.

When we demand that all the analyses of the problems concerning the

Ecumenical Movement for Justice, Peace, and the Integrity of Creation shall include the sin of sexism, then we do so in the knowledge that this is in accordance with the Gospel, which promises peace and justice for all people. A church that is not prepared to take clear note of the relationships we refer to suppresses a vitally important dimension of the worldwide catastrophe and perpetrates the sin of sexism. When we fail to acknowledge and deal with the sin of sexism, then we fail fundamentally to follow the Gospel in its clear demand for justice, peace, and the integrity of creation.

12

Moral Theology, Ecology, Justice, and Development

DREW CHRISTIANSEN, S.J.

International economic policies either force third-world nations into undesirable and ecologically costly development or they reward environmentally insensitive projects. The goal of just and sustainable development is thwarted frequently by the pressures on debtor nations toward economic growth. In this article Father Christiansen reviews recent Roman Catholic teaching on the need for just and sustainable development and asks what tasks confront ethical reflection when ecological thinking is both more holistic and more probabilistic than an ethic based on a static conception of nature. He also reviews other resources that play a major role in ecojustice thinking and evaluates them through their ability to throw light on the complex topic of international economic relations and the biosphere. Finally, he probes the role of ethicists in developing environmental policy.

Since the first Earth Day in 1970, there have been many efforts to make the environment a major public issue.[1] While there have been some revolutionary developments domestically—the Wilderness Act (1964), the National Environmental Policy Act (1969), the Clean Air Act (1970), and the Toxic Substances Control Act (1978)—action at an international level has come more slowly. In the past several months, for example, the United States and Britain blocked agreement on the Antarctic Treaty, President Bush failed to make good on his promises to support strong measures against global warming, and only modest cutbacks have been announced

Permission to publish Drew Christiansen's "Moral Theology, Ecology, Justice, and Development" was kindly granted by Walter J. Burghardt, S. J., for *Theological Studies*, which published a shorter version in the December 1989 issue.

by East Asian nations on driftnet fishing.[2] One major exception has been the 1987 Vienna Convention for the Protection of the Ozone Layer, which gathered swift support even from manufacturers.[3]

Nonetheless, with the lessening of traditional international rivalries, the attention of world leaders has begun to turn to global environmental issues.[4] At the economic summit in July 1989 the leaders of the industrial democracies called for "decisive action" to "understand and protect the earth's ecological balance."[5] In September, 1989, 100 members of the nonaligned movement called for "a productive dialogue with the developed world" on "protection of the environment."[6] The World Watch Institute talks about the nineties as "a turnaround decade" for a sustainable world, and Pope John Paul II looks to the third millennium as "a New Advent."[7] The agenda for this new epoch is "just and sustainable development," a conjunction of worldwide ecological goals with third-world development.[8] While the limits-to-growth debate in the 1970s raised questions of intergenerational equity, current discussions recognize global equity as intrinsically connected to an ecologically sustainable world economy.

ECOLOGY AND DEVELOPMENT

At the 1989 U.N. General Assembly, as Britain's Margaret Thatcher urged the adoption by 1992 of a convention on atmospheric pollution, third-world leaders made clear that environmental collaboration between rich and poor nations must involve greater assistance for the latter's development and greater equity in international economic arrangements.[9] World leaders had three sorts of concern about global environmental quality, development, and international justice: the relative burden of restraint among nations; the effect of international economic activity on development priorities; and the environmental degradation caused by large numbers of poor people.

Burden of restraint. As third-world leaders are quick to point out, responsibility for atmospheric pollution lies largely with the industrialized nations. "Pollution of the environment and other environmental dangers," they contend, "stem mainly from the industrialized world's high standard of living and wasteful consumption of fossil fuels."[10] Accordingly, the burden for reducing pollution ought to fall first on them. So long as the industrialized countries have not made very substantial adjustments in their own economies, efforts to force the developing nations to curtail resource depletion, limit population expansion, or alter strategies of economic growth will be regarded as unjust.

International economic policies. Second, deforestation and the depletion of other resources is very often the result of undesirable patterns of development encouraged by international economic policies. To curb and correct these trends, changes will be needed in international economic arrangements, not only to reward environmentally sensitive projects but also to assure that poorer nations will enjoy economic growth by other means.[11] In a limited way, the environment-development connection has already been made. There have been various schemes, for example, to trade debt adjustment by lending nations for environmental preservation of tropical rain forests in Central and South America and in South Asia.

Poverty and ecological deterioration. Besides the general need to promote just development for third-world nations, there is a special need to assist the poorest peoples. These large populations, eking out a living on marginal lands with inappropriate farming and pasturing techniques, are fast destroying forests and grazing land, resulting in flooding, erosion, and desertification over large areas.[12] "Protecting the global environment is inextricably linked with eliminating poverty," says Richard Benedick, a leading U.S. environmental negotiator.[13]

JUST AND SUSTAINABLE DEVELOPMENT

While the ideal of just and sustainable development has been around since the limits-to-growth debate in the 1970s, it received its most important formulation to date in the 1986 report of the World Commission on Environment and Development, *Our Common Future*.[14] The Commission, headed by Prime Minister Gro Harlem Brundtland of Norway, acknowledged that coordination of international policies is necessary because otherwise rich and poor nations are likely to differ about the relative value of economic growth and environmental conservation. "Sustainable development thus reflects a choice of values for managing planet earth in which equity matters," writes William C. Clark, "equity among peoples of the earth around the world today, equity between parents and their grandchildren."[15]

Paradoxically, further economic growth—growth controlled and redefined—seems necessary to reduce pressures on the environment. The Brundtland commission concluded that a five- to tenfold increase in economic activity will be necessary over the next fifty years to reduce mass poverty. Its best estimate is that a minimum 3 percent annual growth in per capita income in developing countries would be necessary as a transition to sustainable development.[16] At the same time, efforts will need to be made to preserve and restore stocks of environmental resources (soil, water, forests, fish, and so on), to reduce population growth, to develop resource-conserving technologies (especially through recycling and energy efficiency), and to develop new political decision-making procedures served by novel information systems.[17]

In sum, sustainable development poses a number of unprecedented moral and social questions. For one, how do societies balance economic growth with reducing pollution and resource depletion? In particular, what are the morally acceptable (or preferable) mixes of technology, population control, reduced consumption, and resource transfers that will produce such results? For another, if global environmental catastrophe cannot be avoided without concerted political action, are changes in democratic political culture, market economics, and international institutions necessary to provide long-term, authoritative decision making? Again, if ecological policy is a matter of maintaining a dynamic equilibrium, is there a need to rethink ethical methodology along the lines of the principle of totality and proportionalism, to take account of the balancing of goods required for equilibrium? Finally, if ecological viability cannot be attained without greater international equity, is common interest in planetary survival alone sufficient to produce the desired results, or must there be a greater identification with all the world's peoples and development of a global consensus on norms of justice? It is especially in this last area, the vision of human solidarity and the advancement of transnational standards of justice, that official Catholic social theology has made its significant recent contribution to the discussion of sustainable development.

CHURCH TEACHING: *SOLLICITUDO REI SOCIALIS*

Environmentalists greeted the 1988 release of Pope John Paul II's encyclical letter *Sollicitudo Rei Socialis (On Social Concern)* as a landmark in Catholic participation in the environmental movement.[18] For the first time an official Vatican document bearing the pope's own name discusses ecological issues in the context of just and sustainable development. John Paul also appreciates the interconnected nature of the common dangers facing humanity. Noting the numerous factors that deter concerted action against poverty, John Paul concludes nonetheless that "we are *all* called, indeed *obligated*, to face the tremendous challenge of the last decade of the second millennium, also because the present dangers threaten everyone [no. 47]." In number 26, he explicitly argues the "indivisibility" of respect for life with the search for peace and justice. The Philippine bishops in a 1988 pastoral, "What Is Happening to Our Beautiful Land?" echo the indivisibility argument, claiming ecology is "the ultimate pro-life issue."[19]

Like Paul VI's *Populorum Progressio* which it commemorates, *Sollicitudo* is primarily concerned with the issue of equitable and humane development.[20] It focuses on the growth of inequality, the worsening of poverty, and the subversion of development aims by ideological tensions between East and West. Like Paul VI before him, John Paul takes table fellowship to be the root metaphor for a Catholic conception of justice. He argues for "each people's right to be seated at the table of the common banquet [no. 32]" and interprets the lack of North-South collaboration in development as reenacting the indifference of the rich man to Lazarus.

As a religious thinker, John Paul is a "cosmopolitan" whose views on international affairs do not fit the familiar conventions of geopolitics as defined by the East-West conflict. "The present division of the world," he writes in the letter, "is a *direct obstacle* to the transformation of the conditions of underdevelopment in the developing and less advanced countries" [no. 22]. *Sollicitudo* enjoins solidarity within and among nations, demands that political leaders take responsibility for the universal common good, and argues for the need for more effective international organizations. "A leadership role among nations," he writes with not-so-veiled criticism of the cold-war mentality, "can only be justified by the possibility and willingness to contribute widely and generously to the [universal] common good [no. 23]."

Just Development

Although the focus of this essay is the intersection of just development with ecology, since the Holy Father's primary concern in commemorating *Populorum Progressio* was to address the development question, it is appropriate that some space be allocated to this topic.

If there is one sign of the time that emerges as a unifying theme in *Sollicitudo*, it is the growth of inequality over the last two decades. The aggravation of inequality is symbolized by the further subdivision of the globe into four worlds, the Fourth World being the collective designation for the poorest countries. But the pope notes that underdevelopment is not restricted to the so-called lesser-developed countries. "In a process of regression [no. 17]," fast-expanding islands of underdevelopment have appeared in certain regions and among social groups in the most advanced countries. Insult, moreover, is added to the injury of poverty by the conspicuous consumption of the affluent. Material goods themselves, however, are not the problem. The injustice lies in maldistribution: "the ones who possess so much are relatively few and those who possess almost nothing are many [no. 28]."

To redress "the notorious inequalities" that afflict the contemporary world, John Paul, following the teaching of Paul VI, appears to advocate a thoroughgoing redistribution of resources both within and among nations on *the principle of solidarity*. *Sollicitudo* makes clear the aim of redistribution is not simply the alleviation of poverty, but rather an egalitarian sharing in a common level of development. The poor, the Holy Father argues, are neighbors and helpers, "to be made sharers, *on a par with ourselves*, in the banquet of life to which all are equally called by God [no. 19; italics mine]."

While the encyclical's primary emphasis is on the obligations of the rich toward the poor, the solidarity of the poor with one another is nonetheless a significant theme within the letter, too. The Holy Father is especially supportive of nonviolent protests in which the poor claim their own rights. He favors initiative on the part of developing countries and encourages solidarity among developing nations themselves, especially in geographic regions.[21]

The Ecological Dimension of Development

Sollicitudo takes up environmental concerns at the conclusion of its treatment of authentic human development (no. 34). The theme is well integrated within the encyclical as an expression of humanity's moral vocation (nos. 26, 29–30). The pope addresses the anthropocentrism, particularly the biblical motif of human dominion over nature, alleged to be at the root of the environmental crisis. He argues that it is not the unique position of humanity in the scheme of values, but rather a misconceived utilitarianism, that has caused the abuse of nature. In turn, that disordered set of values is a singular example of humanity's persistent sinfulness, a dynamic of human existence that will not be eliminated by any newly contrived ethic. John Paul affirms "the dominion" of humanity over the rest of creation, but insists that this dominion is circumscribed by moral limits. "[D]evelopment," he writes, "cannot consist in the use, dominion over and *indiscriminate* possession of created things ... [no. 29]." For John Paul, environmental constraints are simply a further example of the prohibitions "imposed from the beginning by the Creator [no. 34]." He argues that the primary function of development is to subordinate "possession, dominion and use to man's divine likeness and to his vocation to immortality [no. 29]." In the concrete, human beings fulfill their vocation by working together "for the full development of others [no. 30]."

Unlike many environmental theologians, John Paul, therefore, does not regard the dominion theme as a special source of the environmental crisis. It is, rather, another instance of the checkered human history of sin and achievement. Human history *"is not* a straightforward process, *as it were automatic* and *in itself limitless* [no. 27];"* it is instead an ambiguous succession of developments, constantly threatened with sin and in need of moral guidance to keep it faithful to humanity's essential vocation.[22]

Respect for Nature

Sollicitudo identifies three moral guidelines with respect to the environmental dimensions of development. These precepts have to do with respect for nature, conservation of nonrenewable resources, and restriction of pollution. Only the first is explained at any length, and its formulation is most striking. In development, "one must take into account *the nature of each being* and of its *mutual connection* in an ordered system, which is precisely the 'cosmos' [no. 34]." The formulation is remarkable because it is an affirmation, in the pope's own words, of two strong ecological principles, namely, the independent moral status of other creatures, and the need to think and to act in terms of whole "environments" and ecological systems.

In accepting the nonutilitarian value of nonhuman creatures and in recognizing the demand for ecological thinking, *Sollicitudo* takes some very long and rapid steps to bring Catholics into the march of environmental ethics. The encyclical's contribution to that discussion, however, lies largely in the promotion of the justice and development dimensions of sustainable development. It provides a global vision of human solidarity, environmentally sensitive notions of development in which "being" is more important than "having," an implied asceticism favorable to reduced consumption, and serious consideration of norms of solidarity requiring the transfer of resources from developed to developing world. This contribution is vital because so few public voices seriously address the justice dimensions of the issue.

At the same time, a number of serious problems go undiscussed or are insufficiently examined in the encyclical. First, given our knowledge of the shortcomings of technical fixes — it turns out, for example, that the increase in rice production of the Green Revolution is responsible for the largest portion of methane emissions, and so for global warming — and the difficulties in reducing consumption, population size becomes an even more important part of the ecological balance than had been realized heretofore. Second, while economic development is necessary, knowledge about how to support economic transformation is very fragmentary. Attention needs to be drawn to third-world development, therefore, as a commitment involving protracted experiments, many of which will fail. Third, while an ascetic ethic of reduced consumption appears appropriate and even necessary, policy planners will be on entirely new terrain in learning how to regulate a healthy economy deprived of the engine of consumer-driven expansion. While the Brundtland Commission calls for continued growth, there are reasons to be quite skeptical of the ecological soundness of such proposals. (See "Constructive Efforts," below.) Church support for development needs to argue not just generosity but sustained commitment and sacrifice to cope with the uncertainties of the transition. It also needs to encourage experiment with alternative models of development. (See "Politics of Ecojustice," below.)

Finally, if in thinking about ethics, "one must take into account," to cite Pope John Paul, "*the nature of each being* and of its *mutual connection* in an ordered system, which is precisely the 'cosmos,' " then the recent tendency on the part of the magisterium to think of the natural law primarily in deontological terms will need to be reconsidered. For ecological thinking is at one and the same time both more holistic and more probabilistic than an ethic based on natures statically conceived. To be sure, there is room for a mixed system of norms, as indeed the history of natural law shows, but the overall framework will be more like an ethic of responsibility, in which many factors have to be weighed in different ways, than a code of peremptory prohibitions and injunctions.

HISTORY REEXAMINED

Ever since Lynn White, Jr.'s notorious essay, "The Historical Roots of Our Ecological Crisis," there has been a tendency among environmentalists to blame Christianity for the pernicious anthropocentric attitudes that motivated the Western assault on nature.[23] A new wave of environmental theology, however, has begun to do a more searching and dispassionate evaluation of the resources for environmental theology in the Christian tradition. The most ambitious of these works is H. Paul Santmire's *Travail of Nature*. Santmire has produced a critical survey of the history of Western theology from the perspective of the standing of nature.[24] The problematic feature in Christian theological anthropology, as Santmire sees it, is "a spiritual motif" of humanity's ascent to God in which nature serves only as a means to salvation or as backdrop for the drama of salvation history. To this he opposes "an ecological motif" "predicated on the assumption of a divine and human concomitance with nature."[25] Santmire's use of these models in the assessment of major theological figures can be seen best in his treatment of Augustine's thought, which he regards as "the flowering of the ecological promise of classical theology."[26]

Augustine and Creation History

Santmire's interpretation leans heavily on Augustine's mature theology. He argues that "the ascent motif" that is evident in the Latin Father's early theology was displaced over time by an increasingly historical conception of divine action and an affirmative view of the material universe. Subsequently, Augustine's theology of history became "creation history," the narrative of the unfolding of God's goodness in the physical cosmos. *"Human redemptive history,"* Santmire writes, *"happens within the broader milieu of the all-comprehending framework of creation history."*[27]

From his exegetical studies, Santmire claims (I believe correctly) Augustine also gained a respect for the diversity of God's creatures. According to his theocentric aesthetic, other creatures do not exist solely to serve humans but rather to glorify God.[28] Heretics, he objects in *The City of God* (22.24),

> do not consider how admirable these things are in their own places,
> how excellent in their own natures, how beautifully adjusted to the
> rest of creation, and how much grace they contribute to the universe
> by their own contributions, as to a commonwealth. . . ."

From passages like these, Santmire concludes that Augustine propounded a theological aesthetic that respected the value of nonhuman creatures and the harmonious (ecological) relationships of the natural world.

Santmire's treatment of Augustine as a precursor of ecotheology deserves serious comment. I would like to address three issues: the interpretation of Augustine's development; the contention that Augustine's cosmology is "world-affirming"; and the assertion of the equality of nature and humanity in light of contemporary biological thought.

First then, what are we to make of Santmire's version of Augustinian cosmology? Does contemplation of the goodness of creation displace the orientation to God as the Good that satisfies human life? To begin with, one must acknowledge that at times Augustine takes delight in the physical universe, and further that he makes exceptional theological moves with respect to the worth of natural creatures. These positions, however, do not unambiguously constitute an Augustinian theology of nature that overturns his earlier convictions. For one thing, Augustine's delight in the natural world wanes with the passing years.[29] For another, his concern for the natural world takes up only a small space in a cosmology largely concerned with spiritual realities. He was far more preoccupied with the status of angels than with plants and animals and landscapes and from the hardships nature placed on human beings drew lessons about the appropriateness of human ingenuity.[30]

Second, does the Augustinian cosmology really surrender the dualism of "the ascent motif" for affirmation of the natural world? To be sure, the marvels of nature are occasion to glorify God, but they are not enough to keep Augustine from longing for the life to come. For Augustine, the pertinent metaphor for the human journey in the confines of history is *peregrinatio*, that is, living out one's allotted time like a resident alien or exile, living in the world without being attached to it. Those who belong to the City of God are set apart by a holy yearning for the heavenly Jerusalem.[31] Such an attitude is most unlikely to provide the affirmation of the natural world required to undergird a modern-day environmental ethics. Indeed, it is more likely to advise willing endurance of "the necessities" of a degraded environment rather than to preserve and restore a rapidly changing ecology. The loss of ecosystems, the extinction of species, and the poisoning of air and water are just the kind of evils that admonish, "We have here no lasting garden of Eden."

Santmire makes much of "the overflowing goodness" of God displacing God "as the Good" in Augustine's mature thought. True, Augustine's late thought does show greater pluralism. Life in glory is not so much the union of the individual soul with God, for example, as the *vita socialis sanctorum*. Fulfillment, however, still lies in union with God. In a justly famous image, Augustine compares humanity to a woman who has received a ring from her beloved. Something is profoundly wrong, he argues, if one loves the ring more than the lover.[32] The goodness of creation, therefore, when properly understood, should draw humanity to God. Thus, a wholesale rejection of ascent for an immanentist cosmic piety is unfaithful to Augustine's intention.

Last, one must ask whether even contemporary science and experience any longer warrant thinking of nature, at least on this planet, apart from humanity. Is it possible to talk of a three-way encounter — nature, humanity, God — in an ethic of "concomitance"?

In planetary terms, I would assert it is less and less possible to see nature as an independent reality. Human intervention has become so enmeshed in the cycles of the biophysical world that one biologist speculates that we have seen "the end of nature."[33] Biologically speaking, there is no one stable reality called nature. Ecosystems themselves are constantly evolving in natural succession. Species other than humankind alter large ecosystems: the beaver, the lamprey eel, the harbor seal, and so on. To maintain a preferred balance in nature (secure a flowing stream, preserve fish stocks, rescue a mountain landscape, and so forth), humans must intervene in natural processes. Likewise, to arrest the depletion of the ozone layer, to check global warming, or to control acid rain, human beings must plan together and collaborate. On this planet, then, there is no longer any nature apart from humanity. If the future of the earth itself is so entwined with conscious human decision, then one cannot avoid granting a special place to human beings in the cosmos. Respect for nature must be, therefore, as much an act of intelligence and reason as an act of contemplative awareness.

Francis and the Ascetic Tradition

Francis of Assisi remains an icon of the environmental movement. For Santmire, Francis represents "the flowering of Christianity's ecological promise."[34] Roger Sorrell, *Saint Francis of Assisi and Nature*, provides a careful analysis of sources of Poverello's nature mysticism in the medieval spiritual traditions.[35] He situates Francis's development within the ascetic spirituality of the eremitic tradition. Francis's familiarity with nature seems to have grown with his recourse to remote and rugged sites for prayer.[36] Much of his response to the natural world consisted in stock elements of medieval ascetic spirituality and hagiography. Some of it, however, was original: nature mysticism, familiarity with natural creatures, chivalric address, insistence on the goodness of nature, extension of alms-giving to birds and animals.[37] Sorrell concludes that Francis resolved "the medieval ascetic ambivalence to the natural world" into "a burst of positive reactions to creation."[38]

Sorrell's historical scholarship gives the lie to sentimentally romantic interpretations of Francis's life and Franciscan spirituality. Leonardo Boff's *Saint Francis* makes the case that Francis's reverence for the created world was rooted in the severest sort of asceticism. He became a reformer only after "a long and demanding novitiate" in which he lived with the poor and lepers. Boff concludes,

> Whoever tries to romantically imitate [*sic*] Saint Francis in his love for nature without passing through asceticism, penitence, and the cross falls into deep illusion. . . . It was at the end, not the beginning of his life that Francis composed the hymn to the sun. To begin where Francis ended is a disastrous illusion.[39]

Penance, Boff writes, "apparently so inhuman, was the price he had to pay for his profound humanity."[40] If Boff is correct, and I think he is, then environmental ethics will need to learn from Christian asceticism rather than discard it as a life-denying spirituality.[41]

Michael and Kenneth Himes, drawing together the figures of Augustine and Francis, argue that creatureliness per se is the source of equality with the rest of God's creation. What Augustine and Francis grasped, they write, is that

> When one grasps the "iffiness" of one's existence, the shocking fact that the source and foundation of one's being is not in oneself, then one knows oneself as truly poor. . . . This poverty unites all creatures.[42]

The Himes brothers' argument points to a theological affirmation that many environmentalists deny, at least implicitly — the ontological difference between God and creation.

An overlooked aspect of the Franciscan nature ethic is its tie to love of the poor. Francis's humility developed from his engagement with the little people (*minores*) and the lepers and grew to embrace all God's little creatures. Perhaps the most inspiring role for Francis as patron of the environmental movement would be to join ecology with an option for the poor. "Only the *vere expropriatus*, the person who has truly disappropriated himself, can become a *frater menor*, a brother of all."[43] "It is the concept of need that is essential in formulating a new understanding of Francis as the patron of an ecological movement," writes Paul Wiegand. In choosing Francis, he contends, ecologists "have gotten more than they bargained for. . . ."[44]

CONSTRUCTIVE EFFORTS[45]

Deep Ecology[46]

Deep ecology is the name radical ecologists give their movement. It is an eclectic vision drawing from Gandhi, process philosophy, Teilhard, Buddhism, and ancient religions of the earth. It is, according to the bible of the movement, "Earth wisdom . . . [the] unity of humans, plants, animals and the Earth."[47] Both a philosophy and a social program, it is above all a spirituality rooted in "biocentric equality," that is, "the intuition" that "all things in the biosphere have an equal right to live and blossom and to reach their individual forms of unfolding and self-realization within the larger Self-Realization."[48] The movement, accordingly, advances a radical program of moral and religious transformation. Its platform includes the affirmation of the intrinsic value of nonhuman "life" (including inanimate things), preservation of ecological and cultural diversity, an economic standard of "vital needs," and a measure of "life quality" rather than "standard of living" for the evaluation of development.[49]

The Norwegian philosopher Arne Naess, the most articulate spokesman of the movement, sees the tenets of deep ecology as antithetical to the goal of "sustained development" advocated by the Brundtland Commission and the World Conservation Society. The nub of the disagreement lies in the value each ascribes nonhuman life. For the mainline environmental movement, Naess believes, "Conservation, like development, is for people"; it is essentially anthropocentric. Deep ecology, by contrast, values nonhuman life "independently of human life," and it adheres to "a policy of non-interference with continuing evolution, for example, the evolution of mammals demanding vast territory, and of highly different landscapes with their special organisms."[50] Thus, "the satisfaction of nonhuman needs and the improvement of life quality for any nonhuman kind of being" are central to the deep-ecology platform.[51]

The Ethical Program

Several principles of deep ecology deserve further reflection even for those who hold reservations about the necessity of biocentricity. To begin with, *ecological diversity* also has utilitarian value, for example, in providing the variation in the gene pool needed for adaptive survival.[52] Wetlands prove valuable not only for flood control but also as breeding grounds for marine life and as natural filters to cleanse polluted waters. Over the long term, then, a diversity of ecosystems is more than an amenity, it is a source of replenished life. A conservative respect for the worth of other creatures and ecologies may serve as a barrier against a narrow or shortsighted economic calculus that has proved dangerous even for human ends.

Second, the *vital needs standard* raises serious questions about worldwide economic growth as a tool of just and sustainable development. The basic needs strategies advocated by mainline environmentalists looks to continued economic growth to supply the necessities of the poor. By contrast, the vital needs standard gives a signal to the affluent that environmental reform in the long run will require cutbacks in consumption on their part.[53] The principle, of course, bears some similarities to the patristic idea of autarky, which has become a consistent theme of Catholic social teaching since Vatican II.[54] While basic needs are a matter of justice to other human beings, an economy of vital needs would be required for the preservation of a viable ecosystem. For if past experience can be a guide, then new efforts to ensure that growth does not augment current levels of pollution can be expected to yield unforeseen yet large-scale problems of their own.[55] A standard of vital needs for everyone, not just the poor, therefore merits consideration as a referent point to spur discussion about reduction in consumption as a necessary component of a prudent environmental policy.

Third, the *standard of life quality*, even more than that of vital needs, suggests that development does not have to be measured in GNP per capita. "Reverence for life," Naess argues, "implies reverence for the richness and diversity of human cultures and subcultures." Replacing a material standard of living with a new measure of life quality is intended to indicate that there are patterns of life that do not entail intensive consumption or high technology and that are humanly very satisfying. By weighing more heavily those things other than material growth that contribute to quality of life (environmental quality, leisure, education, friendships, and so on), it may be possible for diverse cultures to exist subject to "local, regional, and national particularities."[56] Again, such a standard would coincide with what Pope John Paul refers to as the distinction between "being and having."[57]

Thus, while biocentricity may be unsatisfactory as an ultimate standard of value, the ethical principles articulated by the deep-ecology movement point nevertheless to plausible standards for sustainable development with which traditional Catholic spirituality and contemporary Catholic social teaching will be sympathetic. As to biocentricity, given the evolution of human-nature interactions and the need for conscious human direction, it appears to me that biocentrism is an exaggerated principle. Humans need to be respectful of environmental systems, to be sure, but reverence for nature can and ought to be combined with intelligent action. Furthermore, traditional Christian concepts like sin and conversion are better able to deal with moral failure and renewal experienced in the environmental crisis than neo-gnostic notions about earth wisdom. Anthropocentrism, in the aggressive form known by Western industrial society, needs a corrective, but biocentrism is not the answer. Whether humanity succeeds or fails in meeting the environmental crisis will depend upon the intrinsically ambiguous character of human beings themselves. To meet that challenge, humanity needs to look more searchingly at itself as it is embedded in nature, not turn away to look at nature alone. Finally, the theocentric tradition in Christian theology (Augustine, Edwards, H. R. Niebuhr, Gustafson), with its insistence on responsibility to the God of all being, seems better able to generate a properly ordered sense of moral responsibility than the natural piety of deep ecology with its emphasis on the undisturbed evolution of the natural world.[58]

POLITICS OF ECOJUSTICE

Before significant progress can be made toward a just and sustainable world, it appears a series of innovations will be necessary both in political culture and in the structures of political decision making.[59] The market mechanisms, the political philosophy of self-interest, and the interest-group politics of the industrial democracies are obstacles to long-term global and regional decision-making, particularly when they demand restraint.[60] Both scientists and political analysts are clear about the need for stronger political institutions as a way to meet the current crisis.

Political institutions need to be strengthened at all levels to meet the global challenge. Even domestic institutions, when a nation is a major actor, like the United States, the Soviet Union, or China in carbon emission, or Nigeria and Egypt in population growth, can make a serious difference on larger problems.[61] But action by single nations, even large ones, will be insufficient; regional and global coordination will be needed, as well. Europe has made significant progress toward regional decision making and enforcement, but acid rain, ozone depletion, and atmospheric warming have made clear the necessity of greater regional and international collaboration.

Improved collaboration, wrote the World Commission on Environment and Development, "is the chief institutional challenge of the 1990s."⁶² Treaties and existing international organizations, such as the U.N. system, have roles to play. Much of the literature emphasizes use of the current political structures, and some authors warn of the proliferation of forums and agencies, arguing that coordination and focus are becoming urgently necessary.⁶³ All urge that environmental policy ought to take its place at the top of the foreign-policy agenda. Differences exist, however, as to the kind of methods that ought to be used: government regulation, market incentives, coercive sumptuary laws, transnational environmental authorities. Some believe, for example, that more coercive policies and institutions will be necessary to produce change.⁶⁴ Others argue that economic incentives can be used to restructure growth.⁶⁵

As I indicated above, recent events suggest that while constructive international agreements on the environment have been few, at least political leaders have begun to put ecology on their agenda and begin negotiation. In the field of development, however, there is no comparable evolution of policy. Yet, we have seen how necessary third-world development (in some modified sense) is to meet the environmental challenge. The Brundtland Commission recommended a series of measures to assist development, from reorienting multilateral and bilateral aid to providing new sources of revenue and automatic financing. These proposals include international taxes on the commons, such as ocean fisheries and seabed mining and taxes on international trade.⁶⁶ The commission recommends automatic financing because the current mix of voluntary aid and minimal financing of international organizations simply is not up to the enormous task ahead.⁶⁷

Automatic financing of this sort would involve a significant derogation of authority to transnational organizations. While it would be desirable to institute such an authority by conscious design to prevent deleterious delays in meeting the environment-development agenda, it is more likely that, as with the European Economic Community, it will evolve over time as a result of efforts to integrate environmental and development activities on a world scale. What is clear is that even within the present international system leaders will have to take the initiative in setting global needs on their national agendas.⁶⁸

Responsibility falls on ethicists as well as politicians. The profession, writes Denis Goulet, cannot "remain content with portraying ideals and passing adverse judgment on the means used by politicians, planners, or others to achieve social justice." Goulet is dissatisfied with two sorts of moral thinking. The first is that practiced primarily in the academy, where there is analysis of ethical issues but no willingness to draw a judgment about the morality or immorality of certain policies and practices. The second is practiced in the church and appears in the form of prophetic denunciation and preemptory moral prescription. The first fails because, out of intellectual reticence, it retreats from the quintessential moral act, judgment of good and evil. The second fails because it restricts itself to declarations and does not join in the endeavor of building a different social order. Ethics, Goulet proposes, ought to be a praxis in which ethicists take responsibility with others for the design and direction of social institutions. He concludes that just and sustainable development requires that ethicists "versed in the constraints surrounding vital choices promote values for which oppressed and underdeveloped groups struggle: greater justice, a decent sufficiency of goods for all, and equitable access to collective human gains realized in domains of technology, organization, and research."[69]

Behind Goulet's critique, of course, lies a debate about whether social ethics, especially a religious social ethics like Roman Catholic social teaching, can do without an ideology, understood as an ensemble of ideas about the social world, and a preferred future that together enable one to work for alternative social structures. I will not discuss this larger question, but I do want to comment on the practical proposal that ethicists ought to be engaged with others in social planning.

When ethicists refrain from judgment or merely set limits as to what is permissible, then social change is left to technicists, whose one-dimensional thinking sets up social dynamics that are very difficult to reverse. Social change requires more conscious moral reflection, and ethicists ought to work alongside lawyers, economists, engineers, and, yes, policy analysts too, in planning and experimenting with new institutions. It would properly be the role of moral theologians to explore such new arrangements, understanding that policy ethics conceived in this way is tentative, pragmatic, and experimental. By contrast, and here I probably depart from Goulet, it would not be the proper role of the magisterium to undertake such reflection precisely because church authority might become wrongly identified with one political program or another. At the same time, church officials should understand their role as encouraging such participation on the part of moral theologians and others in the same way as Paul VI encouraged all Christians, in *Octagesima Adveniens*, to play an active part in communities of discernment. But just as discernment is properly the duty of all communities of Christians working in their own social and political context, so social design would be the work of ethicists working with others.

What Goulet has in mind, it seems to me, is that moral theologians should be willing to join with others in constructing social inventions that satisfy their best judgment of what would be an ethically permissible (or desirable) outcome, so that rigid technical concerns (cost-benefit analysis, quarterly profits, avoiding legal liability) are not the driving factors in our social institutions. An analogy can be found among lawyers who do policy analysis and draft legislation. Given a public problem, their instinct is not simply to draw up a law to forbid something, say the dumping of toxic wastes; rather, they set out designing mechanisms to effect that end: reporting requirements, compliance deadlines, a Superfund to pay for clean-ups, and so on. Likewise, ethicists should consider the alternative ways in which the evils they oppose can be averted or corrected and the goods they desire be effected. In a sense, such social design is only the classic linkage of ethics and politics as we find it in Aristotle. Goulet's own pioneering work in development ethics offers a model of such study, as does the work of the sociologist Amitai Etzioni.[70] Provided ethicists understand that planning is a tentative, pragmatic enterprise and that they accept a pluralism of possible designs in a dialogue among many actors, then one need not fear the onset of an ethical authoritarianism.

There continues to be room for more traditional forms of ethics and moral theology, elaborating and testing principles, examining difficult cases, and illuminating the connections between moral virtues and principles and the Christian faith. But in a new age, when circumstances force hard choices and the shape and direction of the institutions that will guide a sustainable world are still to be discovered, the suggestion that ethicists ought not leave the formulation of policy and the design of institutions to others deserves a serious hearing. Freed from the misconception that Christian faith warrants only one pattern of society and sensitive to what they can learn from all men and women of goodwill, it should be possible for Christian moralists to join in the design of institutions that will make for a world of just and sustainable development.

NOTES

1. I extend my thanks to Rev. Daniel Kroger, O.F.M., and Rev. Lawrence Njoroge, my graduate assistants, for their generous help with background research for this article.

2. On the impasse over the Antarctic Treaty, see "Antarctic Plea by Rocard," *Manchester Guardian Weekly*, October 15, 1989, p. 8, and "Britain and US Block Antarctic Conservation Deal," *Manchester Guardian Weekly*, October 29, 1989, p. 5. For the status and future of the Antarctic environment, see M. J. Petersen, *Managing the Frozen South* (Berkeley: University of California Press, 1988); on acid rain and global warming, "Senators and Administration in Pollution Pact," *New York Times*, November 12, 1989, p. 19, and "Global Warming Means Global Politics," *New York Times*, Section 4, November 12, 1989, p. 5; on driftnet fishing, "Ban on 'Walls of Death' Gaining," *Christian Science Monitor*, November 13, 1989, p. 3, and "Citing Data on Damage to the Pacific, Groups Seek Drift-Net Fishing Ban," *New York Times*, November 14, 1989, p. 1.

3. For details of the Ozone Convention, see Department of State/Environmental Protection Agency (FRL-3295-1), "Environmental Impact Statement on Protocol to the Vienna Convention for Protection of the Ozone Layer," *Federal Register* 52:229 (November 30, 1987): 45520; on the growth of voluntary compliance by business, "More Companies To Phase Out Peril to Ozone," *New York Times*, October 11, 1989, p. 21.

4. See "A New Item on the Agenda, Special Report on the Greening of Geopolitics," *Time*, October 23, 1989, pp. 60–62 and "Global Warming," note 2 above.

5. "A New Item," p. 61.

6. Ibid.

7. Lester Brown et al., *State of the World 1989*, a World Watch Institute Report on Progress toward a Sustainable Society (New York: Norton, 1989), pp. 192-194. The *State of the World* series (1984-1989) is perhaps the best survey of environmental developments, although it does not ordinarily follow the justice dimensions of ecological transition. But, see H. Jeffrey Leonard et al., *Environment and the Poor: Development Strategies for a Common Agenda* (Washington, D.C.: Overseas Development Council, 1989).

John Paul connects the New Advent to the coming of the third Christian millennium (John Paul II, *On Social Concern: Sollicitudo rei socialis* [Washington, D.C.: USCC, 1988], p. 7). According to John Paul's intellectual biographer, George Hunston Williams, the pope's earlier uses of this theme held strong overtones of last judgment (*The Mind of John Paul II* [New York: Seabury, 1981], pp. 305-311), but *Sollicitudo* exudes an uncharacteristic spirit of hopefulness about the human prospect (see below, note 20).

8. On the goals of just and sustainable development, see William C. Clark, "Managing Planet Earth," *Scientific American* 261:3 (September 1989): 48.

9. See "Thatcher Urges U.N. Pact to Protect Climate," *New York Times*, November 9, 1989, p. 4.

The present state of knowledge about how to induce and assist economic development is not precise. Development planning today is characterized by an eclectic pragmatism. See John P. Lewis et al., *Strengthening the Poor: What Have We Learned?* (Washington, D.C.: Overseas Development Council, 1988), and John P. Lewis and Valeriana Kallab, eds., *Development Strategies Reconsidered* (Washington, D.C.: Overseas Development Council, 1988).

10. "Thatcher," above, note 9, and "A New Item," above, note 4, pp. 61–62. For scientific arguments on the need for greater first-world adjustments, see Clark, "Planet Earth," pp. 51–53. On needed changes in political attitudes, see William D. Ruckelshaus, "Toward a Sustainable World," *Scientific American* 261:3 (September 1989): 166–174, esp. 168–169.

11. "A New Item," p. 62.

12. Sandra Postel, "Halting Land Degradation," in Brown et al., *State of the World 1989*, pp. 21–40; Jim McNeill, "Strategies for Sustainable Economic Development," *Scientific American* 261:3 (September 1989): 157.

13. "A New Item," p. 62.

14. World Commission on Environment and Development, *Our Common Future* (Oxford: Oxford University Press, 1987).

15. Clark, "Planet Earth," p. 48.

16. *Our Common Future*, pp. 49–52.

17. McNeill, "Strategies," pp. 157–164.

18. While the encyclical letter was dated December 30, 1987, to coincide with the commemoration of the twentieth anniversary year of *Populorum Progressio*, it was not actually released until some weeks later. For one Christian environmentalist's appreciative reception of the document, see J. Ronald Engel, "Introduction: The Ethics of Sustainable Development," in J. Ronald Engel and Joan Gibb Engel, eds., *Ethics of Environment and Development: Global Challenge, International Response* (Tuscon, Arizona: University of Arizona Press, 1990), p. 4.

For recent surveys of religious responses to the environmental crisis, see Martin J. Palmer, "The Encounter of Religion and Conservation," in *Ethics of Environment and Development*; Freda Rojda, "Creation Theology at the WCC," *Ecumenist*, 26

(September-October 1988): 85–89; and Diane E. Sherwood and Kristin Franklin, "Ecology and the Church: Theology and Action," *Christian Century*, May 13, 1987, pp. 472–474.

19. I have not located the Philippine bishops' 1988 pastoral. It is cited by Robert J. Moore, "A New Christian Reformation," in *Ethics of the Environment and Development*, p. 112. Moore writes that the bishops' theology gives "a totally healthy meaning to the doctrine of dominion." Also see, in the same volume, Henryk Skolimowski, "Reverence for Life."

20. *Sollicitudo* represents a significant stage in the evolution of Pope John Paul's teaching ministry. To start, its reading of the signs of the times has more balance than earlier letters. It manifests greater trust in human capacities (nos. 30 and 31) and confesses greater confidence in humanity's abilities to meet the global crisis (nos. 38, 47). It is more affirmative about the action of grace in society (no. 48) and adopts a servant as well as a sacramental model of the church (no. 31). Most of all, John Paul appeals to a "Christ the Consummator" theology of history (nos. 31, 48), a view he rejected at the council in favor of a redemptive christology because the former appeared to him to be overly optimistic.

What accounts for this change of tone and theology? The pope's careful study of *Gaudium et Spes* and the writings of Paul VI partly explain the change, but other influences are not so readily apparent. In any case, *Sollicitudo* is less personal in idiom and concept, and it is wholly consistent with the major lines of the liberal social teaching of Vatican II and Paul VI (nos. 2–3, 6–10).

21. On nonviolence, see no. 47; on solidarity among the poor, nos. 44–45. On self-help efforts, see Sheldon Annis and Peter Hakim, eds., *Direct to the Poor: Grassroots Development in Latin America* (Boulder, Colo.: Rienner, 1988), and Alan B. Durning, *World Watch Paper 88, Action at the Grassroots: Righting Poverty and Environmental Decline* (Washington, D.C.: World Watch Institute, 1989).

The idea of solidarity among the poor is continuous with the formulation used in *Laborem Exercens* (1981), but in *Sollicitudo* the idea is closer to the usage of Paul VI, in which solidarity expresses an intergroup obligation in which the affluent are obliged to make sacrifices to share with the disadvantaged.

Another noteworthy development is that John Paul seems to distinguish between solidarity as a human virtue (no. 39) and a Christian virtue (no. 40). In his earlier theology, "the human" is understood wholly by light of the redemption.

22. *Sollicitudo*, nos. 30–31, 38.

23. Lynn White, Jr., "The Historical Roots of Our Ecological Crisis," *Science* 155 (1967): 1203–07. Unfortunately, most theologians interested in ecology adopted uncritically White's thesis that environmental destruction was the result of the dominion theme in Genesis. For more dispassionate readings of biblical and historical theological texts, one had to turn to nonbelievers. See especially Clarence Glacken, *Traces on the Rhodian Shore: Nature and Culture in Western Thought from Ancient Times to the End of the Eighteenth Century* (Berkeley: University of California Press, 1967).

For recent treatment of biblical themes, see Bernhard W. Anderson, "Creation in the Bible" and "Creation and the Noachic Covenant" in Philip N. Joranson and Ken Butigan, eds., *Cry of the Environment: Rebuilding the Christian Creation Tradition* (Santa Fe, N.M.: Bear, 1984); Richard J. Clifford, S.J., "Genesis 1–3: Permission to Exploit Nature?," *Bible Today* 26, pp. 133–45; and Norman K. Gottwald, "The Biblical Mandate for Eco-Justice Action," in Dieter T. Hessel, ed., *For Creation's*

Sake: Preaching, Ecology and Justice (Philadelphia: Geneva, 1985). The last essay is especially valuable not only because it combines ecological with justice concerns but also because it provides a succinct yet sophisticated hermeneutic for use of scripture in preaching on these topics.

24. H. Paul Santmire, *The Travail of Nature: The Ambiguous Ecological Promise of Christian Theology* (Philadelphia: Fortress, 1985).

25. Ibid., pp. 189–90.

26. Ibid., p. 73.

27. Ibid., p. 71.

28. Ibid., pp. 60–61.

29. See Peter Brown, *Augustine of Hippo: A Biography* (Berkeley: University of California Press, 1969), pp. 117, 259. Brown's comments on Augustine's waning delight in nature are pertinent because Santmire relies on Brown to make his case for Augustine's world-affirming cosmology.

30. See Eugene Te Selle, *Augustine the Theologian* (New York: Herder and Herder, 1970) pp. 208–223, esp. p. 216, on the spiritual character of Augustine's cosmology.

31. See Brown, p. 323, on the longing for the heavenly Jerusalem.

32. See Augustine's Second Homily on 1 John, no. 11, in John Burnaby, ed., *Augustine's Later Works* (Philadelphia: Westminster Press, 1955), p. 275.

33. Bill McKibben, *The End of Nature* (New York: Random House, 1989). For more scholarly treatments of the place of human intervention in natural history from professional ecologists, see Stephen Boyden, *Western Civilization in Biological Perspective: Patterns in Biohistory* (Oxford: Oxford University Press, 1987) and David Crew, *Man-Environment Process* (London: Allen and Unwin, 1983).

From the side of Christian ethics, theocentric programs seem to offer foundations for an ecological ethic consonant with our scientific knowledge of human-nature interactions. See William C. French, "Ecological Concerns and the Anti-Foundationalist Debates: James Gustafson on Biospheric Constraints," in Diane Yeager, ed., *The Annual of the Society of Christian Ethics, 1989* (Washington, D.C.: Society of Christian Ethics/Georgetown University, 1989), pp. 113–130; and David G. Trickett, *Toward a Christian Theology of Nature: A Study Based on the Thought of H. Richard Niebuhr* (Ph.D. dissertation, Southern Methodist University, 1982).

34. Santmire, p. 117.

35. Sorrell, *Saint Francis of Assisi and Nature: Tradition and Innovation in Western Christian Attitudes Toward the Environment* (New York: Oxford University Press, 1988). Sorrell's summary of the various streams of tradition flowing through medieval spirituality (pp. 9–38), and particularly the Cistercian tradition (pp. 28–38), is highly useful. Because it was willing to combine both aesthetic and utilitarian considerations, the Cistercian tradition seems a more appropriate model for emulation by modern society than Francis's eremitic style.

36. Ibid., pp. 38–44.

37. Ibid., p. 139.

38. Ibid., p. 141.

39. Boff, *Saint Francis: A Model for Human Liberation*, trans. John W. Dierksmeier (New York: Crossroad, 1984), p. 40.

40. Ibid., p. 22.

41. Also see Paul Weigand, "Escape from the Birdbath: Saint Francis as a Model for the Ecological Movement," in *Cry of the Environment*, pp. 148–160.

42. Michael J. Himes and Kenneth R. Himes, O.F.M., "The Sacrament of Creation: Toward an Environmental Theology," *Commonweal*, v. 117, 2 (January 26, 1990), pp. 42–49. On the sacramentality of nature as approached from contemporary biology, see Arthur Peacocke, *God and the New Biology* (San Francisco: Harper and Row, 1987), chapter 7, "Nature as Creation," pp. 108–115.

43. Boff, p. 72.

44. Weigand, p. 156.

45. Because of space considerations, I deal with only one of the three systematic constructive programs I would have liked to review. The second would have been theocentric ethics (see note 33 above). The third would have been Sallie McFague's feminist metaphorical theology; see her *Models of God: Theology for an Ecological, Nuclear Age* (Philadelphia: Fortress, 1987).

46. I also do not consider here the thoroughgoing theological reconstruction proposed by Thomas Berry. See Ann Lonergan and Caroline Richards, eds., *Thomas Berry and the New Cosmology* (Mystic, Conn.: Twenty-Third Publications, 1987); Thomas Berry, "Creative Energy" and "The Dream of the Earth: Our Way into the Future," *Cross Currents*, Summer/Fall 1987, pp. 178–217; and Kenneth L. Woodward, "A New Story of Creation," *Newsweek*, June 5, 1989, pp. 70–72. While I regard Berry's work as thought provoking, my comments on the place of humanity in nature, the significance of sin and redemption, and the like will indicate that I am out of sympathy with his program.

47. Bill Devall and George Sessions, *Deep Ecology: Living as if Nature Mattered* (Salt Lake City, Utah: Gibbs Smith, 1985), p. 64.

48. Ibid., p. 67.

49. Ibid.

50. Arne Naess, "Sustained Development and Deep Ecology," in *Ethics of Environment and Development*, p. 89.

51. As Naess presents the concept of vital needs, the standard would permit a transition toward a sustainable environment, as well as permission for some natural excesses (for example, feasting or large families) within the parameters of ecological viability (see *Ethics of Environment and Development*, p. 91).

52. Naess willingly acknowledges utilitarian assessments of environmental values on condition that they are accompanied by a recognition of the intrinsic worth and diversity of nonhuman life (see *Ethics of Environment and Development*, pp. 94–95).

53. Advocates of just and sustained development contend that energy efficiency, recycling, and population control will allow for transformation of the economy in the direction of sustainable growth (see McNeill, "Strategies," pp. 157–163). Technological fixes, however, may prove unreliable (see note 55 below).

54. I refer to *Gaudium et Spes*, no. 69, *Populorum Progressio*, no. 22–23, and *Sollicitudo*, no. 31.

55. Some unexpected negative feedbacks from recent environmentally designed technologies include the increase in acid rain stemming from the nitrous oxide emitted by energy-efficient auto engines, growing numbers of nuclear-waste sites as a result of attempts to replace fossil fuels, and residue plastic bits from failed efforts to make biodegradable plastics.

For an extended critique of the technicism implicit in the mainline view of sustainable development proposed by the World Conservation Society and the Brundtland Commission, see Rajni Kothari, "Environment, Technology and Ethics," in *Ethics of Environment and Development*, pp. 34–35.

56. *Ethics of Environment and Development,* pp. 94–95.

57. *Sollicitudo,* nos. 28, 31.

58. See James M. Gustafson, *Ethics from a Theocentric Perspective;* vol. 1, *Theology and Ethics,* chap. 6, "Man in Relation to God and World," and vol. 2, *Ethics and Theology,* chap. 7, "Population and Nutrition," especially pp. 218–250. H. Richard Niebuhr's theology provides a more hopeful and Christocentric outlook than Gustafson's (see note 33, above).

59. A provocative exploration of the changes in conceptualities and thought processes needed to meet the global ecological challenge is Robert Ornstein and Paul Ehrlich, *New World, New Mind: Moving toward Conscious Evolution* (New York: Doubleday, 1989).

60. Ruckelshaus, "Sustainable World," pp. 168–69.

61. Lester Brown and Edward C. Wolf, "Charting a Sustainable Course," *State of the World 1987* (Washington, D.C.: World Watch Institute, 1987), esp. pp. 209–13.

62. *Our Common Future,* p. 317.

63. On the need for consolidation and coordination of efforts, see Clark, "Planet Earth," p. 54.

64. See Richard O. Brooks, "Coercion to Environmental Virtue: Can and Should the Law Mandate Environmentally Sensitive Lifestyles?," *American Journal of Jurisprudence* 31 (1986): 21–64. Much of the best literature on political decisions and social design in an era of environmental constraints comes from the 1970s. See, especially, Dennis Clark Priages, *The Sustainable Society* (New York: Praeger, 1977). More recently, see his *Global Technopolitics: The International Politics of Technology and Resources* (Pacific Grove, Calif.: Brooks/Cole, 1989).

65. Ruckelshaus, "Sustainable World," pp. 170–71; McNeill, "Strategies," pp. 163–64.

66. *Our Common Future,* pp. 340–342.

67. Ibid., pp. 340–341.

68. While Pope John Paul sees political will as a necessity for just and sustainable development, he sees determination to work for global change lacking on the part of leaders—particularly, it seems, in the West (*Sollicitudo,* 24, 35).

69. Denis Goulet, "Development Ethics and Ecological Wisdom," in *Ethics of Environment and Development,* p. 41. Also on page 41, see: "Under ideal circumstances ethicists would share responsibility for the practical consequences of joint decisions taken by teams of development planners, economists, and technicians. . . . [T]hey need the critical input made by problem solvers if they are to avoid purely extrinsic moralism."

70. For example, see Denis Goulet, *Mexico: Development Strategies for the Future* (Notre Dame, Ind.: University of Notre Dame Press, 1983), and *The Cruel Choice: A New Concept in the Theory of Development* (Washington, D.C.: University Press of America, 1985); and Amitai Etzioni, *The Moral Dimension: Toward A New Economics* (New York: Free Press, 1988), and *The Active Society* (New York: Free Press, 1971).

13

The Rights of Farmers,
the Common Good,
and Feminist Questions

CAROL S. ROBB

Do farmers who cannot make a living deserve social support to remain farmers, or do they simply have to leave farming? In this article, Dr. Robb contends that the answer to this question depends upon which theory of justice and human rights is most compelling: bourgeois justice or biblical justice. She argues that biblical justice is more conducive to the common good; she then enters into dialogue with other feminist theorists who develop the theme that justice is a male principle and one in which women do not have a stake. Her conversation partners in this collection are Marti Kheel and Martha Ellen Stortz.

I carry in my personal history the history of agriculture in the United States. It is largely through the lens of my family's history that I read the developing literature of environmental theology and ethics, looking for perspectives that will address the lives of my parents, aunts, uncles, and cousins. I will describe some of this history as a preface to an argument for a right to farm for farmers on small and moderate-size farms. Then I will examine this claim in feminist perspective before hazarding some theological reflections that address our environmental instability and the decline of farming communities.

Both my parents came from farm families; they met, courted, and married while they and their families lived on neighboring farms in southeastern Kansas. The soil isn't really rich there, and unlike the terrain in central and western Kansas that is mostly level and prime for agriculture, the fields share the territory with hills and black oaks. My parents farmed for a while after they married, with my father in the fields and my mother at the bank, but the farm was not a viable operation, and they rented it to a neighboring farmer who needed more cropland. With one, then two, then three children, my parents began the "migration" first to a small town, then to the city, where my father became a machinist and my mother a teacher. We never really left the farm, however, for most of my mother's family stayed in that area. So we went back for weekend trips and summer vacations, arriving late at night to a cold farmhouse, lighting the kerosene lamp, smelling the house the mice thought was theirs. My relatives and their neighbors lived very modestly, and, with few exceptions, had to brace themselves for the stringent seasons. But at get-togethers we pooled our resources and ate and laughed. Before and after, the women worked in the kitchen, the men talked in the living room.

One exception to the life of stringency was Aunt Nell. The eldest of eight children, she had gone to a teachers' college and taught for a while. Then she married a wealthy man, who, though simple in his style, was on the board of directors of the town's bank during the depression and had amassed a large holding of farms when the bank foreclosed. He considered himself a shrewd businessman and passed along to Nell the advice to refrain from making any capital outlays that were not absolutely essential. When he died, leaving Nell a widow at a rather young age, she took over the administration of the land and continued his rather stingy ways. She didn't need money, so she refused to allow oil drillers on her land, saying they just made a big mess. Oil was the second most important commodity of that territory, and nearly every farm had one or two barely alive or dead pumps on it when I was growing up. But not on Nell's land.

When Nell died more than a decade ago, members of the family went with one of her neighbors to survey the holdings. For the first time, I realized that the land I always went by to get to Nell's house, and the creek where we went swimming in the summers, and the land out west of town was all Nell's. When I was a child, it never occurred to me to ask why we could swim in the creek at that spot. I didn't have to ask, because my mother knew that we had access to the creek there. There were no fences for long stretches of territory because it was all grazing land that belonged to Nell. She rented it out, she had ponds dug and roofs put on buildings, but she didn't develop it any further because she didn't need to.

In settling the estate, all the land was sold, and my mother used her share of the estate to buy one of Nell's farms. Mom and Dad had finally sold their own farm while I was in college so that they could buy a larger house in the city. Now my mother was reinvesting in her family's home territory, against the advice of most of her siblings. There was a beautiful Victorian house on this one farm, and it had some good fields, pastures, and meadows. Other than our old farm, Mom had always liked this farm the best in the whole county.

The pastures were overgrazed and needed to be left alone for a while, but Mother found some renters to mow the hay or plant crops and later to pasture cows. As an investment for steady income, however, the farm was not adequate. The rental income did not meet expenses, so she signed a lease with an oil-drilling company, which then changed the looks of the countryside. It was another oil boom time in that area, the first since the twenties, and the price of oil was high after the OPEC oil embargo. Geologically, the pressure on the oil had been allowed to build after the boom of the twenties, so once again farms had working oil pumps on them. Ours had four at one time, and my folks felt pretty good, although there were two roads on the land that had never been there before, gas smells in the air, noises of the pumps in the night, and someone in a pickup every day or so to check the tanks and look at the line and whatever else oil people do.

The ground pressure did not last long, nor did the oil boom, so oil checks no longer buy groceries for my folks. Recently times were especially hard, and Mother sold thirty-five acres across the road to an engineer from Wichita, two hours away. He wanted to build a vacation home down on the creek. The cash helped my folks out of their pinch, at least temporarily, and now they have more land on the market. The engineer has not hit it off with people too well so far. Neighbors told him the low land floods during heavy rain, but he assured them he could take care of that and built a dam of sorts upstream from his house. When it rained hard, the road was flooded and the main way into town was impassable for several families. Someone from the county had a talk with him and told him he could not dam the creek like that. His is the first instance of someone's buying land to use as vacation property; most people there cannot afford the home they live in, much less build another.

Down the road from our place is a bridge that has been condemned. We used to drive that way from our old farm to get to town. There weren't many families along the road, so the county decided not to repair it when it became dilapidated. The people on that road just drove the long way to the highway to get to town. The bridge could support foot traffic, and one day during Christmas vacation I hiked over it to visit Uncle Clyde and Aunt Lila. Clyde was Mother's brother, who raised his own family with Lila on the homestead of my grandparents. Mom said as children they used to go out into the fields and see oil oozing up through the soil, so during the last oil boom one of Clyde and Lila's grown children drilled in the cornfield. In the farmhouse, my grown cousins, all with jobs elsewhere, except one who was helping his father farm, were using a CB to communicate about how the pump was doing. That one cousin, Doc, said to me during the visit, "What do people in Boston [where I lived at the time] think about us farmers?" It had not occurred to me that people in Boston think anything about farmers. He was referring to increases in the cost of foodstuffs and assumed city people were hostile to farmers. He told me how much he was getting for corn, soybeans, wheat, and hogs. Then he told me how much bread and pork chops cost and wanted me to know that there was a big difference between what he gets and what we pay, and that most of that difference goes into middlemen who process and package and distribute the food. Within four years, Clyde's and Lila's health became fragile and they moved into town. Doc farmed awhile longer and then gave it up and took a job selling advertising for a newspaper. He said it just wasn't worth it. Farming is hard work. You have to be out every day and night if you have livestock. You cannot control the price of the inputs—the seed and fertilizer—nor can you control the price you get for the crops or livestock. He could not make enough money to make ends meet. The homestead farm was rented out, but the house where Mom and Clyde were born and raised deteriorated.

If I walked in the other direction from my folks' farm, I could reach Nell's farmhouse, bought by a young couple along with some of her fields. They didn't farm full time. He had a job in town, and the last I heard they had their place up for sale. He had lost his job, they had a new baby, and they thought he could find some work if they went to Colorado.

Mr. Rowe bought some of Nell's prime agricultural land, but he bought it at top dollar in the early eighties for speculation. Now the value is down. He could not sell it and make any money, so he decided to harvest the trees down by the creek, where we used to swim. It was wrenching to take a curve in the road where the big trees once provided a canopy from which we used to swing out over the creek and then drop into the water. They were gone. Some grinning guy with a power saw was trying to burn the stumps.

Trees are important in Kansas, as elsewhere. They buffer the winds and snow and help control soil and wind erosion. The trees provide shelter for deer and small animals and mitigate the summer heat. One time my parents consented to selling some of their trees to a local woodcutter. When Dad walked the area, he discovered that the small brush had been left in the creek bed, where it dammed up the flow during the heavy rains. Poor people have to look at their timber as a resource to be sold—although they can never get anything much for it—and cutters are poor enough that they will cut corners in order to keep costs down.

The farmer next door had a stroke this year and died. He was in his early eighties and had lived a hard life. Yet, he made things a bit easier for us. He kept an eye on the place and told my folks if he saw any wild turkeys down in the fescue. He rented the fescue and another pasture from Mom, and they made decisions together about fertilizer and whether or not to mow or graze the fescue. Mom always felt that his long-term interests and hers coincided. It was a comfort knowing that he would read the electric meter if she were not there. He had two children; but neither of them wanted to farm, so we don't know what will happen to his place.

It is depressing. Most farmers got caught in the crazy cycle of the seventies when land value was high, and the eighties, when it slumped badly.

Farmers took out loans for equipment, home improvements, and more land, using their land for collateral. Oil prices were up then also. Then the economy pulled the rug out. Lots of neighbors had to declare bankruptcy. One farmer who used to rent from Nell bought a lot of what had been her acreage, built a new house for his wife and himself, and lost it all. Now he's working as a foreman for someone out of state. They were two of the most responsible farmers in the county. The only ones, it seems, who didn't lose their shirts during that time were the people so poor the banks would not give them loans in the first place.

My father says that the area around their farm is a dying community. It appears that he is right. Some farm-policy analysts have said the agricultural crisis presents an opportunity for young, new farmers to get started up. I don't see it that way. In this area, the farm economy is limp and no longer provides a foundation for the county's economy. With the older farmers moving off the land and dying, the towns are losing business for machinery and farm products, never mind the movie theaters and cafés. The clothing stores have been replaced with secondhand stores and empty storefronts. If people want clothes, they drive forty-five minutes to Bartlesville, where there are cut-rate, high-volume stores like K-Mart or Wal-mart. Town houses for sale stay on the market for *years*.

This is the story of one area in Kansas, not of the whole state. In the central part of the state live my cousin and his family, who have a diversified farm — so diversified that part of his business is to go to the big agricultural shows in order to market his computer software. He didn't grow up in this part of Kansas; he grew up in the Pacific Northwest, was college educated, served in the military, then moved to central Kansas to be near his grandmother and farm her land.

Another cousin in western Kansas bought his family farm from his mother. With a college degree in agriculture, as well as an active family and a wife who teaches, he continues to farm. In that part of the country, however, farmers must irrigate in order to get high crop yields. The groundwater is from the Ogalala Aquifer, and he is counting the years that the Ogalala will continue to supply water. Great Plains agriculture has been steadily draining the Ogalala, and the lower it gets, the more farmers will turn to dry cropping, which means lower crop yields. In turn, that will mean more fiscal fragility for farmers. As it is, my cousin does not feel well entrenched in farming. Although he grew up as a farm boy, gained a degree in agriculture, and has been farming for more than twenty years, every year the economics of farming places him in a delicate position. Each time a combine or a tractor breaks down, as they do, a major expense is required to get it going again. His farming uses some of the latest capital equipment. He custom farms land for others in addition to his own; yet, still, with the magnitude of his operation, he wonders whether or not he can keep going.

FROM PERSONAL HISTORY TO ANALYSIS

I know that agriculture looks different in some other parts of the country, but I believe that what I see in the lives of my family is well represented in every agricultural state. My personal history reflects the changes in U.S. agriculture as a way of life. In the time of my grandparents, farming was the occupation of at least one-third of the people. Since then, the sector of the population making a living on the land has decreased to 3 percent. What happens to the land as farm families move to the towns and cities? It changes hands as people invest in land for speculative reasons, it gets mined for its resources—sometimes in a quick and dirty fashion. It also gets deserted.

For the land to be deserted may not be all bad. Since farm families have left the rural areas to live in towns, the deer and the wild turkeys have begun to reproduce. Now opossums, badgers, and skunks have more of a chance. Yet, in the absence of farm families looking over their shoulders, their habitat is freshly assaulted by oil drillers, who accidentally and carelessly leak saltwater into creeks and ponds. City dwellers who want a vacation home are assaultive when they get a chance, as for them hunting is a leisure sport.

I am profoundly convinced that environmental ethics is economic ethics at its core and that every vision of an economic order is a moral statement that includes a value stance regarding open space, environments for "every person" and for nonhuman creatures. I am disturbed, then, to witness in my own lifetime the dissolution of whole communities and of farming as a way of life. I am disturbed for personal reasons, in that I see land on which I have history being misused and overused in the absence of the people who see their long-term future to be on specific plots of land. I see people living in poverty and near poverty because their roots are on the farm; worse yet, they have a notion that their work is not valued in the community.

I am also disturbed for political and economic reasons. I am convinced by research on patterns of land ownership conducted in the forties, suppressed by the U.S. Department of Agriculture, and then replicated in the seventies that indicates that rural and town communities are directly and positively affected when surrounding farmland is owned by the farmers who work it, and negatively affected when surrounding farmland is owned by people who do not live directly on the land.[1] At stake is the tax base by which small communities finance schools and public works, a network of small businesses that support farming and farm households, a range of churches with their theological diversity, and the democratic involvement of citizens in the sustenance of their communities. Communities surrounded by absentee-owned land have a polarized class basis, fewer taxes to support a healthy community, and an alienated citizenry. Our public policy should support farming as an economic venture for small- and moderate-size farmers to sustain those communities and slow down the rate of urban migration—or at least this is my argument.

For agricultural reasons, too, I would support policies that keep family farmers on the farm. Large landholdings are not the most efficient and productive basis for agriculture. Agribusiness is undermined by soil compaction of heavy machinery, soil erosion from overfarming, and the pollution of ground water from overuse of chemical fertilizers and pesticides. A 1981 study by economists at the USDA examined wheat, feed grains, and cotton farms in seven regions of the country. It concluded that on average the most efficient farm is not the one with millions in gross income, but a sale level of $133,000 and an acreage of 1,157. Furthermore, a farm with $46,000 in sales and 322 acres was large enough to provide 90 percent of the maximum economies of size.[2]

Agricultural policy is not the only economic issue involved in environmental ethics. The sources of acid rain, ozone depletion, and toxic waste are linked more to manufacturing and to urban automobile use than to agriculture. Yet, urban policy and farm policy are inextricably tied, for when people leave the farm they often go to urban areas. Who is left behind to run the tractors if not the hired hands of holding companies that have as much interest in petrochemicals as in wheat? The oil business is very centralized in major metropoles where public transportation is underfunded and underused.

It appears to me that land reform should be as much on the public-policy agenda of the United States as it is in Peru or the Philippines. We are living in a period that has seen consolidation of land ownership in the U.S. analogous to the period of biblical history that Marvin Chaney describes in eighth century B.C.E. Palestine.[3] In 1920, the 32 million people living on farms made up 30 percent of the nation's population, but by 1979 only 3 percent of the population (6.2 million persons) were farm residents. Five percent of the farmland owners—about 0.14 percent of the total population—owned 48 percent of the agricultural acreage. Farms are becoming fewer in number and larger in size.[4]

Few, if any, policies limit farm size and ownership, and many public policies have encouraged consolidation. Credit, tax, and commodity-price-support programs have promoted concentration, because they remove a considerable amount of risk from farming, encourage existing farmers to expand, and entice nonfarm investors into agriculture.

Policies could, however, be designed to turn around the process of concentration. They would include restricting price-support programs to farms that are actively managed and operated by their owners; limiting farm ownership by non–family farm corporations and foreign purchasers; establishing a land bank for acquiring available farmland, with resale or lease in moderate-size parcels; limiting federal loans only to farms no larger than the size needed to achieve reasonable efficiency; and capping commodity programs to a payment limit of $20,000 per farmer. In other words, social policies could turn around the tendency toward land consolidation—if we want to do that as a nation.

Farm owners are also becoming whiter. Black-operated farms are disappearing at a rate faster than white-operated farms. Between 1900 and 1978, the number of black farms declined by 94 percent, while the number of white farms fell by 56 percent. In 1920, one in seven U.S. farms was owned or run by blacks, but in 1948 that proportion had fallen to one in forty-five.[5] This loss of black farmers may primarily stem from movement by black families from southern rural areas to northern urban areas, a movement that is continuing to occur, spurred in no minor way by the failure of the Farmers Home Administration to provide services to black farmers comparable to those provided to whites. In that movement, black farmers leave behind an opportunity for self-employment, managerial experience, considerably larger discretion over their lives, and, overall, the structural underpinnings for self-reliance, nutrition, and psychological security. Racial justice is also at stake in the concentration of farmlands.[6]

FROM ANALYSIS TO ARGUMENT

Fred Kirschenmann is right when he says our national inheritance is a value system that is ambivalent; we honor the development of resources as an index of responsible use of the land, but we also honor the responsibility to protect and preserve the environment on behalf of God. In addition, our cultural language is far more developed in moral discourse about rights to private property than in moral discourse about responsibility to the community's well-being. I propose that farmers have a right to sustain themselves through farming, not solely because they have a qualified right to private property, but because sustaining farming as a way of life and as the mode of agricultural production contributes more to the common good than does agriculture based on concentrated land ownership.

In order to make this case, I need to discuss "rights" and the relationship of rights language to the principle of justice. Then I will explore whether or not this argument is relevant to a moral agenda focused on the well-being of women and children. I will take this latter step as a means for discussing recent contributions to environmental ethics by ecofeminism. Finally, I will locate rights and justice theory in the context of biblical theology.

Rights Language and Justice Theory
In one sense, it is a good strategy to formulate a moral agenda with respect to farming by using rights language, since that language is so "American." Human rights language characterizes the eighteenth-century political theory in the foundational documents of the U.S. Constitution, particularly in the Bill of Rights. This eighteenth-century theory, known technically as liberalism, claims rights to civil and political liberties that might be conceptualized as fences around individual persons. We have fences to keep out people who would infringe upon our abilities to worship, participate in political discussion, have a trial by jury, and whatever else is guaranteed in the foundational documents. My liberty within my fence is my human right. Our nation is not about to tear down those fences casually; and I hope we

will continue to honor that tradition, while at the same time acknowledging its weaknesses and building a better tradition.

The main weakness is that liberalism emphasizes negative rights, that is, the freedom *from* being impinged upon, but it says little about positive rights, or what we have the justifiable expectation to have or to do. In our particular context, this liberal tradition has led to an emphasis on the right to private property in the face of communities suffering depression, hunger, and homelessness because of the way their neighbors are using their rights.

We should be wary of employing traditional liberal human rights theory to develop a moral argument in support of protecting family farmers. As it is, such a theory guarantees farmers the right to decide what crops to grow, how to fertilize, when to harvest, and, ultimately, when to sell to a real-estate developer who has plans for a shopping center or a subdivision. Liberal theory will not by itself provide the basis for arguing that small- and moderate-size farms have a right to be the main way, or even an important way, the nation's food is grown.

An alternative mode of human rights language is emerging, however, that promises more in this direction. Based on reflection upon the United Nations Charter of Human Rights, on weaknesses in the political systems of the United States and the Soviet Union, and on the inability of law and public policy to protect women and families, this alternative direction in moral theory defines human rights as the minimal concrete conditions for participation in community with dignity.[7] A "right" in this discourse is not a fence, but rather a channel for participation in a community. Such conditions are different from one geographical and cultural context to the next, although some conditions may be shared universally. In this sense, human rights are discerned in sensitive reflection upon a particular context, where the concrete conditions of life and possibilities for participation are scrutinized.

In this alternative framework of human rights, one would still proclaim the importance of civil and political rights, but would want to add that some material conditions are necessary in order to enable people to exercise such liberties. For example, if someone does not have access to food, clothing, and shelter, then the right to worship or to vote is vacuous. There are some material conditions that provide the basis for a life directed autonomously (that is, without coercion) to sustain human dignity.

Further, a right can be a human right only if it is consistent with the principle of justice. All rights language asserts what justice requires in a particular context. The principle of justice itself must be determined by reflection upon the historical context. The principle of justice requires us to give someone her or his due. Many standards are used to determine what is your due or my due. While we use each of them at one time or another, we cannot use them all at the same time because they conflict with each other. Hence, the moral task is to determine which measure of justice is most morally relevant at any one time, when two or more incompatible measures of justice may compete. For instance, equality as a measure of justice dictates that we treat each person the same. Strict equality is illustrated in the division of a bushel of apples such that each person has the same number.

Work as a measure of justice would have us determine what is owed on the basis of what is produced—for example, five apples owed for five brooms made, four apples for four brooms. Need as a measure of justice would have us determine what is owed, not on the basis of strict equality nor by what is produced, but rather on the basis of what is needed. If you have five mouths to feed, you are owed five apples; if your neighbor has two mouths to feed, then two apples are owed your neighbor.

Merit is yet another measure of justice and is more subjective in quality. There is no one determinant of what constitutes merit, or what qualifies one as *deserving*. One illustration is in terms of *effort*, regardless of results. We intuitively affirm that persons with handicaps and who have high motivation and have to expend great effort are due recognition for their contributions, even at the expense of equality, work, or need.

Rank is a further determinant of what is owed. Rank, either earned or ascribed, says something about what is owed. Higher education and the military are two institutions that use rank to determine what is owed (rank itself is usually justified by prior work and accomplishment). The very young and the very old also have a certain rank in our society that may be related to need or work or merit, but is at the same time independent of these other measures of justice.

Finally, the law is a measure of justice. It is not the whole measure, as we change laws so they will conform with new perceptions or standards of justice; however, the law is nevertheless important in determining what is owed.[8]

These ways of determining what is owed all have a place in our moral reflection, but with changing priorities. This treatment of the meaning of justice is primarily philosophical. The biblical notion of justice as right-eousness, on the other hand, means the fulfillment of the demands of a relationship, whether with other people, with God/ess, or, by extension, with nonhuman creation. The demands of one kind of relationship, say a parent to a child, may be very different from the demands of another, say a teacher to a student. As with the philosophical notion of justice, however, biblical righteousness has no norm outside the relationship itself. Biblical texts call upon all the above measures of justice at one time or another as measures of righteousness.[9] Biblical justice, and philosophical justice are both historical principles, not only because their meaning is derived from communities that have passed down their wisdom to later generations but also because their meaning has to be debated and discerned in any particular time in history within the context of conflicting or competing claims upon the community.

The righteous or just person in Israel preserved the peace and wholeness of the community, because she fulfilled the demands of communal living. This image is not the dominant one of the just person in the twentieth-century United States. The philosophical definition of justice, however, is quite consistent with the biblical image, *if* there is a high value given to the demands of communal living. Surely, we must acknowledge that the demands of communal living are ever present, although not highly valued in our culture, which is imbued with individualism. Nevertheless, the notion that a human right is a minimal condition for participation in community with dignity is a step beyond bourgeois liberalism and toward a notion of justice much closer to biblical righteousness.

In sum, there is a legacy of justice theory that is much older than liberal political thought, with its individualism. Biblical justice is more accurately the fulfillment of the demands of a relationship, including relationship to the community. Justice, in part, works to preserve the community and in this sense is defined in relationship to the common good. A notion of human rights consistent with biblical justice is that these rights are the minimal conditions for participating in community with dignity. The requirements of dignity will surely coincide with liberal rights, but will involve attention to some material conditions. In this framework human rights are a possibility because of the structural support given by the community. How different from the contemporary liberal perspective in which human rights protect the individual from the forces of the larger community.

A theory of justice lies behind every farm policy, and I believe a farm policy that functions to preserve family farms is closer to the biblical notion of justice than it would be to a liberal notion of justice. In the liberal view, the sum of all individuals making decisions about their own individual self-interest will result in the common good. In order for those individuals to make their self-interested decisions the marketplace should be as unfettered as possible.

This theory of justice may appeal implicitly to work—in that people who have the money to buy out other people probably deserve to because they have earned it—or to the law. The law guarantees the freedom of business transactions among freely consenting adults as the preeminent determinant of justice. If market forces result in the demise of small- and moderate-size farms and the growth of agribusiness and other corporate consolidation of agricultural holdings, then that must be consistent with the common good. I do not want to slight the reasons behind this stance, which refer primarily to the efficient allocation of labor in different sectors of the labor market. However, it is surely the case that those who support the market as the mechanism for making these decisions would agree that when agriculture passes into the hands of corporations agricultural production and investment *must* be concerned primarily with percentage growth in profits or in the vertical consolidation of the agricultural process. They are not primarily concerned with sustainable agricultural practices, the health of rural economies, or the stability of farm communities. Preserving peace and wholeness of the community is not the goal of any corporation, although such peace and wholeness may be desirable and good for business.

To recapitulate an earlier discussion, owner-occupied farms contribute to the common good in several ways. Owner farmers are more concerned with sustainable agriculture than with short-term profits, although they need some profits in order to stay in business. They contribute to the local community government, businesses, churches, and schools, while absentee owners do not. By staying in rural areas they counteract urban migration and centralization of the population. In measurable ways, a farm policy that encourages the viability of small- and moderate-size farms contributes more to the common good than does the unfettered market because it makes rural communities possible. It is more consistent with the definition of human rights as a minimal condition for participating in community with dignity. Also, the measure of justice that would be given a higher priority would be need—the need of farm families for more economic security, the need of the nation for a healthier system of agriculture to produce our foodstuffs, and the need of the ecosystem for responsible stewardship of soil and water and the space for diverse plant and animal species to thrive.[10]

Challenges to the Argument

This argument provokes some issues that are interesting in the practical, as well as theoretical, spheres. Because of the complexity of these issues, some people may be reluctant to agree with my perspective that farmers should have rights to farm. For instance, we have testimony from some environmentalists that raising cows and hogs for the mass market is in itself contradictory to sustainability. The impact of animal grazing and feed lots on the biosphere is more negative than positive, calling into question the practice of all livestock farming.[11] It is in fact a test of the definition of human rights proposed here to ask whether or not human rights are relevant to environmental ethics at all. What is the usefulness of this definition? What are the minimal conditions for participation in community with dignity for cows, pigs, or turkeys? What is the morally relevant community here? Is it the community of cows? the community of meat-eaters? or is it the community of all animals and people?

I think it is fairly easy to say that one condition would have to do with the quality of animals' lives and that, as an illustration, the process of raising veal meets no conditions of dignity for calves. There even may be existent strands of cattle that have been bred to be passive and not complain when their dignity is assaulted. Would an expanded definition of rights that includes farm animals prohibit such breeding practices? It would appear so. Would an expanded definition prohibit all raising of livestock for slaughter? It is not a big leap to imagine that the answer is yes. It would appear that the same kind of moral argument that would lead to public policy in support of small- and moderate-size farms would also, by extension, lead to a major reorientation in the treatment of livestock. For some, it would lead toward vegetarianism. For others, it would lead toward a new community with livestock that does not preclude meat eating, but that may curtail it drastically or set conditions upon it. The practical impact of such new eating patterns would affect the viability of all livestock farming as a business.

Another issue that emerges is whether the definition of justice and its measures should be expanded, in light of this discussion, to include "participation" as a seventh measure, along with equality, work, merit, and the rest.[12] There is reason to include participation as a measure of justice; the Roman Catholic social teaching that went into the U.S. bishops' 1986 pastoral letter on the economy, *Economic Justice for All*, moved in this direction.[13] So has the recent work of the Presbyterian Eco-Justice Task Force.[14]

It is a bit of a mind bender to define justice as that which guarantees (human rights or) the minimal conditions for participating in the community with dignity and then not to evaluate policies or social structures by whether or not affected parties adequately participated in their formation. All notions of the common good or of what is necessary for the preservation of the community will be suspect by minorities if the latter continually pay the price for the stability of a particular society.

However, to the question, what is one owed? Can we answer according to how one has participated? Not really, for that use of the word "participate" implies work or merit. Perhaps we mean one is owed the right to participate in the setting of policies, defining justice, or in constructing a new society. But wouldn't we then also request that policies, definitions, and visions be accountable to justice?

I conclude that participation is a necessary condition for justice, but does not function in the same way as the other aspects of justice we considered. Participation is not inherently in conflict with those other aspects of justice, while, generally speaking, they are mutually exclusive, unless compromise or equity is managed. We can participate in the debate of which measure of justice to emphasize when we next consider farm policy; if we do not, the resulting legislation will be considered unjust. In this sense, participation is a procedural requirement of justice that has become normative, as we have struggled to move out from under paternalism. There are other procedural requirements for justice in addition to participation — that is, in part, what we mean by due process. Justice is a principle of content, particularly in biblical perspective, in addition to a procedural matter, and it could well be that nothing is to be gained by treating participation in the same vein as, say, equality or merit or need.

Feminist Perspectives on Justice Theory

A third issue is whether or not justice theory can be appropriately considered to be consistent with feminist theory, which exposes the levels to which theories of justice have been masculine. For instance, Mary Daly proposes:

It is hardly necessary to review here in detail the long struggle of women to obtain "equal rights" within patriarchy in order to know that the patriarchal devisers of this definition of *justice* had in mind something substantially less than "right" when they created the device of such a concept. ... The "just" king, president, pope, physician, boss, husband, father knows with certainty the proper place and "rights" of the touchable class."[15]

Daly posits a feminist principle, *Nemesis*, "the object and process of internal judgment that sets in motion a kind of new psychic alignment of energy patterns." She relegates justice to the realm of abstract, nonimpassioned rationality into which people with power are cornered.

Carol Gilligan's *In a Different Voice*[16] and her following work have inspired a large tendency in psychological, educational, moral, and environmental disciplines that challenges the centrality of justice to women's moral reflection. According to Gilligan, the morality of care and responsibility, in which the central preoccupation is a responsiveness to others, is more characteristic of women's moral sensitivities than the morality of rights and justice. Justice tradition is characterized in terms very similar to those I would use to describe the liberalism that undergirds U.S. foundational documents:

> Because people are capable of moral autonomy, they are morally entitled and ought to be legally entitled to conduct their lives as they see fit. Their rights protect them from others' aggression and free them to do what they want, provided that they do not violate others' rights. Locke's list of natural rights—the rights to life, liberty, and property—was seminal. Though variously interpreted and supplemented in subsequent theories, this set of rights captures a constant of the justice tradition. People are surely entitled to noninterference; they may not be entitled to aid. Though it is morally commendable to help the needy, and though justice may require helping the needy, it is disputable whether anyone has a *right* to such positive benefits as medical care, decent housing, or education. In this respect, the justice tradition is individualistic.[17]

In the face of the bankruptcy of liberal tradition's ability to protect the commons, air, water, and soil that affect all people's quality of life, as well as the very existence of nonhuman species, some feminist theorists propose a realignment of moral values to give higher priority to the virtues of caring and women's sensitivities in policy making, since by virtue of their role in the family women are more adept at "caring" than men.

I want to rejoice in the exposure of masculine moral theory and sensibilities that Daly's and Gilligan's work has inspired. Their insights are relevant to virtually every field of study and pattern of social interaction. In addition, feminist theorists should be warned against giving over "justice" to "the men," first, because to do so ignores the scholarship of women who are building theories of justice, and second, because it derails the potential power of the biblical call to justice that envisions right relationships among people as the condition of right relationships with the earth. For instance, Beverly Harrison, working within the Christian tradition, but criticizing the patriarchal bias of biblical sources, claims that the vision of justice as rightly related community is the *central* metaphor of Christian moral reflection.

> You are well aware of the thesis of liberation theology that structures of power and privilege thwart and dehumanize not merely individuals, but groups of persons who as a result live out their lives without the degree of self-direction appropriate to the human person, and without the necessary participation in the human community which would make it possible for "community" to be understood as genuinely encompassing them. From such a position, or rather, from such a commitment, justice appears not merely as a juridical notion, nor as a "regulative ideal," nor even as the "first virtue of social institutions." ... For me, justice is more than all of these—it is our central theological image, a metaphor of right relationship, which shapes the *telos* of a good community and serves as the animating passion of the moral life. ... [A] radical conception of justice as rightly related community may be claimed legitimately as *the* core theological metaphor of a Christian moral vision of life, in much the same way that many have claimed love, in the form of *caritas* or *agape*, as Christianity's central theological moral metaphor.[18]

The animating passion Harrison speaks of is justice, recovering the emotional and connectional spirit of a community that required full participation for its survival. We may be able to fool ourselves for a little while that contemporary communities can survive with a high degree of alienation and lack of participation, but not for long. In fact, the social structure consistent with healing the biosphere will undoubtedly be one that is decentralized, requiring high levels of participation.

Adding further to the recovery of justice is Margaret Farley's work using justice as the criterion for evaluating love relationships. In her description of a "just love" are found the moral sensitivities Carol Gilligan characterizes as typically women's:

> A just love of persons will, for example, affirm their essential equality as human persons, but it will also attend to the differences among them in terms of capabilities and needs. It will take account of and respect the essential autonomy of persons and the meaning and values that they themselves give to their lives (though it will not thereby abdicate its own responsibility for discerning meaning and values in

the concrete lives of the ones loved). It will also take account of and respect the relationships that are as essential to persons as is their freedom or autonomy. . . . [L]ove will be just, in the sense of "accurate," when it does not destroy or falsify the reality of the person loved (either as human or as unique individual). It will be *more* or *less* just, in the sense of "adequate," as it more or less adequately reaches to the full and complex reality of the one loved. In this second sense justice in love admits of degrees.[19]

Justice is a condition of love, and it depends upon first knowing and then affirming the concrete reality of oneself and of the other. This discussion of justice merges neatly with Gilligan's description of women's moral sensitivity as tuned to conflicting responsibilities, rather than competing rights. It requires for its resolution a mode of thinking that is contextual and narrative, rather than formal and abstract. The males described by Gilligan (and Lawrence Kohlberg) have been socially prepared to take their leadership positions in bourgeois and liberal society, while the women have been prepared to take care of the relational sphere (for most, the family) out of the public-policy arena. I contend it is the better task to criticize the individualistic political economy in place and the particular theory of justice that sustains it rather than to abdicate our power to do so in the name of a caring ethic. In its stead, I propose a political economy accountable to democratic participation, not only in the political but also in the economic arena. A retrieval of the biblical notion of right relationship should be the goal of every worshiping Christian community and the center of theological education, for retrieval will remind us of a moral sensibility for such participation.

On this basis, I believe that to bring the meaning of justice for our time into the public-policy arena is essential to a social agenda that cares about the personhood and well-being of women and children. We can participate in that arena without any rigidly defined inheritance of the definition of justice. What is "due," says Karen Lebacqz,

> is not due in the abstract but in the concrete. And that concrete is determined by history—by exchanges made, by contracts forced, by covenants broken, by disrespect, by exploitation, by all the myriad ways in which human beings violate the fundamental covenant of life with life. Violations of the covenant of mutual responsibility result in the need for correctives. Relationships in history create demands in justice.[20]

In the matter of wages, justice for women requires the corrective of equality. In the matter of work, justice for parents and children requires more attention to their needs for flexible hours and supportive child care. In the area of agriculture, justice for farmers involves more attention to their need for economic stability, the nation's need for healthy food, and the need for considerate treatment of the land. In this respect, justice theory is a component of feminist *and* enviromental ethics. In both cases, we cannot escape having to argue for a new emphasis or a new priority in measures of justice in order to approach right relationships in community.

It is with some ambivalence that I tie the agenda of environmental ethics so closely to farm policy, as my experience indicates that rural culture is very hard on women. Sex roles seem more rigid than in urban areas, although there is very little basis for such rigidity. In rural cultures, men do men's things and women do women's things, unless, of course, men need women to do men's things. Men rarely do women's things.

Sex-role rigidity is apparently related to control of the business operation of the farm. Sarah Elbert's research indicates that in the early stages of the farm as a business, which usually corresponds to the early years of marriage and child bearing, women are more involved with management decisions on the farm, even though they also juggle responsibilities for child care and household duties. Without their participation, the farm will not make it. Whether or not women obtain ownership rights is likely to be very important for their involvement later on in the farm as a business. If and when the farm becomes a larger business, new forms of labor management and control, involving more bureaucratization and specialization, are likely to be employed, as they would be in any growing firm. The farm wife is likely to be displaced as a farmworker or manager at this stage to make room for hired workers who will not challenge the farm husband as head of the business. If it happens, the farm wife not only loses her share of control of the family production forces but also is shuttled back into the house to the realm of domestic tasks. Agricultural production is not *naturally* sex segregated, particularly as women can obtain skills in farm management, engineering, and agronomy in college agricultural programs and through extension services. The sex segregation is social, and the theologically conservative and charismatic churches found in most farm communities do their share to reinforce husbands' paternal authority and role segregation.[21]

The research from which Elbert draws, however, indicates that when women and men share in farm ownership and management their families are more likely to share equitably domestic and child-caring tasks in the households. She believes that such sharing on both fronts is crucial to the economic survival of small- and moderate-size farms.[22]

Also of note are the women who own 15 percent of the total farmland. More than 50 percent of such ownership involves women age sixty-five and older, and it is often controlled by their spouses in partnership, family corporation, or lending institutions. While female-owned land is less valuable per holding and per acre than male-owned farm holdings, women's access to farming as a business still appears to be tied to the sustainability of family farms.[23] Women's participation in agriculture will certainly not increase if control of farmland is further concentrated.

In spite of my ambivalence about the culture of rural communities, I stand by the original claim that we as a nation will do best to support that struggling sector of the agricultural economy — small- and moderate-size farms. Using moral language, I would claim that these farmers have a right to such structural support, because it is necessary for their participation in the national (and international) community with dignity. Farmers make a just claim on us for this support in order to restore right relationships with them. In the past, the nation has adopted previous tax and farm-support policies that have been disproportionately favorable to large landholders and to speculation in land, and that have contributed to the consolidation of farmland in fewer and fewer hands. We will know that right relationship has been restored by its signs: increased participation of women and racial and ethnic minorities in farming, respectful treatment of the land in terms of diversified crops and conservation of soil and water, decentralized and diversified food products available to consumers, and revivified governments and economies in rural communities.

NOTES

1. John Hart, in *The Spirit of the Earth* (New York: Paulist, 1984), cites Walter Goldschmidt's 1944 "Analysis of California Agriculture," showing the greater benefits of family farming. Goldschmidt's study was replicated by Trudy Wischemann, of the Macro Social Accounting Project, University of California, Davis, and discussed at the Western Jurisdiction Agriculture/Rural Life Hearing, Woodland, California, July 26, 1986, organized under the auspices of the General Board of Church and Society of the United Methodist Church.

2. Joseph N. Belden, *Dirt Rich, Dirt Poor: America's Food and Farm Crisis* (New York: Routledge and Kegan Paul, 1986), p. 25.

3. Marvin L. Chaney, "Systemic Study of the Israelite Monarchy," *Semeia*, 37 (1986): 51–76.

4. Belden, p. 23.

5. Ibid., p. 29.

6. Ibid., p. 30.

7. Two different perspectives that corroborate the value of this definition are David Hollenbach, *Claims in Conflict: Retrieving and Renewing the Catholic Human Rights Tradition* (New York: Paulist, 1979), and Beverly Wildung Harrison, *Our Right To Choose: Toward a New Ethic of Abortion* (Boston: Beacon, 1983).

8. This typology is from Chaim Perelman, *The Idea of Justice and the Problem of Argument* (London: Routledge and Kegan Paul, 1963).

9. My colleague Robert Coote made this point in conversation with me.

10. I want to alert readers to another source, C. Dean Freudenberger, *Food for Tomorrow?* (Minneapolis, Minn.: Augsburg, 1984), where "a new ethic for agriculture" is developed in a somewhat different way. Freudenberger concurs that the family farm is a structural necessity for the conservation of soil, the nation's health, and other measures of the common good. He also appeals to the principle of justice in making his argument, although he does not define the way he uses this principle.

He appeals additionally to participation and sustainability as discrete principles. In a somewhat different way than I will later, he extends the idea of justice to non-human creation.

11. John Robbins, *Realities 1989*, facts excerpted from *Diet for a New America* (EarthSave, P.O. Box 949, Felton CA 95018-0949). Robbins claims 85 percent of all U.S. topsoil loss is directly associated with livestock raising and that livestock production consumes more than half of the water used for all purposes in the United States.

12. We should resist the temptation to define justice as all positive values, thereby blurring the distinctions between values and principles. Americans already tend, if asked, to say that justice means *freedom*, which is why to many people the unfettered free market is the only conceivably moral economic system. It would be a similar intellectual confusion to broaden a definition of justice to include participation without sufficient reason.

13. Pastoral Letter on Catholic Social Teaching and the U.S. Economy, *Economic Justice for All* (Washington, D.C.: National Conference of Catholic Bishops, 1986). In this pastoral letter one finds: "Basic Justice demands the establishment of minimum levels of participation in the life of the human community for all persons" (p. 39). Much of the justification for this assertion can be found in David Hollenbach's *Claims in Conflict* (New York: Paulist, 1979).

14. Presbyterian Eco-Justice Task Force, *Keeping and Healing the Creation* (Louisville, Ky.: Committee on Social Witness Policy, Presbyterian Church, 1989).

15. Mary Daly, *Pure Lust* (Boston: Beacon, 1984), pp. 274-75.

16. Carol Gilligan, *In a Different Voice* (Cambridge, Mass.: Harvard Press, 1982).

17. Diana T. Meyers and Eva Feder Kittay, *Women and Moral Theory* (Totowa, N.J.: Rowman & Littlefield, 1987), p. 5.

18. "The Dream of a Common Language: Towards a Normative Theory of Justice in Christian Ethics," *Annual of the Society of Christian Ethics*, ed. Larry L. Rasmussen (Dallas, Tex.: Perkins School of Theology, 1983) pp. 3-4.

19. Margaret A. Farley, *Making, Keeping, Breaking Personal Commitments* (San Francisco: Harper and Row, 1986), pp. 82-83.

20. Karen Lebacqz, *Justice in an Unjust World: Foundations for a Christian Approach to Justice* (Minneapolis, Minn.: Augsburg, 1987), p. 151.

21. Sarah Elbert, "The Farmer Takes a Wife: Women in America's Farming Families," in Lourdes Beneria and Catharine R. Stimson, eds. *Women, Households, and the Economy* (New Brunswick, N.J., and London: Rutgers University Press, 1987), pp. 173-197.

22. Ibid., p. 192.

23. Ibid., pp. 194-95.

Contributors

Alexandra Allen has lobbied on federal environmental legislation and worked with grassroots environmental groups as an attorney with the U.S. Public Interest Research Group. In 1989 she spoke with and listened to dozens of community activists at two STP (Stop the Poisoning) Schools at the Highlander Research and Education Center in eastern Tennessee.

Ann Marie B. Bahr is Assistant Professor of Religion at South Dakota State University. Her doctorate is from Temple University in New Testament Studies. Her research interests are in the Bible, Comparative Religion, and Psychology of Religion.

J. Baird Callicott is Professor of Philosophy and Natural Resources at the University of Wisconsin — Stevens Point. There he has taught the world's first philosophy course in environmental ethics since 1971 and has helped to build a literature in environmental philosophy. He is author of *In Defense of the Land Ethic: Essays in Environmental Philosophy* (State University of New York Press, 1989). He is editor of and principal contributor to *Companion to "A Sand County Almanac": Interpretive and Critical Essays* (University of Wisconsin Press, 1987); co-editor, with Roger T. Ames of *Nature in Asian Traditions of Thought: Essays in Environmental Philosophy* (State University of New York Press, 1989); and co-editor with Susan L. Flader of *The Ecological Conscience and Other Essays by Aldo Leopold* (University of Wisconsin Press, 1991).

Carl J. Casebolt is Health and Environmental Policy Advocate of the National Council of Churches in Washington, D.C. His M.Div. degree is from Union Theological Seminary in New York, and he is an ordained minister and a member of the United Church of Christ. Previously, he was Director of the Peace and Environment Project, Chief Executive Officer of Work Right Products, Inc., and General Manager of Agalite Bronson Co. His publications include *A Polaris for the Spirit: Toward Ideological Reconciliation in a Nuclear Age* (Oakland, Calif.: Concern for the Fulfillment of Life Foundation, 1982); "Toward Organic Security: Environmental Restoration or the Arms Race?," with Steve Rauh, in Sierra Club *Yodeler*, June 1986; and "An Eco-Justice Perspective on *An Environmental Agenda*" in *The Egg*, Fall 1986.

Drew Christiansen, S.J., is Bannon Scholar and Visiting Fellow at the Center for Applied Ethics, Santa Clara University. His writings on social justice and Roman Catholic social teaching have appeared in *Theological Studies*, *Quarterly Review*, *Social Thought*, and other journals. He is preparing a collection of his essays on international justice, *Lazarus at the Gate: Gospel Justice in a Divided World*.

Herman E. Daly is senior economist for the Environmental Department of the World Bank and formerly was Professor of Economics at Louisiana State University. He holds a B.A. degree from Rice University and a doctorate from Vanderbilt

University. He has published a number of articles in professional journals on population growth and ecological constraints on economic growth.

Ina Praetorius Fehle is a graduate of the University of Heidelberg, majoring in German Language and Literature and Theology. She presented a thesis at the University of Zurich in 1989 on "Menschenbild und Frauenbild in deutschsprachigen theologischen Lehrbuchern seit 1945" in fulfillment of requirements for a Th.D. She is a member of the Swiss Preparatory Committee for the Ecumenical Assembly in Basel, May 1989. As such, she took the initiative for the Feminist Theological Theses.

Irene Gysel-Nef teaches elementary school, Christian education, and religion, and shares parish work with her husband. She took an active part in the Basic Movement of the Church of Zurich, 1984–87, and the Swiss Evangelical Synod, 1983–86. She has responsibilities for the Church Center Helferei Grossmünster Zürich.

Marti Kheel is a writer and activist in the areas of animal liberation and ecofeminism and cofounder of Feminists for Animal Rights. Her articles have been translated into several languages and have appeared in a variety of journals, including *Environmental Ethics, Between the Species, Creation*, and *Woman of Power*, as well as in several anthologies. Currently, she is a doctoral student at the Graduate Theological Union, Berkeley.

Frederick Kirschenmann is the manager of Kirschenmann Family Farms in Windsor, North Dakota. He is involved at various levels in the development and administration of the Farm Verified Organic (FVO) program and currently serves as chair of the FVO Technical Committee. He holds a Ph.D. in Historical Theology from the University of Chicago and is the author of several articles in the areas of church history and sustainable agriculture.

Susanne Kramer-Friedrich studied German and French literature in Geneva and Zurich and writes for the largest church periodical of Switzerland, *Kirchenbote für den Kanton Zürich*. She is one of the founding members of the Oekumenische Frauenbewegung Zürich, together with Irene Gysel-Nef and Monika Wolgensinger, and takes an active part in the Justice, Peace, and Integrity of Creation (JPIC) movement, including the Assembly of Basel.

James Lockman, O.F.M., is a Franciscan friar of the Santa Barbara Province. He works to promote the Franciscan way of life as an ecological and social, as well as a religious, alternative. He holds an M.A. in Theology from the Graduate Theological Union, Berkeley, in addition to an M.S. in Horticulture and a B.S. in Botany from the University of California at Davis.

Charles S. McCoy is Robert Gordon Sproul Professor of Theological Ethics, Pacific School of Religion and Graduate Theological Union. He is also Senior Fellow at the Center for Ethics and Social Policy. Among his publications are *When Gods Change: Hope for Theology* (1980), and *Management of Values: The Ethical Difference in Corporate Policy and Performance* (Ballinger, 1985).

Alan S. Miller is a member of the faculties in Conservation and Resource Studies and Peace and Conflict Studies at the University of California, Berkeley. Teaching on the Berkeley campus since 1973, he is the author of numerous articles and books, including *Gaia Connections: Ecology, Ecoethics, Economics*, published August 1, 1990, by Rowman and Littlefield; *Global Stakes: The Linkages of Peace*, published by the Pacific Institute of Resource Studies in Wellington, New Zealand, in 1986 and 1988; and *A Planet To Choose: Value Studies in Political Ecology*, published by

Pilgrim Press in 1978. Twice nominated for Berkeley's distinguished-teaching award, Dr. Miller gives courses on global environmental issues, environmental philosophy, bioethics, nuclear safety, and world order and the environment. He is Academic Coordinator and Lecturer in the Department of Conservation and Resource Studies. He has been parish minister, campus minister, director of an ecumenical higher-education agency, community organizer, antiwar organizer during the Vietnam era, and editor with Pacific News Service in San Francisco.

Carol S. Robb is Associate Professor of Christian Social Ethics at San Francisco Theological Seminary, San Anselmo, California. She has served on the board of the Center for Ethics and Social Policy at the Graduate Theological Union, Berkeley, for several years. Her research interests and publications concern economic, environmental, feminist, and sexual ethics.

Martha Ellen Stortz teaches Historical Theology and Ethics at Pacific Lutheran Theological Seminary in Berkeley, California. She is a laywoman in the Evangelical Lutheran Church in America. Her current research interests are friendship and issues of power and leadership.

Monika Wolgensinger graduated from the University of Zurich as a pastor (VDM) and has had a variety of pastorates, including working for several years with the POS/mentally and physically handicapped. She was director of the Church Center Helferei Grossmünster Zürich, 1984–89, and took the initiative for several hearings and consultations to bring the Divinity Department of the University of Zurich into dialogue with feminist theologians of the area.